CRYSTAL HEALING

The Complete Practitioner's Guide

CRYSTAL HEALING

The Complete Practitioner's Guide

by Hazel Raven

Disclaimer:

The information in this book is not intended to be a substitute for medical advise, diagnosis or treatment. If you have any concerns about your health consult a qualified medical practitioner. Neither the publisher nor the author accept any liability for readers who choose to self-prescribe.

Crystal energy is subtle, but powerful. If you are in any doubt about their use, consult a qualified crystal therapist. The Affiliation of Crystal Healing Organisation has a list of qualified therapists and approved crystal schools. All approved courses should be at least two years in duration.

ISBN 0 9538890 0 9

First Published in 2000 by
Raven & Co. Publishing
http://www.raven.org.uk
Printed by T. Snape & Co. Ltd., Boltons Court Preston Lancs.

Cover Design by Martyne Raven
Chakra Illustrations by Hazel Raven
All Other Illustrations by Graham and Hazel Raven
Photographs by Graham Raven

For information on purchases, bulk purchases or group discounts for this and other titles by Hazel Raven or details of crystal therapy courses - please contact the Hazel Raven College of Bio-Dynamics or Raven & Co Publishing at

http://www.raven.org.uk

For information on Martyne Raven's art work, jewellery designs and cards please contact the HRCB at:

http://www.raven.org.uk and go to the links page.

Other Books by Hazel Raven

Crystal Healing - A Vibrational Journey Through the Chakras
Angel Therapy - The Complete Practitioner's Guide
Heal Yourself with Crystals
Secrets of Angel Healing
co-author of
Book of Stones - Gemstone Encyclopaedia

Dedication

This book is dedicated to my life partner and husband Graham, my daughter Martyne and my son Marc. They are the ones who have truly loved me unconditionally; they have taught me so much, as we have shared our search for truth and empowerment together.

Secondly, to the rest of my family, especially Gary and Andrea, Gabriel and my 'spiritual sister' Jacqui Malone.

Finally, I would also like to dedicate this book to all who seek simplicity, truth, wisdom, compassion and joy in our uniqueness of being. May your light shine brighter to illuminate even the darkest corners of our minds and world.

For Avalokiteshvara

Acknowledgements

I would like to thank my daughter, Martyne Raven, for choosing me to be her mother and for being the gifted artist who has allowed me to use 'The Angel of Light' Archangel Seraphiel as the cover of this book. Her visionary art is transformative and inspirational.

I also wish to thank my husband, Graham Raven, for his patience during the book's birth process.

Thank you, Graham, for walking the path with me.

Foreword - Crystal Magic

Crystals bring wholeness to every area of your life when you apply them with commitment and love; from the simple act of placing a crystal within your environment, as in feng shui, to wearing a beautiful gemstone as a piece of jewellery, to the ancient healing art of laying stones on your body, crystals embrace you with their love, encouragement, joy and structure.

Crystals have delighted, inspired and been used for protection since the dawn of time. Their perfect resonance helps you conquer physical dis-ease, emotional suffering and spiritual illusion. They gently guide, nurture, empower and support your mind, body and spirit.

Crystals bring joy and unity to our world. They are gifts of the Goddess. They are for everyone and anyone. They are free spirits knowing no boundaries or limitations.

Crystals reflect the workings of the universe and your unique place within it. They help you conquer the elements of earth, water, fire, air and ether.

Crystals have countless uses; they generate, focus, store, amplify, regulate and transmit subtle-energy. They dispel stagnant energy and attract positive energy. They harmonise your psyche with their subtle but measurable electromagnetic field. They re-establish homeostasis, by restoring the body's self-healing mechanism.

Crystals hold the imagination allowing you to step into the magic of manifestation.

Preface

I am eternally grateful and totally delighted for the constant faith and encouragement of my devoted family, friends, clients, students and, of course, the crystals, that this book is now achieved. This book has been a labour of love and endurance. It is not that I am a slow writer, rather I have been so busy devising and teaching crystal courses and working as a holistic therapist.

The book will work for you on many levels, from the absolute beginner to the advanced 'Crystal Light Worker'. I have worked with thousands and thousands of people over the last twenty-seven years as teacher and facilitator of Crystal, Yoga, Angel and Enlightenment courses. I have used the knowledge gained from these experiences to weave this Web of Crystal Enlightenment.

Please take what wisdom you need and feel resonates with you as your truth. That which does not quite fit you yet, do not discard it; place it in your heart and perhaps one day you will feel guided to use it. Everyone has a God/Goddess - given right to their own opinions, feelings, thoughts and emotions. All too often, for millennia, we have given our power away to others; not only have we given our power away, we have allowed others, however well meaning, to manipulate control and dis-empower us.

I am aware that it is early days in subtle-energy research. Even though many people have felt the positive benefits of crystal therapy, we need regulated studies conducted under scientific conditions. The Hazel Raven College of Bio-Dynamics has been instrumental in gathering information and in practical research; it has also been involved with setting the United Kingdom standards for crystal therapy. This has led me to offer this knowledge in the form of seminars, training courses and lectures to the wider public. I have been teaching professional crystal courses since 1988, and I now have a dedicated team of qualified therapists and tutors who are able to offer these approved training courses.

My own official spiritual quest started 29 years ago, with Yoga. It has been a joyful, fruitful and truly enlightening process. I hope this book gives wisdom, love, joy and encouragement to all who read and apply the crystal knowledge contained within its pages. The journey to wholeness begins with a single step, a first dawning of realisation; by allowing the magic to happen, you open yourself to your true eternal perfect nature.

As the 'Wish Fulfilling Jewel' of Ratnasambhava, the Buddha of the South, I hope you let crystals guide you, as they have guided me, towards your highest spiritual goal this lifetime. I hope you allow them to heal you into wholeness and fill your world with color, harmony, vibrancy, wisdom, compassion, love and personal power.

I personally can never fully express my gratitude and appreciation to the crystal kingdom. Crystals have fascinated, nurtured, supported, transformed and enlightened me and given me a life filled with wonder. I have never, in all these years, been disappointed in the crystal kingdom.

Hazel Raven
Spain
11 November 1999

About the Author

Hazel Raven is a respected writer, teacher and holistic therapist - specialising in subtle-energy medicine - with over thirty years experience in this field. She is the founder member and course director of the Hazel Raven College of Bio-Dynamics.

Hazel Raven has been instrumental in gathering information and in practical research; she has also been involved with setting the United Kingdom standards for crystal therapy. She has been teaching crystal therapy since 1988 and has trained a dedicated team of professional crystal therapists and qualified tutors who are able to offer these approved training courses.

Hazel is clairvoyant, clairaudient and clairsentient and uses these gifts to enhance her healing work. Her style of teaching is inspriational and empowering.

Hazel is a qualified educationalist, who is a former vice-chair of the Affiliation of Crystal Healing Organisations and was previously treasurer for four years, is well respected by her colleagues in the field of complementary therapies and has served on the Inner Council of the British Complementary Medicine Association for many years as its crystal therapy representative for education.

Initiated as a Reiki Master in 1994, Hazel served on The Reiki Federations's Steering Committee as representative for obtaining validation for courses.

In May 1999, Hazel was asked to attend the Foundation for Integrated Medicine conference at the Commonwealth Institute in London, which was also attended by HRH The Prince of Wales, the Foundation's patron.

Hazel has always been aware of subtle-energies and the spiritual powers of flowers, trees, crystals, herbs, colour and sound to expand human consciousness. She has had a series of articles published and has appeared on television and radio, in the press and national women's magazines, including the Christmas 1997 edition of Cosmopolitan magazine, which featured her Angelic experiences.

For more details of the Hazel Raven College of Bio-Dynamic training courses, Angelic or Master essences please contact:

e.mail - info@raven.org.uk

http://www.raven.org.uk

Table of Contents

Part Two:
Working With Crystals **43**

Illustrations List

Part One

Crystallography - The Basics

"The cloud-capp'd towers, the gorgeous palaces,
The solemn temples, the great globe itself,
Yea, all which it inherit, shall dissolve
And, like this insubstantial pageant faded,
Leave not a rack behind. We are such stuff
As dreams are made on, and our little life
Is rounded with a sleep."

William Shakespeare: 'The Tempest', act if, scene one, lines 152-8 in the Arden Shakespeare.

What is a Crystal?

The rocks which form the earth, the moon and the planets are made up of minerals. Minerals are solid substances composed of atoms having a regular and systematic arrangement. This orderly atomic arrangement is the criterion of the crystalline state and it means also that it is possible to express the composition of a mineral as a scientific chemical formula.

Crystals

When minerals are free to develop without restriction they are bound by crystal faces which are invariably disposed in a regular way, such that there is a particular relationship between them in any one mineral species. A crystal is bounded by naturally-formed plane faces and its regular outward shape is an expression of its regular atomic organisation. It has grown during the cooling, formative stages of the earth's development.

The Structure of Minerals

The internal structure of minerals has been resolved only this century, by the use of X- rays, although for about 200 years it has been acknowledged that crystals are almost incredibly regular. This is not at once apparent, for crystals of the same substance, such as quartz, have faces that seem almost infinitely variable in their size and shape: it is only when the angles between corresponding pairs of faces are measured that the regularity becomes apparent. The angle between the same two faces in all crystals of the same mineral species is constant. It is now known that this is because the constituent atoms pack together in a definite and orderly way. Crystals were studied long before this was appreciated, however, and from a study of external shape alone it was supposed that crystals were symmetrical and could be grouped according to their symmetry.

Crystal Symmetry

We are accustomed to symmetrical objects such as boxes, furniture and even ourselves. Close examination of such objects will reveal that they can be symmetrical about a plane such that, if the object were to be cut in half along the plane, one half would be the mirror image of the other. The human body is symmetrical externally about a vertical plane arranged from front to back. Objects can also be symmetrical about a line or axis which is considered to pass through the centre. When crystals are rotated about this axis, they present the same appearance twice, three times, four times or six times during a complete revolution. This axis is called an axis of two-fold, three-fold, four-fold, or six-fold symmetry. Crystals never have a five-fold symmetry. Finally, crystals can be said to be symmetrical about a centre if the face on one side of the crystal has a corresponding parallel on the other.

Mineral Aggregates

Most minerals occur as aggregates of crystals that rarely show perfect crystal shapes. Evaporates, tektites and obsidian will be discussed in the relevant sections.

Identification

The identification of gem materials depends to some extent on whether they are in the rough state or whether they are cut and polished. Further, if the stone is set in jewellery you will have to rely on the knowledge of the retailer. There is no single cause of color in minerals.

Internal Structure

To fully understand the structure of crystals it is useful to know something of the atom itself. An atom is said to be the smallest part of an element, giving the term element the meaning more commonly assigned to it in practical chemistry. However, each atom is now known to be a complex system consisting of planetary particles each with a unit of negative electrical charge, which are called electrons, surrounding a heavy nucleus containing a number of positively charged particles called protons. There are a similar number of protons to electrons, so producing, by balancing the positive and negative charges, an electrically neutral atom. Except for the hydrogen atom, all the nuclei of atoms also contain a number of uncharged particles called neutrons, whose possible function is to act as a cement against the repulsive action of the positively charged protons to each other. An atom contains three elementary particles, two of which, the proton and the neutron, have approximately equal weight or mass, and the electron has a mass much smaller. An atom may be considered as consisting of a core - small and compact - surrounded by a 'cloud' of electrons describing orbits which may be circular or of varying elipticity. The electrons, the protons and the neutrons spin on their own axes, so that the atom is a highly dynamic system.

Each of the chemical elements is made of like atoms, atoms which have the same nuclear charge or, as it is better known, atomic number; that is, they have the same number of protons. While the number of protons determines the nature of an atom, not all the atoms of a given element possess the same number of neutrons, therefore such atoms will vary in their weight. The configuration of the planetary electrons around the nucleus is important, for the chemical properties of an element, chemical compounds, and the formation of crystals depend a great deal upon the disposition of the electrons. The electrons circle the nucleus in all directions as a 'cloud' in given orbits which may be described as the average of their movements, the radius of which defines a 'shell' or energy level. If the atom gains or loses one or more electrons it ceases to be electrically neutral and becomes what is known as an ion, the gain of electrons producing negatively charged ions called anions and the loss producing positive ions called cations.

This is the simple basis, as all substances are built upon this foundation. In nature we find no more than 83 different, stable atoms; they are distinguished from each other only by the number of their elementary particles. Not all of the elements in a chemistry book can be found in minerals. Some are absent because they do not form bonds (noble gases) and some because they were created by humans in laboratories and atomic reactors (plutonium etc). From the compounds of these few elements, the majority (over 95%) of the 4,000 known minerals are formed. These elements in fact make up over

99.9% of the earth's crust. Each of them has its own unique properties and the compounds of these elements formulate the characteristic features of minerals.

Atoms and molecules are not themselves geometric shapes. However, they are organised spatially in exact geometric patterns, known as 'crystal lattices'. This perfect order is explained by the fact that individual atoms and molecules of the mineral are packed together as tightly as possible during their growth, which is partly due to the strong electromagnetic forces exerted on them at this time, and partly due to the pressure around them as they form. The internal structure of any crystalline substance is constant and the outward shape of a crystal must have a definite relationship to this structure. Therefore, ideally, a crystal shows a symmetrical arrangement of the various surfaces, which are usually flat but in diamond and a few others may be curved. These plane surfaces are called faces: they may be of two kinds, like and unlike. Crystals made up of similar faces are termed simple forms. A cube or octahedron is an example of a simple form.

Habit

The characteristic shape of a crystal is known as its habit. While the interfacial angles are always the same for crystals of the same mineral, the form of crystals can differ greatly, and for reasons which are not clearly understood. In gem minerals it has been noticed that a different habit can occur in crystals of the same mineral which come from different localities or are of a different color. For example, aquamarine is usually found as long prismatic crystals, while pink beryl (morganite) usually forms crystals which are short and tabular.

Polymorphism

When a mineral has a chemical composition the same as another mineral, but crystallises in a different system, the effect is termed dimorphism, or collectively polymorphism. For instance, diamond and graphite are both carbon, but crystallise in the cubic and hexagonal system respectively, and the rhombohedral calcite has the same chemical make-up as the orthorhombic aragonite.

Crystal Systems

On the basis of their symmetry, crystals can be grouped into seven crystal systems. One other 'crystal' system, amorphous, is not technically crystal: this is because it is without structure, due to the formation, which is so rapid that no crystal structure has had a chance to form. The systems are:

Cubic
Tetragonal
Orthorhombic
Monoclinic
Triclinic
Hexagonal
Trigonal
Amorphous

Hardness

Bound up with the atomic bonding of a substance is the property of hardness. A high degree of hardness in a precious stone is necessary, for only hard substances can take and retain a good polish. A practical means of assessing hardness was proposed by the German mineralogist Friedrich Mohs (1773-1837), who in 1822, after extensive experiments, chose 10 well-known and easily obtainable minerals and arranged them in order of their 'scratch hardness' to serve as standards of comparison. Albeit the numbers of Mohs' list have no quantitative meaning, it is commonly called the Mohs' scale and still forms a universally accepted standard of hardness amongst mineralogists, gemmologists and crystal healers. The Mohs' scale is as follows:

10. Diamond
9. Sapphire
8. Topaz
7. Quartz
6. Orthoclase
5. Apatite
4. Fluorite
3. Calcite
2. Gypsum
1. Talc

The numbers on Mohs' list are not quantities, they represent an order only. Diamond is enormously harder than any other mineral and the gap between 10 and 9 on the list is far greater than that between any other of the numbers. The number 7 on the Mohs' scale is an important one, as any gemstone must be at least as hard as this if it is to withstand being regularly worn in jewellery. Stones such as peridot or green demantoid garnet are only suitable for occasional wear. Opal, pearl, amber and coral are also very soft and great care should be taken if they are worn as pendants.

Growth Conditions

Gem materials, except for those which are of organic origin or due to man's artifice, are found in the rocks forming the upper accessible levels of the earth's crust. Rocks are usually classified under three broad headings:

a) igneous
b) sedimentary
c) metamorphic

Igneous Rocks

The igneous rocks were produced by the solidification of hot molten matter (magma), which was pushed into fissures in the earth's crust, or was extruded on the surface as lava flowing from a volcano. During the cooling of magma, the individual minerals crystallise out around local centres. Some minerals do so at an early stage and are able to develop good crystal outlines. One fruitful source of gem material is a pegmatite. The pegmatites of Madagascar provide an interesting collection of gem materials such as beryl, tourmaline, garnet, topaz, kunzite, iolite and transparent golden-yellow feldspar. Hollow spaces caused by gases and fluids trapped in the solidifying magma produce cavities lined with free-growing crystals of such high temperature minerals as topaz and beryl. From these so-called miarolitic cavities gem crystals have been recovered. The cooling of certain minor intrusions and lava flows extruded out of the earth's surface was so rapid that there was no time for crystallisation to take place: in this manner obsidian was formed.

Sedimentary Rocks

The second group of rocks, sedimentary, results from the breaking down (denudation) of earlier formed rock masses. There are three stages in the formation of typical sedimentary rocks: first, the chemical and mechanical weathering of source rocks by the action of wind, rain or ice; by changing temperatures; by the chemical breakdown of unstable material; or by chemical action of the atmosphere. The second stage is the transportation of the products of weathering by moving water or wind. Thirdly comes the deposition of the debris, or simple evaporation of mineralised water in places favouring rapid evaporation, which is how gypsum is formed. Coal and jet are formed by the accumulation of plant remains and are classed as sedimentary rocks. Brecciated jasper occurs when pebbles are cemented together by secondary mineralisation. The sorting of the detritus (gravel, sand, silt and so forth) of broken-down rocks is commonly carried out by the action of streams and rivers. Such sorting by water may depend greatly upon the density of the mineral being carried along. The more important gem minerals, being relatively heavy, tend to fall into any depression in the river bed, forming placer deposits. The river beds may be ancient, having long since ceased to carry water, and are now covered and obliterated by more recent soils. It is in such old river courses that the water-worn pebbles of many gemstones are found. A typical example of this are the gem gravels of Sri Lanka, where sapphires and rubies are found. Sedimentary rocks may also accumulate where life is possible and wood opal or silicified wood is produced by the replacement and impregnation of the woody tissues of trees by silica.

Metamorphic Rocks

Heat and pressure from intrusions of igneous rocks, or from the folding of rock masses during deep-seated disturbances in the earth's crust during the birth of mountains, may alter the surrounding country rocks, whether they be igneous or sedimentary, so that a new type of rock is produced. Such an alteration is termed metamorphism. When extensive areas - some hundreds or thousands of square miles - are affected by deep-seated igneous activity, regional or dynamothermal metamorphism is said to occur, and under these conditions rocks such as schists and some crystalline limestone and quartzites are produced. During alteration by metamorphism, any impurities in the original rock, the so-called accessory minerals, may crystallise out as separate minerals which are disseminated through the newly-formed rock. Thus green fuchsite mica may form from crystals throughout quartzite, producing green aventurine.

Rocks Formed by Vapour Action

By the action of chemically active vapours (pneumatolysis) or fluids, often assisted by heat from the intrusion of molten matter, new rocks may be produced from old ones. New minerals are formed by the action of the vapours, particularly boron and fluorine, which produce such minerals as tourmaline and topaz in granite rocks.

Mineral-Rich Water

Much mineral-rich water travels through cracks and fissures in the country rock and deposits low-temperature minerals in them. Such veins or loads, the latter term being used for metallic veins, may open out into cavities, called vughs (vugs). The vughs may be lined with crystals deposited from the water. Many of the deposited minerals have gem significance. In a vugh, the minerals deposited are of a different nature from the surrounding rock. When this happens in a cavity the minerals are often called drusy. Geodes are hollow cavities lined with crystals deposited from mineral-rich waters which have percolated into stream cavities in lavas, or into cavities in sedimentary rocks, and even into fossils. Such geodes are a common source of gem crystals, particularly rock crystal and amethyst. In caves, the mineral-rich water dripping from the roof forms hanging masses called stalactites; similar but upstanding masses may form on the floor of the cave as stalagmites. Further deposits of minerals may well occur in irregular sheets over the floor of the cave and these are often banded in structure. It is from such formations that the banded calcites and rhodochrosites are obtained. A gemstone is the naturally occurring crystalline form of a mineral: there are more than 30 popular varieties and some come in more than one color.

The Structure of the Earth

The earth is made up of layers like an onion: the crust, mantle, core and inner core. We live on the crust, which is about 30km deep, but under the oceans it can be as thin as 10km deep. The first layer, the crust, is made mostly of rocks. The crust is the thinnest of the three layers. Just under the crust is the layer called the mantle. The mantle is very thick: in fact, if you drove from the east coast to the west coast of the USA you would have travelled as many miles as through the thickest of the earth's mantle. Most of the mantle is solid. Beneath the mantle, and at the centre of the earth, is the core. The core has two parts, the inner core and the outer core. Scientists believe the outer core is liquid and the inner core is solid. The core is believed to be shaped like a ball with a temperature of about 5,500 degrees centigrade. The earth's temperature dispersion is intimately connected to problems of the structure, composition, dynamic state and evolution of the planet. The high temperatures in the interior provide the driving force for the earth's convective engine and are ultimately accountable for the dynamic geological activity on the surface of the planet. The past quadrennium has witnessed major progress in our understanding of the thermal structure of the earth. While considerable advancement has been made, a number of aspects of the earth's temperature structure remain highly controversial.

Ecological Implications

The ecological implications of mining are not fully understood by some crystal therapists. I have heard that many of them are incredibly worried about how we are stripping the earth of her minerals, but the truth is, and I personally know dozens of miners from all over the world, most of the crystals and gemstones crystal therapists use are removed by a man or woman with a pickaxe and a shovel. The huge scars we see on the earth are the result of mining by industry for industrial use, such as coal, iron, copper etc. Crystal therapists can rest easy, with a clear mind, for we use only a tiny fraction; in fact more gemstones are used for fashion jewellery than crystal therapists use.

Quartz Crystals - Sacred Geometry - Technical Terms used in Crystallography

Quartz is crystalline silicon dioxide (silica) which has the formula $Si0_2$ and a hardness of 7 on the Mohs' scale. Quartz crystallises in the trigonal (rhombohedral) system. Ideally quartz forms doubly terminated crystals consisting of a hexagonal prism capped at each end by what can be assumed to be, from their appearance, hexagonal pyramids. These twelve triangular-shaped faces are not, however, pyramidal faces but equal development of the faces of two rhombohedra of opposite hands or, more correctly, positive and negative rhombohedra. Usually one of the rhombohedra predominates and the crystal shows clearly the trigonal nature of the crystallisation. Occasionally the predominating rhombohedron and the prism face; the crystal then assumes the form of a rhombohedron and an aspect nearly that of a cube. Some crystals may have equal development of the rhombohedral faces but with a complete absence of the hexagonal prism; this gives a bi-pyramidal form which is called quartzoid.

Quartz crystals are characterised by the horizontal striations which appear on the prism faces. These striations are due to oscillation between the faces on the prism and the different rhombohedra, and it is to this oscillatory effect that the tapering of some quartz crystals is due.

Other factors do cause distortion in crystals and, indeed, it is rare for a crystal to show perfect form; this can be readily comprehended when the growth conditions are understood. Crystals are forced to grow in rock cavities and usually commence their growth from any nucleus which may be present on the rock wall; hence, as the crystals grow from the wall, they will have only one termination. Also, the silica-bearing solution which feeds the crystal is always in more or less rapid movement and may be richer in silica in some flow directions than others. This causes some faces to grow faster than others. The slower, growing less fast, become the larger faces. However, whatever the irregularity of the faces, the angle between any two like faces is always the same as in the perfect crystal. Owing to pauses in the growth of the crystal due to lack of mineral-charged mother-liquid, or to a change in the constitution of that liquid, ghost-like outlines may be seen in some quartz crystals; such specimens are called phantoms.

X-ray study has shown that the atomic structure of quartz, unique among the gem minerals, is helical, and that this spiral arrangement of atoms can be either right-handed or left-handed. This right-hand or left-hand nature of quartz, termed enantiomorphism, is occasionally manifested in crystals by the position of the small trigonal pyramidal faces, if present. This is shown in the 'Time link' section - from which it will be clear that the left-handed crystal is an exact counterpart of the right-handed one, but that each is a mirror-image of the other. Such a spiral structure causes a crystal to rotate the plane of polarisation of light, and this circular polarisation, as it is termed, is made manifest by this peculiarity.

Rock crystal is found all over the world. These are only some of the most important localities: fine specimens, usually crystal groups, come from the Swiss and French Alps and from Hot Springs, Arkansas, USA. Doubly terminated crystals, often containing black inclusions of petroleum, are found in Herkimer County in the State of New York. The most important source for rock crystal is in Brazil, where the best technical quartz is obtained in Goyaz, Minas Gerais and Bahia. Another source is Mount Kimpu in the Kai Province and elsewhere in Japan. Large crystals are found in New South Wales and rutilated quartz is found in Tinga in the same Australian state. Very large quartz crystals are found in Sakangyi in the Kathe district of upper Burma.

Rock Crystal

The water-clear colorless quartz is known as rock crystal and receives its name from the hardy mountain climbers of ancient Greece, who first came upon it gleaming in hidden caves near their sacred mountain, Mount Olympus. They called it 'krustallos', meaning ice, for they believed it to be water forever frozen by the Gods. Colorless clear quartz crystals are profuse and show extraordinary irregularity in size, from crystals so tiny that it would take a hundred thousand to make an ounce to gigantic crystals weighing more than a thousand pounds.

Attunement Crystal

These crystals are used for opening, balancing, aligning and attuning the chakras before a healing or meditation session. They hold a very strong pulsing energy which works like a tuning fork to quickly bring the chakras back into a resonant state of balance and harmony by using a powerful sweeping cleansing process. They are always slender and water-clear, holding a positive male energy within their vibratory pattern.

Barnacle Quartz

The barnacle crystal is recognised as a quartz crystal covered or partially covered with a host of smaller crystals. This crystal is a teaching crystal. The large crystal is the teacher, whose knowledge, wisdom and experience has attracted the attention of the smaller crystals. This crystal will teach you to facilitate others' learning when the time is right. (When the student is ready, the teacher will appear).

Bridge Crystal

The bridge crystal is instantly recognised by a small to medium crystal which penetrates the main larger crystal. It is partially located within the crystal and partially located without. It is used for inner bridges, linking of energies and parallel realities and universes. It is also used at crossroads in your life, when you are ready to step out into unknown territory and need divine guidance. Sometimes we must let go of the old before we can bring in the new; the letting go process can be painful and fear of the unknown can seem overwhelming. Just allow this crystal to help you make the transition into a new and better, more wholesome and abundant way of life that nourishes your soul.

Candle Quartz - see elestial.

Cathedral Crystal

The quartz cathedral crystal usually has one termination which, on closer inspection, actually is many small terminations. They are very often female in appearance and clarity, but sometimes a natural clear smoky golden color is exhibited and a brilliant display of rainbows. They have a sacred energy of worship and devotion which has accumulated through eons of time. They are very often used for meditation and prayer. They usually instruct their keeper to place them in a sacred setting, normally outside in nature, but some of these crystals prefer to work with groups of people and live very happily in healing centres and retreat centres, where their influence is beneficial to all who come into their vibratory purity and presence. They bring the message to humanity that through devotion comes the ecstasy and bliss vibration which is humankind's natural God/Goddess-given state of perfection.

Celestial Writer

This crystal can be recognised by the inclusion of an angel or deva (natural or man-made) or even a Host of Angelic Beings. This crystal has one of the purest clearest energies of all quartz crystals. It is used for meditation, prayer, divine intervention and cosmic understanding. It can truly only be recognised by its angelic signature of energy. It has also been used as a channelling tool. This crystal should be kept on an altar or in a spirit box to protect its divine energies from outside unwanted intrusive energy. It is not really for use in healing, it is more a meditation aid and for personal spiritual growth. This crystal will accelerate your vibrational rate, bringing wisdom and understanding to the tasks of this lifetime and the karmic implications of leaving the required work undone or ignored.

Channelling Crystal

The channelling crystal is recognised by the sacred configuration of a large seven-sided face, located in the centre front position of the terminated end of the crystal. A triangular face is located on the opposite side of the crystal. This crystal is dedicated to channelling information from the Angels and Ascended Masters. It is also used for channelling healing energies.

Cluster or Group

A group of connected crystals is usually joined at the base, one or more crystals growing from the same host. A very special type of cluster is known as the star-burst, where the growth looks like a star-shaped formation. Each termination or point may be programmed for a specific function. They are also useful for group work, with each termination being programmed for a specific group member. In feng shui they are often used to generate large amounts of energy for space clearing or energy amplification, particularly where the energy may be dead or stagnant. Clusters are also useful in healing rooms to clear and balance the energy space. A group or cluster will cleanse the environment of large amounts of stuck or blocked energy, easily raising the overall vibratory level to a much higher frequency of light, which is always beneficial to health.

Cultured Crystal

Cultured quartz has recently been used for energy balancing, but the process used to produce it originated in Germany some fifty years ago. Although chemically identical to natural quartz SiO^2, it has a greatly refined nature, due to its flawlessness and vibrant colour (doping is the process used to add colour). Colours include blue, gold, purple and green, as well as clear. Cultured ruby, sapphire, emerald and alexandrite are also freely available to therapists. These gems are chemically the same as natural gemstones, also exhibiting the same vibrant colours as the most expensive natural gemstones and, in the case of alexandrite, a mystical colour change. They are more affordable than equivalent size natural gemstones. The cultured crystals are cut and faceted into jewellery or sacred geometric shapes such as platonic solids, precision healing wands, the star of David, Merkaba, Star tetrahedron (this consists of two interpenetrating tetrahedrons), spheres and pyramids. Therapists are experimenting with these specimens for their flawless refined energy transmission. It is advisable, if using these cultured quartz crystals for healing, to clear, charge, dedicate and programme them first and infuse them with the required bioinformation; this is because they do not contain the memory of natural devic energies. This makes them free from any outside influences and clean energetically. Some crystal purists do say that these cultured crystals are devoid of life force, which does not make any sense at all, as they are the same chemically (SiO^2) and contain a refined crystal lattice. In truth, cultured quartz is actually a purer form of quartz which has no inclusions and a more stable pattern of rotation in the molecules, which experienced crystal therapists find speeds up the energy movement within the crystal. (This is the reason why the electronics industry also uses lab-grown quartz).

The Merkaba or Star of David design, cut from clear quartz (generally), is a symbol dating back before the Jewish religion. It is composed of two triangles on top of each other, one with the point up, the other with the point down. The design is triangular in shape, with smaller triangles on each face. A vortex of female pranic energy, which spins anticlockwise, is pulled in through the female side and travels through the body of the cut stone. This pranic energy is then amplified by the energy movement through the cut crystal and is radiated out of the male side clockwise. When one looks through the stone one sees the Star of David. This is symbolic of the spiritual and physical trinities fusing to create balance. It is also symbolic of the Merkaba vehicle, which is the male/female interlocking three-dimensional star tetrahedron energy field that surrounds our body. It is also represented in the centre of the heart chakra (Anahata) and as the symbol of your 'Holy Guardian Angel'. The Merkaba cut crystals come in several sizes: the larger ones are suitable for using as meditation pieces or for room gridding and the smaller ones are often set in gold or silver and worn over the thymus at the witness point. They need to be programmed first with bioinformation or energy resonance patterns. These are placed into the crystal by the focused human mind holding the intent of healing, harmony and happiness. The effect of wearing a programmmed Merkaba is to protect and shield the wearer by making their aura more luminous; this stabilises the personal aura, making the wearer feel secure, focused and balanced.

Curves on a Crystal

These teach you to go with the flow, to bend rather than break. They are a feminine shape and, like a woman, are yin in nature. They are good for spinal problems and issues of support. They help you understand how 'inflexible attitudes' and rigid thought patterns only hinder your evolution and spiritual growth. They take you beyond your limiting belief system, allowing you to find growth and evolution even in difficult circumstances. They also help you to overcome a lack of self-confidence and enable you to learn to stand up for yourself in a positive constructive way. Rather than lashing out in anger, they teach you to find your inner strength and power, regardless of the outside circumstances.

Dead Crystal

These crystals are lifeless; they have usually been abused in some way, either by irradiating, dyeing with different substances, soaking in salt water until their internal structure is damaged, or negative programming, intentional or unintentional. They will be useless for healing or spiritual work. The other reason crystals become 'dead' is due to someone selling or using crystals who is only in it for the profit. Their intention has become known to the crystal devas. When someone only wants to use the crystals, rather than becoming their partners, the crystals probably will stay 'dead' or their energy may withdraw.

Part of the spiritual work of the crystal devas is to work with the human spirits. If our intention is to become partners, much more of their 'magic' manifests in our lives. Ask for divine guidance from the crystal devas, before attempting to use them for healing and spiritual work.

Dendritic Quartz

Dendritic quartz contains a branching marking or figure resembling a tree or leaf form. It usually contains chlorite or manganese. This crystal connects you to the 'Grandmother' earth energy which makes it feel very ancient, wise and nurturing. Due to the crystal's amazing imitation of the plant kingdom it brings a synergy of energies, allowing for a deeper connection to the source of plant wisdom; it allows you to reach even deeper into plant lore. For those of you who are healing hereditary genetic disorders from every level it will help you to tune into your family tree. This allows you to follow the karmic path back to discover the source of the problem. It has also been used for healing lung, circulatory and nervous disorders.

Devic Temple Crystal

This is any quartz crystal that has the inclusion of a deva (natural or man-made) or even a host of devic beings. It has one of the purest clearest energies of all quartz crystals. It is used for meditation, prayer, divine intervention and cosmic understanding. It can truly only be recognised by its devic signature of energy. It has also been used as a channelling tool. This crystal should be kept on an altar or in a spirit box to protect its divine energies from outside unwanted intrusive energy. It is not really for use in healing, it is more a meditation aid and for personal spiritual growth. It will accelerate your vibrational rate, bringing wisdom and understanding to the tasks of this lifetime and the karmic implications of leaving the required work undone or ignored.

Diamond Crystal (Window)

The diamond crystal is recognised by the presence of a diamond-shaped 'window' located usually in the centre front face of the crystal, although I have seen some diamond crystals with several contained in the same stone. This crystal configuration will help you to see beyond illusion, to read the different layers in a person's aura: the physical, emotional, vitality, mental, spiritual and etheric. It will also allow you to define your and others' life purpose or divine mission. Use this window to see into other dimensions. This is done by gazing into the window and allowing visions, thoughts or impressions to form within your mind.

Double Terminated Crystal

The double terminated crystal is recognised as having a complete and perfect termination at both ends. True double terminated crystals are really rare. Their energy flow is powerful, due to the energy's dualistic vibration that allows for the flow both ways. They have traditionally been used for protection, also for linking up the energy of other crystals in a full body layout. Double terminated crystals can be used in any situation where a build-up of energy has disadvantages. Often one termination will be very clear and the other termination quite milky; these crystals are a perfect balance of yin and yang energies and can be used to restore equilibrium, harmony and balance to the energy field when used with conscious intent. Doubly terminated crystals, often containing black inclusions of petroleum, are found in Herkimer County in the State of New York.

Elestial or El (Candle Quartz, Hopper Quartz, Skeletal Quartz)

The El crystal is recognised by small natural terminations all over the body and face of an etched and indented or multi-layered crystal, which look as though one crystal has grown over another; sometimes this is so pronounced that they almost look like a candle where layer upon layer of wax has dripped down over the side. They are usually smoky in color, but rose, amethyst, citrine and aquamarine crystals have also displayed the El features. These crystals are known as 'gifts from the angels' and you will find that they will gently remove all negative energy blocks. They release fearful vibrations from the human energy field and will ease fear and nightmares. Els are full of wisdom and cosmic understanding. These crystals work with the Solar Lords of Light, Wisdom and Karma and they also assist in activating the third eye, which naturally will increase all abilities associated with clairvoyance, clairaudience and clairsentience.

The smoky quartz variety is very powerful and the darker the color the more potent the energy. They have been used to heal stress and stress-related conditions, including addiction to drugs (prescribed and otherwise) and alcoholic-related liver conditions. They also appear to balance the male and female polarities within the brain and help with schizophrenia and epilepsy. In addition, they have greatly helped with all diseases of the stomach and intestines and can give quick release from pain when placed over a painful area. Additionally they are used for strengthening the physical body and cleansing the auric shell of unwanted negative emotional ties. (They are currently energetically directed for earth healing - healing all pain contained within this 'earth walk' and the path of service - by Archangel Sandalphon).

Rose quartz Els are the heart attunement stone. They really do ease the burdens associated with the heart chakra and can quickly release the emotional blockages that stop our spiritual growth towards the state of perfection and joy. (They are currently energetically directed for healing, mercy and pain relief - or for those who wish to have children - by the Lady Ascended Master Quan Yin, loosely translated as 'She who observes and pays attention to all prayers').

Amethyst Els are probably the most potent meditation tool to be manifested on the planet at this time, quickly releasing the karmic blocks which stop our spiritual growth. (They are currently energetically directed for healing , creative visualisation and transmutation, using the violet flame of purification, by the Ascended Master Saint Germain).

The citrine Els are an absolute joy to work with. They balance the mental body, bringing renewed hope in times of mental confusion or burn-out. Their energy can hardly be contained in words and truly words can never express the full potential these crystals have for upliftment and light. (They are currently energetically directed for healing, protection and devotion by Archangel Michael).

The last of the Els manifested on the earth plane at this time are the aquamarine version. These have surfaced in the last two years and usually come from Brazil. They are extremely powerful metaphysical healing tools for the new millennium. They work primarily on the emotional body and ease all or release all dis-ease. They are being used at the moment for releasing all negative vibrations from the physical, emotional, mental and spiritual bodies. (They are currently energetically directed for the full potential of a balanced expression of love, the primary energy location being the thymus or witness area situated between the heart and throat chakras, by the Ascended Atlantean Master Maha Chohan).

Enhydro

The chalcedony enhydros, or water agate, have a unique significance; they are masses which consist of a shell of cloudy-white chalcedony within which is sealed a quantity of water. This can often be heard splashing about when the pebble is shaken. Sometimes the water is visible. These enhydros are found in Brazil. They are very useful for healing emotional trauma; this is facilitated by holding the enhydro in the receptive hand, or placing it over any painful area of the body until all painful sensation has stopped. Enhydros can be used to heal all fluid functions of the body. They work very quickly and have been successfully used in the treatment of liver disorders. The cleansing effect is very beneficial on all organs of the body. Enhydros have a cleansing, supportive, watery, female energy. They equate to the primeval waters, the symbol of the collective unconscious. They have been carried as talismans by pregnant women since the dawn of civilisation.

Herkimer Diamonds are not diamonds at all, but water-clear quartz from Herkimer County, New York. They often contain rainbow inclusions, some even contain water and air bubbles. They grew in soft mud, which did not restrict their growth, and so they often show ideal quartz formation of doubly terminated crystals consisting of a hexagonal prism capped at each end by what may be assumed to be, from their appearance, hexagonal pyramids. These twelve triangular-shaped faces are not, however, pyramidal faces, but equal development of the faces of two rhombohedra of opposite hands or, more correctly, positive and negative rhombohedra. This makes Herkimers quite extraordinary to work with. They have a very balanced flowing energy that is full of light. Herkimers are a joy to work with. Herkimers are wonderful little dream and vision crystals. With conscious attunement to the light, high, joyful energy you will find they stimulate visions in meditation and dream work. They give access to your unlimited potential and growth, owing to their unique properties, which are due entirely to the formation of Herkimer diamonds, their own birth process being in soft mud which did not restrict their growth and potential.

Faden (Faden is the German word for thread)

Fadens grow under tremendous stress within the mountainous regions of the earth. In the process of their life they have been broken and have healed themselves dozens of times. They usually are small, flat and dirty looking and must have a thread of white 'cotton' type material within them to be true Fadens. They are used for distress, depression, despair, fatigue and burn-out. They contain the 'Mother of all Mothers' energy and really help with severe emotional problems where you feel at the end of your strength and endurance.

Fashioned Stones

The bright faces seen on the more regularly formed crystals and the crude polish given to water-worn pebbles by being rubbed against one another in running water may well have been the incentive to produce a polish on other brightly colored minerals used by early man for utility and decoration. Whoever first learned to polish the rough surfaces of these hard substances is lost in the mists of pre-history, but these early attempts may have been to give a sort of polish to the irregular surfaces by rubbing one stone against another. Grinding the stone to symmetrical shapes did not come until much later; indeed, shaping was most probably first carried out to give an edge to stone tools, rather than give symmetry to ornaments. The beautiful symmetrical and highly polished gemstones of modern production may be said to emanate from the original work of the lapidaries and diamond polishers of medieval times. Curiously, the engraving of gems was carried out in times far earlier than the fashioning with symmetrically arranged flat facets.

Tumbled Stones

Small rough stones or small pieces of rough stone are often tumble polished until they are smooth and free from surface imperfections. A tumbler is a very simple machine which is rotated by a motor with finer and finer grades of grit. The time the process takes depends on the hardness of the material being tumbled. Many people feel that the tumbling process increases the radiance and beauty of stones that would otherwise not be so attractive. They are used as pocket stones or worry stones, for jewellery and in body layouts.

Cabochon Cut

The earliest form of cutting simply gave a curved surface to the stone, collectively known as the cabochon cut. This cutting process generally increases the value and energy of the stone. They are used for jewellery and body layouts.

Faceted Stones

Most transparent gemstones can be faceted, which enables them to carry a higher and more focused vibration of light and intensity. This becomes very apparent when this is carried out by a highly skilled and 'tuned in' cutter. Each facet enables the gemstone to capture more light, which will be internally reflected, displaying the stone's innate depth and color. A skilled and sensitive stone artist will be able to take a rough piece of stone and transform it into a precious precision piece of jewellery that can reflect greater amounts of healing energy and light. This aids the stone's consciousness evolution and growth. Faceted stones have a very intense energy and are used for jewellery, body layouts and meditation or mandala pieces. When we wear a faceted gemstone and it 'catches the light', that little flash of light it emits reminds us of our true nature as brilliant flashes of cosmic light. Let your light shine even into the darkest corners of our world.

Wand

Faceted wands are designed to focus, direct and cohere energy. They can be manufactured from any natural gemstone or quartz material. Smoky quartz wands are traditionally used for loosening pain, or negative or stagnant energy, by gently unwinding the trapped obstruction. Amethyst is used for transmutation, transformation and release, being especially good for releasing addictions. Rose quartz wands are gentle, soothing and excellent for balancing the emotional level of the aura by gently nourishing the emotional body. Rose quartz is revitalising and stimulates healing by helping to maintain energy levels to protect against unwanted influences from the outside world, which many sensitive souls find overwhelming. Wands in clear quartz cohere, amplify, focus and transmit energies: it is the master healer and the only programmable crystal. Rutile quartz wands intensify the powerful quartz vibration, giving protection. Citrine wands clear and balance the solar plexus chakra; bringing personal power, spontanaiety, positive mental attitudes, joy, hope and freedom from emotional hang-ups. Obsidian wands draw the quality of our Divine essence into our physical body; which purges the negativity, quickly dissolving blocks, trauma, shock and fear. Fashioned wands are often long and have six straight sides with a small point at each end, which makes them behave similarly to natural double terminated crystals. Others have one end rounded and smooth and these are used for deep tissue massage or as energy or blockage shifters. Then there are wands with multiple facets which greatly cohere and amplify the potential energy transmission. Cutting and faceting also increase the information storage capacity. Some wands are distinguished by their faceting being very precise, with a larger yin termination; this end draws in pranic life force, which spirals down the length of the crystal, being amplified each time it comes into contact with a facet. The Prana, suitably amplified, flows throught the opposite yang termination. The more facets there are, the greater the coherence and power. Some innovative new faceted wands are composed of a combination of two facets. One is slender and flat and the other is wide and concave; this new generation of wands is extremely focused.

Feng Shui Crystal

Small-faceted crystal spheres, these round prisms used in feng shui are one of the *nine* basic 'cures'. They will adjust a home or office's chi, symbolically resolve design imbalances and enhance ba-gau positions. They work by refracting light, converting strong, threatening chi, both exterior and interior, and dispersing it throughout the room. Thus, symbolically, they are sources of power. They are also used to break up stagnant or stuck chi, thereby improving the occupants' lives. Many people also hang a round faceted feng shui crystal in their bedroom to bring sparkle and life into their relationship. If you use a red ribbon or thread it is said to increase the effectiveness of this cure. Most commercially available faceted spheres are made of glass.

Crystal Ball

Rock crystal is ground and polished, mostly by low paid workers in Third World countries, into crystal-gazing balls, although most of the crystal-gazing balls are moulded and polished glass. Clear quartz spheres over three inches across are very rare, but there is an exceptional specimen in the United States National Museum, which has a diameter of 12.75 inches and weighs 107 pounds. One way to tell a quartz sphere from those made of glass is that quartz feels much colder to the touch and does not have the air bubbles of glass. Crystal balls have been historically used for scrying. The uniform radiant energy of the crystal ball facilitates easy access to past, present and even future events. Other uses are deep tissue massage and meditation. Crystal balls and crystal ball pendants can be used in healing, as they quickly fill gaps in the auric field, due to their shape and their sympathetic correspondence to the overall structure of the human energy field. They can be worn or carried. They will also afford total protection of the integrity and structure of the human aura during stressful or negative encounters where a breach of the energy field would result in illness. In ancient times crystal balls were used in sacred ceremonies for divination and they can also be charged with positive energy. (See scrying, part five, for full instructions).

Jewellery

Humans have always searched for ways to adorn and beautify themselves. Carrying stones as amulets, or wearing them as jewellery, is one of the most simple and effective ways of utilising their powerful healing vibration. Evidence has been found of the use of gemstones as jewellery as long ago as the Palaeolithic Age. Gems have traditionally been worn on the fingers to symbolise eternity or union or to carry specific energies to certain parts of the body; around the wrist and arm to influence and affect the side of the body you wear them on; and around the neck. Lapis, malachite and carnelian were used by the ancient Egyptians, emerald by the Incas, jade by the Chinese, smoky quartz by the Celts and turquoise by the Native Americans.

Ancient rulers would also wear crowns of sacred gemstones to assist them in ruling wisely. Unfortunately a lot of this wisdom and ancient knowledge regarding enlightened leadership using precious gemstones has been lost, distorted or hidden. Rubies and deep red garnets were also worn in the navel of belly dancers to excite and activate deep sexual interest and passion; this tradition is being revived due to the current interest in body piercing. The tradition of ear piercing dates back to antiquity, when earrings were worn to protect the ears from entities and ghosts. Ear ornaments were part of the large number of amulets used to protect the openings of the body from dangerous malevolent spirits. Earrings also serve to balance the right and left hemispheres of the brain and will work on acupressure points of the ear itself. If you decide to wear earrings, please be aware of the properties of the gemstones you are using and make sure that it would be appropriate to wear them on the ears. Some crystals do not apply to the throat or third eye chakras' energy fields.

When you choose to wear a pendant around your neck, try to wear it over the witness area to heal and integrate the whole body and aura. This also stimulates the thymus gland, boosting your immune system. Also be aware of the stone or stones you choose for your pendant: are they appropriate for your energy field? Many pendants being made today are exquisite pieces of art; they combine beauty, craftsmanship and crystal empathy, bringing a synergy of energies to empower their custodians. When you decide to wear a pendant you can choose a simple 'off the shelf' piece or have a power-piece specifically made to suit your energy field and your soul's true requirement. Please choose very carefully one that will enhance your highest spiritual purpose/achievement this lifetime. Also ask when you buy a pendant, who made it? What kind of a person are they? Are they energetically aware, with sympathy, empathy and crystal wisdom, or are they a retailer/jeweller who thinks of crystals as lumps of inanimate rock and the New Age crystal therapists as 'healie feelies' to be exploited, laughed at and ridiculed as they take your money (energy)?

Wearing a quartz pendant around your neck will heal, balance and protect your energy field from harmful negative hostile environments. Remember, the point of the crystal will direct and focus the energy flow, so decide which way the stone should be set for optimum benefit for you. When pointed upwards in the setting, the stone will energise, activate, cleanse, balance and stimulate the upper chakras of the throat, third eye and crown. This is wonderful for those who otherwise would be too grounded, materialistic and heavy. This position is also good for those who get depressed or for those who are working on meditation, channelling or out of body experiences. When pointed down, the crystal has a grounding, draining effect. A double terminated crystal is often best for everyday wear, or choose one that has two stones, one pointing up and one pointing down, to balance and protect the integrity of your energy field.

Whatever you choose, please be aware of the effect your pendant has on your energy field, be aware of your emotions, thoughts, feelings etc. Very often I have seen people wearing totally inappropriate pendants that do not enhance their energy field. Sometimes these same people have paid a lot of money for their pendant. I have even seen people who have been 'sold' a lie: they have been told their pendant is a type of crystal when, in fact, it is not that type of crystal at all. Choose your setting with care: gold will strengthen your energy field with a very powerful male yang energy, while silver is balancing, soothing and yin - perhaps you will choose a piece fashioned using gold and silver combined?

Female Crystal

The female crystal is recognised as being cloudy, as opposed to brilliantly clear. It contains milky, soft, feminine energies. It is also known as white quartz. It owes its milkiness to the presence of a multitude of very small cavities containing water or carbon dioxide in liquid condition. Sometimes the milkiness is only skin deep on the crystal and such crystals are called 'quartz en chemise'. Much vein quartz is white quartz and this type is often gold bearing. They truly are a gift from the Goddess. This crystal will heal all hurts and especially emotional pain which has lodged within the emotional body. It has a very strong yin energy and will cool down hot or inflamed emotions and stressful conditions.

Fire Crystal

Sometimes clear quartz crystals seem to contain an inner fire. This can be due to inclusions of other minerals, especially haematite or even rainbow inclusions, which give them their own interior fire elemental; they are strong and intense, giving a powerful cleansing vibration. Use them to transform any old or negative belief systems that may have lodged within your cellular structure. They can also be used for stressful situations that may burn you out.

Generator Cluster

Generator clusters of clear quartz are normally very large crystal groups ranging in size from a large dinner plate to several feet across. They are typically used in healing centres or for group work, where each termination is programmed for a specific function or group member. They teach us to live peacefully together, facilitating the understanding of equality and inclusion. This is not some vague utopian concept, it is our true reality and the sooner we understand the energies of equality and inclusion, the easier our true soul expression will fully manifest in our daily lives and the lives of everyone on the planet. Unless we recognise this fact, our world will remain full of disagreement, exclusion, war, famine, hatred etc. These clusters are also excellent for energising other crystals and jewellery or for placement as clearing, energising, life-enhancing tools. They are also traditionally used for absent healing ceremonies.

Generator Crystal

The generator crystal is recognised by a configuration of crystal faces, all joining equally at the top of each crystal face, in the same location, in order to form the termination of the apex. They are mostly fabricated. They are used to focus, cohere, amplify and direct positive energies, or to generate vast amounts of focused energy, and are useful for groups and earth healing.

Geode or Crystal Cave

Sometimes weathered-out cavity linings, called geodes, are lined with well-shaped crystals and many fine specimens of amethyst occur in such associations. These can range considerably in size and shape, from the size of a football to large enough to accommodate a human occupant. They have traditionally been used for healing and protection. They aid spiritual growth and understanding, purifying on all levels, giving relief from addictions and addictive traits within the personality. The geode works as an amplifier of healing and spiritual energies. When consciously directed it will break down and transform blocked or stuck energies. It also helps protect from over-indulgences and calms the mind. Amethyst is a powerful positive meditation stone and master healer. It treats hearing disorders, the skeletal system, nervous system, digestive tract, stomach, heart, skin and teeth, insomnia, mental disorders and headaches. Geodes can be used for protection by placing a name inside and asking the crystal consciousness to give complete protection from all outside negative malevolent influences.

Goddess Crystal

The Goddess crystal is recognised by the configuration of a large five-sided face, which must be the main face or the most dominant as you view the crystal point. It is very pointed, looking almost like an arrow head. These crystals are used for healing broken bodies, emotions and the mind. Those who are drawn to this crystal feel very comfortable and easily link into the feminine Goddess energy. They also hold the five vibration of the electronic pattern of the Goddess of Mercy, Quan Yin.

Healing Crystal

Clear quartz healing crystals are any configuration, structure or size that appear to you to be specifically attuned for healing.

Hieroglyph Crystal

The hieroglyph crystal is easily recognised by any totally unique markings or etchings. These will usually be all over the crystal and can include the termination. Use these crystals to access the ancient knowledge stored within. This is normally relevant to you personally and may give past life information or specific ways of working with the crystalline vibration.

Kabalistic Crystal

Kabalistic crystal cut vibrational healing wands are specifically cut from quartz. This crystal healing 'device' amplifies and coheres energies, structuring them in the frequency of the perfectly balanced water molecule. They are usually available in a variety of quartz material, such as clear, smoky or amethyst quartz, and cut with facets numbering from 8 to 33. They are an advanced healing tool and great care should be taken when using them for crystal therapy work.

Key Release Crystal

The key crystal is recognised by a three-sided or six-sided indentation located on the crystal. The six-sided indentation becomes narrower as it goes within the crystal and ends within the crystal. The difference between the three and six sides depends on how the release key has been caused. Basically the release key is caused by the clear quartz crystal releasing its neighbour. It is used to unlock the answers to hidden concepts, which may lie behind the locked 'doors' of the unconscious mind. It also facilitates a deeper understanding of the letting go process, allowing us to painlessly release that which no longer serves our highest good. This process can sometimes be very painful, through fear and ignorance. The fear is due to the unknown and unknowable. How many times do we see others hanging on to negative out-dated fears, relationships, careers etc., when we can see very clearly that if they were to release themselves from these negative situations their lives would instantly take a turn for the better? Remember, we must let go of what we are, to allow the space for growth into what we can become. We also use this crystal for cutting ties that bind us to the past, ignorance and negative conditioning of the conscious and sub-conscious mind. These crystals are useful when programmed with positive affirmations; remember to always word your affirmation in a positive way.

Laser Wand

The laser wand crystal is recognised as a very long slender crystal, with small faces constituting the termination. The angles of the sides of the crystal can be curved, in many instances, rather than straight and parallel. This development pattern is due to its growth conditions, whereby the oscillation between the faces of the prism causes the tapering. New Age legend has it that the laser wands were specially grown by the consciousness of highly evolved Lemurians and that they are manifesting at this time to be used by the same Lemurians who evolved them eons ago. There is no doubt that they constitute a very advanced healing tool. This is due to the length of the crystal in relation to the size of the terminations. The extreme length to ratio of termination allows a vast amount of female energy to be drawn into the body of the crystal ready for direction via the male termination. Laser wands will:

* Minutely focus and cohere energy
* Dramatically amplify your healing power and healing potential
* Stimulate harmonious brain activity during healing practice
* Protect and restore the energy structure of your body
* Activate and stimulate personal healing and spiritual growth
* Align your inner levels of awareness
* Create powerful carrier waves of pure vibrant energy
* Heal and rejuvenate your body
* Surround the body and aura with protection
* Facilitate psychic surgery
* Transmute unwanted information that may be locked in your bones, tissues and your unconscious mind

Library Crystal

Library crystals are storehouses of information and knowledge. They usually contain this library already, but some people use them to store even more information, very much as a computer. They are useful for students and anyone who needs to work with the intellect or heal their mental body. They have a strange appearance, with multiple terminations instead of one termination, and will contain record keeper markings and, more than likely, diamond-shaped windows.

Lines on a Crystal

These striations denote fast-flowing power - the more lines, the faster the energy.

Male Crystal

The male crystal is recognised as being totally water clear. It transmits powerful, vibrant, focused healing energy. Use this crystal when you need a very strong yang or male energy, but be sure to use your crystal wisdom to regulate the flow of energy, to allow your client to absorb the healing at the correct level, otherwise you will 'blow' (over-stimulate) your client's chakras.

Manifesting Crystal

The manifesting crystal is recognised by a small crystal or several smaller crystals totally enclosed within a larger crystal. You will be able to use this amazing crystal for manifesting your goals. Such crystals are extremely rare, beautiful and remarkably powerful manifesting tools. If you are lucky enough to be the earth-keeper of one, please use it for the highest good of all.

- Use for meditation
- Use for visualisation
- Use for planetary healing
- Use for group work

Phantom Crystal

Owing to pauses in the growth of the crystal by lack of mineral-charged mother liquid, or to a change in the constitution of that liquid, ghost-like outlines may be seen in some quartz crystals; such crystals are called phantoms. These pauses can happen numerous times. The phantom crystal has experienced many lifetimes of learning, through eons of time, while continuing in the same physical configuration. This crystal is a 'living' example of the evolution of consciousness and the ultimate continued growth of the eternal towards total perfection of the being. This crystal is without a doubt very useful for those of us who feel we have reached a 'brick wall' and do not know how to continue, or even if we have the strength and courage to continue to 'evolve' and grow. A must for those who search for perfection within this lifetime.

- Use for healing and stress
- Use for past life exploration
- Use for ascension

Rainbow Crystal

When clear colorless quartz is permeated by cracks, these, if thin enough, produce rainbow colors by interference of light at the films of air in the crack. Such stones are called 'rainbow quartz' or 'iris quartz'. A corresponding result can be artificially induced by suddenly cooling a heated rock crystal. Sometimes this cooling is carried out in water colored with red or green dyes; the color dries in the fractures, producing the so-called firestone. The natural rainbow quartz crystals bring joy and happiness to the owner. They have also been beneficially used in the alleviation of depression.

Record Keeper Crystal

The record keeper crystal is recognised by one or more perfectly formed raised triangles on one or more faces. This clearly indicates sacred fire knowledge of creation which, at a vibrational level, is stored within them. It can be released with a candle flame meditation. They are also used to improve energy levels and stop burn-out, due to overwork and stress.

Reversed Sceptre

Reversed sceptre quartz has a small, fine, delicate tip and a larger stone growing out of the base. They are used to find balance and harmony and are especially useful for those who give their 'power' away and are easily controlled or manipulated by others. Use it to find your own space again.

Rutilated Quartz (Maiden Hair Quartz or Venus Hair Quartz or Hair Crystal)

Rock crystal is often remarkably clear from internal imperfections, but sometimes other crystals are found enclosed in quartz which, forming later, has grown round and enveloped them. In this category come the sagenitic quartzes, so named from the Greek for net, for the criss-crossing needles seem like a net. When the enclosed crystals are long, hair-like needles of red or golden-colored rutile, the material is called rutile quartz. Other more popular names such as 'Venus hair stone', 'Cupid's darts' and 'Fleches d'amour' are applied to the material. A similar type of quartz may have included crystals of black tourmaline, or green actinolite fibres, to which the name 'Thetis hair stone' has been applied. If the actinolite crystals are so dense as to color the quartz green, it forms a variety called prase. It has been reported that some forty different minerals have been found to be included in quartz, but only a few have gem importance. Rutile within the quartz intensifies the energy of the quartz, providing a synergy of energies. The energy seems to be intensified on the astral body. It has been used for astral travel. It is also very protective in hostile situations, the hostile energy being completely dissipated by the power of light. It is excellent to use for 'channelling' and 'automatic writing'. Most users of this crystal for 'channelling' report excellent results. It creates positive life patterns and has been used to heal the lungs and improve the function of the immune system. It will elevate the energy centres it is placed upon. It has also been carried to improve self-esteem and confidence.

Sceptre Quartz

Sceptre quartz looks as though it has one crystal growing over the top of another crystal or crystal rod. They look like ancient symbols of power, vitality and life force. New Age legend has it that they were used in Atlantean and Lemurian times as a symbol of authority. They can obviously be used for infertility problems. (They are a natural Lingam). These are very useful tools for those who wish to find a balanced yang or male energy to work with, in order to balance their own yin or female energies.

Scrying Stone

Any kind of reflective surface can be used for scrying, which is one of the best known forms of divination. It is an ancient technique of contacting and gaining guidance from the divine. The use of crystals and crystal spheres to gain access to other dimensions, the astral plane or the Akashic records, goes back to pre-history. Crystal divination or scrying normally requires a clear quartz crystal as clear as possible and as large as possible. (See part five for complete instructions on how to scry).

Seer Stone (Dragon's Egg, Dragon's Eye)

The seer stone is a natural river-tumbled quartz which has been cut and polished on one end. This is used for gazing deep into the inner structure of the crystal. Using this stone facilitates a deep going within process. This stone also makes a powerful dream crystal ally. (Remember, dragons hoard treasure and ancient knowledge). Use this crystal to find your buried treasure, your hidden knowledge, which is very often deeply encoded within your dreams.

Self-Healed Crystal

The self-healed crystal is recognised by small (usually less in size than the main termination) crystalline structures at the location where the crystal was broken off from its base. It was damaged during its growth; undaunted, it grew a new and smaller group of terminations over its original wound. This is the crystal's quest, to grow and heal. It teaches us that, however broken we may be, we can always heal our pain and disease. This crystal is the personification of the wounded healer. By using this crystal in your healing and self-healing work you will gain many insights into the true purpose of healing into wholeness (enlightenment) and the understanding that the source of all pain is the illusory world (maya), which gives rise to feelings of separation and wrong mental processes (duality).

Singing Bowl

Fabricated quartz crystal bowls are claimed to be the sound of light. Those who work with them say they are a deeply transformative vibrational experience. They bathe the listener in harmonic waves which deeply effect healing in every cell. Quartz crystal bowls re-balance and cleanse abnormal functioning or 'blocked' chakras. Dysfunctional chakras affect the subtle energy bodies: the sounds of the crystal singing bowls release the 'blocked' energy, allowing healing to occur. Crystal singing bowls are also used to aid meditation and develop deeply spiritual experiences. They have been used for space clearing and earth healing at the times of the full moon. They will also create structured water, which is beneficial to radiant good health. Care should be taken, however, never to place a quartz crystal singing bowl on the body of your client. If the quartz was to shatter it could very seriously damage your client, who would be showered in thousands of sharp pieces of glass-type quartz. (I have never see this happen for myself, but I have been told of this happening by a very reliable source). Two more cautionary notes are: quartz crystal singing bowls should never be played too close together, as the vibration from one could shatter the other. Finally, some very sensitive people find them too intense when played indiscriminately, especially at New Age fairs. Remember, the bowls will amplify the players' thoughts and energies and send them out to pollute the atmosphere; it is much better to only play them in a sacred way for healing and meditation.

Singing Crystal

Clear quartz singing crystals have a particular high pitched sound or musical note that resonates when you use them for healing, meditation etc. They can also be identified physically by their appearance. They are usually long and slender, with a high pitched sound like tinkling glass when they are touched together.

Transcendental Crystal (Tabby, Tabulator)

The transcendental crystal is recognised as a slim, flat crystal. It always has horizontal striations which appear on the prism faces. These striations are due to oscillation between the faces of the prism and the different rhombohedra, and it is to this oscillatory effect that the growth configuration is due. These striations are energy lines for storing information within. The information they contain acts as a connecting device. They allow you to connect energy centres on the human body, for fast connection and realignment of information. Transcendental crystals definitely allow for the connection to your higher self, as well as connection to other worlds and realities. They also allow for the rapid transference of energy between other crystals when used in body layouts or crystal healing configurations.

Tantric Twin Crystal

The tantric twin crystal is recognised as the growing together of two crystals, perfectly balanced in size, shape, form and clarity. They facilitate working as an equal with another person, or inner self-outer self, in perfect symmetry, harmony and balance. Sometimes you may find a perfect double terminated tantric twin crystal. These are very rare and highly prized tools for ascension. They are used to align completely with your higher self, to access your true soul purpose.

Time Link (Left-Handed and Right-Handed Quartz Crystal)

X-ray study has shown that the atomic structure of quartz, unique among the gem minerals, is helical, and that this spiral arrangement of atoms can be either right-handed or left-handed. This right-hand or left-hand nature of quartz, termed enantiomorphism, is occasionally manifested in crystals by the position of the small trigonal pyramidal faces, if present. This is shown in a diagram from which it will be clear that the left-handed crystal is an exact counterpart of the right-handed one, but that each is a mirror-image of the other. Such a spiral structure causes a crystal to rotate the plane of polarisation of light, and this circular polarisation, as it is termed, is made manifest by this peculiarity. These crystals, which are known in New Age terminology as time-link crystals, may point right (forwards) or left (backwards). They will allow you to travel forwards or backwards in time and space, giving access to different dimensions. Time is merely an illusion of the physical plane, in fact all time is now, but this crystal will allow you, because of its growth conditions, to understand this information clearly and incorporate this concept within your conscious awareness. This will bring a new level of enlightenment to your overall structure of the universe. The way we view the world 'colors' our experiences.

Toning Crystal

Clear quartz toning crystals have a particular high pitched sound or musical note that resonates when you use them for healing, meditation etc. They can also be identified physically by their appearance. They are usually long and thin, with a high pitched sound like tinkling glass when they are touched together.

Transmitter Crystal

The transmitter crystal is recognised by the dominant face being a perfect triangle. On either side of the triangle is a seven-sided symmetrical face. The triangle signifies the Trinity and the importance of the three vibration is recognised by many religions and faiths. It is for transmitting to the universe the awareness of the user, or to transmit healing or absent healing.

Trans-Channelling Crystal

The trans-channelling crystal is recognised by 7-3-7-3-7-3. This is a configuration of three seven-sided faces, each adjacent (on both sides) to a three-sided triangular face. This crystal combines the energy of the channelling and transmitter crystal and is extremely rare. If you are lucky enough to attract one of these crystals into your life you would be advised to meditate with it to find how you should use it within your healing regime.

Transformation Crystal

This crystal is recognised as any type or configuration of clear quartz crystal. You do not know it is a transformation crystal until it happens to start transforming and beginning its metamorphosis. This usually happens as you start to work with it. It helps you to transform, change and evolve into a higher state of consciousness, allowing you no limitations within your realm of cognizant awareness and personal reality. You may well have your belief systems challenged as this process unfolds.

Twin Crystal

The twin crystal is recognised as two crystals growing together, but not the same size or shape. This can be useful for working with another person, in a relationship such as mother/daughter, father/son, etc.

Crystal Enhancement

Crystal enhancement is a vast and specialist subject, one that could fill the whole of this book, so we will just touch on the subject with regard to crystal therapy and the effects it may have on the stones crystal therapists will purchase for their healing practice. Heat treatment is used to enhance or change the color of gemstones and crystal. It also removes flaws, which would otherwise reduce the price of the gemstone. Irradiation - radiation by alpha, beta or gamma rays is used. The verneuil process is a method that produces artificial sapphires; they are so good that it takes a trained expert to recognise them. Diamonds are often enhanced using a secret process that makes imperfections invisible. I have tried to deal with the common enhancements in Part Seven: Properties of Crystals A-Z. Due to the nature of human beings, there will always be new ways of enhancing crystals, to improve the color, clarity, price etc. This is a specialist subject and one that would be constantly on-going. If you wish to study this subject in greater depth I would strongly suggest undertaking a course as a gemmologist.

Part Two

Working with Crystals

"To see a World in a Grain of Sand,
And a Heaven in a Wild Flower,
Hold Infinity in the palm of your hand,
And Eternity in an hour."

William Blake

Crystals

Hold a quartz crystal, examine it carefully, admire its beauty, see its radiance and perfection. As you hold it gently in your hand it is possible to begin to feel the very subtle vibrations or oscillations, not only in the hand but also at various points in the body as the vibrations move to the parts which perhaps need alignment or strength. As you become more aware of its energy, feel the synchronised vibration it programmes into your energy field. Quartz crystals, these miraculous forms of nature, are an outward expression of the atomic orderliness that exists in their inner structure. Quartz crystals or silicon dioxide (SiO_2) occur in profusion throughout the earth's surface. They are a white, transparent substance when found in their pure state (no impurities - inclusions, crevices, fractures and different mineral particles). They have a hexagonal form and broadcast the complete spectrum of wavelengths - the visible colors and the low and high frequencies not perceived by us, such as radio waves, infra-red radiation and ultraviolet light etc.

Crystals have a natural allure to everyone, especially children. This is understandable when you comprehend the influence of light and subtle magnetic fields on the human energy structure and on the cellular level of the physical body. (Even if you are not consciously aware, your sub-conscious and superconscious are). As crystals can go into a state of resonance with you, you will feel their instinctive appeal and they will respond positively to you. They are marvellous life-forms of mother-nature in the process of divine evolution, just like you, just like me, just like the cosmos. Crystals resonate with the liquid crystals in your body and transfer to your bloodstream and to your circulatory system vital elements, in the form of intelligent energy fields which are essential for your health and for the rejuvenation of your body, while transmuting unwanted information that may be locked in your bones, tissues and unconscious mind. You can also programme clear quartz with a thought of love, a thought of prosperity, healing, compassion or protection.

Crystals:

* Focus, cohere and amplify energy or prana
* Relieve and release stress
* Amplify your healing power and healing potential
* Stop burn-out and energy depletion
* Stimulate harmonious brain activity
* Restore the energy structure of your body and mind
* Stimulate healing, personal growth and spiritual development

* Re-connect you with inner levels of your being and aura
* Create carrier waves of pure vibrant energy
* Improve your health and rejuvenate your body by stimulating the energy flow of the meridians
* Transfer intelligent encoded information to the bloodstream
* Transmute unwanted information that may be locked in your bones, tissues and your unconscious mind

Where to Find Crystals and Gemstones

Acquiring your crystals and gemstones will be an enjoyable adventure. It is a journey of discovery and self-discovery that can last a lifetime. Once you have been initiated into the crystal world and have made your very first contact with the devic stone consciousness you will never view the world the same. Crystals and gemstones cost very little in their tumbled form, but you can pay much more for an exquisite or rare specimen such as phenacite. Some of the sources for stones are rock shops, mineral shows, the Internet and metaphysical fairs: New Age stores are springing up everywhere as the consciousness of the planet shifts into a higher vibration. Try to find a place that has a wide variety and choice of beautiful crystals and gemstones and whose owners know the correct names, mineral content and vibrational properties. Perhaps you may be lucky enough to find beautiful stones while walking on the beach, or along the side of a river or even up in the mountains. Remember, the earth is full of crystals and gemstones.

Most crystal therapists are aware how important it is to know not only the source but where crystals and gemstones come from and by what means they were mined: for example, strip mining is the cheapest, but also causes the most destruction to our planet. It goes against the harmony of the devic kingdom. When you are selecting stones for personal healing, ask the salesperson questions such as: Where were the stones mined? What are the therapeutic properties? Buying crystals and gemstones must be a beautiful empowering experience, one that is not only enjoyable, but educational. Don't be rushed or intimidated into buying a crystal just because you feel browbeaten by the salesperson. I would suggest looking at the list below, which gives you tips on buying:

1. Damage - The more blemishes a crystal has, the less effective it will be, especially in the case of quartz crystals. If they are chipped, cracked or broken, primarily on the tips of the terminations, then they are useless for directing energy and may well even damage your energy field.

2. Clarity - For certain types of vibrational healing a crystal or gemstone must be as pure and clear as possible. This rule holds for all semi-precious gemstones and especially quartz points.

3. Shape and size - Does the shape attract you? If you are buying stones for body layouts, flat shapes or cabochons are best. The size of your clear quartz crystal is also important; you should find one that fits your hand. If you are practising chakra cleansing techniques, it is no use having a crystal that makes your arm ache because it is too heavy.

4. Rarity - Rare stones are more costly, especially if they are currently mined out, so be aware of this fact and be prepared to pay more for these special purchases.

5. Inclusions - Sometimes inclusions are very attractive. If the stone is full of rainbows it brings light and joy to the owner; often you will find 'pictures' of animals, landscapes or Angels inside a stone which make it more attractive for you personally. The great exception to this rule is if you follow Vedic astrology: then the clearer and purer the gemstone the better and it is best to buy these from specialised dealers only.

6. Vibration - Does the crystal resonate with your energy field, harmonics and frequency? If it does, you will experience sensations of harmony, balance, clarity and positiveness. Also with clear quartz the type can make a lot of difference; the list of different types is in part one of this book.

Selecting a Crystal

All crystals and gemstones are naturally tuned to particular vibrations, frequencies and energy harmonics. See which crystal captivates your eye or attracts your attention. It is usually the first one that we feel drawn to that will be 'our' crystal. When you are in attunement with a crystal, you will experience sensations of resonance, balance, harmony, joy, compassion, wisdom or love. It will give you a feeling of wholeness and completion.

Sensations Experienced

* Energetic charge or tingling on your skin or in your hands
* Humming sensations
* Electric charge
* Dampness or sweating, a moistness in your hand on rubbing the stone
* Breeze or cool wind-like energy across your skin
* Flow of energy from the termination of the crystal
* Cold
* Heat
* Pulsing or vibration
* Heat from the termination of the crystal
* Twitching in your fingers or hand
* Immediate sense of being centred and balanced
* Sound or audible humming in your ears
* Glowing light or a visible energy field
* Odour or scent
* Flush or wave of heat through your body
* Feelings of being enclosed by the crystal energy field

How to Choose a Crystal

Choosing crystals and gemstones is an intuitive act of love. So take a very deep breath and release all negative thoughts and emotions, still your mind and focus completely on the crystals as you hold them one by one. Your intention will be known. If you only wish to use the crystals, rather than becoming their partners, the crystals probably will stay 'dead' or their energy may withdraw. Part of the spiritual work of the crystal devas is to work with the human spirits. If your intention is to become a partner, much more of their 'magic' manifests in your life.

Allow yourself to notice which stones feel good to you. If a stone feels good to you it probably will be the right one for you. You may like to use a pendulum, or ask a friend to help with muscle-testing techniques. Also allow your inner guru and the crystal devas to be the teachers. Do not listen to or be too prejudiced by other people's thinking and advice, however well meant. Ask for guidance from the point of love and wisdom within yourself. If you are working from the point of love and humility you will always be helped by the crystal devas. In the West we have a very superior attitude and, in our ignorance, we tend to believe we are the highest evolved energy in the universe.

Selecting Personal Stones

A cautionary word - it is wisest not to tune in to unclean stones. The implications of tuning in to uncleaned crystals and gemstones are immense. You will run the risk of absorbing any residual negative vibrations which have been left on the stones from whoever has handled them prior to you, be it the miner, wholesaler, retailer, jeweller or any previous customer. It is very important that all crystals are cleansed before you attune to them. Cleansing is important and will ensure that any residual disharmonies are removed from the stones. There are many New Age shops and suppliers who understand how important it is metaphysically for their crystals and gemstones to be cleansed before they sell them. If the shop you buy your crystals from is not energetically aware, only choose by sight and leave the 'tuning' in till later, after you have had time to cleanse them completely. The other places to avoid attuning to crystals and gemstones are museums, where they have never had any cleansing.

Method One: Vibration

Because all crystals and gemstones are naturally tuned to a particular frequency, vibration, resonance or energy harmonics, when you attune to a stone you will experience a sensation that is appropriate to that stone's harmonic range: this very often is a feeling of harmony, peace, compassion, balance, love or wholeness.

Selecting a crystal or gemstone by its vibration:

1. Raise the sensitivity in your hands by washing them in warm water, then dry them thoroughly.
2. Begin to sensitise your hands by shaking them; this releases blocked energy.
3. Briskly rub your hands together; this begins to concentrate the chi or Prana into your hands and begins to sensitise them.
4. Hold your hands with your palms facing each other, about nine inches apart. Feel the energy radiating and vibrating between your hands; play with this energy.
5. Begin to form this energy into a ball and visualise it yellow in color. When it feels right, place this yellow ball into the solar plexus area. This energises your mental body, allowing you to perceive the energy of the crystals more easily.
6. Take a deep breath and relax. Release all negative thoughts and emotions, still your mind and focus completely on the crystals as you hold them one by one. Your intention will be known.
7. Hold several different crystals, allow plenty of time with each stone. Normally you will find your receptive left hand (if you are right-handed) finds this process easier than your right hand. The reverse will be true if you are left-handed.
8. Make a mental note of which stone feels good to you personally. If it intuitively feels 'right' to you it is definitely the 'right' one for you at this time.
9. When you have finished, ground, centre and focus yourself. Then write down the experience, for future reference.

Method Two: Intuition

1. Take a very deep breath and release all negative thoughts and emotions.
2. Still your mind and focus completely on the crystals as you look at them one by one. Your intention will be known to the crystals.

3. Hold each crystal or gemstone in your mind and feel the energy or vibration; if it intuitively feels good to you, it has a natural affinity with you.

4. When you have finished, ground, centre and focus yourself. Then write down the experience, for future reference.

Method Three: Scanning

Another method is scanning, passing your hand slowly over several crystals until you can detect a crystal that feels hotter/cooler/stronger vibration/pulse etc.

1. Raise the sensitivity in your hands by washing them in warm water, then dry them thoroughly.

2. Begin to sensitise your hands by shaking them; this releases blocked energy.

3. Briskly rub your hands together; this begins to concentrate the chi or Prana into your hands and begins to sensitise them.

4. Hold your hands with your palms facing each other, about nine inches apart. Feel the energy radiating and vibrating between your hands; play with this energy.

5. Begin to form this energy into a ball and visualise it yellow in color. When it feels right, place this yellow ball into the solar plexus area. This energises your mental body, allowing you to perceive the energy of the crystal more easily.

6. Now take a very deep breath and release all negative thoughts and emotions, still your mind and focus completely on the crystals. Your intention will be known to the crystals.

7. Pass your left hand slowly over several crystals and begin to feel and see their energy. Gradually work along each crystal, observing the energy in any way you can, via heat, cold, tingling, vibration, pulse, etc. If you are left-handed, work with your right hand.

8. When you have finished, ground, centre and focus yourself. Then write down the experience, for future reference.

Method Four: Kinesiology

Kinesiology, or muscle testing, is one very effective means of selecting personal stones. This very simplified version really is extremely useful.

1. You need to find another person to work with.

2. Extend your right arm at shoulder height.

3. First test your normal muscle strength by having the other person rest two fingers on your extended arm and press down gently but firmly while you resist.

4. Then with your left hand, hold the crystal or stone on your witness area, which is at the thymus, the area where your physical and etheric bodies meet.

5. Ask the question "Is this the right crystal for me to wear or carry?" or "Is this a good gemstone for me to use for self healing? Is this good for meditation?" "Is it good for channelling?"

6. After each question, have the other person do the same finger test on your extended arm, while you resist.

7. If your arm remains strong, you have made the right choice. If your arm becomes weak, try again with another stone.

8. When you have finished, ground, centre and focus yourself. Then write down the experience, for future reference.

Method Five: Resonance

There are many other methods of choosing your crystal or gemstone. My favourite is to use resonance, which is connected breathing technique. I 'discovered' this technique as a child, using rhythmical, connected, fine breaths which are long, slow and deep, allowing us to connect to, and experience, the vibrational aspect of the energy that drives the breath. This energy is our divine essence. When using this technique you will reach a point where you feel as though you are 'being breathed'. As you continue with this breathing practice you will experience it aiding you in maintaining and restoring health and vitality and increasing longevity. This is due to its pure and perfect nature.

Step one: Hold a clear quartz single terminated crystal in your right hand with the termination pointing away from you.

Step two: Take a long deep breath in and breathe out very slowly as though a candle flame is in front of you and your breath must be so gentle as not to blow it out.

Step three: Begin to breathe in a connected way, where each inhale flows naturally into each exhale with no pause. The Buddhists call this 'chasing the breath'. The re-birthers call it rhythmical breathing.

Step four: Breathe finely and slowly, through the nostrils, until you feel the resonance or oscillation.

Step five: Slowly bring your right hand and crystal to the witness area at the thymus - this area is where your physical and etheric bodies meet - and continue to breathe slowly and calmly.

Step six: Allow the crystal consciousness to merge with your energy field.

Step seven: When you have finished, ground, centre and focus yourself. Then write down the experience, for future reference.

The Buddhists say that correct breathing keeps the body calm - calm breath, calm body, calm mind. The crystal consciousness is much slower and calmer than our normal everyday vibration. This is one of the reasons why we, as humans, find it so very therapeutic and beneficial to our health, vitality and well-being to work with the crystal consciousness. The crystal energy is also much more focused than most human minds; crystals do not scatter their energy as humans do. Using connected breathing resonance allows us to access the crystal vibration with greater ease.

Method Six: Breath

Step one: Another way to find a crystal you feel empathy with is to hold your crystal in your right hand and take a deep breath.

Step two: Hold your breath until you feel your body begin to shake, vibrate or oscillate.

Step three: As you exhale and relax, point the termination of the crystal towards the palm of your left hand, at a distance of two to six inches.

Step four: Begin slowly to move the crystal in a clockwise circular motion. You will begin to feel a sensation in your left hand reflecting the movements of the crystal.

Step five: Begin to move your right hand further and further away from your left hand, keeping the circular motion intact. Move your hand as far away as you can, until you no longer feel the crystal sensation in your left hand, then begin slowly spiralling the crystal back in, then out.

Step six: Continue in this manner until your left hand feels a sensation of lightness, tingling or heat.

Step seven: When you have finished, ground, centre and focus yourself.

Method Seven: Hand Activation

Another technique is hand activation and attunement.

1. Hold your breath until you feel your body shake, tremble, vibrate or oscillate.
2. As you exhale and relax, point the termination of the crystal towards the palm of your left hand, at a distance of two to six inches, and slowly move the crystal in a clockwise circular motion. You will begin to feel a sensation in your left hand reflecting the movements of the crystal. Begin to move your right hand further and further away from your left hand, keeping the circular motion intact.
3. Move your hand as far away as you can, until you no longer feel the crystal sensation in your left hand, then slowly spiral the crystal back in, then out, then in.
4. Continue in this manner until your hand feels very light and full of energy.
5. Repeat the process on the back of your left hand.
6. Then trace round the outline of your hand three times with the termination of the crystal.
7. Put your crystal down, close your eyes and feel the difference between your left and right hands.
8. Repeat the whole process, this time on your right hand, holding your crystal in your left hand.
9. This crystal technique will remove all the energy blocks within your hands and will aid you in your crystal healing practice. It is also good for those who work as Reiki or spiritual healers. Regular use of this technique will enhance your health and well-being also. The hand represents the whole of the body, so in fact you are carrying out a crystal healing session on yourself each time you use this simple technique.
10. When you have finished, ground, centre and focus yourself.

Cleansing Your Crystal

This is the next stage. No matter who may have given it to you, always cleanse your crystal to remove any negative vibrations or physical dirt. It is very important that all crystals are cleansed before and after use. This will ensure that any residual disharmonies are removed from the stones. This you can do with water, smudging etc. Again, be guided by your own inner knowledge. Only use a technique that truly resonates with your energy field.

Natural Water Cleansing (this is particularly suited to those born under a water sign)

First find a source of pure, clean, fresh water. This may be a stream, waterfall, river or spring. Hold your crystal under the flowing water until you feel all the dirt or stored negative vibrations have left it. When this process is complete you will feel your crystal is pure and vibrant. It is now ready to be used or, if it is a clear quartz crystal, programmed, charged or dedicated. Please check that your crystal is safe in water. Some crystals, such as talc, halite or selenite, are water soluble.

Saltwater Cleansing

Purely from a scientific angle, I would never use saltwater on a crystal, as this process will, in a short time, damage the crystalline structure and split the crystal or make it appear cloudy, dull, or change color. Remember, salt is also a crystal. Salt will get into any other crystalline structure, causing irreparable structural damage. If you do want to try cleansing with the salt vibration, I recommend you place the crystal in a large bowl of sea salt, allowing enough salt to completely cover the crystal. Leave it buried for as long as your intuition tells you. You could also dowse for the correct amount of time. Wash your crystal with plenty of fresh, clear, clean pure water after its salt immersion. Laying an Opal in salt will damage it by extracting the water. You can lay the Opal or any crystal that might react negatively to salt - in a small glass dish that is embedded in a larger glass dish full of salt.

Smudge Cleansing (this technique is particularly suited to those born under an air sign)

The burning of herbs or incense is a sacred practice held in common by many traditions. In American Indian tradition the practice is called "smudging" or sometimes "smoking" even though the herbs may not be inhaled. Smudging, practised traditionally, takes many forms. Sometimes the herbs are tied in a bundle and called a "smudge stick". There are certain herbs that lend themselves to braiding, such as sweet-grass. To smudge cleanse a crystal or gemstone you need a safe container that is heat-proof. Ceramic and glass bowls or abalone shells work well. There are also special chalices designed for smudging. Unless you use a chalice, place a layer of soil, sand or salt in the bottom for insulation, before adding your charcoal and herbs. Some people place the herbs on quick-lighting charcoal, which is available from many New Age shops, health food stores and Bible and Christian supply shops. (Smudging is similar to Catholic and Orthodox incense burning, for which Bible and Christian supply shops carry prepared charcoal blocks). Place either sage, cedar, copal, lavender, fennel or sweet-grass into the container and light the herbs using a candle or lighter. Matches are not very efficient because it takes a while to get the herbs smoking. If you prefer to light your whole bundle or braid, hold it in a candle flame until the smudge glows red hot. Blow out the flame; it will smoulder for at least a few minutes. You will need a bowl or shell to catch the hot ashes. The bundle or braid of herbs will eventually go out by itself. Should you need to put it out before it does, you can tap it out as you would a cigarette or cigar. Putting water on it to put it out is messier and considered disrespectful to the fire spirits. The idea of burning herbs is to release their fragrance and energy, not to fill your room or lungs with smoke. Burning excessive amounts of smudge can lead to respiratory distress and other respiratory problems. Show consideration for other people when burning smudge. Avoid burning smudge in the same room as infants and anyone who is pregnant and those who suffer from respiratory problems, or those who have asthma or respiratory allergies. Avoid fire hazards; never smudge around flammable substances and never leave burning smudge, charcoal, candles or fires unattended. Smudging is also used during healing work and prayer. The Native Americans believe it helps them to connect to their spirit helpers. The smoke carries their intention to the sky world. Allow the smoke to pass around the crystal, gently carrying away any harmful, stagnant vibrations to the elements of air to be dispersed and transmuted. If you are using this technique indoors, be sure to keep a window open to allow the stagnant vibrations a place by which to exit.

Bay leaf - used in the autumn to protect from colds, flu and infections
Cedar, Cypress, Juniper - to consecrate and make sacred
Fennel - repels evil energies
Lavender - protection, relaxation and cleansing
Mint - cleansing, invigorating and uplifting
Mugwort - healing, divination and dream work. Unsafe for pregnancy
Pine - purifying and disinfecting
Resin, Copal, Balsam, Gum, Sap - embodying the four elements for balance
Sage - clears negative energy, foreign energy and entities from oneself
Sweet-grass - grounding, protection and making sacred
Wild tobacco - traditionally used to connect with sacred beings and wisdom

Earth Cleansing (this technique is particularly attractive to the earth signs amongst us)

This technique is extremely useful when you feel your crystal is particularly negative. By placing it in the earth you are returning it to its 'Great Mother' for realigning, nurturing and cleansing. Crystals love this experience; they simply enjoy the whole process of earth placement. After you have buried your crystal in the earth, please mark the place with a twig or other marker if you want to find it again. Also be aware that if your pet has watched you enact this ceremony it may try to dig up your crystal to help you! This cleansing process can take some time. Once again, allow your inner guru to let you know how long to leave your crystal in the earth. Please note, however, that you may have a soil that will damage your gemstone. Some soils are very acid, so please check before you bury it, otherwise you may find your crystal has been damaged.

Fire Cleansing (fire signs love this one and it's quick, which also appeals to fire signs)

Simply pass your crystal very quickly through a small candle flame, taking care not to burn yourself or the crystal. I always use a white candle for this 'Grandfather' fire ceremony. This is a quick dynamic process, which is instant and very effective. Please note, however, that you must never put an Opal near fire, as fire will damage it. Another technique with fire is to surround your crystal or crystals that need cleansing with small tea lights, normally four, one for each direction. You can leave them in place until the candles burn out, which is normally four hours or for as long as you feel is the right length of time. This process also works very well to burn off negativity from the human aura. In the case of humans you may need up to 12 small candles. Begin by lighting one, then two, three, etc. until you can feel the effect of the flames in your auric shell. You may even hear hissing sounds from the candles as negative energy is burned away. I like to use this technique often.

Flowers or Petals for Cleansing

Gather petals or flowers of any kind you feel attracted to. Very often you may feel a particular vibration is needed for each crystal or gemstone. Obvious flower choices would be lavender for cleansing, roses for love, chamomile for soothing: the list is endless. Place your flowers or petals in a clear glass container and leave the crystals completely covered by the flowers for at least twenty-four hours. This process is gentle and nurturing.

Rice Cleansing

Fill a clear glass bowl with plain brown rice (uncooked) and place your crystal or gemstone in the rice. Make sure your crystal is completely covered. Leave it for twenty-four hours and safely discard the rice afterwards (do not eat it). The rice will have absorbed the negative vibration from the crystal, leaving it clean and ready for re-use in whatever way you choose.

Sound Cleansing

For this process you will need a crystal singing bowl, bells, a gong, ting-shaws, rattle or drum. Simply allow your chosen sound to 'wash' over the crystal, purifying, cleansing and freeing it of any stuck or negative vibrations. This process can take a little time, but it is very effective for large quantities of crystals which may all need cleansing at the same time.

Toning

You may use a mantra such as Om to cleanse a crystal or gemstone. This is quick and efficient, bringing a powerful cosmic vibrational energy to aid you in this way, which is very empowering to both you and your crystal. You may also charge or energise your crystal with your favourite mantra.

Breath Cleansing

This technique was given to me by a Native American elder. Simply breathe into your crystal three times with the view of clearing any unwanted vibration from your crystal or pendant with your breath. I would never use this technique on a crystal I was using in healing others, but I feel it is fine for my own personal crystals; it imbues them with my energy and my pure vibration and stops other vibrations from intruding into the crystals' energy fields.

Crystal Cleansing

You may decide to cleanse your crystal by placing it on an amethyst bed or cluster. This is a very powerful and effective method, but please be aware that if your crystal is softer than amethyst (7) it may become scratched and dull. The other problem with this technique is that the amethyst cluster is so powerful it will remove other vibrations completely. In other words, if you leave the crystal on it too long it will have lost its original vibration and have absorbed the amethyst signature, which may take some time to dissipate from your crystal.

Care of Your Crystal

When you purchase or are given a crystal or gemstone, you have to 'care' for it. Remember it is a sacred unique piece of Mother Earth that you will be able to cherish for ever. This means finding a position for it where it is safe, secure and is in harmonious surroundings. This facilitates its vibration to work with you and for you. Please make sure your crystal is content and honoured. Do not put it in your pocket, to be scratched, chipped and knocked by your keys and loose change, but maybe in a small pouch or on a special healing shelf or altar. If it is a pendant, please take very special care of it. Do not allow others, however well meaning, to touch your pendant or personal crystals. Please do not wear a pendant in the shower or bath. Wearing pendants in the sea or swimming baths is not a good idea, as your pendant chain may break. Also, take your pendant off at night and place it on your bedside table or altar.

Control or Master Crystal

Crystal vibrational therapists normally work with a 'control' or 'master crystal'. This is your own personal crystal. You may use this for all your crystal healing work. It is your main crystal. It is your best friend and your guide into the crystal kingdom. It usually is a clear quartz single terminated point, between 3" and 10" long, 1" to 3" thick. It may be a powerful masculine focused water-clear laser quartz or the type of milky quartz crystal from Madagascar which has a soft feminine energy. Perhaps you will be attracted to a clear quartz point from Arkansas, USA, with a balanced male/female energy. You will try not to let anyone touch your control crystal, because it will be tuned into your energy vibration. You may have more than one control crystal in your life. As you grow in knowledge and understanding, another control crystal may be attracted to you. When this happens, release the original control crystal with love and pass it on to do other work. If you do not have a control crystal as yet, be assured that one will be attracted to you in the course of your crystal healing work, if you so desire.

Attuning to Crystals - Activating

Crystals oscillate to a natural 'healing' frequency that is fully activated by the concatenated power of the focused human mind. This is achieved by techniques such as meditation and visualization. Crystals are consequently compatible tools with which to harmonise, heal and balance the human energy field. All you need to do to unlock this vibrational 'healing' potential is to focus your mental energy on the crystals when using them.

Dedicating Your Crystal

Simply dedicate your crystal to your highest good and the good of all, then fill it with the appropriate image, finally filling the crystal with love and compassion. These are the vibrations you are best to work with and the only vibrations to use when healing others. You may prefer to enact a simple ritual and dedicate the crystal, asking that "from this point on this crystal may only be used in the name of love and compassion and always for the universal highest good of all".

Programming

Please note that only clear quartz crystals can actually be 'programmed'. All other crystals, minerals and gemstones automatically contain their own specific programme, via their mineral and vibrational make-up. That is why you must choose your crystal with great care for the specific purpose you have in mind. It is always wisest to consult a qualified crystal therapist who has completed a full professional crystal course, before committing yourself to an expensive purchase. You can also take a course yourself. There are excellent courses run by many organisations worldwide. Allow yourself to be guided to the course that resonates with you. In other words, follow your heart: if you feel joy and excitement, this will be the right course for you. When you enquire about courses, always ask how long the facilitators have been working with crystals, how long they have been running crystal courses, are they qualified tutors and, most of all, how their course will develop your inner knowing, wisdom and compassion. To programme your clear quartz crystal, simply hold your cleansed quartz crystal between your hands in a prayer position at your heart chakra, concentrate on the energy of your choice and fill your crystal with this energy. Say "I intend this crystal to be an effective tool for healing/meditation/dream interpretation, etc". You may enact a simple ceremony. Or you may like to programme your crystal during a meditation. Please remember, positive emotions strengthen your energy field, bringing health, balance and vitality, whilst negative emotions bring sickness, instability, mood swings and low energy. So always remain positive emotionally when programming your clear quartz crystal.

Tuning

When you have cleansed your crystals you 'turn them on', like switching on a radio, but to receive a 'broadcast' you must tune the dial to the appropriate station. Also the 'frequency' you choose when 'tuning' depends on your purpose. Say "It is my focused pure intention that this crystal be an effective tool for healing/absent healing/meditation/scrying/dream interpretation, etc".

Energising Crystals

This is like "programming" and it is useful when you feel your crystal needs a positive charge of energy, filling the clear quartz crystal with sunlight, moonlight, sound or storm energy, Reiki, Angel energy, Karuna or Pranic healing. You can even place your crystal under a pyramid.

Charging Crystals

Charging is like "programming", filling the clear quartz crystal with sunlight, moonlight, storm energy, Prana, Karuna or planetary energy. You may even feel that you associate your particular stone or crystal with a totem or power animal. Many people also fill their crystals with Angelic healing energy, which instantly lifts the vibration of any stone. It is also possible to fill your crystal with a specific sound or color vibration for more individual healing energies. Clear quartz will also hold the charge of air, earth, fire and water or any combination of the four.

Moonlight

Moonlight is feminine, liquid, yin, calm, intuitive, still, mysterious, hidden. To energise your clear quartz crystal with moonlight, simply place your cleansed crystal outside during the three days of the full moon. If you wish to have a banishing energy within your crystal to help you let go of negative thoughts, habits, people or situations, simply place your quartz crystal out of doors in the three days of the dark moon. You may enact a simple ceremony of dedication and thanks to the moon during this process for more immediate results. The moon influences certain crystals naturally: these are moonstone, labradorite, pearl, snow quartz and mother-of-pearl.

Sunlight

Sunlight is associated with fire, personal power, agni (Lord of fire), ambition, intellectual activity, combustion, anger, joy, laughter, expansion, movement, yang. To energise your clear quartz crystal with sunlight, simply place your cleansed crystal outside on a sunny day. You may enact a simple ceremony of dedication and thanks to the sun during this process for more immediate and powerful results. The sun influences certain crystals naturally: these are ruby, garnet, citrine, gold, golden labradorite and sunstone.

Starlight

Starlight is associated with cosmic awareness, universal energies, brightness, expansiveness, wishing and wish fulfilment. To energise your clear quartz crystal with starlight, simply place your cleansed crystal outside on a clear night, or you may wish to fill it with a particular star energy. Maybe you already have a guiding star or star-being contact. You may enact a simple ceremony of dedication and thanks to the stars and the star-beings during this process for more immediate and powerful results. It is also possible to use your clear quartz crystal for wish fulfilment. Simply go outside on a clear starry night, look up to the stars and think about the wish you want fulfilling. If it is in the name of love and light and the highest universal good of all beings, your wish will be fulfilled. The stars influence certain crystals naturally: these are iolite, moldavite, star sapphire and asterised quartz.

Angel Energy

Angel energy is associated with hope, protection, warmth, love, compassion, universal energies and guidance. To energise your clear quartz crystal with Angelic energy, simply hold your cleansed crystal in your left hand; left is for receiving. You may enact a simple ceremony, asking the Angels of light, love and protection to place their pristine energies within the crystal. Alternatively you may already work with a particular Angel, such as Archangel Michael for protection, or Archangel Raphael for healing. Simply ask your Angel to place their energy within the crystal. Please give thanks after the dedication ceremony. This process is immediate and powerful. The results are always swift and pristine. The Angels influence certain crystals naturally: these are angelite, seraphinite, selenite and danburite.

Karuna

Karuna is the energy of compassionate action. To energise your clear quartz crystal with Karuna, simply hold your cleansed crystal between your hands in a prayer position at your heart chakra and meditate on the energy of compassion and compassion for all beings. Remember the most compassionate thing you can do for all beings is to become enlightened. This then raises not only your vibratory rate, but the vibration of all who come into contact with you. You may enact a simple ceremony of dedication and thanks to all enlightened beings, both in the physical realm and those from other realms during this process for more immediate and powerful results. The influences of the Karuna energies are contained in certain crystals naturally: these are morganite, rhodocrosite and aquamarine.

Storm

The element of storm is the most transformational of all the elements. It is a combination of air, earth, fire and water. This synergy of energies is very powerful and not to be worked with lightly. It is sudden and powerful and embodies the creative and destructive forces of nature. It also combines the yin yang vibration and, as such, has a point of perfect balance. The earth is renewed by the storm vibration as it quickly cleanses and purifies the environment. If you wish to work with this powerful rebirth energy, place your crystals outside before a thunderstorm reaches you, allow them plenty of time to absorb the energies and wait for the storm to finish before you go outside again to retrieve your crystals. Some 'stones' are already working with this vibration, such as herderite, fulgurite, moldavite, Tibetan tektite and phenacite.

Earth

Earth energy is associated with physical energy, gravity, self-preservation, being grounded and deep healing. To energise your clear quartz crystal with the earth element when you wish to work with the energy of abundance, strength and deep healing to reconnect you to your roots, or when you feel spacey or detached from reality, simply place your crystal back into the earth. By placing it in the earth you are returning it to its 'Great Mother' for realigning, nurturing and the magic of abundance. Crystals love this experience; they simply enjoy the whole process of earth placement. After you have buried your crystal in the earth, please mark the place with a twig or other marker if you want to find it again. Also be aware that if your pet has watched you enact this ceremony it may try to dig up your crystal to help you! This cleansing process can take some time. Please note, however, that you may have a soil that will damage your gemstone. Some soils are very acid, so please check before you bury it, otherwise you may find your crystal has been damaged. You may enact a simple earth healing ceremony of dedication and thanks to the Earth Mother for deep healing and connection; if you do this during the process you will find a more immediate and powerful result. The earth influences all the crystals she has given birth to.

Water

The water element is associated with emotions, cleansing, tears and all fluid functions of the body. To energise your clear quartz crystal with the water element, simply find a source of pure, clean, fresh water. This may be a stream, waterfall, river or spring. Hold your crystal or place your crystal under the flowing water. You may enact a simple ceremony of dedication and thanks to the element of water during this process for more immediate and powerful results. The water element influences certain crystals naturally: these are enhydros, water sapphire, river-tumbled pebbles, aquamarine and aqua aura quartz.

Fire

The fire element is associated with heat, personal power, agni (Lord of fire), ambition, intellectual activity, combustion, anger, joy, laughter, expansion, movement and yang. To energise your clear quartz crystal with the fire element, simply light a white candle and place your crystal in front of it. Ask the crystal to absorb the energy of fire or you may use any source of the fire element that will not damage you or the crystal and is appropriate to the fire element. You may enact a simple ceremony of dedication and thanks to the fire during this process for more immediate and powerful results. Fire influences certain crystals naturally: these are fire agate, fire opal, pumice, Mexican fire opal and sunstone.

Air

The element of air is associated with movement, breath, lightness, freedom and spirit. To energise your clear quartz crystal with the element of air, simply place your cleansed crystal outside on a windy or breezy day. You may enact a simple ceremony of dedication and thanks to the element of air during this process for more immediate and powerful results. The element of air influences certain crystals naturally: these are amethyst, selenite (with air bubbles in) or any crystal that contains air bubbles. Moldavite and other tektites very often contain air bubbles; this is ancient air, which is full of prehistoric memories.

Color

To energise your clear quartz crystal with a particular color vibration, simply hold your cleansed crystal between your hands in a prayer position at your heart chakra and meditate on the energy of the color you wish to work with. Feel the crystal begin to radiate the color vibration of your choice. Alternatively you can wrap your clear quartz crystal in a cloth of the color you wish it to absorb, or place it on a colored gel. You may enact a simple ceremony of dedication and thanks to the elements of color during this process for more immediate and powerful results. The influences of color are contained in all colored crystals and gemstones naturally.

Tree

To energise your clear quartz crystal with a particular tree vibration, simply hold your cleansed crystal between your hands in a prayer position at your heart chakra and meditate on the energy of the tree you wish to work with. Feel the crystal begin to radiate the tree vibration of your choice. Alternatively you can place your clear quartz crystal in or near the tree you wish it to absorb, or place it on a leaf, blossom, fruit or photograph of the type of tree. You may enact a simple ceremony of dedication and thanks to the elemental/deva of the tree during this process for more immediate and powerful results. The elementals of certain trees naturally influence fossilized wood and amber; this is ancient energy, which is full of prehistoric memories.

Flower

To energise your clear quartz crystal with a particular flower or plant vibration, simply hold your cleansed crystal between your hands in a prayer position at your heart chakra and meditate on the energy of the flower or plant you wish to work with. Feel the crystal begin to radiate the flower or plant vibration of your choice. Alternatively you can place your clear quartz crystal in or near the flower or plant you wish it to absorb, or place it on a leaf, blossom, fruit or photograph of the type of flower or plant. You may enact a simple ceremony of dedication and thanks to the elemental/deva of the flower during this process for more immediate and powerful results. The elementals of certain flowers and plants influence amber, which may contain pollen or pieces of flower or plant material; this is ancient energy, which is full of prehistoric memories.

Prana or Reiki

To energise your clear quartz crystal with Prana or Reiki, simply hold your cleansed quartz crystal between your hands in a prayer position at your heart chakra, meditate on the energy of Prana or Reiki and fill your crystal with this energy. You may enact a simple ceremony of dedication and thanks to all enlightened beings, both in the physical and those from other realms, during this process, for more immediate and powerful results. You can then carry your crystal around with you, or give it to someone else who needs healing. Another traditional way crystals are used with Reiki is to write down on a piece of paper any problem you are experiencing and place it under the Reiki crystal, intending that the Reiki energy flows constantly into the problem to create a solution or healing that is to the highest possible good of all. You must charge the crystal once a week to maintain the strength and integrity of the energetic link. Another way to use crystals and Reiki is the Reiki web of light.

Reiki Web of Light

Reiki is a powerful, mysterious healing energy and by combining crystals with the Reiki we have seen amazing, tremendous positive results from this technique. The Japanese word REIKI means power and a Reiki attunement can only be facilitated by a Master who has personally been attuned to the Reiki energy. For those crystal therapists who are not attuned to Reiki, the following crystal web of light will still be effective, especially if you use Prana or chi for activation.

A crystal web of light can be established and charged with Reiki to heal, protect or manifest a goal for 48 hours or longer after it has been charged. In addition, the Reiki web can be used by your guides and higher self as a connection to transmit healing and help your clients. Don't rush choosing your crystals for the web of light; we often find that it is better to allow the 'right' crystals to come into your life. You may already possess some clear quartz crystals. If so, these should be considered as possible candidates for your Reiki web. One more question you should ask yourself before you begin is: do the crystals you have chosen wish to participate in the web of light? Do they feel right for this device?

When you are ready to create your web of Reiki light you will need 8 clear quartz crystals:

6 small (2")
1 medium (4")
1 double terminated (2-3")

Your clear quartz crystals should be totally cleansed before using them by placing them under running water for one hour. Say a prayer over them during this process of purification, asking the crystal Angels to help guide you as you set up this web of light. Also ask the spirit of the water to cleanse your crystals. Then ask the crystals to help you manifest your highest spiritual purpose this lifetime.

You may also attune your quartz crystals to the energies of the sun, moon and earth by placing them in the earth with the terminations pointing out for the three days of the full moon. Do this in a safe place where they will be bathed in the appropriate energies. Say a prayer over them each evening, asking for the creative powers of the universe to help you.

Next, you must prepare a special place for your Reiki web of light. It should be a place that only you have access to, or at least a safe place. It could be your Reiki altar or shelf, a desk top or window-sill. From your 8 crystals, the medium-sized one is your control or master charging quartz crystal. Place the 6 small quartz crystals at equal points around a circle of about 12" in diameter pointing inwards. This will create a hexagon or six-sided figure. This is the optimum web for working with quartz crystals. Clear quartz crystals contain the full spectrum of white light energy (white light contains all colors and all energies, so this enables you to help yourself and your clients on every level of their bodies and minds). Clear quartz crystals are master healers and are the only programmable crystals on the planet at this time.

Lastly, place the double terminated crystal in the centre. This completes the web of light. The next steps are:

1. Choose a photograph of yourself and sign your name on the back.

2. Draw the four Usui Reiki symbols on the back, along with their names.

3. Include a powerful affirmation such as: "I am perfectly protected with divine love, compassion and wisdom; I now allow myself to heal on every level of my being, as I fulfill my highest spiritual goals this lifetime" or "Reiki guides and Angels, heal and guide me in all I do" or "I am a channel for Reiki healing, love and compassion, the more I use my Reiki the stronger it becomes until I am of great service to all I meet" or " I now connect with the divine essence that dwells within me, as I allow the Reiki energy to flow into my life". Use any of these or a combination of them or be creative and make up your own affirmation to suit you personally.

After your crystals have been purified and blessed and you know how you will arrange them and your photograph is ready, your next step is to charge your crystals with Reiki. Take each quartz crystal individually and hold it in your hands; allow Reiki to flow into the crystal, filling it with Reiki energy for at least 10 minutes. As you do this, say a prayer asking your Reiki guides and Angels, Archangels and all beings of love and light to assist you in the process of charging your quartz crystals with Reiki energy. You can also do a Reiki attunement on each crystal if you are a Reiki Master. This gives them an even greater charge of higher frequency energy. As you charge each crystal, place it in its correct position on the Reiki web of light. After the crystals are in position, do not move them, as this will weaken their energy connection. Then charge your master crystal in the same way.

Your master crystal will be used to keep your Reiki web charged with positive healing energies. Charge it with Reiki the same way as the others. Then, while holding it in your right hand, begin drawing out pie-shaped sections above the web, imagining the energy coming out of your master crystal and charging the web of light. Start with the central double terminated crystal and move to an outer crystal, then move counter clockwise to the next outer crystal and back to the centre, then back out to the same outer crystal you just came in from, and so on, making pie-shaped movements and moving around the web in a counter-clockwise direction.

As you do this, repeat an affirmation/mantra/prayer such as: "I empower this web with love, with light, with compassion, with healing, with wisdom; I empower this web with love, with compassion, with light, with healing, with wisdom, to heal, to heal, to heal; I empower this web with joy to heal, to heal, to heal; I call on my Reiki guides and Angels to empower this web with love, with love, with love, to heal, to heal, I am filled with compassion for all beings". Again feel free to create your own positive affirmation/mantra/prayer that feels perfect for you.

Meditate with your master crystal each day or night and use it to charge your Reiki web of light each and every day. If you miss the odd day, do not worry, but you must keep your web charged for it to remain activated.

You must work with it regularly to obtain the best positive results. For greater empowerment you may draw the four Usui Reiki symbols over the web with your master crystal and charge the web regularly with your master crystal.

If you have a person to whom you would like to send Reiki or a project or goal you would like to empower with Reiki, write it out on a piece of paper and draw out the four Reiki symbols. Then Reiki it between your hands and place it within your web of light. Your crystal Reiki web will continue to send Reiki to the person or to manifest your goal or project.

You may also place other crystals in the centre of the Reiki web of light and I would suggest looking up the properties of the different crystals and gemstones in the relevant section of this book to find which crystal would help you.

Part Three

Subtle Anatomy

Because the eye gazes but can catch no glimpse of it,
it is called elusive.

Because the ear listens but cannot hear it,
it is called rarefied.

Because the hand feels for it but cannot find it,
it is called infinitesimal.

Its rising brings no light;
Its sinking no darkness,
It is called chi.

Tao Te Ching

The Chakras

Chakra is a Sanskrit word. It literally means wheel, ring or circle. *Prana* (energy) is said to flow through the human body along the three main *nadis* (channels), namely, *susumna* (fire), *pingala* (male) and *ida* (female). Susumna is situated inside the spinal column. Pingala and ida start respectively from the right and left nostrils, move up to the crown of the head and course downwards to the base of the spine. These two nadis intersect with each other and also with the susumna. These junctions of the nadis are known as chakras or wheels, which regulate the mechanism of the bodies. Even to think of a chakra as a wheel is merely not enough. It is, in metaphysical terminology, a vortex. Chakras pick up cosmic vibrations, or Universal Life Force and distribute them throughout the body via the *nadis, dhamanis* and *siras*.

The body is a replica of the universe, a microcosm of the macrocosm on the physical and spiritual levels. As you develop your inner guru, you will become aware of your own chakras. Although there are literally hundreds within the human body, we are most familiar with the seven main ones, which are aligned or 'embedded' within the spinal column. These moderators of subtle energy are envisioned in classic lore as a 'lotus' flower. Each chakra's lotus has a different number of petals. The number of petals is related both to Sanskrit symbolism concerning the configuration of subtle nerves, called nadis, that emanate from the particular region of the spinal column where the chakra is located, and also to the meaning of particular vowels and consonants in the Sanskrit alphabet.

These seven main chakras are called 'master' chakras. They are also gateways between various dimensions, physical, emotional, spiritual, etc. On a physical level, chakras correspond to nerve ganglia, where there is a high degree of nervous activity, and to the glands in the endocrine system. Each person's chakras are unique, yet there are basic similarities among us all. When they are clear and free-flowing, vital optimum health results. When the energy centres (chakras) are blocked, distorted or inactive, we find ill health or dis-ease occurs. The aim of all of us is to maintain the free-flowing energy within the body, keeping it as clear as possible to maintain a happier healthier life. In the ancient yoga tradition it was important to conserve the energies generated within the body and prevent their dissipation, therefore *asanas* (postures) and *mudras* (hand positions), *pranayamas* (life-force-breath) and *bandhas* (seals or locks) were used. The heat so generated causes the *Kundalini Shakti* (Divine cosmic energy) to uncoil. The serpent lifts her head, enters the susumna and is forced up through the system of chakras one by one to the *sahasrara* (chakra at the top of the head). This journey upwards through the chakras is spoken of as 'Kundalini rising' the Kundalini Goddess is represented as a coiled snake wrapped around a phallus, or *Lingham*, which represents male sexuality. Female sexuality is located primarily in the Sacral (second) chakra.

1. Root Chakra

Sanskrit name *muladhara* (*mula* = root, source; *adhara* = support, vital part). Also known as the base or earth chakra.

Located in the perineum, the base of the spine, between anus and genitals.

Associated with physical energy, physical health and fitness, gravity, self-preservation, survival, being grounded, adrenal glands, spinal column. All the solid elements of the body.

Energy location: feet, ankles, legs, knees, thighs and large intestine. Energetic gateway between us and the earth, also energies of childhood and the past. When this chakra is developed, we are more grounded, solid and powerful at physical levels of survival. Knowledge of the past, present and future are bestowed when this chakra is fully activated.

Malfunction: osteoarthritis, obesity, haemorrhoids, constipation and problems associated with the feet, legs, bones and teeth. Mental lethargy, 'spaciness', incapability of inner stillness.

The first chakra (Earth) is masculine; solid; earthly; yang.

Element and ruling planet: earth, Saturn.

Astrological association: Capricorn.

Intake: protein.

Symbol: 4-petal crimson-red lotus flower, around a yellow square containing a downward-pointing white triangle containing the *Bija* Lam. Here also is the *Brahma granthi*, or knot of *Brahma*, which must be forced open through rigorous *sadhana* and intensive purification for the *Kundalini* to rise. The colors red, scarlet and crimson are associated with this chakra.

Names of petals: vam, sam, sham, sam.

Sensory channel: smell.

Sound - *Bija* Mantra: Lam (female) or Lang (male).

Musical note - C

Associated creature: elephant.

Developmental age and lesson: 1-8 years. Standing up for oneself.

Sephira: Malkuth.

Archangel: Sandalphon.

Gemstones: ruby, garnet, zircon, ruby aura quartz, hematite.

Incense/Oils: cedarwood, patchouli, myrrh, musk.

Red Ray:

The deep sub-conscious (which we find hard to access) issues of abuse. This chakra helps one to live on the physical plane. Growth and destruction. Strength, courage, perseverance, stamina. It is also the location of the resting *Kundalini* Goddess: she is said to lie coiled three-and-a-half times around this chakra which is represented as a phallus, or *Lingham.* The three coils represent the three stages of *avastha* (mind), namely *jagrt* (awake), *svapna* (dreaming) and *susuptiin* (deep sleep). There is a fourth level, *turiya*, combining and transcending the others, which represents the last half coil. It is attained in *samadhi* (enlightenment). Before the word *'Kundalini'* became fashionable, the term used to represent this Divine power was *agni* (fire), that purifies and rises upwards like fire.

2. Sacral Chakra

Sanskrit name *svadhisthana* (*sva* = vital force, soul; *adhisthana* = seat or abode). Also known as the water, or sexual chakra or sweetness.

Located in the sexual organs and upwards towards the navel.

Associated with vitality, attraction, magnetism, desire, emotion, creativity, sexuality, water.

Bodily parts: all fluid functions of the body, ovaries, testes, womb.

There is great cleansing potential in this chakra associated with personality disorders related to the emotions. Unbalanced sex drive, emotional instability, feelings of isolation. Social awareness and partnerships.

Malfunction: frigidity, impotence, bladder, kidney and uterine disorders, prostate problems, lower back pain, fertility. Also fear, shock and guilt.

The second chakra (Sex) is feminine; liquid; flowing; yin.

Element and ruling planet: water, Pluto.

Astrological association: Cancer, Scorpio.

Intake: fluids.

Symbol: 6-petal orange-red lotus flower, containing a second lotus flower and an upward-pointing crescent moon. Within the moon lies the *'Makara'*, a fish-tailed alligator with a coiled tail. The colors orange, peach and pink are associated with this chakra.

Names of petals: bam, bham, mam, yam, ram, lam.

Sensory channel: taste.

Sound - *Bija* Mantra: Vam or Vang.

Musical note - D

Associated creature: water dragon or fish-tailed alligator with a coiled tail *(Makara)* or crocodile.

Developmental age and lesson: 8-14 years. Challenging motivations based on social/tribal conditioning.

Sephira: Yesod.

Archangel: Gabriel.

Gemstones: carnelian, red jasper, orange sunstone, aragonite, hessonite, amber, tangerine quartz.

Incense/Oils: jasmine, rose, sandalwood.

Orange Ray:

The color orange is for creativity, wisdom and benevolence. When this chakra is balanced you will 'flow'. Use this chakra as a primal spiritual centre. When this chakra is activated fully you become healthy and full of vitality. Meditation on the crescent moon gives control over the water element and confers psychic powers, intuitional knowledge and knowledge of astral entities. Many impure qualities are annihilated.

3. Solar Plexus Chakra

Sanskrit name *manipuraka* (*manipura* = navel), situated in the navel; *manas* (mind) and *surya* (the sun). Also known as the power chakra or lustrous gem.

Located between the navel and the solar plexus centre.

Associated with fire, personal power, ambition, intellectual activity, combustion, anger, joy, laughter. Astral force, mental power, pancreas and adrenals. Also central nervous system.

Malfunction: stomach ulcers and other digestive disorders, also diabetes, low vitality, chronic fatigue and allergies. Oversensitive to criticism, need to be in control, low self-esteem. Addictive personality, aggression.

The third chakra (power or *agni*) is masculine; wilful; yang.

Element and ruling planet: fire, Mars and the Sun.

Astrological association: Aries, Leo.

Intake: starch, complex carbohydrates.

Symbol: 10-petal lotus flower. The petals are deep yellow and the centre contains a deep red downward-pointing triangle surrounded by three *'svastikas'*, symbolic of fire. The colors yellow and gold are associated with this chakra.

Names of petals: dam, dham, nam, tam, tham, dam, dham, nam, pam, pham.

Sensory channel: sight.

Sound - *Bija* Mantra: Ram or Rang.

Musical note - E

Associated creature: ram.

Developmental age and lesson: 14-21 years. Self-esteem/self-confidence/self-exploration.

Sephiroth: Hod and Netzach.

Archangels: Michael and Haniel.

Gemstones: yellow sapphire, citrine, golden sunstone, sunshine aura quartz, amber, amblygonite, tiger eye, yellow jasper.

Incense/Oils: vetivert, rose, bergamot, ylang ylang, cinnamon, carnation.

Yellow Ray:

The color yellow is for meditative analytical thought, intellectual activity, abundance, manifestation of your dreams. If you meditate on this chakra you will become dis-ease free and have no fear of fire, being able to control this element. There is another important chakra (manas) which lies between the manipuraka and anahata chakras. It is the seat of the emotions, igniting imagination and creativity. When the manas and anahata chakras are activated together, they strengthen the heart and help you develop devotion to your spiritual path or goal.

4. Heart Chakra

Sanskrit name *anahata* (= unbeaten or unstruck. A sound that is made without any two things striking).

Located in the cardiac area, in the region of the physical and spiritual heart.

Associated with compassion, love. Beliefs about love and relationships. One-ness, heart, thymus and the immune system.

Malfunction: lung disease, asthma, heart disease. Shallow breathing, high blood pressure, cancer. Problems with arms, hands and fingers. Fears about betrayal, co-dependent, melancholic.

The fourth chakra (Heart) is feminine; loving; integrating; yin.

Element and ruling planet: air, Venus.

Astrological association: Libra, Taurus.

Intake: vegetables.

Symbol: 12-petal green lotus flower, the inner centre containing two intersecting triangles making up a perfect six-pointed star, demonstrating the balance between the downward-pointing spirit descending towards matter and the upward-pointing matter ascending towards spirit. The colors green, pink and gold are associated with this chakra.

Names of petals: kam, kham, gam, gham, nam, cam, cham, jam, jham, nam, tam, tham.

Sensory channel: touch.

Sound - *Bija* Mantra: Yam or Yang.

Musical note - F

Associated creature: black antelope.

Developmental age and lesson: 21-28 years. Forgiveness and compassion.

Sephira: Tiphareth.

Archangel: Raphael.

Gemstones: emerald, green jade, green tourmaline, green aventurine, moldavite, peridot, malachite, chrysoprase.

Incense/Oils: rose, bergamot, melissa.

Green Ray:

The color green is for soothing, healing, growth, balance, discrimination, ecstasy, unconditional love. Merging the physical with the Divine. Transmutation with love. Marriage of physical and spiritual. Meditation on the heart chakra gives the primal sound of *anahata* sound, the primal sound of

Sabdabrahman. It also bestows pure qualities, cosmic love and various psychic powers. This central heart chakra within the sevenfold system is the heart of our journey on the physical plane. It balances between the worlds of spirit and matter. Through this balance we relate compassionately and unconditionally with all life, with love. Remember, this 'love' is not dependant on others. It is not the tribal love of the root chakra or the sexual love of the sacral chakra, or the materialistic love of the solar plexus chakra, but is a state of being, enduring and constant. It also means self-love, self acceptance.

Pink Ray:

The color pink is for love and harmony in all relationships, hope, receptive, intimate, affection, kindness. It melts and dissolves resentment. Activation of *Karuna* (compassion, pity, tenderness; it also implies devoted action to alleviate suffering).

Gemstones: rose quartz, morganite, pink tourmaline, watermelon tourmaline, rhodochrosite, kunzite, smithsonite.

5. Throat Chakra

Sanskrit name *visuddha* (= pure), which means purification. It is also known as the 'communication' chakra.

Located in the throat region at the base of the neck.

Associated with communication, self expression, sound, voice, speech, writing. Active listening, thyroid gland, parathyroid, lungs, vocal cords, jaw, breath. Dreaming, imagination and out of body experiences. The power of choice, harmony with others.

Malfunction: stiff necks, colds, sore throats, thyroid and hearing problems, tinnitus, asthma. Masks of the self. Perfectionism, inability to express emotions, blocked creativity.

The fifth chakra (Throat) is masculine; manifesting; logical; yang.

Element and ruling planet: ether (akasha in Sanskrit), Moon and Mercury.

Astrological association: Gemini, Virgo.

Intake: fruit

Symbol: 16-petal blue lotus flower, containing within the flower a downward-pointing triangle within which is a circle representing the full silvery-blue moon.

Names of petals: (am, am, im, im, um, um, rm, rm, im, im, em, aim, om, aum, am, ahm).

Sensory channel: sound

Sound - *Bija* Mantra: Ham or Hang.

Musical note - G

Associated creatures: white lion and *Airavata*, the many-tusked elephant.

Developmental age and lesson: 28-35 years. Personal truth and self expression.

Sephiroth: Geburah and Chesed.

Archangels: Khamael and Tzadkiel.

Gemstones: lapis lazuli, blue sapphire, chrysocolla, blue calcite, azurite, blue lace agate, larimar, aquamarine, turquoise, aqua aura quartz.

Incense/Oils: chamomile, myrrh.

Blue Ray:

The color blue gives communication with Divine guidance. When this chakra is fully activated you have a beautiful voice and your speech is clear and fluent. Your intellect increases, as does your understanding of the Divine scriptures. You have complete knowledge of the past, present and future.

6. Third Eye Chakra

Sanskrit name *ajna* (= command), which means to know. Also known as the brow chakra or intuitive chakra.

Located right between and just above the physical eyes, it corresponds to the space between the eyebrows, the *trikuta*.

Associated with intuition, pituitary gland, left eye, the base of the skull. The mind is looking directly at itself. The combined interaction of the pineal with the pituitary gland activates this chakra. The element is *Avyakta*, the primordial cloud of undifferentiated energy and matter.

Malfunction: headaches, nightmares, eye problems, poor vision, neurological disturbances, glaucoma. Learning difficulties, hallucinations.

The sixth chakra (Brow) is feminine; intuitive; mysterious; yin.

Element and ruling planet: mind, light - telepathic energy, Neptune and Jupiter.

Astrological association: Sagittarius, Pisces.

Intake: air.

Symbol: 2 large pure white lotus petals on each side of a pure white circle, within which is a downward-pointing triangle containing the *bija* seed letter Om. The color indigo is associated with this chakra.

Names of petals: ksham, ham.

Sensory channel: light, sixth sense.

Sound - *Bija* Mantra: Om.

Musical note - A

Associated creature: white owl.

Lesson: Integration of Consciousness

Sephiroth: Binah and Chokmah.

Archangels: Tzaphkiel and Ratziel

Gemstones: amethyst, tanzanite, sugilite, charoite, lepidolite, purple fluorite.

Incense/Oils: hyacinth, violet, rose geranium.

Indigo/Violet Rays:

The color indigo (dark blue and dark violet) represents devotion to the truth - idealism, obedience, intuition and perception. The ability to look to the future. Indigo transmutes and purifies; it is the transformer. Indigo is the color of the priest or priestess. When you meditate on the third eye chakra and it becomes fully activated you can successfully destroy the karma of all past lives and become a liberated soul. Intuitional knowledge is obtained through this chakra; it is the seat of primordial power and soul. It is here that yogis consciously place their Prana at the time of death.

The color violet represents those who search for the spiritual truth in all life. This is the seat of true wisdom, through deep meditation. When this chakra is fully activated you are filled with joym and develop a spiritual aura.

> *In the Gospel of St Matthew the following statement is attributed to Jesus: "If therefore thine eye be single, thy whole body shall be filled with light."*

This is where the un-manifested and manifested meet. This is where yin and yang merge. This is where we move beyond dualism.

6a. The fourth Eye Chakra

Sanskrit name *soma* (= water). The colors violet, white and indigo are associated with this chakra. It is located just above the third eye chakra in the centre of the brain. This chakra controls the body temperature and balances the power chakra in the solar plexus, bringing the male-female balance to the whole body system. The balance is maintained via the breath. Erratic breathing causes imbalances in the body and upsets this polarity.

6b. The Fifth Eye Chakra

Sanskrit name *lalata* (= forehead). The colors violet, white and gold are associated with this chakra. It is located at the top of the forehead. Its full activation brings man to be master of his own destiny.

7. Crown Chakra

Sanskrit name *sahasrara* (= thousand), which means 'to multiply by a thousandfold'.

Located at the crown of the head, known as the anterior fontanelle in a new-born child; is called *Brahmarandhra*, the "hole of Brahma". At the time of death the advanced meditator separates him/herself from the physical body, it bursts open and the Prana escapes through it.

Associated with enlightenment, cosmic consciousness, right eye, cerebral cortex, pineal gland, upper skull, skin.

Malfunction: confusion, lack of clarity, depression, obsessional thinking, sensitivity to pollutants, chronic exhaustion, epilepsy, Alzheimer's.

The seventh chakra (Crown) is masculine; pure bright light; yang - violet, gold, white.

Element and ruling planet: thought, cosmic energy, Uranus.

Astrological association: Aquarius.

Symbol: The thousand-petal lotus flower on which are repeated the fifty letters of the *Sanskrit* alphabet. It is the abode of *Shiva*. The colors violet, white and gold are associated with this chakra.

Intake: fasting (Prana), breatharian.

Sensory channel: experience - beyond self.

Sound - *Bija* Mantra: of silence or silent OM.

Musical note - B

Lesson: Pure Consciousness.

Sephira: Kether.

Archangel: Metatron.

Gemstones: diamond, clear quartz, danburite, phenacite, azeztulite, petalite, clear calcite, selenite, Herkimer diamond.

Incense/Oils: lavender, frankincense, rosewood.

Clear Ray:

Color clear, brilliance, bringing enlightenment, cosmic awareness, blissful reunion with source. Allowing the 'Holy Spirit' to flow downward into our lives for the ultimate healing and inspirational power of the universe. We transcend our individual minds and enter into perfect conscious harmony with the infinite wholeness of the universe. Infinite love, infinite bliss. Enlightenment is to be filled with light, to comprehend the light, to function in the light, to radiate the light and merge with the light. When *Kundalini Shakti* is united with *Shiva* at the *sahasrara*, the *yogi/yogini* experiences extreme bliss. He/she attains the superconscious state and the highest knowledge.

Crystal Therapy - Working Directly on the Chakras

The following section gives three very different methods of working directly on the chakra system. As with all other subtle systems, and even the gross physical system, a tiny change in one area will create a larger overall effect. This puts responsibility on the crystal therapist to be aware of the equilibrium of the overall energy systems of the client. To keep the chakra system in balance it is important to make sure there is not an excess of energy or a lack of energy in the system. Individual chakras may be performing outside their standard ranges, but in a balanced system general equilibrium is kept by an overabundance in one chakra being balanced by a shortage in another. The following three methods will allow you to connect each energy centre on the human body, for fast correlation and realignment of potency. Crystals definitely allow for this connection to your higher self, also connection to other worlds and realities. They also allow for the rapid transference of energy between each chakra.

Method One - Alignment and Healing

Uses: Complete chakra healing and realignment to restore wholeness, health and well-being. This specific system produces an energy vortex of healing over each chakra, which results in higher octaves or frequencies of energy and light becoming more pronounced within them.

Crystals: 4 clear quartz medium-size points are needed.

Use 3 medium clear quartz points in a triangle configuration - to form a crystal web of light. (2 level with the ankles, 1 at the soul star chakra about six inches above the crown chakra).

Use 1 clear quartz point (known as the control or master crystal) held in your hand with the termination pointing towards the client.

1. Raise the sensitivity in your hands, wash them in warm water, dry them thoroughly, then rub your hands together vigorously and rapidly several times to build up the surface chi in your hands. Then begin to align yourself with the source of healing energies you will be using.

2. Make sure your own personal energy system is flowing smoothly and you are grounded, centred and in balance.

3. Ask your client to lie down on the therapy table. Make sure that they are comfortable.

4. Relax the client and give reassurance on the procedure.

5. Begin by scanning your client's energy field using your left hand approximately 3" above the physical body. Start at their feet and legs, then the hands and arms, going finally over the body scanning the seven major chakras. Finish at the crown chakra. (You will be working on the vitality layer of the aura).

   Keep scanning until you are satisfied that you have a good knowledge of your client's energy field. Always move your hand in the same forwards direction when scanning; never go backwards. If you need to re-check, lift your hand upwards and then go back to the beginning.

6. Place a clear quartz triangle web of light around your client, about 6" distance from the body. You will be using single terminated clear quartz crystals. First place two crystals at the feet. This will act as a grounding for the client, to stabilise the crystal triangulation's energy field. Then place one crystal above the head, with the point facing away from the client, to act as a release for any negative energies. This will also prevent overloading of the client's energy field.

7. Join up the quartz triangulation with your clear quartz control crystal. This is done clockwise, using your right hand and holding the left hand up to receive the healing energies.

8. Remove any negative energies anti-clockwise (unwinding), using your control or master crystal in your left hand and keeping your right hand pointing at the floor. This procedure will act as a drain for any negative energies. Start at the feet, then knees, hips, hands and arms, then work up through the seven major chakras in the body. Finish at the crown chakra.

9. Now change your control or master crystal over to your right hand and begin to place the crystal healing energies into the client's body. Place the healing in clockwise. Start at the feet, then knees, hips, hands and arms, and then go through the seven major chakras of the body. You must finish at the crown chakra.

10. Place your control crystal on the therapy couch between your client's feet with the termination of the crystal pointing towards your client.

11. You will now scan your client's body again, using your left hand and keeping your right hand pointing at the floor.

12. By scanning your client's body again you will decide if you need to perform any more crystal therapy on the client, or if all your crystal healing therapy is complete.

If complete, proceed to No. 13; if not, go back to No. 9 and give your client more crystal therapy.

13. When the crystal therapy is complete, seal the healing around the patient clockwise, using your right hand. Go round your client three times at least.

14. Remove the triangulation from around your client, taking away the quartz crystals in reverse order of placement (starting at the head).

15. Ground your client by very gently holding the ankles and directing the energy downwards.

16. Make sure that you and your client are fully grounded, centred and balanced.

17. Finish by giving thanks and asking mentally that all the work you have just accomplished is closed, sealed and protected with Divine love and wisdom.

18. Give your client sufficient time to integrate the crystal therapy session. As a general guideline it is suggested a period of twice the length of time your client was actually receiving crystal therapy be allowed for integration.

19. Wash your hands and control crystal in cold water to release any unwanted energies - cold water does not open your pores, therefore it gives protection from absorbing your client's negative energy release, and cleanse the other crystals used.

Outcome: You may use this technique as many times as needed. Try not to overdo this procedure though; remember to allow your client's body time to integrate the new flow of energy before attempting another session. Please also recognise that everyone heals at their own pace. Some people choose to take the crystal energy and integrate it very quickly, others may take longer. We are all unique and each disease is unique, so allow the healing to be natural to the person you are helping with the crystal healing vibration.

Method Two - Basic Chakra Layout

Crystals:
1 smoky quartz, tumbled or faceted - place on the base chakra.
1 carnelian, tumbled or faceted - place on the sacral chakra.
1 citrine quartz, tumbled or faceted - place on the solar chakra.
1 green aventurine, tumbled or faceted - place on the heart chakra.
1 rose quartz, tumbled or faceted - place on the heart chakra.
1 lapis lazuli, tumbled or faceted - place on the throat chakra.
1 amethyst quartz, tumbled or faceted - place on the third eye chakra.
1 clear quartz, tumbled or faceted - place on the crown chakra
6 clear quartz medium-size points

Uses: Complete chakra healing and balancing to restore wholeness, health and well-being. This specific integrated system produces an energy vortex of healing over each chakra, which results in higher octaves or frequencies of energy and light becoming more pronounced within them. The crystals act as energetic gateways, opening communication not only between the different layers of a person's aura, but between other dimensions of light, love and inspiration.

1. First begin to align yourself with the source of healing energies you will be using.
2. Make sure your own personal energy system is flowing smoothly and you are grounded, centred and in balance.
3. Ask your client to lie down on the therapy table. Make sure that they are comfortable.
4. Relax the client and give reassurance on the procedure.
5. Lay the stones on the body at the 7 master chakras (using two at the heart chakra).
6. Place the 6 medium clear quartz points in a Star of David - crystal web of light (first 2 level with the knees, 1 at the soul star chakra about six inches above the crown chakra, then 1 at the earth star chakra beneath the feet and the remaining 2 at shoulder height on each side of the head).
7. Allow 20 minutes to facilitate the integration of the crystal vibration.
8. On no account must you leave your client unattended. Be ready to remove the crystals sooner, if your client has integrated the crystal energy very quickly.
9. Remove the 6 medium clear quartz points in a Star of David crystal web of light, from around your client, taking away the quartz crystals in reverse order of placement (starting at the head).
10. Remove the chakra stones, in reverse order of placement (starting at the head).
11. Ground your client by very gently holding the ankles and directing the energy downwards.

12. Make sure that you and your client are fully grounded, centred and balanced.

13. Cleanse your crystals (using your chosen method).

14. Finish by giving thanks and asking mentally that all the work you have just accomplished is closed, sealed and protected with Divine love and wisdom.

15. Give your client sufficient time to integrate the crystal therapy session. As a general guideline it is suggested a period of twice the length of time your client was actually receiving crystal therapy be allowed for integration.

Outcome: Balance and harmony are restored to the physical, mental, emotional and spiritual bodies. Used once a week for general healing and well-being, this will result in overall improvement in any imbalance or disease. Please note: when using faceted stones the energy will be much more intense; this is due to the higher vibration contained within the faceted gemstone.

Method Three - Dowsing to Balance the Chakras

Crystals: 3 clear quartz medium-size points
1 clear quartz pendulum

Uses: Complete chakra healing and realignment to restore wholeness, health and well-being. This specific system produces an energy vortex of healing over each chakra, which results in higher octaves or frequencies of energy and light becoming more pronounced within them. This method is good for identifying which chakras are dysfunctional, not only by being too open but also by vibrating or spinning sluggishly. Your pranic energy flows into the clear quartz pendulum and into its energy field; this energises it. This combined field of the quartz pendulum and your energy then interacts with the field of the client, causing the clear quartz pendulum to move.

3 medium clear quartz points in a triangle crystal web of light (2 level with the ankles, 1 at the soul star chakra about six inches above the crown chakra).

1. First begin to align yourself with the source of healing energies you will be using.

2. Make sure your own personal energy system is flowing smoothly and you are grounded, centred and in balance.

3. Ask your client to lie down on the therapy table. Make sure that they are comfortable.

4. Relax the client and give reassurance on the procedure.

5. Place a clear quartz triangle crystal web of light around your client, about 6” distance from the body. You will be using single terminated clear quartz crystals. First place two crystals at the feet. This will act as a grounding for the client, to stabilise the crystal triangulation’s energy field. Then place one crystal above the head, with the point facing away from the client to act as a release for any negative energies. This will also prevent overloading of the client’s energy field and place a protective barrier around your client that will stop any outside unwanted energies from interfering with the healing process.

6. Begin by scanning your client’s chakras using your pendulum. Hold your pendulum in your right hand (or left, if left-handed) approximately 3” to 6” above the physical body.

7. Start at the base chakra and methodically work upwards over the seven major chakras. Finish at the crown chakra.

8. Hold your pendulum over each chakra and allow it to ‘balance’ each chakra.

Pendulum movement over each chakra:

a. No movement - chakra may be balanced already

b. Anti-clockwise spin - removal of negative energy or too much energy (un-winding)

c. Clockwise spin - putting healing energy in

d. Swinging from left to right - wait and see if the pendulum begins to spin or stop

e. Swinging up and down - wait and see if the pendulum begins to spin or stop

f. Erratic movement - wait and see if the pendulum begins to spin or stop

g. Figure of 8 movement - healing movement, allow the pendulum to continue

9. Once you have placed the crystal healing energies into the client's body, your crystal healing therapy is complete.

10. Remove the triangle crystal web of light from around your client, taking away the quartz crystals in reverse order of placement (starting at the head).

11. Ground your client by very gently holding the ankles and directing the energy downwards.

12. Make sure that you and your client are fully grounded, centred and balanced.

13. Cleanse your quartz crystals and pendulum (using your chosen method).

14. Finish by giving thanks and asking mentally that all the work you have just accomplished is closed, sealed and protected with Divine love and wisdom. Give your client sufficient time to integrate the crystal therapy session.

Outcome: You may use this technique as many times as needed. Try not to overdo this procedure though; remember to allow your client's body time to integrate the new flow of energy before attempting another session.

The Aura

The peoples of ancient cultures, knew and understood, that beyond its physical material form the human body is a pulsing, moving, dynamic field of energy. They developed a deep understanding of these basic fundamental energies, called Universal Life Force, prana or chi. This pool of energy is drawn into and surrounds and permeate the human body and surrounding energy field known as the aura. (Aura is a Greek word meaning breeze). The aura consists of seven levels, subtle bodies or kosas (body sheaths). The seven levels correlate to the seven master chakras. The aura begins with the seen (physical body) and progresses to subtle and more refined vibrations as we go further away from the physical. Awareness of the levels of the aura is gained through meditation, attention, intention, contemplation and realisation.

Very often, as we open spiritually, we begin to perceive a glow around the physical body. This is the first level and the most easy to view. The seven levels are as follows: each has a particular function, energy, awareness and realisation, which is reflected in the consciousness and is observable in all individuals. In Yoga it is known as the sevenfold knowledge and is to be integrated between the seen (prakrti) and the seer (purusa). They are: integration of the body (sarira samyama), the senses (indriya samyama), energy (prana samyama), mind (mano samyama), intellect (buddhi samyama), consciousness (citta samyama) and soul (atma samyama). The Yoga Sutras of Patanjali (written 2,500 years ago) were the earliest - and are still the most profound and enlightening - study of the human psyche. In 11.27 he wrote "tasya saptadha prantabhumih prajna". This roughly translates as "its sevenfold province holds supreme knowledge of consciousness". He was referring to the seven sheaths or levels of the aura.

The aura of an un-evolved person will be very different to the aura of someone who is self-realised. All the stages in between these two vast polarities give myriad kinds and types of aura. When we progress spiritually we begin to find vast differences in the color, quality, texture, resonance and vibration of each person on the planet. We have at the moment no totally accurate devices for measuring the aura. I am sure this will happen soon, but in the meantime we have our own awareness which is automatic. I am sure we all know when we like someone or when someone is angry or sad: this we sense by direct contact of our aura with theirs.

All auras are different and change constantly as our thoughts, moods, environment and state of health change. The aura may become damaged by ill health, negative thought patterns, environmental pollutants, stress or poor breathing techniques. This can be 'viewed' and the damage may be repaired with the correct use and placement of crystals and gemstones. Sometimes we find debris in the aura when someone repeatedly holds a negative thought pattern or addiction for a long time. Some of these thought patterns and addictions take on a life of their own and act as a possession, negative entity thought form or negative entity thought form shape; in time these can influence not only the person they are attached to but control other people's behaviour too. Colors and shapes are clearly visible within the aura, the colors reflecting which chakras are the most active or under-active, also where the person needs to pay special attention to restore pure color or vibrancy. Any imbalances will cause trouble in the overall vitality of the energy field. If a person regularly has spiritual thoughts the aura can be a very clear yellow or even gold, while a thought charged with anger and hatred is dark red.

The shapes and patterns in the aura represent energies which will block the spiritual, mental, emotional and physical health of a person. These can be removed with crystal energies and other vibrational healing techniques. Karmic burdens and karmic pre-dispositions or miasms (crystallized patterns of karma) are also viewed within the aura. This debris is a past-life carry-over and will cause problems, misery and mental or emotional instability. Very often we find damage in the aura caused by attachments, cords or ties. These are usually from outside causes, where one individual has damaged another. This can be very nasty to deal with, as it causes energy leakage or vampirism. These cords and energy drains need to be very carefully removed and the spaces where they have been need to be filled with positive vital loving healing energy.

The Seven Kosas

(Body Sheaths or Aura) and Corresponding States of Consciousness:

Sheath One

Element of earth

Sheath - physical body (annamaya kosa)

Related chakra - Root

State of consciousness - emerging consciousness (vyutthana citta)

Knowledge of body - integration of body (sarira samyama)

Appearance - Pale blue or light grey with tiny sparks of light moving very fast

State - Fixed

Close to the physical body

Level - One - Etheric (lower aspect)

Sheath Two

Element of water

Sheath - physiological body (pranamaya kosa)

Related chakra - Sacral

State of consciousness - restraining consciousness (nirodha citta)

Knowledge of energy - vitality, integration of senses (indriya samyama)

Appearance - Vibrant colors (when healthy and emotionally balanced)

State - Moving

1-3 inches around the physical body

Level - Two - Emotional/vitality body (lower base emotions aspect)

Sheath Three

Element of fire

Sheath - psychological body (manomaya kosa)

Related chakra - Solar Plexus

State of consciousness - individualized consciousness (nirmana citta)

Knowledge of energy - integration of energy (prana samyama)

Appearance - Yellow to Gold depending on spiritual development

State - Fixed

3-8 inches around the physical body.

Level - Three - Mental body

Sheath Four

Element of air

Sheath - intellectual body (vijnanamaya kosa)

Related chakra - Heart

State of consciousness - tranquil consciousness (prasanta citta)

Knowledge of energy - integration of mind (mano samyama)

Appearance - Pastel colors, when fully developed a pastel rainbow infused with rose pink

State - Moving

6-12 inches around the physical body

Level - Four - Astral

Sheath Five

Element of ether

Sheath - the body of joy (anandamaya kosa)

Related chakra - Throat

State of consciousness - attentive consciousness (ekagrata citta)

Knowledge of energy - integration of intellect (buddhi samyama)

Appearance - Vivid bright blue

State - Fixed

12-24 inches around the physical body

Level - Five - Etheric Blue Print

Sheath Six

Element of spirit

Sheath - the body of consciousness (cittamaya kosa)

Related chakra - Third eye (brow)

State of consciousness - fissured or rent consciousness (chidra citta)

Knowledge of energy - integration of consciousness (citta samyama)

Appearance - Bright gold light flowing down from the higher self, when fully developed

State - Moving

24-30 inches around the physical body

Level - Six - Celestial

Sheath Seven

Element of thought

Sheath - the body of the self (atmamaya kosa)

Related chakra - Crown

State of consciousness - pure consciousness (paripakva citta or divya citta)

Knowledge of energy - integration of soul (atma samyama)

Appearance - Silvery-blue to shimmering-gold (the original blueprint)

State - Fixed

30-44 inches around the physical body (until self-realisation)

Level - Seven - Luminous Egg

Crystal Healing Technique - Clearing Stress From the Aura

Everyone has at some time in their lives experienced a stressful situation. Whether it is a visit to the dentist or a driving test, perhaps a job interview or a person or situation that regularly stresses you out, don't worry, help is at hand. When we become stressed, our bodies no longer function with a balanced flow of energy. Very soon we find we can no longer cope with the stressful person or situation. The stress builds and builds until we either become ill, or can no longer cope at all. This may take place over many years. The following application will clear stress from the physical, etheric, emotional, mental, astral, and etheric blue print bodies, etc. - the auric shell or luminous egg.

We will use an amethyst or clear quartz crystal; this is a really effective and totally safe procedure even for a beginner in crystal therapy.

Prepare and cleanse your crystal ready for use and place it at your left side as you:

Sit in a comfortable steady posture, with the spine and neck held erect but not tense. This helps steady the mind and aids concentration. The psychic current must be able to travel freely from the base of the spine to the top of the head. Any comfortable cross-legged posture provides a firm base for the body. It makes a triangular pathway for the energy flow, which must be contained rather than dissipated in all directions and keeps the lungs free to move naturally with as little effort as possible.

Place the hands in the lap, with the right hand resting on the left, and pull the shoulders back ever so slightly and the chin in a little so that there is a small pull on the back of the neck, this will ease the blood-flow to the brain. Close your eyes and, with the mouth ever so slightly open, rest the tip of the tongue on the roof of the mouth just behind the teeth. This placement of the tongue is vital because it naturally maintains the flow of energy to the head whilst keeping the jaw relaxed. There are two major energy channels (acupuncture meridians) The Yin channel (the conception Vessel) begins at the perineum and flows up the front centre of the body and ends at the tip of the tongue. The Yang channel (the Governing vessel) begins at the perineum and flows up the back centre of the body, over the top of the head and back down to the roof of the mouth. The tongue connects these two important currents when touched to the highest point in the roof of the mouth.

(An easy way to open this energy channel is to sit in a relaxed posture. Allow your energy to complete the loop by letting your mind flow along with it. Start in the mouth and mentally circulate your attention with the energy. Eventually the current will begin to feel warm in some places as it loops around. Relax, try to bring your mind directly into the part of the loop being focused on. Experience the actual feeling of the flow of chi in that part of your body. Once the circuit is going smoothly, inhale as you go up the spine and over to the third eye, and exhale as you go down from the third eye to the perineum).

Now - consciously, regulate the breath. Begin with five minutes of deep abdominal breathing to bring oxygen to the brain. Then slow it to an imperceptible rate. Now simply turn your full attention to the movement of your breath. Do not try and control your breathing, simply be aware of the breath. Then begin to follow the breath entering and leaving your body, and gradually feel the effect this conscious breathing has on your body.

Next, with your right hand, tap the witness point three times (which is on your breastbone between your heart and your throat, just at the thymus point). Then return your right hand into your lap and become aware of the witness point. You may feel a tingling or throbbing sensation as it begins to activate.

Then, pick up your amethyst or clear quartz crystal, hold it in your left hand with the termination pointing towards your head and gently hold your crystal to the witness point.

Begin to think about the stressful situation you have chosen to 'heal'. Really feel all the emotions associated with the stress, remember everything you can, actually bring the full memory back into your conscious awareness, allow the stress to really well up in your body - what happens next is nothing short of miraculous. You will feel all the stress draining away and your emotions will quickly become calm and focused. Keep holding the crystal at the witness point, because very often you will feel another surge of energy as the crystal goes even deeper to 'heal' the stress. This process may happen several times as your body takes the healing energy from the crystal. Each time you feel the surge of energy be aware that your body has chosen to use the healing crystal vibration to go to deeper and deeper levels. This will remove the stressful memory which has become encoded deep within your cellular structure. This facilitates healing to take place on all levels, physical, emotional, mental, etheric etc.

We use the witness point on the human body as this is the area where the etheric blue print joins all the other levels. Whether you are aware of it or not, the etheric blue print body was formed before the astral, mental, emotional and physical bodies, and by using this point healing will occur on all lower levels.

You may use this technique on yourself and others, as many times as needed. Try not to overdo this procedure though; remember to allow your body time to integrate the new flow of energy before attempting to heal another stressful situation. Please also recognise that everyone heals at their own pace. Some people choose to take the crystal energy and integrate it very quickly, others may take longer. We are all unique and each disease is unique, so allow the healing to be natural to the person you are helping with the crystal healing vibration.

Allow yourself or your client to return to everyday awareness and normal breathing.

Finally, drink plenty of pure fresh clean water; this will flush any toxins from your physical body that may have been released during the crystal therapy session. Sometimes the witness point may feel sore, tight or tingling for several hours; this is quite normal and will pass.

The Meridians

The ancient Chinese meridian theory, based on acupuncture meridians, was first discovered many thousands of years ago. It is a system of energy that flows throughout the body, providing protection to its inner mechanisms. The word meridian, as used in Chinese medicine, came into the English language through a French translation of the Chinese term jing-luo. Jing means 'to go through', or 'a thread in a fabric'; luo means 'something that connects or attaches' or 'a net'.

In traditional Eastern medical systems - notably the Chinese healing system and the Indian Ayurvedic system - it has long been accepted that health is based on the continuous harmonious flow of energies. These systems believe that an intricate realm of subtle energy flows permeates the universe and that the physical, material world is but a gross manifestation of these energies. In Chinese and Ayurvedic medicine, health is seen as the fluent and harmonious movement of energies at subtle levels. In the East, energies have various names. The Indian yogis call it Prana; to the Tibetan lamas it is lung-gom. It is known as sakia-tundra or ki to the Japanese Shinto and the Chinese call it chi. In the West it is loosely translated as 'vital energy', 'vital force' or 'life force'. This energy is considered as having clearly distinct and established pathways, definite direction of flow and characteristic behaviour as well defined as any other circulation, such as blood and the vascular system.

The body has twelve pairs of meridians that flow each side of the body, as well as two specific meridians known as vessels. All meridians flow near the surface of the skin. These twelve regular meridians correspond to each of the five yin and six yang organs. Together these constitute the body's energy system, which works to maintain the health of the whole organism. There are also many finer smaller net-like meridians called luo meridians. These meridians are pathways through which the energy of the universe circulates throughout the body organs and keeps the body and the universe in harmony. Illness or pain occurs when the pathway becomes blocked, disrupting the energy flow and breaking the body's harmony.

Although it is one integrated system, each meridian has a starting point and an end point, which indicate direction of flow and function. Each meridian is named after an organ or function, such as lung or kidney, but these 'names' can be very misleading to the student, as the physical organ is only one tiny aspect of the type of energy over which a meridian has influence. The functions ascribed to physical organs by the Chinese rarely have any recognisable correlations to Western medicine and it is difficult not to get completely confused by trying to tie in the two very distinct systems. Meridians are not straight lines, their pathways have curves; they curl and sometimes zig- zag across the body. The Chinese in acupuncture developed the use of needles to unblock these pathways. In shiatsu, the Japanese use direct thumb and finger pressure on acupuncture meridian points to achieve similar results. Reflexologists also work on acupuncture and acupressure points, but only those found in the feet. Through increased awareness of meridians one can practise crystal therapy more effectively, as meridians provide profound insight into the disease pathway and are therefore a most useful diagnostic tool. Crystal therapy encourages positive changes throughout the body by stimulating the body's own healing potential, which is believed to be the result of stimulating and revitalizing this energy flow. Once you have identified which meridian(s) are dysfunctional it is easy to bring them back into balance. However, always remember to think of the meridian system in its entirety and how each one works in harmony with the others to bring a complete sense of well-being. Each meridian operates at a unique, optimum frequency, which determines its vibrancy and flow. However, this frequency can be detrimentally affected through receiving too much or too little from the Universal Life Force. There are various schools of thought as to why such dysfunctions or miasms occur. Some say they stem from Karmic patterning - that is, we come into this life with a certain set of life challenges factored into our energy systems. This 'prior programming' or predisposition determines our subsequent attitudes and behaviours. Similarly, many therapists and healers believe that the deficient or excessive energy patterning of our energy systems, chakras, aura and meridians stems from our childhood and cultural/tribal experiences. They say that one way in which we cope with certain repeating situations is to try and protect ourselves by closing down the relevant chakra; this then would affect the meridian system. Another school of thought relates to miasms. Planetary miasms are stored in the collective consciousness of the planet and in the ethers. They may penetrate the physical body but are not permanently stored there. Acquired miasms are acute or infectious diseases or petrochemical toxicity acquired during a lifetime. After the acute phase of an illness, these acquired miasmatic traits settle into the subtle bodies and the molecular and cellular levels, where they ultimately may cause other problems. Whichever explanation resonates with you, never forget we always have a personal choice. We have the choice as to whether we accept or attempt to transcend the challenging situations which our predisposition causes us to attract. Knowledge is power, wisdom is applying that knowledge and love is transcending these predispositions with self-realisation.

Yin and Yang

Yin is seen as negative, passive, female, interior and dark.

Yang is positive, active, male, exterior, light.

They are a pair of complementary qualities, constantly interacting and changing, and neither can exist in isolation from the other. Their affinity to each other has a direct effect on health, harmony and well-being. The meridians connect the interior of the body with the exterior. Positive thoughts, feelings and emotions strengthen the meridians, whilst negative thoughts and emotions weaken the meridians. The two most important channels are the Governing and Conceptual Vessels, so we shall look at these first.

Central Meridian (Conceptual Vessel)

Begins at the perineum and flows up the front centre of the body and ends just below the lower lip on the outside of the body, but actually ends at the tip of the tongue. This is a yin vessel which has a governing effect on all the other yin meridians. It has a major effect on conception. The yin meridians and organ functions - heart, pericardium, spleen, lungs, kidneys and liver - are related to storing vital essence. They are associated with generation, regulation, transformation and storage of energy, blood, fluids and spirit (shen). The specific connecting point for all yin meridians is the base of the sternum, where according to the Nei Ching all the energies are collected. This area of the solar plexus is very important for the overall well-being of the body.

Governing Meridian

The Yang channel (the Governing vessel) begins at the perineum and flows up the back centre of the body, over the top of the head and back down to the roof of the mouth. On the outside of the body it ends at the centre of the upper lip. This is the main yang meridian and as such has a governing effect on all the other yang meridians and organs - small intestine, bladder, triple burner, stomach, large intestine and gall bladder. The yang organ functions are primarily active and relate to breaking down food and fluids and the absorption of nutrients from them, the circulation of the derived 'nourishing energies' around the body and the secretion of unused materials. Located right at the crown of the head, known as the anterior fontanelle in a new-born child, is a unique connecting point for all yang meridians. The name of the point is 'Baihui' which means 'meeting point for 100 points'. This point governs all other points and all meridians in the body; according to Chinese philosophy it is a point of contact of the heavenly yang.

The tongue connects these two important currents when touched to the highest point in the roof of the mouth. An easy way to open and connect this energy channel is to sit in a relaxed posture. Allow your energy to complete the loop by letting your mind flow along with it. Start in the mouth and mentally circulate your attention with the energy. Eventually the current will begin to feel warm in some places as it loops around. Relax, try to bring your mind directly into the part of the loop being focused on. Experience the actual feeling of the flow of chi in that part of your body. Once the circuit is going smoothly, inhale as you go up the spine and over to the third eye, and exhale as you go down from the third eye to the perineum.

Gall-Bladder Meridian

Begins at the outer edge of the eye and finishes at the outer end of the fourth toe. It has a descending pathway (yang). As it circulates around the ear, it therefore directly relates to the ear.

The gall-bladder meridian penetrates the lungs, liver, gall-bladder, spleen, large intestine and hip area. Meridian disorders include problems with the lungs, liver, gall-bladder, spleen, large intestine and hip area.

Liver Meridian

Starts at the outside of the big toe and ends just above the bottom of the ribcage either side of the sternum. It has an ascending pathway (yin). It has an internal branch which runs through the throat and affects the thyroid. Meridian disorders include eye pain; obstructions in the throat; chest tightness; lung conditions; tightness in the solar plexus area.

Bladder Meridian

Begins at the inner canthus of the eye and ends on the outer edge of the little toe. It has a descending pathway (yang). It is the longest meridian line in the body. Meridian disorders are eye weakness, for example, red, itchy, weak or squint eyes; headaches in the crown of the head, in the forehead crossing over the head, and headaches caused by neck tension; forehead sinus; hair loss; pain and stiffness along the spine; haemorrhoids; bladder and kidney problems.

Kidney Meridian

Begins at the ball of the foot and ends where the collarbone and breastbone meet. The kidney meridian also penetrates the uterus/prostate in the body and according to Chinese medicine the kidneys store the Jing, a vital essence involved in reproduction. It has an ascending pathway (yin). Meridian disorders include uterus/prostate disorders; bladder weakness; digestive problems in the small intestine or colon; solar plexus and diaphragm problems; breast problems; lumps in the breast on the inner side; asthma; lung conditions and kidney pain.

Large Intestine Meridian

Begins on the face by the outer edge of the nostril and ends on the inner edge of the index finger. It has an ascending pathway (yin). Problems associated with this meridian are herpes; cold sores; colic; toxins; constipation or diarrhoea.

Lung Meridian

Begins just below the coracoid process on the shoulder and ends on the inner end of the thumb. It has an ascending pathway (yin). The lungs regulate respiration and are therefore responsible for the chi of the entire body. Imbalance in this meridian will result in all kinds of chest and skin problems; also asthma.

Stomach Meridian

Begins below the eye at the inner edge of the orbit and finishes at the outer end of the second toe. It has a descending pathway (yang). It affects the sinuses, throat, lungs, diaphragm, spleen, liver, gall-bladder, stomach, pancreas, duodenum, adrenal glands, kidneys, large intestine, small intestine and pelvic region; also the appetite and digestion. If the stomach is out of balance, whatever is taken in, be it physical or psychic food, will not be utilized correctly; energy depletion, lethargy, weakness and debilitation are the results.

Spleen Meridian

Begins at the inner edge of the big toe and ends at the side of the chest just below nipple level. It has an ascending pathway (yin) and affects the spleen and pancreas. It is the crucial link in the process by which food is transformed into chi and blood. Emotional problems are also related to this meridian, for example, depression, PMT, irritability and concentration problems.

Heart Meridian

Begins at the forward edge of the armpit and ends on the inner edge of the little finger. It has a descending pathway (yang). The heart and small intestine meridians are coupled. The heart meridian gets its chi from the spleen meridian and in turn passes it to the small intestine meridian. If the heart meridian is strong and healthy, the emotions will be balanced. Imbalances in this meridian will affect the skin and cause weak wrists, angina and palpitations.

Small Intestine Meridian

Begins at the outer end of the little fingertip and ends at the start of the upper edge of the ear in a small hollow of the cheek. It has a descending pathway (yang). Meridian disorders are any heart condition; abdominal distension; headaches; poor circulation in the legs; indigestion; constipation; feeling cold and weakness in the legs.

Circulation-Sex Meridian (Pericardium, Heart Protector)

Begins at the outer edge of the nipple and finishes at the inside of the middle finger. It has an ascending pathway (yin). Meridian disorders include hot flushes and rapid heartbeat; heart pain; endocrine-related problems.

Triple Warmer Meridian (Triple heater)

Begins at the outside end of the ring finger (third) and ends at the outer edge of the eyebrow. It has a descending pathway (yang). Meridian disorders include ear problems - loss of hearing and earache; spontaneous perspiration for no reason; mental confusion; weakness; lack of energy.

Crystal Therapy for the Meridians

As with all other subtle systems, and even the gross physical system, a tiny change in one area will create a larger overall effect. This puts responsibility on the crystal therapist to be aware of the equilibrium of the overall energy systems of the client. To keep the meridian system in equilibrium it is important to make sure there is not an excess of energy or a lack of energy in the system. Individual meridians or even sections of a meridian may be performing outside their standard ranges, but in a balanced system general equilibrium is kept by an overabundance in one area being balanced by a shortage in another.

Crystal Healing Method One:

What follows is a safe procedure for working on the meridian system with crystals and gemstones, but you would be wise to become totally familiar with the meridian system before attempting the technique on others:

1. Use a list of the meridians to dowse or muscle test which meridian is out of balance. Remember that, apart from the Central and Governing meridians, all meridians are in pairs. So you will need to decide which side of the meridian pair needs balancing, or if both pairs require balancing.

2. A practical illustration of an unbalanced meridian can be to gently touch one end-point with the first two fingers of your right hand. If that half of the meridian is out of balance a previously strong muscle test will go weak. Muscle testing all meridians in this way will quickly show where crystal therapy is needed. By testing again, using a crystal, you will be able to check on the effectiveness of the re-balancing.

3. It is unimportant which end-point is touched, so select the most convenient point for you or your client. You may even allow your client to touch the end-point if that is more convenient.

4. All twelve yin and yang meridians should be tested thoroughly using a systematic approach, as well as the Governing and Central vessels.

5. Find which crystal or gemstone will be effective in re-balancing a meridian. If you are dowsing, use a suitable list of gemstones (such as the one at the end of this section) or use a suitably 'programmed' clear quartz crystal.

6. Once you have established which crystal will be the most effective, place the crystal on the end-point of the meridian, either at the beginning or end, whichever is indicated by the dowsing or muscle testing. You may even need to place a different crystal on each end of the meridian. You can even tape the crystal in place using 'medical tape'.

7. Once the re-balancing is complete, recheck all the meridians by either dowsing or muscle testing.

The length of time it takes to rebalance a meridian will differ for each person. Some people integrate healing energy very quickly, others may take longer to fully consolidate the process. It is quite normal for this process to take several months for total integration. It is also vitally important to allow a rest period of several months which are free from any other form of healing. This ensures the correction has not only been fully integrated into the meridian system, but the body has stabilized to a balanced sustainable level.

Crystal Healing Method Two:

Placing crystals or gem essences on acupuncture points is another way of balancing meridians. This process is very powerful and great care should be taken not to over or under-stimulate any meridian. Once again, the length of time a crystal is left on the acupuncture point will vary from person to person, as we are each unique in the way we handle and assimilate energy. It is advisable to take a break from other forms of healing whilst undergoing crystal healing using the acupuncture points. Always allow plenty of time for the body to integrate the crystal healing energy and advise your client to drink plenty of pure fresh water.

Acupuncture Points

1. Find out using dowsing or muscle testing which meridian is involved.
2. Find out whether the right or left channels need working on.
3. Find the exact point on the meridian by tracing the path with your fingertips until the arm or pendulum indicate the exact right point. You must follow the natural flow of the meridian by tracing the normal direction (going in the wrong direction will weaken the meridian). It is quite common for the meridian to deviate from what is considered normal.

You may wish to work with diagrams of the meridians.

4. After you have marked the point, gently hold or place the crystal on the exact spot (take care to be aware of the energy assimilation by dowsing or using your fingertips to feel the energy flow). Sometimes the energy flow will be very subtle and at a deep level, which means you may have to rely on feedback from your client. It is important to ask your client to be aware of thoughts, feelings, sensations or emotions.
5. When the assimilation is accomplished, re-test to check that all your work is complete.
6. Ground, centre and earth your client after all the treatment is finished.

Crystal List

Amethyst
Aquamarine
Blue lace agate
Carnelian
Citrine
Danburite
Emerald
Green aventurine
Garnet
Lapis
Moldavite
Moonstone
Morganite
Pyrite
Quartz
Rose quartz
Snow quartz
Sunstone
Turquoise

Meridian List

Conceptual -Yin
Governing -Yang
Bladder -Yang
Gall bladder -Yang
Heart -Yang
Large intestine -Yin
Liver -Yin
Lung -Yin
Kidney -Yin
Pericardium -Yin
Small intestine -Yang
Spleen -Yin
Stomach -Yang
Triple warmer -Yang

Part Four

Crystal Therapy

Mahatma Gandhi said:*"The human body is the best portrayal of the universe in miniature. Whatever does not exist in the human body cannot be found in the universe, and whatever exists in the universe can be found in the human body."*

Yes, we truly are the substance stars are made of …

Since the dawn of civilisation the human race has collected shells, stones, pebbles and rocks; they have enchanted us. Their beauty, brilliance, color, texture, feel and shape draw us like magnets. Our distant ancestors valued them very highly as talismans and objects of immense beauty. Archaeologists have found them in ancient burial grounds, tombs and graves. Though we may not know for sure how they were used, there are ancient texts relating to the application of crystals from different civilisations. Many cultures around the world, including Chinese, Native American and Celtic, have used and still use crystals in their healing ceremonies. The beautiful violet gemstone amethyst has been professed to protect the wearer from intoxication and over-indulgence and to spiritualise the intellect. It was mentioned in Exodus as one of the stones in the twelve-jewelled breastplate worn by the High Priest Aaron, brother of Moses, the law giver. Amethyst is still worn to this very day by bishops in the Catholic Church.

The extremely high and exact rates of vibration contained within quartz crystals has given them the important role they play today in modern technology, ranging from the liquid crystal diodes in our calculators and clocks to their use in computers, credit cards, fibre-optic phone lines and laser technology - which enables everything from new surgical techniques to the playing of compact discs. For the precision cutting of optical lenses, diamonds are used.

How Does it Work? - Clear Quartz Crystals

Those of us who are 'tuned in' to the forthcoming 'new age of enlightenment' or 'golden age' have become aware of the unique properties of organic natural clear quartz crystals. Clear quartz has a natural allure to almost everyone. This is understandable when you comprehend the influence of light and subtle magnetic fields on the human energy structure and on the cellular level of the physical body. As clear quartz crystals can go into a state of resonance with you, you will feel spontaneous appeal to them and they respond positively to you. They are marvellous life-forms of nature in process of evolution, just like you, just like me, just like the cosmos. They resonate with the liquid crystals in your body. These are called biocrystalline and refer to the network of cellular elements in the body which have liquid crystal or quartz-like properties. These areas include cell salts, lymphatics, fatty tissue, red and white blood cells, and the pineal gland. Crystals transfer information to your bloodstream and to your circulatory system - vital elements, in the form of intelligent energy fields which are important for your health and for the rejuvenation of your body, while transmuting unwanted information or miasms that may be locked in your bones, tissues and your unconscious mind. You can also programme clear quartz crystals with a thought of love, a thought of prosperity or protection, and give them to your friends and family.

Clear Quartz Crystals:

* Focus, cohere and amplify energy or prana
* Relieve and release stress
* Amplify your healing power and healing potential
* Stop burn-out and energy depletion
* Stimulate harmonious brain activity
* Restore the energy structure of your body and mind
* Stimulate healing, personal growth and spiritual development
* Re-connect you with inner levels of your being and aura
* Create carrier waves of pure vibrant energy
* Improve your health and rejuvenate your body by stimulating the energy flow of the meridians
* Transfer intelligent encoded information to the bloodstream
* Transmute unwanted information that may be locked in your bones, tissues and your unconscious mind

Using Crystals

The one thing we can be sure of is that we all have a right to use the crystal energies in whatever way is appropriate for us. The New Age movement has seen thousands of people drawn to the crystal energies; they have become part of a vast spiritual and environmental awakening. Crystals bring unconditional joy and beauty to our world. Like each human being, each one is a unique representation of God/Goddess and as such they should be treasured.

The crystal magic begins with each tetrahedral molecular unit of quartz oscillating at the same frequency. Therefore, in a single crystal there are millions of identically vibrating units. They are arranged in a helical pattern. Like-vibrational oscillating systems have an inherent momentum towards vibrating in unison. With crystals in general and quartz in particular, these conditions are maximised, throughout the matrix. When in a state of activated resonance, the crystal molecules vibrate and pulse in energy waves. The crystal body and terminations have distinctly different functions in the quartz matrix. Basically, the body serves as a mixing chamber, inputting and formulating energy flow. The termination is where the focused energy flows out. In addition, there are significant amplification factors mainly occurring in the body, the specifics of which will depend on the sacred geometry of the crystal structure.

As a general rule, the larger the crystal and the greater the overall clarity, the higher will be the amplification. The inward slope of the six facets towards the tip will amplify and focus the energy. Very often when people use quartz crystal for some time they are aware of a laser-like beam projecting out of the tip of the quartz crystal as they are using it for healing, meditation etc.

The Cosmic Dance

The whole universe is a constant dance of energy. Everything vibrates with its own unique vibration or frequency. Crystals and gemstones have a special place in human evolution and healing. Crystals and gemstones work with the energy field of the human body. We all have a male/female polarity or balance within our bodies and when these two finely-tuned aspects are out of balance dis-ease occurs. With each breath we take we balance these two polarities. With each heart-beat balance these two polarities.

Under Pressure

What goes wrong with this process, which allows illness to occur? When our organism is under stress, we do not breathe properly, or our breathing may become laboured or shallow; we may even hold our breath in fear, trauma or shock. Whatever causes our breathing to become irregular, stressed or erratic, the result is dis-ease. Other factors which we do have control over also come into play, such as poor air conditions, pollution, bad diet, stress, anger, wrong mental or emotional attitudes: the list is endless. The results are the same; we become ill or our natural balance is disturbed.

The ancients described the energy flows of Prana along the nadis, dhamani and sira. These energy channels control the flow of life force or Prana. As the energy flows, each cell is bathed in superior life force when the crystalline energies are applied. As the superior life force bathes each cell, it wakes it up and floods it with powerful positive energy. Healing occurs as each cell vibrates at a higher frequency (Disease or sickness is a lower vibration, bringing ageing and eventually death). The main nadis are: ida, pingala and susumna; other very important well-known ones are citra, gandhari, hastijihva, pusa, yasasvini, alambusa, kuhu, saasvati, varuni, visvodhari, payasvini, samkhini, kausiki, sura, raka, vijnana and kurma. Some nadis, dhamanis and siras will correspond to arteries, veins and capillaries of the circulatory and respiratory systems. They are also nerves, channels and ducts of the nervous, lymphatic, glandular, digestive and genito-urinary systems of the physical and physiological body. Others carry vital energy (Prana) to the mental body, intellectual energy (vijnana) to the intellectual body and spiritual energy to the causal or spiritual body (soul). The terminating point of each nadi is to be found in cell, follicle or hair. They act as inlets and outlets of the various energies which make up all the different bodies or layers. In all, 5.9 billion of them flow in the gross, subtle and causal bodies. We are full of nadis. By identifying the imbalance and applying the correct crystal or crystals we can immediately start the re-alignment process which will bring the body, soul and spirit back into perfection and balance.

Because crystals are multi-functional energy systems which work in many different ways, this has caused some confusion amongst the many people who have been drawn to use them for their healing and spiritual growth. They work with their color vibration or color therapy, structure (crystal system) or energy pattern, mineral composition (many mineral- forming substances have a vital function in the human body, vital to the formation of certain enzymes, which are substances that control and make the chemical processes in the body possible and guide them, thereby regulating our entire metabolism), growth conditions (birth or formation), vibration, sound? (yes, there are people who hear the gemstone vibration, but I will write about that in the next book) and inspiration (the X factor). Another way of using them is to make gem essences, which work on similar lines to flower or tree essences.

How Does it Work? - Color Therapy

Color, crystals, gemstones and light are ancient methods of intuitive natural healing. The first detail you will notice about a crystal or gemstone is indisputably its color. Color plays a large part in our lives and whether we are aware of the effects or not it is an extremely powerful force. The colors that surround you can make you happy or sad, healthy or sick, tense or relaxed. Crystals and gemstones (a gemstone is the naturally occurring crystalline form of a mineral: there are more than 30 popular varieties and some come in more than one color) obviously are conveniently color-coded and at a very basic level of awareness we can use them in color healing, by either choosing the appropriate colored stones from the list below which will rebalance our energy system, or by intuitively allowing ourselves to be drawn to the crystal or crystals that attract us and holding or placing them within our environment.

Introducing Color

Our bodies are aroused and energized by some colors, or calmed and relaxed by others. Colors can be healing - and they can make you agitated, depressed, suicidal or ill. The health of all our internal organs, the circulation of the blood, the nervous, lymphatic and endocrine systems, in fact all the workings of the body are constantly altered by the color vibrations to which we expose ourselves. Mentally, emotionally, and spiritually color works on a deep level, changing our mood and our sense of well-being. Humans are not the only creatures on our planet who are affected by color. In the animal and plant worlds color can mean survival or extinction. Color is used to attract, repel, camouflage, ward off danger and send sexual signals. Color is intrinsic to life, and it is important to our species as it is to the survival of the plant and animal kingdoms. We must become consciously aware of the language of color for our own health, happiness and spiritual growth. Nature has furnished us with light and color to support not only the body, mind and emotions, but also the spirit. It nourishes our whole system, supplying a vital energy that is an essential part of life. We respond to color actively or passively in all that we do. Light waves affect us every minute of our lives and penetrate our energetic system whether we are awake or asleep, blind or sighted. Our growth, blood pressure, breathing, body temperature, muscular activity, sleep patterns and immune system are all affected by light rays. The colored rays affect not only our physical bodies but our emotions, moods, mental faculties and our spiritual nature. We all have a intimate relationship with light and color. We often give ourselves an instinctive color treatment by choosing jewellery, or clothes of a certain color, or by surrounding ourselves with certain colors in our homes, offices and gardens. Most of our reactions are, however, unconscious and it is only when we start to use the qualities of light and color vibration in an informed way that we harness this wonderful vital force to improve the quality of our lives and our overall well-being.

Stop reading this book, pause for a moment: I want you to imagine a clear blue sky and right in the middle of the blue appears a beautiful rainbow.

How did it make you feel, which color or colors did you feel most drawn to?

What is Color?

The subject of color is a vast and complex one and in these pages only certain aspects of it can be suitably addressed.

Electromagnetic Spectrum

The universe is a magnetic field of positive and negative charges, vibrating constantly to produce electromagnetic waves. Each of these has a different wavelength and speed of vibration: this forms the electromagnetic spectrum. We can see about 40 per cent of the colors contained in sunlight. So although white light looks colorless it is made up of assorted definite color vibrations, which have not only wavelengths but also a "corpuscular structure." The radiant energy of pure sunlight is a vital component in nourishing our bodies, minds and spirits. Each color vibration has its own quality. As shown by Newton, white light is composed of all the colors of the rainbow intermingled. By passing a narrow beam of white light through a glass prism it can be spread out into a whole series of spectrum colors according to their wavelength. There are only six main color names (or seven if one includes indigo). Red is the longest wavelength we can see and has the slowest frequency and vibration. Its energy is passionate, hot and stimulating. Violet has the shortest wavelength and the quickest vibration. It is calm, cold and purifying.

Beyond the Visible Spectrum

At either end of the visible spectrum of light are very many wavelengths we, as humans, cannot see. Ultraviolet light is just beyond violet, and further beyond this are electromagnetic rays with increasing frequencies as the wavelengths get progressively shorter: these include X-rays and gamma rays. At the other end, infra-red light is found just beyond red light. Just as red has warming qualities, although it gives off more concentrated heat (these qualities are utilized in infra-red lamps), beyond this are electromagnetic rays with increasing wavelengths and decreasing frequencies: these include radio waves. The ancient Yogic mystics have long been able to see colors outside the 'normal' range, during meditation.

The Human Eye and Color Vision

The human eye consists essentially of a flexible lens of changeable focal length, limited by a diaphragm (the iris), through which light is focused to form an inverted image as the retina, which lines the back wall of the eye. The retina is connected with the brain (where all messages of light and color are translated into sensations) by the optic nerve. Impulses from the right eye travel to the left side of the brain, while those from the left side travel to the right half of the brain. This action of the nerve fibres means that they actually cross over, in part of the brain called the optic chiasma. The sensory layer of the retina consists of small rod-like structures interspersed with shorter conical bodies, which are known respectively as rods and cones. Only the cones are thought to be sensitive to colors and only the cones are capable of acute vision. A small central area known as the yellow spot near the emergence of the optic nerve contains cones only, and it is here that the image of an object is focused for the clearest possible vision. The cones that are sensitive to green light are situated directly in the middle of the retina, allowing light to fall in the centre of the eye. This will make the green color the most relaxing on the eyes and, in turn, the mind.

The rods, on the other hand, are the structures which enable us to see to some extent in a dim light: for this reason they are the chief feature in the retina of a nocturnal animal. The rods contain a reddish substance (rhodopsin), commonly called the visual purple, which is rapidly bleached on exposure to light. The visual purple can thus only begin to form in the dark and its presence can make the sensitivity of the eye several thousand times greater than it is in bright light - hence the power of the dark-adapted eye to see objects which would be quite invisible before this transformation has had time to take place. Rods, therefore, are more light sensitive, allowing us to see in dim light, but do not record color, only shades of gray. There have been many theories of color vision and a final answer to all problems connected with this intricate subject is still to be found. For most practical purposes, however, the 'three color' theories, particularly the Young-Helmholtz theory, serves very well. According to the simplest form of this theory, the human retina contains three varieties of cone, which are sensitive to the red-yellow, green and blue-violet parts of the spectrum, respectively. It is assumed that three light-sensitive chemical compounds are present in these different groups of cones, each of which undergoes a breakdown when exposed to light of the correct wavelengths, transmitting messages to the brain. The spectral regions where these receptors are active overlap considerably. Thus, in the central part of the spectrum, all three will be functioning, though the green receptors will be much more active than the other two, which will function alone at the extreme ends of the spectrum. The action of these three receptors in varying strengths permits all familiar sensations of color by persons of normal vision. More recent work seems to indicate the presence of not merely three, but as many as seven, different types of receptors. About 10 per cent of men and less than 1 per cent of women are in some measure color-defective, or are color-blind. In such persons it is supposed that one or more of the red, green or violet-sensitive color receptors is not functioning, thus limiting and distorting to a lesser or greater degree the perception of hue.

However not all the light impulses received through our physical eyes are used solely for the purpose of sight. Nervous impulses from the eyes travel not only to the visual cortex of the brain, but also via the hypothalamus to the pituitary and pineal glands. We find, therefore, that many body functions are stimulated or retarded by light, and different colors of light have specific effects on the brain and central nervous system

How Are Our Bodies Affected by Color?

The pituitary gland, known as the 'master gland' of the endocrine system, is first affected by colored light. It produces substances that regulate the hormones produced by the endocrine glands. These hormones regulate our body functions, which include growth patterns, sleep, our temperature control, our sex drive, our energy levels, our metabolic rate and appetite. It has also been discovered that our pineal gland, located deep within our brain, is also sensitive to light. This gland is our internal body clock, producing a substance known as melatonin, which controls our sleep cycles and also inhibits sexual maturation. Daylight suppresses the production of melatonin and at night the lack of sunlight increases its production. The quality and amount of the light reaching the pineal gland will also alter with the changing seasons. Therefore the proportions of the colors within sunlight, according to the season, cause our body functions, like those of plants and animals, to mimic the energy of the seasons. In summer we are full of energy and life and very active, whilst in the winter months we feel sluggish, depressed and inactive.

Color affects us even when our eyes are closed. Light is required for our cells to function normally and individual colors affect them by causing changes in growth and behaviour patterns. There is a lot of research in progress at the moment into S.A.D. or Seasonal Affective Disorder. You can even purchase SAD lamps that mimic the effects of sunlight on the human body. SAD is typically identified in certain individuals by their symptoms: feelings of deep depression (even feeling suicidal), but only in the autumn and winter months. This is due to the shorter daylight hours and lack of bright light. These individuals may also put on extra weight in winter and lose it in the summer months. Many SAD lamp users have found that they no longer feel depressed in winter or put on excess weight. I have tested several of these SAD lamps for myself and clients, therefore I can personally attest to their effectiveness.

Examples of How Color Can Affect You:-

Red Increases physical energy and can be used if you are feeling tired.

Stones Red jasper, ruby, garnet.

Orange Very motivating, balances body energy levels, increases vitality.

Stones Carnelian, orange calcite, sunstone (orange).

Pink This is the color of love, ideal for developing a loving attitude for yourself and others. Also gives us emotional balance.

Stones Rose quartz, rhodochrosite, rhodonite, pink tourmaline, morganite.

Yellow A very good communication color. Helps to stimulate conversation, prevents shyness and gives courage. Prevents mental confusion.

Stones Citrine, topaz, golden calcite (especially stellar beams), sunstone (golden).

Green This is a major balancing color. Also an emotional soother. It reduces mental confusion. Will aid spiritual awareness.

Stones Emerald, malachite, green calcite, chrysoprase, green aventurine, moldavite, green tourmaline.

Blue Calms the mind. Helps you to think more clearly. The intellectual and mind color. Will soothe your soul.

Stones Blue sapphire, azurite, lapis lazuli, turquoise, blue topaz, blue lace agate, Siberian blue quartz, blue tourmaline.

Violet and Purple Sensitive, intuitive, spiritual colors. They will enhance receptivity and introspection of the one mind. These colors also secure you emotionally. They promote divine growth and awareness.

Stones Amethyst, purple fluorite, sugilite, charoite.

Brown Basic security. Stability. Prevents fear and stress. Tunes you in to nature

Stones Brown agates, smoky quartz, elestial quartz, mahogany obsidian.

Black Protection, acting as a barrier. Prevents negativity from others influencing you.

Stones Black tourmaline, obsidian, smoky quartz, elestial quartz, snowflake obsidian.

White Peace, purity, calming and soothing, healing.

Stones Clear quartz, snow quartz, white moonstone, Herkimer diamonds.

The Chakra System

The chakra system is known to the Hindu yogis and many other ancient native cultures. Basically, according to the teachings, a chakra is the Sanskrit word for wheel. As you develop your inner 'intuition' you will become aware of your chakras. They are the intersections of vital energy flowing through the body. Although there are literally hundreds within the human body, we are most acquainted with the seven main ones, which are aligned with the spinal column. Each of the chakras is envisioned in classic lore as a 'lotus' flower. Each chakra's lotus has a different number of petals. The number of petals is related both to Sanskrit symbolism concerning the configuration of subtle nerves, called nadis, that emanate from the particular region of the spinal column where the chakra is located, and also to the meaning of particular vowels and consonants in the Sanskrit alphabet. The chakras are also gateways between various dimensions, physical, emotional, spiritual etc. On a physical level, chakras correspond to nerve ganglia, where there is a high degree of nervous activity, and to the glands in the endocrine system. In metaphysical terminology, a chakra is a vortex. Each person's chakras are unique, yet there are basic similarities among us all. When they are clear and free-flowing, vital optimum health results. When the energy centres (chakras) are blocked, distorted or inactive, we find ill health or dis-ease occurs. The goal of all of us is to maintain the free-flowing energy within the body, keeping it as clear as possible to maintain a happier healthier life.

Master Chakras

These seven main chakras are called master chakras. As each master chakra gives off its own unique color, which is one of the seven colors of the rainbow, so when a person is healthy, strong and vibrant, so is the chakra color and we find the human body and human aura is a vibrant rainbow. When there is a serious physical, emotional, mental, or spiritual imbalance or illness, certain colors will appear impure, muddy, pale or dull; sometimes a color can even be missing altogether. Healing with crystals and gemstones allows the aura of the crystal or gemstone to mix with our own aura; through the balanced superior color vibration of the crystal or gemstone we quickly find the chakra and aura restored to the original color strength and vibration. Colored light (Chromotherapy) works in a similar way, with the ray of light penetrating our aura.

Red Ray:

Red has an influence on our deep sub-conscious (which we find hard to access) issues of abuse. This color helps one to live on the physical plane. Red is associated with physical energy, passion, gravity, self-preservation, being grounded, suprarenal glands, spinal column and all the solid elements of the body - bones, teeth etc. The red works on the feet, ankles, legs, knees, thighs and large intestine. The red ray is the energetic gateway between us and the earth and also represents energies of childhood and the past. When this color is in balance we are more grounded, solid and powerful at physical levels of survival. Malfunction or lack of the red ray: obesity, haemorrhoids, constipation and problems associated with the feet, legs, bones and teeth. Gemstones of the red ray: ruby, garnet, zircon, ruby aura quartz.

Orange Ray:

Orange is for creativity, wisdom and benevolence. When this color is balanced you will 'flow with your creative feelings'. Use this color as a primal spiritual energy. This color will activate you fully to become healthy and full of vitality. It is associated with vitality, attraction, desire, emotion, creativity, sexuality, water. Bodily parts: all fluid functions of the body, ovaries, testes, womb. Use it also for fertility, impotency, fear, shock and guilt. There is great cleansing potential in this color associated with personality disorders related to the emotions. Malfunction or lack of the orange ray: frigidity, impotence, bladder, kidney and uterine disorders. Gemstones: carnelian, red jasper, orange sunstone, aragonite, hessonite, amber, tangerine quartz.

Yellow Ray:

Yellow is for meditative analytical thought, intellectual activity, abundance and manifestation of your dreams. It will ignite imagination and creativity. It is associated with fire, the sun, personal power, ambition, combustion, anger, joy, laughter; also with astral force, mental power, the adrenal glands and central nervous system. Malfunction or lack of the yellow ray: ulcers and other digestive disorders, also diabetes and low vitality. Gemstones: yellow sapphire, citrine, golden sunstone, sunshine aura quartz, amber, amblygonite, tiger eye.

Green Ray:

Green is for soothing, healing, ecstasy, unconditional love; merging the physical with the divine; transmutation with love; marriage of the physical and spiritual; activation of Karuna (compassion), pity, tenderness. Getting to the heart of the problem or disease. It is associated with compassion, love, oneness, the heart, thymus and immune system. Malfunction or lack of the green ray: lung disease, asthma, heart disease, problems with arms, hands and fingers. Gemstones: moldavite, emerald, green jade, green tourmaline, green aventurine, malachite, peridot.

Blue/Indigo Rays:

These colors give communication with Divine guidance. Use this color to fully activate your voice and your speech will become clear and fluent; your intellect increases, as does your understanding. Blue and Indigo are associated with communication, truth, sound, voice, expression, speech, writing, the thyroid gland, parathyroid, lungs, vocal cords, jaw, breath; also with dreaming, imagination and out of body experiences. Blue will also lower your temperature. Malfunction or lack of the blue ray: stiff necks, colds, sore throats, thyroid and hearing problems. Gemstones: lapis lazuli, blue calcite, blue sapphire, azurite, blue lace agate, larimar, aquamarine, turquoise, aqua aura quartz.

Violet Ray:

Violet represents those who search for the spiritual truth in all life. Violet activates the seat of true wisdom, through deep meditation. It fills you with peace and helps develop a spiritual aura. This color controls the body temperature, giving balance and harmony. It is associated with intuition, the pituitary gland, left eye and pineal gland. Malfunction or lack of the violet ray: headaches, nightmares, eye problems. Gemstones: amethyst, tanzanite, sugilite, lepidolite, charoite, purple fluorite.

Clear Ray:

Color clear, bringing enlightenment, cosmic awareness, blissful reunion with source. Associated with enlightenment, cosmic consciousness, clarity and clear insight, right eye, cerebrum, pineal gland. Malfunction or lack of the clear ray: confusion, lack of clarity, depression. Gemstones: diamond, clear quartz, danburite, phenacite, azeztulite, petalite, clear calcite, selenite, Herkimer diamond.

Complementary or Balance Colors

Very often in crystal therapy we use the complementary or balance color to conclude a treatment. This facilitates easier integration of the missing color or colors into the aura.

Black	White
Red	Green
Pink	Pale green
Peach	Turquoise
Orange	Blue
Gold	Indigo
Yellow	Violet
Pale green	Pink
Green	Red
Turquoise	Peach
Blue	Orange
Indigo	Gold
Violet	Yellow
White	Black

Using Color for the Face

Our face is a microcosm of the body. I have experimented with the following colors using crystals on the various areas of the face, head and throat:

Red: The jaw, chin and bottom lip.

Orange: The top lip and inside of mouth, including the gums, teeth and tongue.

Yellow: The throat, leading down to the intestinal tract.

Green: The nose, leading through nasal passages to the bronchial tract and lungs.

Blue: The eyes and sinuses.

Indigo: The ears, forehead and third eye area.

Violet: The upper forehead, top of the head.

Crystal Light Boxes

Crystal light boxes are square wooden boxes with a small light bulb fitted in one side and a hole in the centre of the lid for the light to shine through. Color filters or gels are placed over the hole where the light shines out of the box. Light box crystals (clear quartz) are placed over the colored filters. When clear quartz crystal is used in this way, it intensifies and projects the color ray into the surrounding environment. This may be used for healing, meditation and emotional upliftment.

In fact colors are shades of light vibrating at different frequencies. Red and black vibrate at a slower rate than, say white or blue, so they register on the human optical scale as darker colors or shades of light. Because of this they will send different signals to the brain of the observer, causing different degrees of emotional reaction.

How Does it Work? - Seeing Auras

There are people who are born with the gift of seeing auras. I am one of them. We can see the colors, shapes, patterns and symbols that surround a person, plant, animal, crystal etc. Other people find that they can feel the aura surrounding a person: some people do it with their eyes closed, others with their eyes open. I use my gift as a diagnostic tool, as do others who share this gift. Basically, by using aura viewing or sensing, we can tell which color is missing or which color needs balancing to return a person to optimum health and well-being. In my teaching of the crystal courses I have discovered that almost everyone can develop this gift to some extent by allowing themselves to sense or feel the energy of the aura. Others have developed their inner vision and still others have completely developed aura vision.

I have developed a very simple technique for experiencing the aura of another person:

1. Stand facing your partner, about three feet away from each other.
2. Begin to sensitise your hands by shaking them; this releases blocked energy.
3. Briskly rub your hands together; this begins to concentrate the chi or Prana into your hands and sensitises them.
4. Hold your hands with your palms facing each other, about nine inches apart. Feel the energy radiating and vibrating between your hands; play with this energy.
5. Begin to form this energy into a ball and visualise it yellow in color. When it feels right, place this yellow ball into the solar plexus area. This energises your mental body, allowing you to perceive auras more easily.
6. Now your partner drops their hands and you take your hands to the top of your partner's head and begin to feel and see their energy. Gradually work down along both sides of the head and neck, shoulders, arms, pelvis, legs and feet, observing the energy in any way you can, via heat, cold, tingling and color.
7. Your partner repeats the same process over your aura.
8. Ground, centre and focus yourself.
9. Share with your partner what you perceived in each other's aura.

How Does it Work? - Toning

Toning refers to sounds which are a language for the multidimensional transmission of light, color, vibration and sacred geometries. These tones break up dysfunctional energy patterns and energy blockages which are the cause of illness and misery. In the section on chakras I have given you the seed sounds I have personally used for twenty-eight years. These are ancient Sanskrit syllables known as varnas. Varna means color, and all sounds have a corresponding color in the invisible world. They are the ones I use in my teaching, group work and with my clients. I can personally vouch for their effectiveness in restoring the human chakras to perfect balance and alignment. By using the seed sounds or *mantras* we can change our frequency or vibratory rate to align with our perfect body and mind, bringing in the energy of our higher God nature. These holy energy forms of meditation restore harmony and much more. Every time I have used them in group work all the participants have made huge shifts in their consciousness and healing awareness. It is said that if we have the name of God on our lips in the last moment of life, our spirit will pass directly to that sacred space of being. That is how sacred and powerful these spiritual sounds are. Experiments have demonstrated that notes produced by certain instruments can trace out in a bed of sand definite geometric shapes. Socrates said "The simple form of maths is music".

Each chakra or energy centre has a corresponding tone which we use to vibrate that chakra. As I have said, the ones I give in this book are the ones I use, but there are many other systems for toning. All ancient peoples used sound as a potent force in their spiritual and healing work. You will derive the most benefit if you tone for yourself, but it is possible to tone for others. Also, toning with others is very effective in group work; the energy produced is magnified and those who are new to toning quickly gain strength from those more experienced in the art. Sound as energy or the theory of *japa* meditation, or *mantra* repetition, holds that repeating the syllables with accuracy will invoke the form of the *mantra's* presiding deity.

To enhance the vibratory effect it is good to hold a clear quartz crystal in your hand. This amplifies and focuses the sound into the chakra or chakras being worked with. During a crystal therapy treatment you can increase the effect by placing a single terminated clear quartz crystal over the chakra being balanced, with the point towards the person's head, and begin to sound the tone for that chakra. Repeat the tone several times until the quartz crystal and the corresponding chakra begin to resonate with the sound. Continue this process until the chakra is re-balanced or the blocked energy is released.

You can do an entire quartz crystal chakra vibratory balancing session in this way for your client, remembering to use only pure clear quartz crystals. You could even have a complete chakra balancing set that you keep only for this technique. When toning for yourself, you can place the tips of your fingers very lightly on the chakra you are toning for until you feel the resonance (vibration) in that chakra, although after a while even that is unnecessary as the effects will be felt throughout the physical body and aura. Other methods of toning are to allow any vibratory sound to come out spontaneously. This method is very good for releasing grief, sorrow, pain, anger, frustration or any emotion that needs clearing which is blocking that chakra.

Toning is used to enhance meditation, for clearing emotional debris, healing and alignment. Some people 'tone' just for the sheer joy of it. The Usui Reiki system of natural healing using the symbols' sounds has also proved very potent; you can even buy tapes of chanting Reiki Masters. Another example of using sound in healing is drumming, which is useful for attaining altered states of consciousness and healing.

How Does it Work? - Structure

After color, possibly the next thing you notice about a crystal is its interesting shape. The geologist divides the rocks of the earth's surface into groups, which are then subdivided into smaller divisions called systems. Some knowledge of these systems may be necessary in order to understand them clearly as holistic healing systems.

The Crystal Systems

On the basis of their symmetry, crystals can be grouped into seven crystal systems. One other 'crystal' system, amorphous, is not technically crystal: this is because it is without structure, due to the formation, which is so rapid that no crystal structure has had a chance to form. The systems are:

Cubic
Tetragonal
Orthorhombic

Monoclinic
Triclinic
Hexagonal
Trigonal
Amorphous

Working With Crystal Systems

I would suggest the serious crystal therapist/researcher would be well advised to cut out the shapes of the crystal systems in paper, or mark them out on the floor. The next step is to meditate or lie down in each shape in turn. This process should be facilitated over several days to get the most from the experience. Doing this will encourage a deeper understanding of each crystal system's energy signature and its effect on modifying the human aura and consciousness. Each system has a very definite effect and you may find some of them are more comfortable for you to 'be' with than others. You may find that your consciousness and perceptions are altered as each crystal system adjusts your energy signature to expand or contract your normal senses and expectations.

Many people find the experience can be likened to similar or parallel experiences that rely on the use of ancient symbols to instigate 'tuning' in to other frequencies. An obvious example of this is Reiki healing using symbols, or Shamanic body postures used for attaining altered states of consciousness. My own first experience of this was in 1990, while I was in the Senora desert in Southern Arizona. It was very easy to find a secluded place and I used a saguaro rib to draw each 'shape' out in the sand; I personally found it a very powerful life-changing experience. I have since used this experiment with many others in groups and in individual meditation experiences. I have found ancient sites, especially the stone circles of Great Britain, to be very enlightening, but I have found we have very interesting experiences wherever this technique has been tried. After all, the universe is made from energy that took on geometric form due to the nature of formation and energy movement.

Many people also report that during meditation they are shown geometric shapes. I remember when I was 21 years old being shown many different geometric shapes and structures during deep meditation. I remember afterwards thinking, 'You have the wrong one here', as I knew nothing of geometry. How little at that time did I realise how very important the sacred geometry was to become to me, or how I would be guided by the crystals to help others using the ancient language of light and form.

There is also the most obvious connection with the seven crystal systems and the cosmic significance of the seven master chakras. It can be likened to those who are drawn to a certain crystal shape, or tend to focus or operate from a particular chakra they feel at ease with. As an example of this belief system, the most obvious would be the cubic crystal system being related to those who are very base (muladhara) chakra orientated and view the world in a materialistic way. The muladhara chakra is located at the base of the spinal column. It has a yellow square in the centre of its mandala representing the earth principle.

How Does it Work? - Hardness

After you have become aware of the shape, another factor to be taken into account when we look at the structure of crystals and their effect as precise healing mediums is the hardness of each crystal. As you will soon discover when you begin to use crystals for healing, this information is vital to the holistic overview. It becomes apparent that crystal systems are not enough to explain the intensity or quality of the energy, so we will now look at what is called hardness and how it relates to the crystal healing experience.

Bound up with the atomic bonding of a substance is the property of hardness. A high degree of hardness in a precious stone is necessary, for only hard substances can take and retain a good polish. A practical means of assessing hardness was proposed by the German mineralogist Friedrich Mohs, who in 1822, after extensive experiments, chose 10 well-known and easily obtainable minerals and arranged them in order of their 'scratch hardness' to serve as standards of comparison. Albeit the numbers of Mohs' list have no quantitative meaning, it is commonly called the Mohs' scale and still forms a universally accepted standard of hardness amongst mineralogists, gemmologists and crystal healers.

The Mohs' scale is as follows:

10. Diamond,
9. Sapphire
8. Topaz
7. Quartz
6. Orthoclase
5. Apatite
4. Fluorite
3. Calcite
2. Gypsum
1. Talc

The numbers on Mohs' list are not quantities, they represent an order only. Diamond is enormously harder than any other mineral and the gap between 10 and 9 on the list is far greater than that between any other of the numbers. The number 7 on the Mohs' scale is an important one, as any gemstone must be at least as hard as this if it is to withstand being regularly worn in jewellery. Stones such as peridot or green demantoid garnet are only suitable for occasional wear. Opal, pearl, amber and coral are also very soft and great care should be taken if they are worn as pendants.

The therapeutic effect related to the hardness of a gemstone can best be appreciated if one does the following experiment:

First hold and feel the vibration of clear calcite (3), then a clear quartz (7), followed by diamond (10).

The clear calcite is gentle, flowing and cleansing; the clear quartz amplifies, focuses and coheres energy, whilst the diamond is exceedingly intense, magnifying and amplifying all other energies, both positive and negative. You can experiment with this information as you work with the crystal vibration and I have included the hardness of each stone in part seven, the A to Z of crystals.

How Does it Work? - Mineral Composition

Perhaps the fourth thing you notice about a crystal is its composition? Well, maybe not! But after a while you may think 'What is this crystal composed of?' There is no doubt of the long-term important effects mineral-forming elements have on our bodies. They have key roles to play in everything from the vital formation of enzymes to regulating brain activity and aiding fertility. Minerals are not produced by the body: they are absorbed from our food intake. Mineral deficiency can easily arise through poor diet or bad eating habits; also the long-term effects of pollution and stress can cause the body to become mineral deficient.

Crystal therapy can give you the opportunity to experiment with the possibility of using crystals for their mineral composition. Perhaps if you have a tendency to be deficient in some minerals you would have the opportunity to use crystal therapy to investigate why you are deficient; perhaps your body needs to work with that particular frequency or vibration. Very often, using the frequency of a particular mineral helps the body to formulate why it does not absorb its mineral vibrational frequency. On no account must you ingest a crystal as a means of correcting an imbalance. You must only take internally vitamins and minerals described as pure which you buy from a health food store or pharmacy.

An example I would like to share concerns one of my clients who had been diagnosed as having anaemia; she had this problem for years and had been prescribed iron tablets. These she had taken intermittently over the years. When she was not taking the iron tablets, her blood count would go down and she would become tired, listless and irritable again. It seemed as though her body had a problem absorbing iron from her food intake. When she came to see me she had just had a blood count taken and was diagnosed once more as anaemic. I decided, after taking a clinical history, to give her a hematite tumbled polished stone to use. I asked her to sleep holding the hematite in her left hand. This allowed her body to become sensitive to the vibration. During this time she found her energy increased and she felt more physically vital. One month later she had another blood test and her iron deficiency was gone; her blood count was normal. She had decided not to take the iron tablets prescribed by her doctor, only to use the hematite stone. Her anaemia never returned and she has been able ever since to absorb fully the iron from her normal food intake. As crystal therapists we find that hematite allows the body, via the small intestine, to absorb iron and aids in the formation of red blood corpuscles.

Another example I would like to share concerns a client who had been taking anti-depressants for several years. After an initial consultation I advised my client to use lepidolite, which is a mica containing lithium. Lithium reduces over-sensitivity in nerves and the motor nervous system. Within a week my client reported a vast improvement in the condition and over a short period of time was able to use the lepidolite crystal alone and completely stop using the anti-depressants. Eventually my client had re-balanced his body and no longer needed the lepidolite. The original depression has still not returned after a duration of six years.

The following is a list of common minerals and their physical healing properties:

Minerals - many of which are metals - are not found by themselves in food or supplements. In fact, most minerals naturally exist as mineral salts, e.g. iron oxide - the major constituent of iron ore. It is these compounds - known as salts - that are used in most supplements.

Calcium (Ca) - is the most abundant mineral in the body, comprising over 1% of our total body weight. Of this, 99% is found in our bones and teeth, the remaining 1% in soft tissues, including blood, muscles and nerves.

- Needed for strong teeth and bones
- Important for muscle and nerve function
- Helps prevent osteoporosis
- Can help with insomnia

Iron (Fe) - is a vital trace mineral. The chemical symbol for iron is Fe. It is needed to make haemoglobin, the red pigment of blood. Haemoglobin is contained within red blood cells and transports oxygen around the body, from the lungs to the tissues, via the bloodstream. Insufficient iron to meet the body's needs leads to iron deficiency. Iron is also found in the protein myoglobin, the red pigment of muscles, and in certain cell enzymes. The remainder of the body's iron is stored in the liver, spleen and bone marrow.

- Needed for healthy red blood cells
- A deficiency leads to anaemia
- Iron deficiency symptoms are: fatigue, light-headedness, pale skin and weakness

Magnesium (Mg) - is a vital component of bones and teeth, and is sometimes known as the 'anti-stress' mineral because of its intimate connection with the nervous system. Over a half of the body's magnesium is found in our bones, where, along with calcium and phosphorous, it provides skeletal strength and structure. Magnesium is a co-factor in energy producing reactions, and so is closely involved in energy release. It is also important in the correct functioning of our nerves and muscles. A deficiency of this mineral may lead to increased irritability, anxiety or even mild depression, eyelid or facial twitches, 'restless leg syndrome' and other muscle spasms. Magnesium is closely involved with the body's use of calcium. Magnesium also plays a role in regulating blood sugar levels and in the pumping of the heart muscle, where low levels can cause heart palpitations.

* Helps maintain strong bones
* Closely linked with calcium
* May help reduce muscle twitches
* May help with mild depression
* Needed for a healthy heart

Boron (B) - is a trace mineral which has only been found to be important for humans since the 1980s. Our bones contain the highest amounts of this mineral.

* Can slow down calcium and magnesium loss
* May help with arthritis

Zinc (Zn) - is a vital mineral for our health and well-being. It is an antioxidant mineral needed for a healthy robust immune defence system, and for repair and renewal of skin cells. A diet marginally lacking in zinc can lead to problems such as frequent infections, delayed wound healing, reduced appetite, decreased sense of smell and taste, poor skin conditions and white flecks on the nails. Zinc is also important for reproductive health; low levels may result in reduced sperm count. Zinc is commonly taken as a food supplement to help with skin conditions such as acne or eczema. It is needed for the metabolism of fatty acids into important substances which regulate our skin health.

* Needed for a healthy immune system
* Important for reproductive health
* Needed for sense of taste and smell

Selenium - has been known as an essential trace mineral, vital to prevent degeneration of liver tissue, for only the last two decades. About half of the body's selenium is found in the liver. Selenium forms part of a key antioxidant enzyme, glutathione peroxidase, which helps protect the fatty parts of our cells from going rancid. It is also involved in our antibody response to harmful germs, so it helps to maintain our immune system. Low selenium levels are linked to an increased risk of cancer and heart disease. Another selenium function is helping the body produce anti-inflammatory prostaglandins (hormone-like substances), and so some rheumatoid arthritis sufferers find taking selenium helpful. The mineral is also required for production of thyroxine, a hormone made by the thyroid gland which helps regulate metabolic rate.

* Preserves normal liver function
* Helps the immune system
* Used as an antioxidant
* May help reduce risk of heart disease
* May benefit arthritis sufferers

Lithium (Li) - reduces over-sensitivity in nerves and the motor nervous system. It can alleviate neural pains, sciatica or neuralgia. It also affects the blood by reducing cholesterol levels and prevents the deposition of plaques in the blood vessels and joints. Another lithium function is its calming effect which eases restlessness and trembling. It is used to improve the memory and as an anti-depressant.

* Reduces nerve pain
* Reduces cholesterol
* Used as an anti-depressant
* May help reduce risk of heart disease
* May benefit arthritis sufferers

Chromium (Cr) - if severely deficient is known to result in poor glucose tolerance, the precursor to diabetic conditions. Chromium might also play a role in maintaining a healthy low cholesterol level in the blood.

* Helps regulation of blood sugar levels
* Part of glucose tolerance factor
* May help maintain healthy cholesterol levels

Copper (Cu) - will benefit the body functions of enzyme and haemoglobin production. The deficiency symptoms are anaemia, fatigue, weakness and bone fragility.

* Needed for healthy red blood cells
* A deficiency leads to anaemia
* Copper deficiency symptoms are fatigue and weakness
* Helps maintain strong bones

Manganese (Mn) - benefits the body functions of enzyme activity in reproduction, growth, fat metabolism. Deficiency symptoms: poor growth, reproductive and co-ordination abnormalities.

* Needed for reproduction
* Needed for fat metabolism

Phosphorus (P) - benefits these body functions: bone/tooth formation, muscle contraction, kidney function, nerve and muscle activity. Deficiency symptoms: continuous thirst, dry skin, general weakness and weak reflexes.

* Needed for bone/tooth formation
* A deficiency leads to poor muscle contraction, nerve and muscle activity

Potassium (K) - benefits these body functions: pH balance of blood, body-water balance, nerve and muscle function. The deficiency symptoms are: irregular heartbeat, muscular weakness and the build-up of lactic acid.

* Needed for body-water balance
* Needed for healthy muscle and nerve function

How Does it Work? - Growth Conditions

The fifth thing you may notice about a crystal is how it grew? Well, maybe not! But sometimes this question dawns on you when you have the choice of two crystals, both the same color and hardness. You find one behaves in one way and the other behaves completely differently and you feel you need to explore further the fascinating world of crystals, looking to find a deeper explanation. One possible answer could be that they must have had a different birth process. Perhaps one crystal has had a watery birth and the other crystal has had a birth of fire. Very often, as crystal therapists, you become acutely aware that the evolution of the crystal consciousness plays a major role in its interaction within the human energy field.

Gem materials, except for those which are of organic origin or due to man's artifice, are found in the rocks forming the upper accessible levels of the earth's crust. Rocks are usually classified under three broad headings:

a) igneous
b) sedimentary
c) metamorphic

Igneous Rocks

The igneous rocks were produced by the solidification of hot molten matter (magma) which was pushed into fissures in the earth's crust, or was extruded on the surface as lava flowing from a volcano. During the cooling of magma, the individual minerals crystallise out around local centres. Some minerals do so at an early stage and are able to develop good crystal outlines. One fruitful source of gem material is a pegmatite. The pegmatites of Madagascar provide an interesting collection of gem materials such as beryl, tourmaline, garnet, topaz, kunzite, iolite and transparent golden-yellow feldspar. Hollow spaces caused by gases and fluids trapped in the solidifying magma produce cavities lined with free-growing crystals of such high temperature minerals as topaz and beryl. From these so-called miarolitic cavities gem crystals have been recovered. The cooling of certain minor intrusions and lava flows extruded out of the earth's surface was so rapid that there was no time for crystallisation to take place: in this manner obsidian was formed.

Sedimentary Rocks

The second group of rocks, sedimentary, results from the breaking down (denudation) of earlier formed rock masses. There are three stages in the formation of typical sedimentary rocks: first, the chemical and mechanical weathering of source rocks by the action of wind, rain or ice; by changing temperatures; by the chemical breakdown of unstable material; or by chemical action of the atmosphere. The second stage is the transportation of the products of weathering by moving water or wind. Thirdly comes the deposition of the debris, or simple evaporation of mineralised water in places favouring rapid evaporation, which is how gypsum is formed. Coal and jet are formed by the accumulation of plant remains and are classed as sedimentary rocks. Brecciated jasper occurs when pebbles are cemented together by secondary mineralisation. The sorting of the detritus (gravel, sand, silt and so forth) of broken-down rocks is commonly carried out by the action of streams and rivers. Such sorting by water may depend greatly upon the density of the mineral being carried along. The more important gem minerals, being relatively heavy, tend to fall into any depression in the river bed, forming placer deposits. The river beds may be ancient, having long since ceased to carry water, and are now covered and obliterated by more recent soils. It is in such old river courses that the water-worn pebbles of many gemstones are found. A typical example of this are the gem gravels of Sri Lanka, where sapphires and rubies are found. Sedimentary rocks may also accumulate where life is possible and wood opal or silicified wood is produced by the replacement and impregnation of the woody tissues of trees by silica.

Metamorphic Rocks

Heat and pressure from intrusions of igneous rocks, or from the folding of rock masses during deep-seated disturbances in the earth's crust during the birth of mountains, may alter the surrounding country rocks, whether they be igneous or sedimentary, so that a new type of rock is produced. Such an alteration is termed metamorphism. When extensive areas - some hundreds or thousands of square miles - are affected by deep-seated igneous activity, regional or dynamothermal metamorphism is said to occur, and under these conditions rocks such as schists and some crystalline limestone and quartzites are produced. During alteration by metamorphism, any impurities in the original rock, the so-called accessory minerals, may crystallise out as separate minerals which are disseminated through the newly-formed rock. Thus green fuchsite mica may form from crystals throughout quartzite, producing green aventurine.

Rocks Formed by Vapour Action

By the action of chemically active vapours (pneumatolysis) or fluids, often assisted by heat from the intrusion of molten matter, new rocks may be produced from old ones. New minerals are formed by the action of the vapours, particularly boron and fluorine, which produce such minerals as tourmaline and topaz in granite rocks.

Mineral-Rich Water

Much mineral-rich water travels through cracks and fissures in the country rock and deposits low-temperature minerals in them. Such veins or loads, the latter term being used for metallic veins, may open out into cavities, called vughs (vugs). The vughs may be lined with crystals deposited from the water. Many of the deposited minerals have gem significance. In a vugh, the minerals deposited are of a different nature from the surrounding rock. When this happens in a cavity the minerals are often called drusy. Geodes are hollow cavities lined with crystals deposited from mineral-rich waters which have percolated into stream cavities in lavas, or into cavities in sedimentary rocks, and even into fossils. Such geodes are a common source of gem crystals, particularly rock crystal and amethyst. In caves, the mineral-rich water dripping from the roof forms hanging masses called stalactites; similar but upstanding masses may form on the floor of the cave as stalagmites. Further deposits of minerals may well occur in irregular sheets over the floor of the cave and these are often banded in structure. It is from such formations that the banded calcites and rhodochrosites are obtained.

Tektites

The last birth process we will explore is the amorphous tektite. Chemically, tektites comprise nearly pure silica-rich glass, which sometimes is also rich in alumina, potash and lime and can be matched by a few igneous or sedimentary rocks. There are two schools of scientific thought about the true origin of tektites and Moldavite tektites in particular - one holds that they are true meteorites, while the other suggests that they are a fusion of meteoric material with earthly rock. So, they are either a gift from heaven, or a marriage of heaven and earth. Either way, their birth process is sudden impact. As such, they are very fast in their healing action.

One more factor when choosing a crystal for its therapeutic properties, which ties in with the birth process, is the birth process of the dis-ease; after all, the illness was created in the first place, so how did we manifest the blockage in the energy system?

Was it created by fire - anger?

Was it created by water - delusion?

Was it created by ether - grief?

Was it created by air - desire?

Was it created by earth - fear?

As all energy is created by ether and the five properties of ether are grief, desire, anger, delusion and fear, according to the practice of Jnana Yoga meditation - Vedantic practice - these are all generated in the ether which belongs to the space of the heart. (The actual position is slightly higher than the heart, at the thymus; it is the witness point where the etheric body joins the physical vehicle).

Grief is the main part of ether, for with grieving the body feels empty and hollow.

Desire is transitory, restless and fleeting like the wind.

When anger arises, the body becomes agitated and over heated.

Delusion is as pervasive as fast flowing water.

When we become frozen with the fear vibration, the body becomes inanimate as earth.

These feelings or emotions are actually characteristics of the astral body, but we treat them as real and as if they belonged to the physical body, because this is where their influences are directly tangible. Only by releasing these notions of disease-producing negative concepts can we become whole again. If we apply this principle to crystal therapy, very often we find it is better to use a crystal that will ease a manifested health condition rather than inflame it. So for cooling an overheated angry condition it would be wise to choose a crystal that was born out of water to 'put out the fire'. A perfect crystal in these circumstances would be a calcite. (By becoming aware of our speech, we very often we give major clues to the birth process of our dis-ease).

How Does it Work? - Vibration

This is a good one to notice, because at this point you are on your own when you try and tell other people that what they perceive as a lump of inanimate rock is actually a live, pulsing, vibrating mass of energy, which is interacting with your energy field and is having a positive effect on you!! (It is getting better, as more and more people are waking up to vibration perception and admitting that we are in a vast, unlimited, unknown, but not unknowable, sea of energies and in reality nothing is solid - or is it that people are owning up and coming out of the closet energy-wise and speaking their truth vibration without fear?).

> *"That which is looked upon by one generation as the apex of human knowledge is often considered an absurdity by the next, and that which is regarded as a superstition in one century, may form the basis of science for the following one". Paracelsus*

The way your body and aura are organised gives you your perception of reality. Your perceptive ability is preset to certain energy bands or frequencies by your conditioning or belief system. You are most familiar with those we call sound, light, touch, taste, and smell (third dimension). If you were able to alter at will your own bioelectromagnetic signature (vibration) in some way, it would be possible to connect your individual pattern to a slightly different pervading omnipresent model or pattern, thus altering your experiences, signature and comprehension and ultimately realisation. In ancient yogic philosophy, thought, form and sound are all the same just as ice, water and steam are all the same substance.

We use the same process when we lie within a crystal web. This also happens when we hold a crystal in our hand and attune to its refined frequency or vibration. Each crystal modifies the physical and subtle bodies' energy relationship to its environment and allows access to other tiers (levels, worlds or, as the Kabalists would say, spheres) of information and most of all awareness perception. I became conscious of this process many years ago when I discovered that by placing certain crystals on or around the body we could expect and even predict a certain change in comprehension or perception. I have seen thousands of people 'feel' this 'shift' in consciousness or change of perception when using crystals. It usually takes years of meditation practice before this shift in consciousness occurs! So you can imagine my excitement as I watched the speed of awareness development within individuals who were not regular meditators. Some were even downright sceptics. The sceptics very often resorted to denial, although they initially felt the shift, but through fear of change or leaving themselves open to ridicule decided to block their spiritual growth. We all know the fear vibration and have felt it used against us many times by those who wish for their own selfish reasons to control or manipulate us.

We are surrounded by energy and energy patterns. Depending on our awareness, culture, expectations, intellect and perceptive abilities, this gives us our personal reality profile. Any time that changes occur, we become aware of the many billions of different energy currents and energy flows that live alongside us and the different sorts of beings that also inhabit our universe. All energy is omnipresent and all-pervasive; it only requires the correct energy shift or awareness to find it. As a child I was aware of the myriad of different energies and energy systems; in fact I could not understand why others were not aware of these energies. I did not realise that they were not 'tuned' in to the frequencies that were my reality, my birthright. From the age of twenty I have studied these energies and energy realities. The native traditions of many peoples are very unlike those of the average westerner: their belief systems are very different. The more I studied, the more I became aware of the limitations we place upon ourselves. I also realised not only that 'healing' used different energy frequencies within the human body and aura (chakras, meridians, sheaths etc.), but that different frequencies and energy patterns are present and exist within the universal energy frequencies.

All energy begins with a central point which is the source of 'all'. In the Tantric view, sound, as a vibration of undifferentiated Intelligence, is the catalyst that sets into motion the unfolding of the manifest cosmos. This nothingness is comprised of all the energies and forces of the Divine Universe, existing in harmony beyond our understanding at a time before our existence. It has neither mass nor form, but it has the potential to become everything and anything. It is that first point from which we came and to which we will some day return. View, if you will, the first primal movement that awakens the sleeping equilibrium of the Divine Intelligence and arouses the two active principles to carry out creation. This great cosmic vibration splits the Divine Intelligence into two streams of magnetic force, as two aspects are projected outward, male and female. The centrifugal positive male force is the ground from which the centripetal, negative feminine energy springs. It is the female that unfolds the universe into manifestation. They are the Father (Bindu) and Mother (Nada) aspects of the Supreme Power. The act of creation, the act of Divine Intelligence manifesting from a place beyond physical reality and thus beyond our comprehension, as seen within the Kabala, gives a way of perceiving how we can each evolve and attain higher and greater knowledge or gifts. The Divine Intelligence began to manifest through stages its energies, acquiring greater density, much as steam condenses into water and then can change into ice: it is still the same, but different. Everything at some level or another is energy in motion; the electrons and protons that make up every atom of every substance and form have motion. According to quantum theory, matter is never quiescent but always in a state of motion. Macroscopically the materials around us may seem dead and inert, but modern physics pictures matter not as passive and inert but as continuously dancing and vibrating.

This vibrational movement continues as the energy moves further and further away from its source. It becomes heavier and denser and vibrates more and more slowly: but it does have the potential and the content of all the higher and finer vibrations within it. We, as human beings, contain this energy of the all within our energy field. Through meditation and conscious attunement, we can cause our reality to shift into any desired frequency or vibration. This ability will become much more prevalent as we go into the next millennium and the frequencies become available to all within the earth vibration. This has been prophesied by many peoples in many countries. We, who choose to work with multiple frequencies or select the frequency reality of our choice, are the forerunners of the millennium shift. It is no longer appropriate to just go along with the reality map we have been 'tuned' in to through our sentimental tribal conditioning.

Our thoughts and expectations create our reality, whether we are aware of this or not: what we think about or our mind dwells on day after day is brought into existence, along with its opposite quality. The real challenge is to gain control of the internal world we call the mind. This will facilitate our human evolution on a return journey home from the gross physical plane back to our source. In one case the force is centrifugal, in the other centripetal.

How Does it Work? - Inspiration

Inspiration, intuition, flash, idea, revelation, thought, impulse, boost, lift, encouragement, stimulation or Divine guidance. Call it what you will, we have all experienced those moments of pure inspired revelation. Whether we believe we have blessed Celestial counsel, or impressions from the Cosmic Hierarchy, does it matter? Everyone experiences these moments in their life. Even the most ardent sceptic will admit that they happen.

So What is It ?

It usually happens when we are under stress, confused or at our wits' end with worry; suddenly we find the answer. This can be through dreams, chance remarks from friends, or while relaxing in the bath. With inspiration we are not dealing with our normal everyday mind, we are dealing with our superconscious mind. We can access our superconscious mind at will, if we know how. Ideally we should spend some time each day in meditation or contemplation; this would help us to become relaxed and centred. The problem for most people is they are so stressed out and exhausted that this causes their vibration to become even lower, which in turn causes more stress, ill health, etc. They get caught in a trap and their life force slips lower and lower. When we are relaxed and centred, we have access to the universal laws and infinite knowledge and we tap into the frequency we need. We understand another's frequency patterns, too. That is, again, because we are one. In the oneness of this existence we are able to transmit and receive messages and, more importantly, we can become the sender and receiver of messages in perfect understanding.

I have found that this ability to access universal knowledge, wisdom and inspiration always increases as people use crystals for healing, personal development and meditation. This is because the crystalline vibration is focused and unified; this coherent energy will usually stabilise the user's energy field, bringing relaxation, focused concentration and divine inspiration. Some people will struggle their whole lives, never finding their centre of peace and wisdom. Very often it is not until a person reaches a point of great distress that they realise it is time to stop and take stock of what is happening in their lives.

Every person projects some kind of vibration. Some people are a pleasure to be with and are an inspirational force. They have a certain prana, or energy, that they share with others. Then there are those who are negative and depressed; they seem to actually pull energy out of others. The reason for this is that there is a power contained in thought. It is subtle, yet it does exist and it is extremely potent. Whether a person is aware of it or not, they are constantly receiving and transmitting thoughts. The ability to communicate and perceive thought is developed to a higher degree in those who are said to be psychic. All thoughts have size, shape, weight, color and power. Those of us who are experienced in meditating can see this directly. So how can you learn to relax and find inspiration, to become one with your true source of power, love and wisdom, which is your Divine birthright, your higher self, this energy that exists in each being, yet exists independently also? Some call it God. Others call it Goddess, Great Spirit, Jehovah, Allah, Brahma, Cosmic Consciousness, Atman, Holy Spirit or Universal Mind. The names and paths are numerous, but there is one Divine essence which pervades all beings, the-one-thread-soul.

Crystal meditation is simple, easy, safe and effective - see part five for inspirational meditation practice.

How Does it Work? - Gem Essences

How a gemstone essence can help you: gem remedies are specially prepared gem and crystal-based essences; each crystal and gemstone contains a vibratory signature, which will address a different feeling, emotion or physical symptom. They can also be used for spiritual development.

The thoughts or emotions you experience daily surround you and can make you happy or sad, healthy or sick, tense or relaxed. Please remember - positive emotions strengthen your energy field, bringing health, balance and vitality, whilst negative emotions or stress bring sickness, instability, mood swings and low energy. This is called the body-mind connection.

It works with the Universal Law of resonance; basically what we dwell on day after day becomes embedded in our aura. The negative or positive thoughts work with the karmic law of return: what you send out is returned amplified like a boomerang. The reason the energy is magnified is very simple: like attracts like! This makes some people very wary of negative thoughts and rightly so - for if you are not sending out positive loving energy and are instead deeply focused on negativity, the last thing you need is even more negativity! What you focus on attracts even more of the same energy; this law makes you very aware of your every thought, word and deed. What you give out will always be yours, you just attract even more of the same! This law can cause havoc when you consider all the negative emotional states people experience on a daily basis. I know from my own experience that we can change our field of reality. It is as simple as owning your thoughts, feelings, emotions - your vibratory pattern; pure mind control, when you are ready to accept responsibility for owning your own emotional energies and vibratory pattern.

But what happens if illness occurs or you find yourself totally swamped by these negative thoughts? Because these negative thoughts or disruptional energies filter down from the etheric level into the physical, it may take weeks, months or even years before the body breaks down and illness is fully manifested in the physical body. In fact these energies become crystalline or fixed within the body. (They are sometimes referred to as miasms*). One of the best ways to alter these dysfunctional patterns or miasms in the subtle bodies or physical body is to administer therapeutic doses of frequency-specific subtle energy in the form of vibrational medicine. Vibration, frequency, resonance, signature, harmonic range; these are all terms used to describe subtle energy.

When we are experiencing joy, happiness, peace and health, our vibratory pattern will be high; illness is a lower or disrupted frequency. This is where the crystals and gemstones essences can come to the rescue. In order to therapeutically alter our subtle bodies, we must administer energy that vibrates at a higher stable frequency. Healing with crystal and gemstone essences allows the vibration of the crystal or gemstone to interact with our own energy field; through the balanced superior higher vibration of the crystal or gemstone we quickly find the imbalance will be alleviated; this, in turn, stimulates the body's own capacity to heal itself by bringing it back into alignment with the higher self.

Gem essences work in many different ways and on all levels, from the gross physical body through to the highest spiritual level. This is because we store negative thought patterns or miasms in different areas of not just the physical body, but all the levels of the aura as well. Gemstones and crystals have a unique molecular arrangement of geometric symmetry which has a stabilizing energetic influence on cellular systems within the physical body. Their harmonic range resonates with certain points within the human anatomy. This influence affects all levels, as the body and aura are interconnected. Gem essences can also bring about spiritual growth and understanding of universal laws; each gemstone's action is given in great detail in part seven of this book.

A gemstone essence is simple to use and make. Recognising exactly how you are feeling is very important when it comes to choosing the most appropriate gem essence. To choose a gem essence you need to identify precisely how you are feeling in that moment, then match the exact mood you are in with the appropriate gemstone. For example, if you feel mentally, physically or emotionally exhausted and your energy is low, you will find fire agate, which stops 'burn-out'.

If you find it perplexing to exactly express how you feel, why not:

* Use a pendulum and dowse over a list of gemstones to find one that will help you?
* Get a friend or relative to help you with kinesiology?
* Intuitively choose one?
* Look under physical problems in the list of crystals?
* Scan the crystals or crystal essences to find which one is attractive to your hand?

However you decide, it is relatively easy to make an essence for yourself. Before we explore making a gemstone essence , I would like to give just two examples from many hundreds of just how gemstone essence have been successfully used. The first is a combination gemstone essence I made for the Angel workshops I have been running since 1990. Very early on I devised a crystal and gemstone energy web, 'Angel of Light', that would adjust the human energy field to the Angelic frequencies. The crystal web allows for easier contact with your Guardian Angel and other beings from the Angelic Realm of love, light, wisdom, truth, compassion and healing.

The workshops have always been a huge success and many thousands of people have attended and gained insight, protection and healing from the Angelic Realm. But I still felt something was missing. When people attended the Angel workshops they very quickly would adjust their perception to the

Angelic Realms, but on returning home they would find it more and more difficult to maintain the energy shifts. Slowly their vibrations would return to their previous state. After meditating on this problem I was guided by the Angels to make a gemstone essence using the crystals from the 'Angel of Light' energy web. This I did and the results have been not only dramatic, but very positive. Initially I just made an essence, then the Angel essence cream was born and finally the aura spray. Each method of using the original essence brought immediate and positive results. These varied from dramatic spontaneous healings to space clearing of negative energies to easily attainable meditative states. The results were so positive that the name of the gemstone essence was changed to 'Angel of Light (to the rescue)'. The Angel workshops and 'Angel of Light (to the rescue)' essence, cream and aura spray have been featured on television and in the national press, as well as women's magazines. The stones used in this essence are:

Angelite; Azeztulite; Danburite; Morganite; Clear Quartz and Seraphinite.

The second example of the effectiveness of a gemstone essence concerned one of my students. He was on his second year of the two-year professional crystal therapy course. On the crystal course the students make and experiment with a wide variety of gemstone essences. This particular student was very intellectual and very often found his intellect was so powerful it stopped him getting in touch with his feelings. Here we had a classic case of a male/female (yin/yang) imbalance; it is also very common on the earth plane at this time. Early in the crystal course this student decided to balance his male-female polarities to end his dualistic tendencies. He decided to work with the energies of rose quartz. I was aware he was finding it difficult, for as soon as he began to identify with his female polarity his male intellect would sabotage the process and he was finding the situation frustrating. Believe me when I say that there was nothing wrong with the student; in fact he was a very gentle and balanced male when you consider the imbalance that some males display (anger, aggression, war, violence, corruption, machismo, etc). Well, after much frustration and by meditating on his problem, he was guided to make and experiment with a rose quartz gem essence. The result was instant and positive; because the gem essence is taken internally and the effects are felt within the emotional body very quickly, he found he could begin to access his feminine, intuitive nature. This accelerated his emotional and spiritual progress to such an extent that his compassionate nature was fully activated.

To Make a Gem Essence You Will Need:

1. A crystal or gemstone of your choice, physically and metaphysically cleansed and dedicated and, if quartz, programmed.

2. A small bottle of purified water or distilled water (from the chemist). Distilled water is the best as it contains no impurities or energetic signature. This facilitates, when energized by the pranic forces of sunlight, the optimum energetic interaction, which allows the gem essence to fully interact not only with the physical body but all the subtle bodies as well. Water is a universal storage medium of vibrational energy; when activated by the solar energies it allows a therapeutic essence to be made.

3. A clear glass container or gemstone dish. (A quartz crystal bowl is the best, but not essential.) Crystal bowls are usually fabricated. The energy of the crystal bowl will allow the optimum enhancement of the crystal vibration placed within: this is to bring out the purest energy and lessen the transference of unwanted outside vibratory energy to the gem essence being prepared. If you use a colored container you *must* make this part of your gem essence.

4. Brandy or other preservative.

5. Glass dropper bottle (not clear).

6. Three pure quartz crystals with terminations. (These are to be placed around your gem essence

during preparation, to keep out unwanted outside energies.)

7. Glass funnels and labels to put on the bottles.
8. A sacred environment or special area.

Method:

Sterilize the glass or crystal bowl, funnels and bottles. It is essential to understand that preparing a gemstone essence is not just a mechanical process. The whole undertaking should be approached in a calm meditative state. Explain mentally to the crystals exactly what you are doing, be very clear and focused in your intent. Enacting a simple ceremony of attunement to the devic realm is always wise, as is obtaining the crystal's permission to be a co-creator of the gemstone essence. Place your chosen crystal, suitably cleansed, dedicated etc., in a clear glass container.

Surround the container with three clear quartz crystal points in triangulation, pointing inwards, to keep away unwanted outside energies.

Add purified or distilled water from the chemist, enough to cover the crystal if possible (unless the crystal is very large).

If it is a crystal which does not like water or is toxic or poisonous, place it in a glass within another glass container and put the water in the outer one, so that the water does not touch it, but the vibrations can pass through.

Leave your container in a place where it is unlikely to be disturbed by negative energies and away from pets, pests, etc. (not on concrete). Covering it with clean white muslin, net or paper towel is a good idea.

Charge it in sunlight as required.

Dowse, meditate, etc. to find out how long to leave it. Normally three hours is sufficient, but if using the full sun method and the temperature is over 80 degrees, the water will start evaporating, so you will need less exposure time. The normal procedure is to leave it in direct sunlight for several hours during the early morning sun. The solar pranic energies are most potent in the early hours of the day. As with flowers, certain etheric properties from the gems become transferred to the water, which becomes charged with their particular vibration.

N.B. Using any colored container or covering will affect the outcome, so this would have to be appropriate for the remedy and form part of the essence.

The original mixture is used to make the mother bottle.

A stock bottle is then made from the mother bottle.

The dosage bottles are made as required from the stock bottle.

Mother Bottle

Contains one-third of your original mixture and two-thirds brandy or other spirit. You must fill the mother bottle with brandy before placing the water from the bowl into the mother bottle, otherwise the vibration of the gem essence could permeate the brandy bottle where it could enter other storage bottles being prepared then or in the future. This mother bottle will keep for ever if stored correctly.

Stock Bottle

Dowse to find out how many drops of the mother bottle should be placed in the stock bottle. It is wise to add seven drops, whether the size of the stock bottle is several drams or several ounces, because gemstone essences work with the influence of the seven dimensions. If you use less than seven drops to the stock bottle, it will still work, but the effects may not permeate all levels and dimensions. If your gemstone essence is from a very high vibrational crystal you may need to place up to twelve drops to maintain access to the higher chakras above the head and the corresponding dimensions.

Then fill the bottle with one half brandy, one half purified water.

Dosage Bottle

Dowse to find out how many drops of the stock bottle should be placed in the dosage bottle (dark glass, with dropper). This may vary, but as with the stock bottle the number of drops will correspond to the dimensional access. Then fill with one-third brandy, two-thirds purified water (or alternatively all water, in which case the dosage bottle must be kept in the fridge and will only last two weeks).

* Label all bottles with the name of the crystal and state whether mother, stock or dosage bottle.
* Give the date made and, on dosage bottles, the expiry date and the number and frequency of drops required.
* Your name and telephone number should also be added.
* Store with a clear quartz crystal, suitably programmed. The area you store them should be a 'clean space' and it is wise to take special precautions. Before storing the essences, first wash the area with distilled water using an organic cloth, such as linen or cotton. After cleaning the area leave it empty for several days prior to use. You could also store them under a pyramid. If you have a lot of bottles to store you may need four clear quartz crystals, one for each corner of the space. Never leave the bottles in sunlight because extreme heat can damage the gemstone essences; cold temperatures are all right, however. Also remember to keep them away from harmful energies and environmental pollutants. I like to use blue bottles whenever possible, as it is a stabilizing, calming, protective color.
* Do not keep different varieties too close together or, in time, there will be a transference of energy from one to another. This applies especially to quartz.
* Remember - the more you dilute the original mixture, the stronger the vibration.
* You can make color, flower, tree or other energy essences in a similar way.

Using the Gemstone Essences:

Gem Essence

Taking gemstone essences is a very personal process. How often and for how long you take a gem essence will depend on how quickly your body integrates the gemstone essence vibration. This will also depend on the circumstances surrounding the emotions/feeling/dis-ease you are treating. If your mood is merely transitory or you are in a small crisis situation, such as a job interview or driving test, you may require only one dose, but if you have been feeling the same for a longer period, there is no set time limit for how long you can take your chosen essence or essences. If you are using the gemstone essence for treating a long-standing or chronic condition, I have found it is best to review the essence and its actions at least once a fortnight. This is the time when you will decide whether to change the essence for yourself or your client or to continue for another two weeks.

If you are taking a gemstone essence for spiritual development, you may need to review it more often, as they can be integrated very quickly by those who are energy aware (we are talking about minutes and seconds, rather than days). Also, if you are taking the gem essence in a group situation, especially for group meditation or spiritual attunement or alignment, the integration period is very fast, almost instant. This is due to the amplification of the overall group energetic dynamics. If you are taking the gem essence in an Earth 'power' area, such as Stonehenge, Glastonbury, Sedona or the Pyramids in Egypt, the essences will be amplified and the integration period substantially reduced.

Each gem essence will work in its own way, but generally they clear miasms outwards and through the aura, although some discharge downwards into the Earth. Others work through the water element and will discharge the miasm when you are taking a shower or bath. It is fascinating to watch the process. If you cannot see the energy movement yet, you will still be able to feel or 'know' what is happening. They can be taken by anyone of any age; they are safe and effective for pets; even flowers, trees and plants have been known to benefit. As they work in harmony with your body and they are self-adjusting and are 100% natural, they can be used with any conventional or complementary medicines and treatments. These are different methods of taking a gem essence:

1. Place 1 to 7 drops directly under the tongue. For spiritual development you can take up to 12 drops.
2. Dilute 1 to 7 drops in a small glass of mineral water and sip slowly throughout the day until relief is obtained. Up to 7 essences may be taken together if required.
3. Rub a few drops on your palms, then pass your hands through the aura using a sweeping motion.
4. Rub a few drops on your palms, then inhale deeply from your cupped hands.
5. Put a few drops in the bath. For spiritual development you can use up to 12 drops.
6. Put a few drops in your washing, with the washing powder.
7. Add 1 to 7 drops directly to massage oil.
8. Apply to the temples before meditation.
9. Use on the meridian system instead of a crystal. It will be just as effective as placing a crystal or gemstone on the meridian point(s).

Gemstone Essence Body Cream

This is made by placing seven drops of the gemstone essence or essences (you may use up to seven different essences together) into an aqueous cream. (You will need to keep this refrigerated or use a preservative in the cream). Do not ingest this gemstone cream, it is for topical use only. Its effectiveness will be felt in the aura and directly within the body because it is absorbed trans-dermally.

1. Apply to the area of the body that is manifesting a painful vibration or feels sore, tense or congested.
2. Apply to the palms of both hands before giving a therapy session.
3. Apply to the temples before meditation.
4. Apply to the temples before sleep.
5. Apply in a circle around the waist for complete auric integration or protection.

Gemstone Essence Aura Spray

This is made by placing seven drops of the gemstone essence or essences (you may use up to seven different essences together) into a spray bottle filled with purified water. (You will need to keep this refrigerated or use a preservative in the water).

1. Rub a drop or two on the palms of both hands.
2. Rub a drop on the pulse points: wrist, throat, forehead, back of neck, soles of both feet.
3. Rub a few drops on your palms, then pass your hands through the aura using a sweeping motion. (Aura cleansing).
4. Rub a few drops on your palms, then inhale deeply from your cupped hands.
5. Spray directly into the aura, especially any areas that may feel stuck or congested.
6. Spray around your room.
7. Put a few drops in the bath.
8. Put a few drops in your washing, with the washing powder.
9. Add to massage oil.
10. Spray directly on the body.

*Miasm - an energetic state which predisposes an organism to future illness. This can be due to the subtle effects of a particular toxic agent or micro-organism. There are four types - acquired, inherited, karmic, or planetary in nature.

Solarized Water

This is a simple way of drinking sunlight-charged water. You can literally bottle the sun's force by placing a bottle of clear mineral water in the sun for one day. Sip slowly. It is wonderful and natural. It rejuvenates and revitalizes you. The subtle effects of sunlight are critical in charging water: it relates to the prana that is contained in sunlight. The Hindus have known for millennia about the pranic beneficial power of sunlight. So have the Chinese; they call it Chi. Prana or Chi permeates everything; it gives life to every cell in the body and a balanced supply is necessary for maintaining optimum physical health, emotional well-being and mental agility and optimism.

Gemstone or Crystal Solarized Water

You can add gemstones and crystals to solarized water too; this is a wonderful way of using the crystal vibration - by drinking it, allowing the body to gently absorb the crystal energy. The effects may be a little slower than those of the previous methods, though. It is a good way to boost other crystal therapy treatments. Red, orange and yellow (magnetic) gemstones are good 'drinks' in the morning; if you take them later in the day the effects may keep you awake all night. Green (balance) gemstones are perfect at lunch time - but you can 'drink' them at any time. Pink (integration) gemstones are used for attuning to relationship energies at any time of the day or night. Blue, indigo, purple and violet (calming) gemstones are only 'taken' in the afternoon or at night. They are good for meditation or relaxation.

1. Fill a clear glass tumbler, glass jug or bottle with pure spring or filtered water.
2. Place the suitably cleansed, dedicated, programmed etc. crystal or gemstone very carefully into the water.

3. Leave the glass/jug/bottle in a position that allows the sunlight to fall upon it. Even thirty minutes will make a difference to the water. I would suggest seven hours is best. The longer the exposure time, the stronger the effect.

Red, orange or yellow gemstone water must be sipped very slowly. (Yellow gemstone water must not be taken after 6 pm because of its elimination effect). Green, blue, indigo and violet gemstone water can be taken a little faster.

Experiment with your level of sensitivity. Shut your eyes and take a sip of solarized water. Then take a sip of water from the same source without solarization. See if you are able to notice a difference. (If you don't detect a difference, do not worry: you will still get the benefit from solarized water.) Some sensitive people can detect a difference after the water has been instilled with crystals for only five minutes. Try it yourself. Then try it after twenty minutes' exposure and so on up to twelve hours. Some gemstones are easier to detect than others.

Do not solarize gemstone water for longer than twelve hours, otherwise the water becomes too intense.

Preparing for a Crystal Therapy Session

The way you prepare yourself and your client before a crystal therapy session will have an enormous effect on not only the quality of the experience, but also the final outcome. It will also minimise any healing crisis. So to help you get the most from your crystal therapy sessions here is a very comprehensive list of helpful advice.

1. You must keep accurate records of all crystal therapy sessions with clients.

2. Asking your client to drink plenty of fresh pure water, just before and especially just after each crystal therapy session, will ease the removal of energy blocks and toxicity. These are always released with the integration of new energy patterns and information (as you return the body back to the original blueprint of perfection and resonance).

3. You should also drink plenty of fresh water to help your energy field before and after giving a crystal therapy session.

4. Please note, warn anyone who has any 'new device' fitted into their body since birth that they may have problems with it (discomfort). This is due to the original blueprint being reinstated back into the body. Do not worry though, the energy will equal out and healing will still occur. (new device = fillings in teeth, caps on teeth, hip replacements etc).

5. Also, they may need less medication than before. They should tell their GP that they are receiving crystal therapy and that they may need to make the necessary adjustments in managing their medication.

6. It is very important that all crystals are cleansed before and after use. This will guarantee that any residual disharmonies are removed from the energy field of the stones.

7. Always allow yourself and your client plenty of time and space. Never rush a crystal therapy session.

8. Allow your client several minutes of quiet time, before beginning the session. This will allow the possibility of a clearer experience and the increased ability to notice any changes more easily.

9. Your experience will probably differ for each session. Crystals always work in the same way, but your client will always have a different experience. This is due to the different issues, thoughts, feelings, miasms, emotions etc. within each person's energy field.

10. Please make sure you have a clean, safe space to work in. Purify it with incense and have a large amethyst cluster to focus and cleanse the energies.

11. Ask your client to remove contact lenses, glasses, all jewellery, belts, coins from their pockets and any metal objects like keys etc. Also ask them not to wear to the therapy session clothes which have metal buttons or hooks, as metal gives a false energetic field.

12. Be sure to clear all jewellery before wearing it again after the therapy session.

13. Always allow your client plenty of time to come round to everyday activities slowly.

14. Ideally they should have three times the length of time they have been receiving crystal therapy before they need to do anything focused. This will allow their body to integrate the energies it has experienced into its normal everyday functioning.

15. Tell them to allow any feelings of agitation, anxiety, fidgeting, anger, resentment, annoyance, heat, stress, cold, fear or restlessness to dispel before they resume normal activity.

16. The same would apply if you used crystal therapy for self-healing: give yourself plenty of time.

17. I would also strongly suggest using no other therapy at the same time as crystal healing. This applies whether you are working with a client or healing yourself.

18. For self-healing make sure you will not be disturbed during the crystal therapy session or during the rest period afterwards: take the phone off the hook etc.

19. Also, for self-healing sessions, if at any time you feel discomfort whilst in a crystal web, quietly get up and find somewhere to rest and relax until the sensations disappear. Re-enter the crystal web when you are ready, or terminate the session.

20. Please also be aware of the color of the clothes your client is wearing for the crystal therapy session, as it can directly influence the outcome considerably.

21. Also what color clothes do you normally wear to facilitate a therapy session? I would advise white is the best; it represents all the colors of the spectrum and gives the best results.

22. For general grounding and earthing at the end of a crystal therapy session, place 1 smoky quartz point beneath each foot.

23. Unless specified otherwise, all crystal webs should be laid out so that the head is aligned with magnetic north. This places the individual's bioelectromagnetic field in harmony with the flow of the earth's energy field, which will augment any therapy session.

24. Please explore the use of different color cloths to lie on; for some crystal webs certain colors have been suggested.

25. Unless otherwise specified, use white until you gain more experience and confidence with the crystal webs.

26. Establishing rapport and trust by communicating with your client plays an integral part in any therapy session.

27. Start by asking the key question 'Do you want to be healed?' This may seem obvious, but sometimes a person does not really want to let go of a problem and find a cure or resolution.

28. Healing is a very personal process and each person must deal with core issues at their own pace, so be sure you receive an affirmative response.

29. If you receive a negative, fearful or non-committal response in any form, whether verbal, physical or psychic, it is not wise to continue with the therapy session. It would be better to discuss with your client their hesitation. Please do this in a non-judgemental, non-threatening

way. Also it is wise to have completed a counselling course before giving 'advice'. If you have completed a counselling course, you would know not to give advice, all we can do is to facilitate the client in finding a deeper understanding of the cause of their dis-ease.

30. You must take responsibility for your actions and the well-being of your client. Remember, when they are in the crystal web or crystal energy field - you are responsible for maintaining the purity and integrity of the energy field.

31. After receiving a positive affirmation from your client, it is now time to merge with the Divine and make your energetic connection to the source of healing energy you will be working with. Whatever your preference - Crystal Angels, Great Spirit, Goddess, Oneness, Cosmic Consciousness, Angels of Healing, One Heart, Ascended Beings of Light - link yourself with this energy and ask for the highest possible good of all. Ask for help and guidance in all your therapy work.

32. Allow yourself to be completely surrounded by this healing energy and allow yourself to be totally protected and guided with Divine love and wisdom. Please remember that the most important energies to work with are love and compassion. If your heart is not open and loving, you are not coming from the right energy.

33. Do not allow your mind to wander to other things while you are treating your client. Stay focused.

34. If there is no reaction to crystal therapy after several sessions the body could be unreceptive due to external factors such as heavy medication or psychological attitude, blocking the therapeutic process. As long as reactions are positive, there is value in continuing the treatment. (This applies to all healing procedures, not only crystal therapy).

35. Try to develop methods for monitoring/checking quality and depth of the crystal therapy session such as monitoring electrical skin responses (biofeedback), visual observations of physiological change, verbal check with client, touch, pre-arranged distress signal. The client's safety must be monitored at all times.

36. The materials and equipment (therapy couch) you use must be in good working order; you should also have available all the case notes of previous sessions, items for recording the content and aims of sessions (written records or audio records) and items for client comfort, i.e. blankets, tissues.

37. Also be aware of any other factor that may cause discomfort, such as medical conditions which are contra-indications or extraneous noise.

38. Self awareness is essential: the kinds of physical, mental and emotional health issues for the practitioner which can affect therapy, such as coughs, flu, stress, unresolved emotional issues, fatigue or any medical condition which is unresolved.

39. Finally, but most important: you must be able to differentiate between your own internal world and that of your clients.

Working With Crystal Energy Webs

Centering Web:

Crystals required: 5 quartz points (4 clear + 1 milky)
1 natural citrine point or tumbled citrine
1 yellow cloth to lie on

Uses: When a person is not centred, we say that their male and female polarities are out of balance, or their yin/yang balance is not in harmony. Their emotions are all over the place and they probably do not understand why they are reacting 'out of character'. The right side of the body is depicted as the 'male' side (yang), representing strength, courage and stamina: dynamic, powerful, aggressive and dominant qualities. The right hand is traditionally the 'sword' hand, associated with giving a blow, lashing out and defending ourselves. It also represents outer journeys, money, prestige or job issues. To treat a problem on the right side of the body we place a clear quartz point in the right hand, with the termination pointing out, for 20 minutes.

The left side of the body is depicted as the 'female' side (yin), representing inner journeys, intuition, spiritual or psychic issues, gentleness and receiving: feminine, nurturing, creative, receptive, weak, shielding, yielding and stagnant. To treat a problem on the left side of the body we place a milky quartz point in the left hand, with the termination pointing towards the body, for 20 minutes. Really we should always combine the two techniques, otherwise we are not treating holistically.

So to combine:

1 citrine placed on the solar plexus chakra.

1 milky quartz in the left hand, pointing in.

1 clear quartz in the right hand, pointing out.

3 matching clear quartz points in a triangulation round the body, two pointing in at the feet and one pointing out at the top of the head.

Allow 20 minutes for integration of the energies. On no account must you leave your client unattended. Be ready to remove the crystals sooner, if your client has integrated the crystal energy very quickly.

Outcome: Balance and harmony is restored to the body so that neither male nor female polarity is dominant and the person feels centred, focused and at peace with themselves, the world, everyone and everything.

Relaxation Web:

Crystals: 6 amethyst points or tumbled stone
1 sugilite tumbled
1 rose quartz tumbled
1 pale blue cloth to lie on

Uses: If a person has too much unbalanced energy in their head, they are unable to relax and let go. They focus too much on their problems and become confused, baffled, dazed, flustered, muddled and perplexed. They may become over-emotional and eventually unable to cope with reality. Sometimes they will find change or any break in their routine as threatening. This fear of change may hold them back, because they would have to take responsibility for their lives. With this imbalance it has been found that, even when therapy sessions are helping, they may continue to sabotage themselves. In view of this we include a stone to help balance the emotions: this includes heartache, grief, fear, heartbreak, loss, rejection, abandonment.

1 rose quartz placed on the heart chakra.

1 sugilite placed on the third eye area.

6 amethysts in a Star of David configuration (2 level with the knees, 1 at the soul star chakra about six inches above the crown chakra, 1 at the earth star chakra beneath the feet, 2 level with the head). If points used, pointing away from the body.

Allow 20 minutes for integration of the energies. On no account must you leave your client unattended. Be ready to remove the crystals sooner, if your client has integrated the crystal energy very quickly.

Outcome: Promotes deep relaxation, brings the head and heart into harmony and balance. It allows for promotion of feelings of emotional well-being and calm confidence with a renewed sense of optimism.

Visualisation Web:

Crystals: 2 clear calcite
1 blue or purple fluorite
1 lapis lazuli
3 medium-size clear quartz points

1 sky blue cloth to lie on (this represents the blue sky, which is a symbol for shunyata, which means 'emptiness' or 'voidness', one of the most important terms in the whole of Buddhism).

Uses: When a person has problems with their physical eyes they may be refusing to see something they do not like or may not want to be seen. Sinus pain can be due to unexpressed emotions, a build-up of tears waiting to be shed. People who have problems visualising or who are trying to develop their third eye (inner vision) will also be helped by this layout.

1 clear calcite on each eye.

1 fluorite on the third eye chakra.

1 lapis lazuli placed on the throat chakra.

3 clear quartz points in triangulation round the body, two pointing in at the feet and also one pointing in at the head.

Allow 20 minutes for integration of the energies. On no account must you leave your client unattended. Be ready to remove the crystals sooner, if your client has integrated the crystal energy very quickly.

Outcome: Probably several sessions will be required. Where a person has problems visualising, there will be gradual clearing of the third eye, allowing fears to dissipate and any feelings of heat or tightness to disappear. Eventually it will become easier to see colors, images etc. If a person has experienced physical problems relating to the eyes there could be an emotional release, leading to greater clarity of vision and a reduction in pain.

Earthing Web:

Crystals: 2 garnets, tumbled, faceted or natural
1 ruby, tumbled, faceted or natural
4 black tourmaline wands

Uses: This is for when your client feels disconnected from the earth, or if they have been travelling over a long distance and need to rebalance their energy field and clear it of unwanted outside energies and influences. It is also for anyone who has survival or fear issues: it will help them to take positive action in their life.

1 ruby placed on the base chakra (for Kundalini activation).

1 garnet at the top of each leg (where the limb joins the trunk).

1 black tourmaline beneath the feet in the earth star chakra, 1 black tourmaline above the head in the soul star chakra and the remaining two tourmalines placed at elbow level, so that the tourmalines form a cross.

Allow 20 minutes for integration of the energies. On no account must you leave your client unattended. Be ready to remove the crystals sooner, if your client has integrated the crystal energy very quickly.

Outcome: The person will feel more in touch with reality, more connected to the earth and more positive in outlook and over time will develop a greater sense of purpose. They may eventually become aware at a deeper level of their soul's reason for incarnating in this lifetime.

Restoring to Everyday Consciousness Web:

Crystals:
2 boji or shaman stones
3 smoky quartz, points or tumbled
1 citrine, point or tumbled

Uses: People whose energy is all in the head and who resort to escapism because they do not want to be grounded can be helped by regular use of this layout. It will benefit anyone who is feeling ungrounded or 'spaced out' after meditation and will restore a person to everyday consciousness following a healing session. Any problems with the feet suggest that the person will not stand their ground, is afraid to stand up for themselves against others or simply 'cannot stand it' any more; they may even feel suicidal.

1 boji or shaman stone at the base of each foot.

3 smoky quartz points arranged in a triangle beneath the feet, pointing downwards.

1 citrine, point or tumbled, placed on the solar plexus chakra. If point used, pointing upwards.

Allow 20 minutes for integration of the energies. On no account must you leave your client unattended. Be ready to remove the crystals sooner, if your client has integrated the crystal energy very quickly.

Outcome: Following healing or meditation, the person is helped to become fully conscious and in the present, aware of their everyday circumstances and totally in touch with reality. Over time, they may become more accepting of their current situation and more able to take control of themselves and speak their own truth - in fact, to stand up for themselves and what they believe in. Escapism will no longer seem the only way out; they can use their feet to walk away and start a new healthier life.

Healing Heart Web:

Crystals:
4 rose quartz small tumbled stones
1 morganite or rhodochrosite, natural or tumbled
1 aquamarine, natural or tumbled
1 sugilite or amethyst tumbled
12 clear quartz single terminated crystals
1 sky blue cloth to lie on (this represents the blue sky, which is a symbol for shunyata, which means 'emptiness' or 'voidness', one of the most important terms in the whole of Buddhism).

Uses: Excellent for emotional balancing in relationships, friendship and higher love. Helpful for spiritual awakening, compassion, self-acceptance, forgiveness, adapting to changes, tapping into the inner voice, restoring faith. Raises low self-esteem, assists in healing old emotional wounds and enhances creativity.

4 rose quartz placed in a cross on the heart chakra.

1 morganite or rhodochrosite placed in the centre of the Rose quartz cross on the heart chakra.

1 aquamarine placed on the throat chakra.

1 sugilite or amethyst placed on the third eye chakra.

12 clear quartz single terminated crystals, one by the head, one by the feet and five evenly spaced on each side of the body. (If you don't have 12 quartz crystals, place a triangulation of quartz around the body).

Join up the quartz crystals by passing your control crystal around the patient three times clockwise, taking care not to allow it to cut across the patient's body.

Allow 20 minutes for integration of the energies. On no account must you leave your client unattended. Be ready to remove the crystals sooner, if your client has integrated the crystal energy very quickly.

Outcome: Emotional imbalances and stored anger towards the self and others are released. Old energy patterns of grief, pain, sorrow, fear, heartbreak, loss, rejection and abandonment are released, allowing loving energy to flow, whereby you can give and receive love. Awareness of tolerance and gratitude is increased.

Quartz Crystal Web (Triangulation):

Quartz crystal triangulations are very effective healing energy grids.

Place three quartz crystals around the patient, who can be either lying or sitting. If this is used for healing, the one above the head - or, if sitting, behind the back - should point away from the patient.

The other two quartz crystals should be placed in such a position as to form a triangulation, pointing in towards the patient.

Pass your control crystal around the patient three times to join up the quartz crystals.

Allow 20 minutes for integration of the energies. On no account must you leave your client unattended. Be ready to remove the crystals sooner, if your client has integrated the crystal energy very quickly.

Quartz Crystal Web for Meditation (Triangulation):

The same quartz triangulation may be used for meditation, the difference being that the quartz crystal above the head (if in supine position) or behind the back (if in the Yoga position) should point towards the body.

Proceed as before. If used on yourself, do not stay in this longer than 20 minutes, until you are

more experienced with the crystal vibrations.

For a client, allow 20 minutes for integration of the energies.

On no account must you leave your client unattended. Be ready to remove the crystals sooner, if your client has integrated the crystal energy very quickly.

Various quartz crystal configurations, or quartz triangulations, create certain energy patterns which will help the body to re-balance its vibrations and heal itself.

Twelve Crystal Web (Configuration):

1. The most common system is to have the patient lying in a supine position, encircled by twelve clear quartz crystals: one by the head, one by the feet, five evenly spaced on each side of the body.

2. Take a thirteenth, or your control crystal, in your hand and by passing it over the twelve crystals surrounding the patient's body you will create a unified vibrational healing field of energy around the patient.
3. Have the patient lie in this position, allowing 20 minutes for integration of the energies.
4. On no account must you leave your client unattended. Be ready to remove the crystals sooner, if your client has integrated the crystal energy very quickly.
5. This type of crystal formation is used for full body, full energy system healing.

Merkaba Web (Star of David):

Another energy system is to have the patient sit on the floor in a Yoga fashion, holding a quartz crystal in the palm of each hand with the points facing in or out depending on the energy flow of the patient. (If the person is right-handed, the left hand should have the point facing towards the body and the right hand would hold a quartz crystal with the point facing away from the body. If the person was left-handed the reverse would be true. If the patient was ambidextrous you would have to check on the energy flow most suitable for them.)

Place six quartz crystals around them in the formation of a six-pointed star, with one point directly behind them and one point directly in front of them. Merkaba, the star of David, is also known as the seal of Solomon or the symbol for your holy Guardian Angel within your heart chakra. It also equates with yin/yang, agni/soma and the infinity symbol.

This type of healing is specifically used to enhance spiritual vibrations and awareness. Use your control crystal by standing over them and passing your control crystal in a circular motion (clockwise), connecting the six quartz crystals surrounding the client.

Do this twelve times, then allow them to rest in this position.

Allow 20 minutes for integration of the energies.

On no account must you leave your client unattended. Be ready to remove the crystals sooner, if your client has integrated the crystal energy very quickly.

You could also experiment with a rose quartz triangulation or amethyst triangulation: each would give a different experience and outcome.

Re-Polarising the Organs

If you need to re-polarise the organs lying within the physical body, to eliminate disease or to correct any imbalances in the magnetic field around every organ of the body, the following quartz crystal configuration should be used. Have the patient lie in a supine position. Place quartz crystals over the third eye, in both hands, at the navel and over each foot. Corresponding quartz crystals should be placed underneath the therapy table. All terminations should point towards the top of the head (crown chakra).

The control crystal is then passed around the patient's body three times.

The patient lies within this magnetic field.

Allow 20 minutes for integration of the energies. On no account must you leave your client unattended. Be ready to remove the crystals sooner, if your client has integrated the crystal energy very quickly.

Healing Circle

Another energy system is group work. Many successful crystal healing treatments take place within the healing circle.

1. Have a regular time, place and practice.
2. Try to have a special room for group healing work.
3. Keep it free from other vibrations and influences.
4. Purify it with incense and have a large amethyst cluster to focus and cleanse the energies.
5. Allow each group member to sit in the area of the circle in which they feel most comfortable.
6. Each group member must sit in a comfortable position with the head erect and the spine straight; what is needed is an upright but relaxed spine. This means that the base of the spine needs to be higher than the knees, so tilting the pelvis forwards to a position where the spine naturally remains upright when relaxed. The easiest way of doing this is to put a small, firm cushion beneath the base of the spine.
7. Sit cross-legged; this forms a triangular path for the energy field and stops it dissipating in all directions. (Sitting on an upright chair is also acceptable, but please make sure your feet are firmly placed on the floor and, in this case, not crossed).
8. Have the 'patient' sit in the centre of the circle.
9. Each group member should be in the moment, forgetting the past, present and future.
10. The members of the healing circle should place their quartz crystals on the floor in front of them, with the termination pointing towards the 'patient'.
11. The group should then begin to consciously regulate their breath; begin with five minutes of deep breathing.
12. Each person should then allow themselves to be completely surrounded by healing energy and allow themselves to be totally protected and guided with Divine love and wisdom. Please remember that the most important energies to work with are love and compassion. If your heart is not open and loving, you are not coming from the right energy.
13. Each member will then send their healing energies to the quartz crystals, which must first be programmed for the energies to be passed to the patient.
14. Allow up to 20 minutes for the process to fully develop. You can finish sooner if you wish.

It is best to elect a group leader, who can take overall responsibility for the group work; this position could be taken in turn by all the group members. Absent or Earth healing can also be sent using this group method.

Medicine Wheel - Healing Mandala

This healing mandala has been successfully used many, many times, as have all the crystal webs in this section. It is wonderful for self healing, or finding the root cause of a disease or problem. I will give the instructions for a self-healing session, but you could follow the same procedure for a client.

1. For this web you will need to gather all your healing crystals and gemstones together, making sure they are all cleansed.

2. The most effective times are dawn and dusk. Purify your room with incense and have a large amethyst cluster to focus and cleanse the energies.

3. First choose a crystal or gemstone that you feel represents you. You will hold this crystal in your left hand.

4. Sit in the middle of a cloth on the floor. Try to be in a comfortable position with the head erect and the spine straight; what is needed is an upright but relaxed spine. This means that the base of the spine needs to be higher than the knees, so tilting the pelvis forwards to a position where the spine naturally remains upright when relaxed. The easiest way of doing this is to put a small, firm cushion beneath the base of the spine.

5. Choose the color of the cloth by intuition or have a purpose-made cloth (I have a cloth that I hand-painted a 'Medicine Wheel' on).

6. Sit cross-legged; this forms a triangular path for the energy field and stops it dissipating in all directions.

7. Be in the moment, forgetting the past, present and future.

8. Now begin to place your crystals and gemstones around you. Allow yourself to be totally guided by your intuition. If you feel like lying down and placing the stones upon your body, please do so, there are no rules for this session.

9. Begin to consciously regulate your breathing; begin with five minutes of deep breathing.

10. Allow yourself to be completely surrounded by the crystal healing energy; feel yourself being totally protected as the crystal devas bestow guidance, love, and wisdom.

11. Allow up to 20 minutes for the process to fully develop. Be ready to remove the crystals sooner, if you have integrated the crystal energy very quickly.

12. Try to remove the crystals in reverse order of placement. Make sure you are fully grounded, centred and balanced. Cleanse all your crystals and gemstones (using your chosen method).

Healing Wands - An Ancient Art for Modern Times

Over the last 20 years 'Healing Wands' have become very fashionable again. They come in every form, material, substance, size, shape and color, from the most intricate exquisite designer silver and gold wands encrusted with expensive precious gemstones to wooden hand-carved totem wands, from gentle seashell wands to huge power rods, or they can even be carved from quartz or other crystals. They are used in healing ceremonies, or for prayer, meditation and ritual. Ritual is any action, undertaken with intention and belief, that grows powerful through repetition and connection. Personal ritual evolves by paying attention to one's feelings, visions and dreams, as one makes or attempts to make sacred or healing actions. The right actions feel good. A sense of well-being and deep connection, of magic, flows into one's soul.

If you decide to make a 'healing wand' it should be made in a sacred way, with your intention made known to the crystals. Please allow yourself to follow the crystal's instructions. This act alone will weave you into the web of life and the universe. It will connect you to the crystal kingdom and to the ancient ones and to all the people and beings who have lived in a sacred way using crystals. You will find the act of fashioning a crystal wand in a sacred way is a powerful experience and very empowering and healing for your soul. There is no exact recipe for making your healing wand, but with patience and commitment you will find your way.

Many people who choose to use a healing wand purchase theirs from a crystal or New Age shop; this is fine. Very often, after you have made your initial purchase, you will be inspired to create your 'own' wand. When you have made or purchased your wand, place it on an altar or other special place. Invite the spirit of the crystals to join you and guide you in your sacred work. Whether you speak to them silently through your heart, or aloud, is up to you. Do whatever makes the process seem the most real. Use respect, kindness and affection when addressing the spirit of the crystals. Consider having the intention to form a long-lasting friendship and partnership. Your intention will be known. If you only wish to use the crystals, rather than becoming their partners, the crystals probably will stay 'dead' or their energy may withdraw. Part of the spiritual work of the crystal devas is to work with the human spirits. If our intention is to become partners, much more of their 'magic' manifests in our lives. If you want to purchase a 'healing wand' that has been fashioned in a sacred way, ask " who made this wand and how was it done". Ask as many questions about the maker as you can. Eventually you will find a wand that feels good to your heart. If you want to learn to make your own, please follow the recipe below, which has been used by hundreds of my crystal students.

1. The wand should be made from thin copper tube (about 7" long), which has a clear quartz crystal secured at one end and a copper blank at the other end, or quartz crystals secured at each end.

2. Herbs, crystals, symbols, colored ribbons and oils may be placed inside the copper tube before securing the crystals.

3. The wand is then wrapped in leather, or some other natural material, in a DNA spiral.

4. It may be decorated with beads, metallic threads, fur or feathers.

5. You must meditate and pray whilst making the wand, ensuring total empowerment.

6. Clear and programme your wand before use.

   You should hold your wand over your heart chakra and visualise/feel a brilliant sparkling rainbow iridescent white light entering your crown chakra, filling your whole body and aura and opening your heart chakra. Send this light through your wand with the clear intent of removing any negative energies.

   Fill the wand completely with brilliant white light. (Clear white light contains the full spectrum of energies and is the most powerful universal healing energy.)

   Now bring your wand up to your third eye and place your programme into the wand, with the unlimited power of your mind and focused intent. A suitable programme would be "I dedicate this wand to the light and to the highest good of all, for healing on all levels and in all situations. I call on my guides and Angels to be with me in all my work. So be it."

7. Take care of your wand; keep it wrapped in a special cloth, or pouch. Never drop it or leave it lying around. Keep it safe at all times.

Using the Wand for Healing

1. When you are ready to use the wand for healing:

2. Ground, centre and balance yourself, open yourself to your positive healing energies; check that these energies are flowing smoothly and easily through your body and that the earth energies are flowing into your feet and legs. Make sure your chakras are flowing with life force and your meridian system is full of positive energy. Make sure you have a positive loving mental attitude.

3. When you feel you are fully ready, say a prayer of connection to your guides and Angels and ask and allow the healing energy to flow through you. Allow the energy to connect totally with your healing wand. Feel your wand becoming a rod of invincible pristine light.

4. In some healing work it is appropriate to first remove distressed energy (blockages, pain, illness etc). Begin by using your wand in your left hand*, pointing the wand at the area you are working on, and moving the wand in a anti-clockwise circle (un-winding). See the distressed energy being pulled into the wand, just like a vacuum cleaner. Carry on until you feel you have removed as much distressed energy as possible. Feel it contained within the structure of the wand

5. When you feel you have totally removed everything necessary, point the wand towards the Earth and, with a sharp flick of the wrist, send the removed energy into the Earth. (You must ask the Earth if she will accept the distressed energy before you do this). Ask the Earth to transmute the energy into positive energy.

6. Now fill your wand with positive energy. Feel it flowing into your wand. Hold your wand in your right hand, see the energy flowing out of your wand and streaming out of the quartz crystal point. When you are ready, point your wand at the area you have been working on and, moving it in a clockwise circle, go over the area. See a laser beam of light begin to fill the area. Working with your guides and Angels, allow the energy to fill the area.

7. Remember you are only an instrument of the Divine. Do not allow yourself to become attached to the outcome, have no expectations. Only God/Goddess can heal, with the help of the person being 'healed'. Dedicate your 'work' to love and the highest good of all beings.

8. When you have finished, close, seal and protect all work done with Divine love.

9. Seal your 'patient' in light. Ground, stabilise and centre them. Allow them time to fully integrate the 'healing' session.

10. If the healing 'session' lasted 10 minutes, allow 20 minutes of integration (always allow at least double the time for integration).

11. Close, seal, protect, ground and stabilise yourself; bring yourself back to everyday waking consciousness.

    You may use your wand to send healing to the Earth, to groups of people, or to a situation. Do not limit yourself in any way in the use of your wand. Use your intuition, use your inner vision, create your own healing rituals. Your wand is a very powerful tool, to be used with integrity and love. Never abuse the energy you have been gifted to work with.

*if you are left-handed please reverse *all* the hand instructions.

Absent Healing With Crystals

Method One:

For this you will need a clear quartz crystal with single termination. If you can find a self-healed crystal, so much the better. First choose, cleanse, dedicate, energise and programme the crystal for absent healing. You will get better results if you keep your absent healing crystal just for this use.

* Have a regular time, place and practice.

* The most effective times are dawn and dusk.

* Try to have a special room for healing work and keep it free from other vibrations and influences. Purify it with incense and have a large amethyst cluster to focus and cleanse the energies.

* Sit in a comfortable position with the head erect and the spine straight; what is needed is an upright but relaxed spine. This means that the base of the spine needs to be higher than the knees, so tilting the pelvis forwards to a position where the spine naturally remains upright when relaxed. The easiest way of doing this is to put a small, firm cushion beneath the base of the spine. Sit cross-legged; this forms a triangular path for the energy field and stops it dissipating in all directions.

* Sit quietly meditating and begin to focus your mind on the person to whom you are sending the absent healing. (A picture, a piece of their hair, or maybe just their name on a piece of paper will help you focus on them if you have never met them).

* Hold your clear quartz crystal in your right hand, point facing away from you. Now begin to visualise a beautiful beam of the purest white light emanating from the tip of your crystal.

* Continue focusing on the person to whom you are sending the absent healing and you will feel a definite contact being made with the person (this may take a few minutes to happen, but it will happen if they really want you to send them healing). If nothing happens, did you ask their permission? Allow the beam of light from the crystal to make a very strong contact with the person.

* Now you have made the contact, just allow the healing to flow. This usually takes between 20 and 30 minutes. Hold your concentration on the person; the more you focus on them, the stronger the healing energy will be. Be aware of any insights into the reason for the dis-ease. You may also send the person positive loving thoughts, such as "You are perfectly healed, with Divine love and wisdom" or "You are a beautiful being of light, take all you need from this absent crystal healing treatment for your perfect mind, your perfect body, your perfect health".

* When you have finished sending the healing, retract the white light into the crystal.

* Acknowledge that the healing session is over and give thanks for all the help you have received from the crystal and the angels. Close, seal and protect the whole session with Divine love and wisdom. Ask for the healing to be protected.

* Restore yourself to everyday waking consciousness, ground and centre yourself.

* Now cleanse your crystal and keep it in a safe place ready for the next time you need it for absent healing. Always send the healing without any attachments to the outcome. Always ask for permission to send healing.

There are numerous other absent healing methods:

Method Two:

Prepare for a full crystal healing session, just as if the person was in the healing room with you and continue to give a full crystal healing session. You will be amazed at what happens. Always send the healing without any attachments to the outcome.

Method Three:

Use a photograph of the person and place it into a crystal web (triangulation) or configuration and leave it in place for as long as they need it. Always send the healing without any attachments to the outcome.

Method Four:

Write the person's name on a piece of paper and place your absent healing crystal on top of it. This works best with a pyramid or standing point. The point upwards will channel the healing energy to them. Once again, leave it in place for as long as they need it.

Dreams and Crystals for Healing

Method One:

1. For this you will need a clear quartz crystal, as clear as possible, one that you feel is very powerful and containing a lot of yang, or male energy. (Herkimer diamonds are very popular as dream crystals).

2. Cleanse, dedicate and then programme your crystal for dream work. This will transform your sleep into a vast pool of healing for you each night.

3. Now, as you lie in bed, tune in to your crystal. Use the resonance technique, which is connected breathing, with rhythmical, connected, fine breaths which are long, slow and deep, allowing us to connect to, and experience, the vibrational aspect of the energy that drives the breath. This energy is our Divine essence. When using this technique you will reach a point where you feel as though you are 'being breathed'.

4. Hold your clear quartz single terminated crystal in your right hand with the termination pointing away from you.

5. Take a long deep breath in and breathe out very slowly as though a candle flame is in front of you and your breath must be so gentle as not to blow it out.

6. Begin to breathe in a connected way, where each inhale flows naturally into each exhale with no pause. The Buddhists call this 'chasing the breath'. The re-birthers call it rhythmical breathing.

7. Breathe finely and slowly, through the nostrils, until you feel the resonance or oscillation.

8. Slowly bring your right hand and crystal to the witness area at the thymus - this area is where your physical and etheric bodies meet - and continue to breathe slowly and calmly.

9. Allow the crystal consciousness to merge with your energy field. You will feel a definite contact being made with your crystal. Ask your crystal to give you healing dreams, or insights into any problems you may have, using the dream state. (This is a very powerful process; it allows you to tune into the deep subconscious, where many of our answers lie hidden).

10. You may also ask to be taken to meet your Angels or Crystal Guides, perhaps go to other dimensions or past lives. Anything is possible, do not limit yourself. Remember, your intention is the most important object.

11. Now place your crystal point towards you under your pillow and go to sleep.

12. Keep a journal by your bedside and write down your dreams as soon as you wake in the morning.

13. Always use this process without any attachments to the outcome and do not be at all judgemental. If you can, resist looking in dream interpretation books; remember, you are unique, so are your dreams.

Method Two:

You may also sleep inside energy webs or configurations to re-balance and enhance your energy systems whilst you sleep.

Method Three:

If you want to, you could place the web under your bed.

Method Four:

Sometimes we are given symbols in dreams or meditation or even through initiation (Reiki). Make the shape of the symbol under your bed using crystals or draw the symbol on a piece of paper and place a crystal on top of it. This will give you insights into the symbols and why they have a deep significance for you.

Method Five:

Put under your bed a picture of a place that seems to draw your attention, place your crystal on top of the picture and ask for insights into the significance that the picture holds for you.

Method Six: Color Healing

As above, but using the appropriate healing colored gemstones:

1. Rose quartz for a soft pink healing loving energy.
2. Citrine for a golden energising experience.
3. Amethyst to soothe and calm with its beautiful violet ray.
4. Orange calcite to cleanse and energise, bringing vitality with its orange glow.
5. Lapis to allow the blue ray of peace and calm to give you your space back after a hectic day.
6. Snow quartz to bring calm to the troubled mind.
7. Turquoise to enhance your verbalisation. (Heartfelt communication).
8. Garnet to ground and give strength, courage, stamina, vitality, endurance.

Room Balancing and Cleansing

Method One: Balancing

To balance a room using crystals you will need four small to medium-size clear quartz single terminated crystals.

First choose, cleanse, dedicate and programme your four quartz crystals. (The programme you should place into your crystals is for room balancing).

Next take your four quartz crystals and place one in each corner of the room pointing towards the centre of the room. This will balance the energies of the room on an on-going basis and it is useful for rooms or areas that need a permanent balanced energy. Remember to cleanse your crystals on a regular basis, as you feel necessary.

Method Two: Balancing

The other way to balance a room using crystals is to place a large quartz cluster in the room and suitably programme it for room balancing. (The placement of your quartz cluster depends on the energy flow of your room. I would recommend dowsing to find the optimum position for the most beneficial, harmonious effect). Remember to regularly cleanse your quartz cluster.

Method Three: Cleansing

1. Open a window, which allows a place for any negative energies to leave by, or have an alternative means of disposing of the negative vibration, such as a violet flame visualisation or a large amethyst cluster.
2. Sit in the room to be balanced or, if cleansing the whole house, start in an upstairs room and work in a methodical manner through the whole house.
3. Hold your control crystal in your right hand and begin by visualising yourself surrounded by protection. (If you are cleansing someone else's house, it would be wise to 'put your protection' around you before you enter). Focus, centre and ground yourself.
4. Take several deep connected breaths and begin to bring the healing, balancing energies of light (brilliant iridescent clear white light is best) down through your crown chakra and down through your body until you feel the energies flowing strongly throughout your entire body.
5. Check to make sure the energies are flowing freely and strongly. You then send these energies of healing, balance and harmony out of the point of your control crystal, slowly filling the entire room. You can use a sweeping motion, or direct the energies at any areas that feel more 'stuck'.
6. This may take several minutes, or happen in seconds, or take an hour, depending on the negativity and disharmony of the room being cleansed.
7. You are now filling the entire room with healing, balancing light. Continue for as long as required. (Your own inner guidance will tell you when it is complete).
8. When you have finished, close, seal and protect the work you have done with Divine love and wisdom. Also give thanks for all the help you have received.
9. Now make sure you are once more focused, centred, grounded and protected.
10. Do not move until you feel grounded, even if this takes several minutes.

Crystal Massage

Very simply, this is how massage works; touch is both healing and comforting. We can all enjoy the experience of massage - both giving and receiving.

Massage is beneficial to us in several ways:

* it improves blood circulation
* it calms the nervous system
* it stimulates skin function
* it improves muscle tone
* it eases aches and pains in muscles and joints
* it feels wonderful

Massage is a gentle healing art suitable for everyone, from babies to the elderly. However, there are certain times or conditions when it should be avoided (for example when the person has just eaten a heavy meal). Often, this just means leaving out a body area, but use your commonsense and if unsure leave well alone.

Do not massage:

* Any infected area.
* A person who is feverish or has a raised temperature.
* Over an area where varicose veins are present.
* Bruised or broken skin.
* Over any swelling or inflammation.

For those crystal therapists who already have a massage qualification, it is very easy for you to incorporate crystals into your massage practice. If you do not have any experience, here are some simple guidelines.

* In basic terms, massage is a way of stroking the body, with variations in the length and depth of strokes. However, you should always direct firm strokes towards the heart. Long flowing massage strokes with little pressure on the body are the most relaxing and soothing. This type of movement is called effleurage. It is done with the whole hand, using gentle even pressure, and is often used to start and finish a massage.

* Use a massage wand or large tumbled stone. Work very gently using small circular movements over a painful area of the body, anticlockwise (unwinding) first to remove pain, then clockwise to put the crystal healing energy in. If the area is very painful you must work just off the body in the aura; this is known as aura massage.

* Try using two different stones, a smoky quartz, amethyst or obsidian for taking pain out (unwinding) and a clear quartz, citrine or rose quartz for putting healing energy in.

* Try working only in the aura, using massage techniques.

If you are not qualified in massage, I would not recommend anything more than this.

I would also not recommend using crystals for massage to anyone who is not a fully trained crystal therapist. Crystals are very powerful and need treating with respect. They know your intent; they will wonder, if you respect massage enough to gain a qualification, why have you not shown the same respect for the Crystal Kingdom?

Crystal Reflexology

It is not necessary to have any experience of reflexology to use the following crystal 'reflexology' technique, as we do not actually practise *conventional* reflexology. It would be advisable, however, to have a thorough knowledge of crystal therapy. This method of crystal 'reflexology' relies solely on the ancient Chinese Meridian theory (see part three of this book on the meridians). Crystal 'reflexology', by stimulating the feet and hands, encourages positive changes throughout the body, by stimulating the body's own healing potential. The fact that major acupuncture meridians pass through the feet and hands makes even more valid the stimulation of the feet and hands for a therapeutic effect. So the efficiency of crystal 'reflexology' is believed to be the result of stimulating and revitalizing this energy flow. There is no doubt that by combining '*reflexology*' and crystal therapy we dramatically increase the healing potential of the body.

Preparation

For treating a patient with the crystal reflexology system you will need a clear quartz single terminated crystal. (I have been teaching this technique since 1989 and I have found that a reflexology crystal must have a rounded end; to this effect I have had special reflexology crystals cut and polished).

Choose this crystal with great care and do not use this reflexology crystal for any other purpose.

1. First cleanse, dedicate and programme your clear quartz single terminated crystal for crystal reflexology use only.
2. Prepare yourself as you would before giving any crystal healing. Begin by centering, grounding and protecting yourself with white light. Make sure your own energy field feels safe, strong and vibrant.
3. Then check to make sure your own energies are flowing freely through your hands.
4. Sit in a comfortable position with the head erect and the spine straight; what is needed is an upright but relaxed spine.
5. The most important aspect of this specific treatment procedure is that both feet are worked through from top to toe; the same with the hands. In this way all body parts, organs and meridians are worked in turn and woven into the crystal web of healing.

Holding the Foot

It is important to support the foot correctly or the crystal reflexology technique will never be mastered. The hands perform complementary functions throughout the crystal treatment. While one hand uses the crystal, the other braces and supports. The hand holding the crystal is referred to as the working hand, the other hand the supporting hand. Take the foot in the support hand, either from the inside or outside. Always keep the foot bent slightly towards you - never in a tight grip with the toes bent backwards.

Crystal Techniques

Begin the treatment on the sole of the left foot. You may apply crystal aura spray at this point. (Please make your own crystal spray: amethyst would work the best at the beginning of a treatment). Work over the whole of the sole from the heel to the tips of each toe. Work in a gentle rhythmic manner and remember never to apply pressure; we are relying solely on the crystal energy to do the work for us. We never dig the crystal into the foot, only gently touching the foot with the tip of the crystal. This allows a web of light to be woven around the whole of the foot. We also never apply any kind of pressure or use our fingers or thumbs to apply pressure; we only work very gently with the crystal. (Those of you who may be conventionally trained in reflexology may have difficulties in stopping yourselves giving a standard reflexology treatment, but please try this with your clients; we have used this technique on people for whom a conventional reflexology treatment would be too painful and the results were amazing). As we proceed the crystal energies will gently work through the meridians of the feet, releasing any blocked energies along the meridian lines, allowing the body to heal and rebalance.

Then proceed to the top of the foot, working in the same manner, taking care not to touch the anklebone, or apply too much pressure over the bony areas of the feet, or damage the tender areas around the toenails. When you have completed the whole of the foot, gently massage the foot with your hands. You may apply crystal aura spray at this point. (Please make your own crystal spray: citrine would work the best at the end of a treatment). To finish the treatment, take your control crystal and go around the foot in the aura (clockwise) seven times to seal and protect the healing.

Proceed with the other foot in the same manner.

When both feet have been treated, take your control crystal and go around both feet in the aura (clockwise) seven times, to seal and protect the healing energies. (This is very important).

As always, make sure your patient is grounded and in full conscious control before you end the treatment. Also make sure that you feel centred and grounded after the treatment session.

You may use the same technique on the hands.

Length of a Crystal Reflexology Treatment

The length of the treatment and the number of sessions will vary according to the person and the condition. As with all vibrational therapy, each person reacts differently. Please also recognise that everyone heals at their own pace. Some people choose to take the crystal energy and integrate it very quickly, others may take longer. We are all unique and each disease is unique, so allow the healing to be natural.

The first treatment session should take approximately one hour. This is the investigative and exploratory stage which enables you to establish as much as possible about the person. Following treatments would last approximately forty to fifty minutes. If the session is too short, insufficient stimulus is provided by the crystal web that you have woven around each hand and foot. This web will not be strong enough for the body to be mobilized fully, activating its own healing powers; if it is too long, there is a danger of over activation, which can cause excessive stimulation and therefore fast elimination, producing an unnecessary severe healing crisis. A course of treatments is recommended for all conditions - even if one session appears to have corrected the problem - to balance the body totally and prevent a recurrence of the disorder.

Color Reflexology

We can begin to introduce color into our reflexology treatments in several distinct different ways.

Method One

Use a colored gemstone in place of the clear quartz. An obvious stone to choose would be amethyst, which is a transformational healer, bringing spiritual growth and understanding. It purifies on all levels and it works as an amplifier of healing and spiritual energies. When consciously directed it will break down and transform blocked or stuck energies. A powerful positive meditation stone, amethyst is a master healer. It treats hearing disorders, the skeletal system, nervous system, digestive tract, stomach, heart, skin and teeth, insomnia, mental disorders and headaches.

Method Two

You could visualize the appropriate colored light coming out of your clear quartz crystal. Clear quartz already contains the full spectrum of white light and when used correctly it will adjust itself automatically to the correct frequency (color) that is needed by the human body. Bearing this in mind it would seem unnecessary to interfere with the normal process.

Method Three

Whilst I was in the United States of America I saw a 'reflexology wand'. This was a copper tube, which contained two batteries. At one end of the copper tube was a clear quartz crystal and underneath the crystal was a small light bulb. Colored gels were then inserted beneath the clear quartz crystal. This meant that you could just choose one color to come out of the crystal. For example, white light contains all the colors, so if you placed a red gel inside the wand the red gel would filter out all the other colors, allowing only the red ray to be used for healing.

The overall idea was that the human facilitator would be able to change the color for different areas of the foot. You could try to make one for yourself and experiment with it.

Part Five

Practicalities of Crystal Therapy

Grounding and Earthing

It is important as a healer or therapist that you can ground, centre and earth yourself. It is part of the overall process of healing holistically. In part four of this book we explored grounding, centering and earthing crystal webs of light. Whilst some people find it more difficult than others to ground, centre and earth themselves, it is vital to the therapeutic process for both healer and client. If you or your client are not grounded, centred and balanced the 'healing' session is not complete. The reason we became ill in the first place is due to some factor which has stressed our body and thrown it out of its normal balance.

Very often it has been found that strong perfumes, air fresheners, aromatherapy oils, etc. make some people feel very 'spacey', headachy or detached from reality. When the offending strong perfume etc. has been removed, the person has quickly recovered their natural balance, normal health and vitality. Armed with this knowledge and due to the effect strong perfumes, air fresheners, aromatherapy oils and scented products have on the human energy field, all the crystal courses and workshops that I am involved with are free from perfume etc. This has resulted in many previously 'spacey' people finding that they no longer have problems grounding, centering and balancing their emotions. The other result is that people who attend my workshops and crystal courses very quickly develop a greater awareness of their energy fields.

How to Tell If Your Client is Ungrounded Or Not Earthed

1. Headache
2. Fuzzy head
3. Sluggish
4. Too relaxed
5. Incomplete recovery from session
6. Unusual/unexpected physiological states
7. Incomplete recovery of normal mobility
8. Glazed eyes

How to Ground

These suggestions can be used for yourself or a client:

1. Use a grounding or earthing crystal web of light.
2. Focus your attention towards your feet and the earth.

3. Slowly sip a glass of water.
4. Hold grounding crystals in each hand (smoky quartz).
5. Visualize roots growing from the bottom of your feet deep into the earth.
6. Experience your sense of balance as gravity pulls on your body and your muscles respond with perfect precision to keep upright.
7. Suck an ice cube.
8. For the therapist: eat a light snack such as an apple (preferably red as the color red relates to the base chakra).
9. For the therapist: do a boring job you hate, such as the washing up!
10. For the therapist: go for a brisk walk outdoors.

Centering

When a person is not centred, we say that their male and female polarities are out of balance, or their yin/yang balance is not in harmony. Their emotions are all over the place and they probably do not understand why they are reacting 'out of character'. They may even feel asymmetrical. We must treat these symptoms holistically and restore balance and harmony to the body so that neither male nor female polarity is dominant and the person feels centred, focused and at peace with themselves, the world, everyone and everything.

How to Tell If Your Client is Not Centred

1. Headache
2. Fuzzy head
3. Feeling asymmetrical
4. Crying, or very emotional
5. Very aggressive
6. Unusual/unexpected physiological states
7. Incomplete recovery of normal mobility

How to Centre

These suggestions can be used for yourself or a client:

1. Use a centering crystal web of light.
2. Focus your attention on your solar plexus area/chakra.
3. Slowly sip a glass of water.
4. Hold centering crystals in each hand (citrine, turquoise or pyrite).
5. Hold a rose quartz in one hand and a turquoise in the other: keep swapping the crystals from hand to hand.

6. For the therapist: place both hands into warm water until the feelings subside.
7. Suck an ice cube.
8. Cleanse the aura.
9. For the therapist: go for a walk outside.

Restoring to Everyday Consciousness

It is also very important to restore your client to everyday consciousness following a crystal therapy session. If your client is feeling ungrounded or 'spaced out' following a healing session you must help them to become fully conscious and in the present, aware of their everyday circumstances and totally in touch with reality.

How to Restore to Everyday Consciousness

1. Use the restoring to everyday consciousness crystal web of light; it will benefit anyone who is feeling ungrounded or 'spaced out' after meditation and will restore a person to everyday consciousness following a healing session.
2. Use grounding, earthing and centering techniques.

Healing Crisis

Healing crisis or symptom substitution, emotional disturbance, self sabotage etc. - these are all part of the process of natural healing. We will explore the different sensations experienced during and or after holistic natural healing.

Negative Sensations

Aching head - Direct your awareness towards your feet. Use grounding crystals. Use a grounding crystal layout. Check your diet for allergies. Check your environment for strong perfumes etc.

Bloated stomach - Too much energy in the solar plexus. Check your diet and use grounding crystals.

Feeling 'spacey' - Not grounded enough. Use grounding crystals.

Detached from reality - Not grounded enough. Use grounding crystals.

Self sabotage - Do they really want 'healing'? Suggest seeing a good holistic counsellor.

Positive Sensations

Sweating - Normal. A sign that the body is cleansing itself.

Numbness - Normal. A sign that chi is flowing.

Increased urination - A good sign. The kidneys are stimulated to produce more urine, which may be darker and stronger smelling, due to the toxin content.

Symptom substitution - Normal. A sign that natural healing is taking place. But be aware of the deep process your client is undergoing. (In standard allopathic medical treatment, symptom substitution is very common. This is due to the nature of allopathic treatment, which only treats the symptom, not the cause of the disease).

Aggravated skin conditions - Good sign, particularly in conditions which have been suppressed; increased perspiration and pimples.

Improved skin tone - Good sign, due to improved circulation.

Increased secretions - Good sign. Increased secretions of the mucus membrane in the nose, mouth and bronchial area.

Disrupted sleep patterns - Good sign. This means the body is re-balancing itself and old energy patterns are breaking down.

Aggression - Normal, this means that chi is flowing. Anger is a good way to release stored emotions, so healing can begin. Find a safe, positive way to release the anger, though.

Temporary outbreak of a disease which has been suppressed - A sign that chi is flowing.

Tiredness - A sign that chi is flowing and the body needs rest.

Depression - Overwhelming desire to weep. A good sign, this means that chi is flowing. Weeping is a good way to release stored emotions, so healing can begin.

Tingling - Normal. A sign that chi is flowing.

Body heat - Normal. A sign that chi is flowing. When energy flows it heats the body.

Trembling - Normal. A sign that chi is flowing.

Shivering - Normal. A good sign that the body is releasing blocked energy.

Feeling asymmetrical - Normal. A sign that the body is trying to rebalance itself.

Yawning - A sign that you are able to relax but perhaps you are too tired.

Burping - A good sign. The body is discharging toxins.

Flatulence - A good sign. The body is discharging toxins.

Diminished or no sensation - This may happen after a while. This is a sign that the meridian pathways have opened up.

Aching old injuries - A good sign. It means you are healing on a deeper level.

You may also experience other sensations not listed. Everyone is unique. Whatever the reactions, they are a necessary part of the healing process and will pass. The way you prepare yourself and your client before a crystal therapy session will have an enormous effect on not only the quality of the experience, but also the final outcome. It will also minimise any healing crisis. I have found most of my clients do not have a healing crisis. This is due to my way of 'working' to clear as much 'debris' out of my clients' auras as possible; in fact my clients feel really good after a crystal therapy session.

Asking your client to drink plenty of fresh pure water, just before and especially just after each crystal therapy session, will ease the removal of energy blocks and toxicity. These are always released with the integration of new energy patterns and information; it will also minimise the possibility of a healing crisis. It is very important that all crystals are cleansed before and after use. This will guarantee that any residual disharmonies are removed from the energy field of the stones. It should also keep a healing crisis to a minimum. Always allow yourself and your client plenty of time and space to deal with any healing crisis that occurs during a healing session. Always give your client an information sheet which explains very simply the process of crystal and gem therapy, including the physical, mental, emotional, and spiritual process of healing. This could include advice on dealing with a healing crisis, such as allowing any feelings of agitation, fidgeting, anger, heat, cold or restlessness to gently dispel.

Explore with clients factors relating to their health and well-being to support clinical crystal therapy treatments; this also keeps a healing crisis to a minimum event. Facilitate clients' own use of crystals for maintenance between visits, including crystals they could use in a healing crisis. A gem essence is invaluable for giving to a client for use between therapy sessions. (Morganite is excellent as it nurtures the emotional body). Also give the client a contact number for them to use between sessions.

Body Language

When we treat a client we find that they may present themselves as a headache, stiff knee, cancer or depression. This is never the case: no one is ever just the manifesting symptom. We are all complex beings, not just a chest infection, as allopathic medicine would lead us to believe. The body simply is not a machine or a collection of chemicals. When the body develops any form of illness, it is trying to bring something to our attention. The message may be that something is not right in our life, or we are going in the wrong direction, or that we are ignoring lessons that need to be learned. These lessons can be wrong diet, wrong mental or emotional attitude, stress etc.

Many people pay no attention to these messages or body language, not because they do not want to, but because they are simply unaware of it. Most people react to sickness by trying to eliminate the symptoms as quickly as possible with direct conventional medical intervention. There is nothing wrong in seeking relief from unpleasant or frightening symptoms but, if you want your body to truly 'heal', you also need to understand why you are ill. Obviously there can be physical causes for illness, such as viruses and bacteria, but not everyone exposed to a particular virus or bacterium actually develops the illness. Similarly, not everyone exposed to carcinogenic toxins develops cancer. Healing is a very personal process. As we become more attuned to ourselves and our clients we will be increasingly aware that all parts of our being are related to all the other parts.

We, then, as crystal healers, must treat in a holistic way the whole being. The Greeks and the Chinese were probably the first to chronicle the link between physical ill health and mental 'dis-ease' several thousand years ago, but the body-mind connection has been an integral part of almost every civilisation throughout history. The study of psychology and more recently of psycho-neuro-immunology has increased our knowledge of the complex links between our physical condition and our mental or emotional state of health.

The following list is only a guideline, a map to guide you to develop a deeper understanding of the many facets that make up our inner and outer selves. Where appropriate I have suggested stones of balance, but it would also be appropriate to make a gemstone essence from a combination of all or some of the suggested stones. You could also dowse or use kinesiology to ascertain which gemstones and crystals to use for the essence. The results of dowsing and muscle testing may surprise you, in that you need a gemstone or crystal that would not normally be considered 'appropriate' for that particular area. The reason is simple: we, as humans in the twenty-first century, are so busy with our lives that if we have problems or issues to deal with we never have the time. So we store all these unresolved issues *anywhere* we can on our body, or in our auric shell, until one day we have nowhere else to store them, the body system finally breaks down and the day of reckoning (ill-health or dis-ease) is upon us.

Right Side of the Body

Male: strength, courage, stamina, dynamic, powerful, aggressive, dominant, outer journeys, money, prestige or job issues. It is the sword hand, giving a blow, lashing out, defending ourselves. Suggested stone for balance:

Clear quartz. Hold in the right hand with the termination pointing out (20 mins).

Left Side of the Body

Female: receiving, intuitive, gentle, inner journeys, receptive, nurturing, feminine, creative, weak, shielding, yielding, or spiritual or psychic issues. Suggested stone for balance:

Quartz (milky). Hold in the left hand with the termination facing towards the body (20 mins).

Front of Body

Female. Suggested stone for centering:

Quartz (milky). Lay the stone over the solar plexus chakra, with the termination pointing towards the heart chakra (20 mins).

Back of Body

Male. Suggested stone to balance:

Clear quartz (as clear as possible). Use with the patient lying face down. The crystal should be placed on the sacral chakra, at the back position. The termination should point towards the feet (20 mins).

Brain

Imbalance of male/female polarities. Suggested stones of balance:

Clear quartz, azeztulite, phenacite, danburite, clear topaz. Place any combination of these stones in the crown chakra area above the head (20 mins).

Or make a gemstone essence from a combination of all or some of the above stones. You could also dowse or use kinesiology to ascertain which gemstones and crystals to use for the essence.

Head

Balances centre of body. Out of balance - too much energy in head, thinks too much or is in confusion, unable to cope with reality, continues to self-sabotage even after healing sessions have helped. Over-emotional, does not want to change, would then have to grow up and take responsibility for own life and problems. Suggested stones to balance:

Sugilite, amethyst, moldavite, fluorite. Place these stones on the crown chakra above the head, or on the third eye chakra, or make a gemstone essence from a combination of all or some of the above stones. You could also dowse or use kinesiology to ascertain which gemstones and crystals to use for the essence.

Headaches

Too much analysing, anger, confusion, unexpressed emotions. Suggested stones to balance:

Lapis, amethyst, sugilite. Place these stones on the third eye chakra.

Hematite. Place hematite at the soles of the feet to pull the energy down from the head.

Eyes

Not wanting to see, not wanting to be seen, refusing to see, also third eye development area. Eyes reveal how you see things. They are the windows through which life is viewed. The positive eye white glistens and is free from all color and blemish. Yellow is liverish, may be an indication of jaundice. Grey shows catarrh or mucus somewhere in the body. Congestion. Red shows irritation. Inflammation. Sinus pain will be unexpressed emotions, a build-up of tears waiting to be shed. Suggested stones of balance:

Fluorite (blue or purple), clear calcite, rainbow calcite. Place these stones on the third eye chakra.

Ears

High blood pressure, not wanting to hear, not being heard, withdrawal into own world due to trauma. Also lack of self worth. Suggested stones to balance:

Imperial topaz, phantom quartz, clear topaz. Place these stones pointing in towards the ears. (This is very powerful, so only use for 3 mins.)

Throat

Not expressing yourself, blocked feeling, being gagged, talking without listening to (hearing) others. Ego problems, pompous, dogmatic, whining. Stored deep sorrows of the heart, unspoken words/words spoken which cannot be unsaid. Suggested stone to balance:

Aquamarine. Place this stone on the throat chakra.

Spine

Support system of being, feelings of not being supported in family, work, etc. Twisted spine, trying to wriggle out of uncomfortable situations, not wanting to be here. Suggested stones of balance:

Selenite, boji stones. Boji stones: For balance and harmony within the spine it is best to use a pair of bojis, one crystallized male and one smooth female. Use the female on the right side of the body and the male on the left side. Bojis have a balanced polarity, so they may be used on acupuncture or acupressure points. They work through the meridian system of the body.

Selenite: Make a gemstone essence and take as often as needed.

Neck

Rigidity, stiff-necked attitude, over-burdened, no support, too many responsibilities. Thyroid problems related to the emotional body: too heavy in the body - not giving people a mouthful back; too thin - always complaining, giving mouthfuls out without wanting to listen to others' explanation, likes being the complaining victim. Suggested stones to balance:

Siberian blue quartz, lapis, turquoise, pyrite. Place these stones on the throat chakra.

Shoulders

Responsibilities - family, others, self - or overburdened with other people's worries. Sloping shoulders show over burdened. Stiff shoulders show tension and fear. If the left shoulder is raised, you have female issues. If the right shoulder is raised, male issues.

Left - Female. Suggested stones of balance:

Rose quartz, pyrite, morganite, pink tourmaline, kunzite.

Right - Male. Suggested stones of balance:

Emerald, malachite, moldavite. Place the stones on the shoulders.

Upper Back

Right side - Not defending oneself, or over-defending. Imbalance is a sign of stored anger to others, hitting out, striking out at others or occasionally at self. Suggested stones of balance:

Green fluorite, emerald, malachite, moldavite.

Left side - Stored grief, pain, sorrow, also could be sign of painful childhood traumas concerning parents. Suggested stones of balance:

Kunzite, morganite. Place these stones on the upper back, on the area of pain or constriction.

Chest

Heartaches, grief, fear, heartbreak, loss, rejection, abandonment, imbalance of loving energy, cannot give or receive love. Asthma can be unexpressed angry emotions. Drooping, concave chest shows a lack of self-worth. Beaten by circumstances. Big, overpowering chest shows conceit and arrogance even the bully. Suggested stones of balance:

Pink/green tourmaline, watermelon tourmaline, rose quartz, rhodochrosite, malachite, sugilite.

Place these stones on the heart chakra area in balanced configurations.

Adrenals/Kidneys

Shock, trauma centre of the body, immune system problem, adrenal rushes, stress, allergies, emotional imbalances, low energy. The kidneys are our life support system. Suggested stones of balance:

Orange/peach calcite, rose quartz, carnelian, rhodochrosite, moldavite. Place these stones on the heart, solar plexus and sacral chakras.

Lower Back

Sexual abuse, stored anger, barriers, stored guilt. Suggested stones of balance:

Carnelian, black obsidian, smoky quartz, moldavite. Make a gemstone essence from a combination of all or some of the above stones. You could also dowse or use kinesiology to ascertain which gemstones and crystals to use for the essence.

Tailbone

Problems with the activation of 'Kundalini'. Issues of fear, success, action, being alive, not wanting to survive. Suggested stones of balance:

Ruby, garnet, smoky quartz, amethyst, moldavite. Make a gemstone essence from a combination of all or some of the above stones. You could also dowse or use kinesiology to ascertain which gemstones and crystals to use for the essence.

Abdomen

Storage area of uncleared information, or emotions relating to anger, fear, guilt, shame. Suggested stones of balance:

Citrine, golden calcite, imperial topaz, moldavite. Place these stones on the solar plexus chakra.

Liver

Stored anger and fear. Suggested stones of balance:

Yellow jasper, citrine, moonstone, smoky quartz. Place these stones over the liver area or make a gemstone essence from a combination of all or some of the above stones. You could also dowse or use kinesiology to ascertain which gemstones and crystals to use for the essence.

Gall-Bladder

Anger turned sour now becomes bitterness. Suggested stones of balance:

Emerald, green calcite, green aventurine, green tourmaline. Place these stones over the gall-bladder area or make a gemstone essence from a combination of all or some of the above stones. You could also dowse or use kinesiology to ascertain which gemstones and crystals to use for the essence.

Stomach

Upset Stomach: We cannot digest all the things we swallow, such as other people's beliefs - parents, teachers, religious teachings, doctors, friends, family, culture, society. Suggested stones of balance:

Moonstone, amethyst, smoky quartz. Make a gemstone essence from a combination of all or some of the above stones. You could also dowse or use kinesiology to ascertain which gemstones and crystals to use for the essence.

Ulcer: Anger eating us away shows as an ulcer. Suggested stones of balance:

Moonstone, aquamarine. Make a gemstone essence from a combination of all or some of the above stones. You could also dowse or use kinesiology to ascertain which gemstones and crystals to use for the essence.

Indigestion: 'I can't stomach it'. Also, we may have bitten off more than we can chew. Suggested stones of balance:

Snow quartz, moonstone. Place these stones over the stomach area, or the solar plexus chakra.

Pancreas

Being too nice, sweetness gone out of life. (Pancreas means all creation). Suggested stones of balance:

Honey calcite, citrine, imperial topaz. Place these stones over the pancreas, or the solar plexus chakra.

Spleen

Also solar plexus, storage of past problems or trauma. Thick waist shows repressed emotions and feelings, anger. Humiliation. Suggested stones of balance:

Bloodstone, yellow jasper, tiger eye. Place these stones over the solar plexus chakra.

Intestines

Colitis/diarrhoea is letting go of old feelings, ideas or thoughts without dealing with them. Constipation is holding on to feelings of anger, fear and guilt. Suggested stones of balance:

Red jasper, red tiger eye, smoky quartz. Place these stones on the hip bones and between the soles of the feet to make a triangulation.

Ovaries/Uterus

Storage of anger towards men, rape, abortion, miscarriage, incest, abuse, all sexual issues that are unresolved, including fear and guilt regarding sex. Self-judgement over sexual behaviour. Judgement over other people's sexual behaviour. Suggested stones of balance:

Carnelian, malachite, rose quartz, pink tourmaline, morganite. Place these stones on the sacral chakra.

Bladder

Fear around sexuality, unresolved anger, guilt, trepidation, not being able to express joy or happiness. (Cystitis = concentrated emotions). Suggested stones of balance:

Smoky quartz, carnelian, citrine, jasper. Place these stones on the sacral chakra.

Prostate

Unresolved sexual problems with women, sexual abuse, incest, birth trauma, helplessness, abandonment, powerlessness. Suggested stones of balance:

Zincite, smoky quartz, ruby, carnelian, citrine, morganite. Make a gemstone essence from a combination of all or some of the above stones. You could also dowse or use kinesiology to ascertain which gemstones and crystals to use for the essence.

Legs

Hold us up/support us, also associated with progress through life, fear of change, fear of the future. Our legs connect us to our feet, our earthing and security. The right leg and the right side of the body relate to action The left leg and the left side of the body relate to passivity. Very slender legs - vulnerable, unprotected, not grounded. Too heavy legs - stored fear or anger, too grounded, materialistic, greedy. Heavy thighs show childhood shock and trauma. Victim as a child. Dis-empowerment. Suppressed anger. Thin thighs indicate growing too fast. No encouragement from the environment. Suggested stones of balance:

Smoky quartz, ruby, garnet, boji stones. Place these stones on or around the legs.

Hips

The hips are where our life is balanced. The pelvic girdle is the cradle, the vase, that holds who we are. Fear of going forward, imbalance of thoughts and emotions, blocked creativity. Too slender - not a firm foundation. Too heavy - too entrenched in rigid belief system or thought patterns. Suggested stones of balance:

Smoky quartz, ruby, garnet, boji stones. Place a pair of these stones on the hips.

Knees

The knees represent the mechanics of moving forward. Linked with stubbornness, inflexibility, indecision, hesitation, vacillation, irresolution. Suggested stones of balance:

Ruby, boji stones, smoky quartz. Place a pair of these stones on or under the knees and a smoky quartz point between the feet.

Ankles

Analysing, dogmatic, reluctance, uncertainty, doubt, scepticism, questioning, qualms, reservation. Suggested stones of balance:

Ruby, black tourmaline or boji stones. Place these stones on or around the ankles and a smoky quartz point between the feet.

Feet

Grounding, 'can't stand it', will not stand up for ourselves against others or stand our ground against others. Security and survival issues. Right foot problems inclined to intellectualise. Left foot problems blocked creativity. The feet also represent all the parts of our body, as do the hands. Suggested stones of balance:

Ruby, smoky quartz, boji stones. Place a pair of these stones on or under the feet and a smoky quartz point between the feet.

Toes

Fear of stepping out, becoming ourselves, trusting to the future, always tripping ourselves up, low self-esteem, as in athlete's foot. Suggested stones of balance and for grounding:

Hematite, smoky quartz, black tourmaline. Place these stones on or around the feet.

Hands

'Can't handle it', too much to handle, also associated with giving (right hand) and receiving (left hand) or over-burdened with life (the hands are an extension of the heart chakra). The ability to grasp what is our in life. Suggested stones to balance:

Smoky quartz, rose quartz, clear quartz. Hold a crystal in each hand.

Elbows

Unbending, rigid attitude, victim mentality. Unable to express desires and feelings. Suggested stones of balance:

Black obsidian, clear quartz. Place or tape these stones on or around the elbows.

Skin

Emotions, holding feelings, not able to deal with emotions, easily led by others, exploited or weak-willed. Also anger, as in 'rash'. Suggested stones of balance:

Rose quartz, green aventurine, morganite, malachite, rhodochrosite. Place these stones over the heart chakra, or make a crystal solution with distilled (purified) water, or place them over the afflicted area. We also find it very effective to make a gemstone essence from a combination of all or some of the above stones. You could also dowse or use kinesiology to ascertain which gemstones and crystals to use for the essence.

Bones

Storage of information, ancestral memories, including genetic predisposition and family ties, past life and karmic issues. Suggested stones of balance:

Clear quartz, fossilized wood, amber, rhodochrosite, morganite, calcite. Make a gemstone essence from a combination of all or some of the above stones. You could also dowse or use kinesiology to ascertain which gemstones and crystals to use for the essence.

Affirmations and Conscious Reprogramming

We make positive or negative affirmations all day long. Our body (and everyone else for that matter) believes every word we say. How many times during the day have you found yourself making a negative statement about yourself or someone else? For example, a mother who says to her child 'Why do you always misbehave?' is implying to the child that its behaviour is permanent and in this way she is embedding a 'command' that is likely to produce bad behaviour. Early in our education we are taught to use what linguists call nominalizations - that is a verb (a doing or process word) being made into a noun (a static thing). For example, in saying you cannot handle a relationship, you are talking about a relationship as if it were a static physical thing, like a milk jug, rather than talking about relating - a dynamic, active process of communication. The problem arises because the art of relating, when it is referred to as a relationship, is perceived as static and no responsibility is being taken for the active, continuing process of relating to another person. When someone systematically nominalizes, they can restrict the amount of choices they have because they perceive the world in a more static and fixed way.

Never underestimate the power of words. They can put us in good moods or bad moods; even though we know that they are only words, they will deeply affect us. While anaesthetized or unconscious, patients are sensitive to the things said within their environment. This can have a profound effect on their behaviour, recovery rate and even self- esteem. Advertisers, religious leaders, politicians, your peers and numerous other sources are all bombarding your sensory awareness all day long with their messages. You and only you have the power to de-programme yourself. We must understand that the unconscious mind is not logical but purposeful. Often an individual will develop an illness to avoid having to confront something. People who get sore throats before having to speak publicly could well be being protected by their unconscious because they remember when they were humiliated talking in front of a class as a child. No matter how inappropriate the behaviour, it serves a purpose.

Start today to follow the old tradition known as mindfulness. Be aware of every thought you have, be aware of every word you say. Very soon you will see a change in your health, your behaviour, your whole attitude to life. Decide today to change. Be aware of any negative thoughts you have about yourself. Did someone tell you this about yourself? Find out where you store the negative thoughts in your body. Keeping a journal is vital for self-development. We have so many thoughts each day it can be difficult to keep pace with them -unless we write them down - to ascertain the patterns that underpin our attitudes to ourselves and others. Acquire a beautifully bound notebook and write your thoughts nightly for the next month, from moon-cycle to moon cycle. That's the length of time we need to perform a new behaviour in order to turn it into a meaningful ritual habit.

You Are What You Believe

Working with the crystal kingdom is an excellent way of de-programming yourself.

1. First write out a positive affirmation for yourself. Make it as powerful and appropriate to you and your situation as possible.

2. Hold your control crystal (or a suitably programmed clear quartz crystal) in your left hand with your positive affirmation.

3. It is necessary to be seated comfortably, so sit in a relaxed steady posture with the spine and neck held erect but not tense. This means that the base of the spine needs to be higher than the knees, so tilting the pelvis forwards alters your posture into a position where the spine will remain upright but relaxed. The easiest way of doing this is to put a small, firm cushion or rolled up towel beneath the base of the spine, whether you are sitting cross-legged on the floor or on a chair. If in a chair, another small firm cushion in the small of the back prevents lolling into the chair and keeps the lungs free to move naturally. The spiritual current must be able to flow unimpeded from the base of the spine to the top of the head.

4. Place the hands in the lap, with the right hand resting on the left (which is still holding the quartz crystal and positive affirmation) and gently ease the shoulders back ever so slightly and the chin in a little so that there is a slight stretch on the back of the neck, easing the blood-flow to the brain. Keep your mouth slightly open and rest the tip of the tongue on the roof of the mouth just behind the teeth. This placement of the tongue is very important because it naturally maintains the flow of energy to the head whilst keeping the jaw relaxed.

5. Now simply turn your full attention to the movement of your breath. Do not try and control your breathing, simply be aware of the breath. Then begin to follow the breath entering and leaving your body and gradually feel the effect this conscious breathing has on your body.

6. Begin to focus on your positive affirmation. Really feel all the emotions associated with the affirmation. Visualise how this affirmation would change your life. Do you feel comfortable with the changes or is there resistance in your body. Do you really believe your affirmation?

7. Working in this way we become acutely aware that we can use 'lip service' to say an affirmation repeatedly, but if we hold resistance on any level of our being it will never be totally effective. Be honest with yourself, you are fooling no one else. This honesty facilities healing to take place on all levels, physical, emotional, mental and etheric.

8. You may use this technique on yourself as many times as needed to find the right positive affirmation. I have found that normally, when people are very ambitious with their affirmations, their bodies, or minds, resist the positive new programme.

9. Try not to overdo this procedure, though; remember to allow your body time to integrate the new flow of energy.

10. At the end of this session allow yourself to return to everyday awareness and normal breathing.

Finally, drink plenty of pure fresh clean water; this will flush any toxins from your physical body which may have been released during the session.

Meditation

There is a power, an energy, which is available to each of us. We can begin to work with this energy and allow it to guide, inspire, strengthen and encourage us. It is available to all who seek to grow in a positive direction. This Divine source of wisdom is the Self. Once we become aware of our own inner light, our Divinity, our own source of unlimited goodness, we are never dis-empowered again. It will guide and nurture us if we sincerely seek our own truth. Whether a person lives a spiritual life on his/her own, or is part of an organized tradition, the goal is the same: the attainment of peace of mind, purity and perfection or, as some call it, self-realization and enlightenment.

Meditation practice will:

* Unleash your immense potential
* Improve your health

* Rejuvenate your body
* Clear your mind and improve your concentration
* Amplify your personal healing power
* Stimulate harmonious, focused brain activity
* Restore the energy structure of your body and aura
* Awaken healing and personal growth
* Release subconscious hidden knowledge
* Release intuitive forces
* Bring inner peace
* Improve your creativity
* Prevent or minimize the problems of senility

Meditation Practice

The two senses that are the strongest are sight and sound; they are able to hold the attention the longest, so we will work with these, although there are other methods. If you find it difficult to meditate, you may need to find out what kind of person you are, as with anything 'new' we all have different ways of learning. (Head, heart, or hand, otherwise known as cognitive, affective or psychomotor domain, also known as intellectual, emotional or practical in nature).

Remember, no one can do it for you and it may take years to learn to meditate correctly, but it is well worth the effort involved.

Method One: Crystal Meditation

Crystal meditation is simple, easy, safe and effective. The following are practical points regarding the basic techniques and stages of meditation. They are primarily intended for the beginner, although even the most experienced meditator will find a review of them useful.

1. Have a regular time, place and practice.
2. The most effective times are dawn and dusk.
3. Try to have a separate room for meditation.
4. Keep it free from other vibrations and influences.
5. Purify it with incense and have a large amethyst crystal (an amethyst cluster will also work) to focus on.
6. When sitting, face north or east to take advantage of favourable magnetic vibrations.
7. Sit in a comfortable steady posture with the spine and neck held erect but not tense. This means that the base of the spine needs to be higher than the knees, thus tilting the pelvis forwards to a position where the spine naturally remains upright when relaxed. The easiest way of doing this is to put a small, firm cushion beneath the base of the spine. The psychic current must be able to flow unimpeded from the base of the spine to the top of the head.
8. Sit cross-legged; this forms a triangular path for the energy field and stops it dissipating in all directions.
9. Command the mind to be still for a specific length of time.
10. Forget the past, present and future.
11. Consciously regulate the breath; begin with five minutes of deep breathing.

12. Focus on the amethyst crystal, then slowly allow your eyes to close, being aware of any after-image or impression.

13. Become aware of the amethyst crystal begging to relax your whole energy field.

14. Use the mantra 'Om' and gradually allow just mental repetition of the mantra.

15. Repetition will lead to pure thought, in which sound vibration merges with thought vibration.

16. With your eyes closed, concentrate on the space between the eyebrows, the heart, or any of the higher chakras or centres of spiritual energy. Generally speaking, the ajna chakra is best for those of an intellectual nature, while the heart chakra is best for the emotional types. Also, you will find that once your centre of concentration is chosen it should not be changed.

17. With practice, concentration develops, then duality disappears and meditation begins; over time, samadhi, the superconscious state, is reached.

18. Begin the practice of meditation with twenty-minute periods and increase to one hour. If the body is overcome by jerking or tremors, control them and keep the energy internalised.

You can also hold a tumbled amethyst crystal in each hand to cleanse, heal, balance and purify your aura. Other crystals can be used to great effect, such as sugilite, tanzanite, charoite, rose quartz and moonstone.

Method Two: Rainbow Bridge

This next meditation is very powerful: it will change your life if you let it. So let us take a look at the rainbow. We have no need to search in the sky, or look very far, we are the rainbow, it lies within each and every one of us within our chakra system and aura. So we will work our healing meditation through the chakra system. We use the seven master chakras, as each master chakra gives off its own unique color. When a person is healthy, strong and vibrant, so is the chakra color and we find the human body and human aura is a resplendent vibrant rainbow. When there is a serious physical, emotional, mental or spiritual imbalance or illness, certain colors will look impure, dirty, dim or drab; sometimes a color can even be absent altogether.

1. Sit in a comfortable steady posture with the spine and neck held erect but not tense. This means that the base of the spine needs to be higher than the knees, thus tilting the pelvis forwards to a position where the spine naturally remains upright when relaxed. The easiest way of doing this is to put a small, firm cushion beneath the base of the spine. The psychic current must be able to flow unimpeded from the base of the spine to the top of the head.

2. Sit cross-legged; this forms a triangular path for the energy field and stops it dissipating in all directions.

3. Command the mind to be still for a specific length of time.

4. Forget the past, present and future.

5. Consciously regulate the breath; begin with five minutes of deep breathing.

6. Focus on the base chakra and visualise or feel a vibrant red light bringing activation, healing, balance, strength and integration. When all energy movements/sensations are completed allow the red light to change to a beautiful violet color and gently feel/visualise it moving up to the next chakra.

7. Focus on the sacral chakra and visualise or feel a glowing vibrant orange light bringing activation, healing, balance, creativity and integration. When all energy movements/sensations

are completed allow the orange light to change to a beautiful violet color and gently feel/visualise it moving up to the next chakra.

8. Focus on the solar plexus chakra and visualise or feel a glowing yellow light bringing activation, healing, warmth, balance and integration. When all energy movements/sensations are completed allow the yellow light to change to a beautiful violet color and gently feel/visualise it moving up to the next chakra.

9. Focus on the heart chakra and visualise or feel a comforting green light bringing activation, healing, balance, integration and acceptance. When all energy movements/sensations are completed allow the green light to change to a beautiful violet color and gently feel/visualise it moving up to the next chakra.

10. Focus on the throat chakra and visualise or feel a soothing blue light bringing activation, healing, balance, integration and peaceful communication. When all energy movements/sensations are completed allow the blue light to change to a beautiful violet color and gently feel/visualise it moving up to the next chakra.

11. Focus on the third eye chakra and visualise or feel a soothing indigo blue light bringing activation, healing, balance, insight and integration. When all energy movements/sensations are completed allow the indigo light to change to a beautiful violet color and gently feel/visualise it moving up to the next chakra.

12. Focus on the crown chakra and visualise or feel the calming violet light bringing activation, healing, balance, purification, integration and wisdom. When all energy movements/sensations are completed allow the violet light to cascade out of the crown chakra and into the aura. Visualise or feel it like a fountain as it cleanses, activates, heals and purifies the whole of the auric shell.

13. Allow yourself plenty of time to come back to everyday reality.

14. Centre and earth yourself. Keep a written record of the experience.

Scrying

Any kind of reflective surface can be used for scrying, which is one of the best known forms of divination. It is an ancient technique of contacting and gaining guidance from the Divine. The use of crystals and crystal spheres to gain access to other dimensions, the astral plane or the Akashic records, goes back to pre-history. Crystal divination or scrying normally requires a clear quartz crystal, as clear as possible and as large as possible. This will help to maximise the energy field and overall influence of ease of communication. Traditionally, balls, eggs, pyramids and polished quartz have been used, with the optimum resonance being created by crystal balls. The energy field created will vary between each quartz crystal and each shaped piece of quartz, so it is important to find the correct one for your energy field. Very often when I meet people who have tried this technique and failed it was only because they chose the wrong crystal for them, or they did not prepare enough to facilitate clear, coherent communication with the Divine; the other problem can be fear, fear of failure or fear of the unknown. When you are ready to take this step into the world of scrying, first check your motives; why are you drawn to scrying? If you find your motives are pure and you feel in harmony with the idea of Divine communication with your higher self, just follow this procedure:

* Select a clear stone that refracts light well
* Make sure it feels psychically clean.
* Follow the cleansing procedure as outlined in the relevant section of this book

* Charge the crystal with positive energy, preferably on the full moon
* Keep it wrapped in a clean cloth, to protect it from other energies (purple cloth is a good choice)
* Find a safe space where you can sit comfortably and not be disturbed
* Turn off the phone, television, radio etc.
* You can use soothing music or a drumming tape
* Light a white candle and turn off the lights (only if you feel comfortable with it)
* Surround yourself with a sphere of pure white light and place around that a circle of brilliant blue light for Divine communication
* Focus on your breathing, then become aware of your heartbeat; do not try and change your breathing, just allow it to become gentle, smooth and easy
* Allowing the in-breath to follow calmly on the out-breath, continue with 20 connected breaths until you feel your energy field begin to oscillate; allow yourself to fully connect with your higher self
* Now hold your crystal in your hand of preference and allow your energy field to merge with the crystal's energy field
* Begin to focus on your question. Be very clear in your intent; do not allow other thoughts to intrude
* Allow yourself to begin to gaze at your crystal
* Find a place on the crystal that begins to draw your eye to it
* Allow your mind to move beyond the physical form of the stone
* You will begin to see the internal light within the crystal
* Keep looking at the light within the crystal. Very often forms will begin to come into view, somewhat like a mini television screen. Keep watching the images and allow other guidance in the form of thoughts or inspiration to inspire you
* When truly connected you should get impressions and insights
* Do not allow yourself to become exhausted; when you have achieved as much as you can in one sitting, begin the closing down process
* Wrap your crystal back carefully in its cloth and give thanks to your higher self for all the protection, communication and guidance you have just received. Blow out your candle
* Allow yourself plenty of time to come back to everyday reality
* Centre and earth yourself
* Keep a written record of the experience

Relaxation

It is very important that you, as a crystal healer, can relax your client. One of the best ways is by using guided imagery, which is helpful to the patient to teach them to relax. Many people do not know how to relax. They are very tense, so it is up to you to be as calm and relaxed as possible. This will help them relax also. When you use relaxation techniques you are working with the unconscious mind. This contains all the wisdom, memories and intelligence. It is the source of creativity. It regulates body maintenance and autonomic processes like breathing, blood circulation and tissue regeneration.

The conscious mind cannot heal a cut or accelerate your heartbeat to the correct rate; the unconscious mind does. It is the seat of your emotions and directs nearly all your behaviour. Everything that has ever happened, you and everything that you have ever imagined, is stored as a multi-sensory recording in your unconscious mind. You can use relaxation techniques to go into the unconscious mind and reveal details of incidents that happened many years before, all of which are filed away somewhere. You may use relaxation techniques to help your client relax in between crystal healing sessions.

Method One: Relaxation

A good way to help them is by teaching them to relax each part of their body, starting at the feet and working up to the top of the head:

1. Lie flat on the floor or bed, with your eyes closed.
2. Begin breathing deeply, consciously relaxing every part of your body. Begin at the feet and move slowly up the body until you reach the top of your head.
3. Imagine each part becoming heavier and heavier. This may take several minutes.
4. Then allow yourself to become lighter and lighter, until you feel you are gently floating on a beautiful white cloud that is soft, warm and so very comfortable.
5. Allow yourself to stay on this beautiful white cloud for as long as you need to.
6. When you are ready, gently become aware of your breathing again.
7. Take several really deep breaths to bring you back into the world.
8. Allow any feelings of light-headedness to dissipate; this may take a little while.
9. Gently get up. Write down any thoughts or feelings that surfaced during your relaxation time.

Method Two: Breathing

Teach them to breathe more deeply and learn to relax.

You could teach them to use the resonance technique, which is connected breathing. Using rhythmical, connected, fine breaths which are long, slow and deep, allowing us to connect to, and experience, the vibrational aspect of the energy that drives the breath. This energy is our Divine essence. When using this technique you will reach a point where you feel as though you are 'being breathed'.

Method Three: Sound

Suggest to your client that they purchase a soothing music or relaxation tape/CD. They could then lie down and relax for 20 minutes a day whilst listening to the music. You could also give them a crystal to hold for the relaxation session. This would be chosen for its soothing, healing and relaxing properties. Amethyst or rose quartz are ideal.

Visualisation

We will take relaxation a stage further now and go into visualisation. Visualisation is nothing new: Buddhists have been perfecting the techniques for thousands of years and will do so until all beings are free from illusion. Using visualisation in the context of this book, we will only look at specific healing methods. My next book will go deeper into visualisation, visions and meditation for personal and spiritual development. This is a subject very close to my heart, which has fascinated me, inducing my exploration of its possibilities in great depth, for most of my life.

So how can we use visualisation to help our clients and augment their healing experience?

Feel free to use the following techniques on yourself as well as your clients.

Visualisation is basically a process whereby we internalise our view of the world and by using specific techniques alter our outer world; this includes our health and overall experience of life. Nearly all visualisations begin with getting us to view something with our mind's eye. Many people get worried that they cannot visualise. Don't worry, everyone can visualise; just think of a time you were happy. Picture the scene, whether it was a party, holiday, wedding or whatever comes to mind. A mental picture will come into your mind and that is visualisation; you may even be able to remember sounds, smells, feelings and emotions.

Method One: Color

This technique can be used for healing, pain relief or just relaxation. It is an excellent 'tonic' whatever your emotional state. Begin with the relaxation technique, whereby you relax each part of the body, starting at the feet and working up to the top of the head. It is important to take the in-breath through the nostrils. Exhale through the nose - unless the pain or condition is acute, in which case the out-breath should be through the mouth. This is applicable for shock or pain of any kind, physical, mental or emotional. You may use the color breath to fill the whole body or just part of the body. This applies to pain or any area of the body that particularly needs healing. If you wanted to, you could just breathe the color or colors you are intuitively drawn to. There are endless variations and combinations. You could even use the color breath, for instance, in a stressful situation, when blue would be very calming, or for shock, when orange would really help.

1. Make yourself comfortable in a chair or lie flat on the floor or bed.
2. Close your eyes.
3. Begin breathing deeply, consciously relaxing every part of your body. Begin at the feet and move slowly up the body until you reach the top of your head.
4. Imagine each part becoming heavier and heavier. This may take several minutes.
5. Then allow yourself to become lighter and lighter, until you feel you are completely relaxed.
6. Remain in this relaxed state and visualise the air around you filled with the color violet.
7. Breath in for the count of three, visualising yourself inhaling the color violet as you do. Visualise this strongly. Actually see yourself pulling the color in through your nose out of the air and watch it going away into your body.
8. Hold your color breath for the count of three.
9. Exhale for the count of three.
10. Repeat 7, 8 and 9 twice more. This will complete first the three-breath color cycle.
11. Now visualise the air around you filled with the indigo blue color. Breathe in for the count of three, visualising yourself inhaling the color indigo as you do. Visualise this strongly. Actually see yourself pulling the color in through your nose out of the air and watch it going away into your body.

12. Hold your color breath for the count of three.

13. Exhale for the count of three.

14. Repeat 11,12 and 13 twice more. This will complete the second three-breath color cycle.

15. Continue with this process of three breath cycles, going through all the remaining colors of the rainbow in reverse order:

    Blue
    Green
    Yellow
    Orange
    Red

16. When you have finished the process, you can either concentrate on breathing in clear white light, or just relax and allow your body to come back very slowly.

17. When you are ready, gently become aware of your surroundings.

18. Allow any feelings of light-headedness to dissipate; this make take a little while.

19. Gently get up. Write down any thoughts or feelings that surfaced during your color breathing.

20. Be aware of any areas that would not absorb some colors, or any areas that absorbed lots of color; these are parts of the body that may need more attention in the healing process.

Method Two: Ice Cube

This next visualisation uses the ice melting process. Frozen energy, thoughts or emotions become stuck within our bodies causing stress, rigid mental attitudes, blocks and illness. This specific technique can be used by anyone; it is tried and tested and once again extremely powerful.

1. Make yourself comfortable in a chair or lie flat on the floor or bed.

2. Close your eyes.

3. Begin breathing deeply, consciously relaxing every part of your body. Begin at the feet and move slowly up the body until you reach the top of your head.

4. Imagine each part becoming heavier and heavier. This may take several minutes.

5. Then allow yourself to become lighter and lighter, until you feel you are completely relaxed.

6. Notice the coming of the in-breath and the going of the out-breath. Become very aware of that small space that occurs between the in-breath and the out-breath. What happens to you in that space? Do you go anywhere? Just observe and let go.

7. When you are breathing gently and without strain, the body relaxed and the mind at rest, go on to the next step.

8. Begin to visualise in an area of your body that has manifested pain or constriction a small ice cube. Don't analyse the process and if you are unsure where to place the ice cube just go with your first impression or instinct.

9. Look at the ice cube. Is it cloudy or clear? Is it thick and heavy or light and clear? Do not worry yourself what these aspects mean. It is not necessary for your conscious mind to understand - something far deeper has taken over.

10. The next step is easy; your body heat is melting the ice cube. This may take a few minutes but the ice will melt. As it does so you feel the gentle warmth of your body spreading even deeper and stronger, healing and balancing the area where the ice cube was. Your body has a tremendous capacity to heal itself. Strong feelings or emotions may come up; if they do, just acknowledge them and let them go.

11. You can repeat this process as many times as you like: first the ice cube, then the warmth melting the ice cube, then the warmth of your body healing itself.

12. When you have finished the process, you can just relax and allow your body to come back very slowly.

13. When you are ready, gently become aware of your surroundings.

14. Allow any feelings of light-headedness to dissipate; this make take a little while.

15. Gently get up. Write down any thoughts or feelings that surfaced during your visualisation.

Method Three: Crystal

For this next 'visualisation' you will require a crystal. Rose quartz, amethyst or clear quartz are good to begin with, but you could use any crystal or gemstone (even your favourite gemstone pendant). Just allow yourself to be intuitively guided. This technique can be used for healing, relaxation or even 'tuning' in to your crystal. As with all the other techniques in this book you know that this format has been used hundreds of times by thousands of people. It is safe, effective and very powerful and has always brought relaxation and healing. This process relies on the crystal kingdom to initiate and activate your relaxation and healing process. The crystal kingdom is very good at working with the human vibration to initiate healing. Please cleanse and energise your crystal before you begin the visualisation.

1. Make yourself comfortable in a chair or lie flat on the floor or bed.

2. Hold your crystal in your left hand with the termination pointing towards the body. If it is a tumbled stone just cradle it gently in your hand.

3. Allow your eyes to slowly close.

4. Begin breathing deeply, consciously relaxing every part of your body. Begin at the feet and move slowly up the body until you reach the top of your head.

5. Imagine each part becoming heavier and heavier. This may take several minutes.

6. Then allow yourself to become lighter and lighter, until you feel you are completely relaxed.

7. Notice the coming of the in-breath and the going of the out-breath. Become very aware of that small space that occurs between the in-breath and the out-breath. What happens to you in that space? Do you go anywhere? Just observe and let go.

8. When you are breathing gently and without strain, the body relaxed and the mind at rest, go on to the next step.

9. Your intentions will be known by the crystal, be assured of this. The crystal wants to help you regain your health and will work very hard to ease your physical, mental or emotional pain and help you tune in to its 'perfect' vibration. So very gently begin to visualise or feel the crystal's vibration in your left hand.

10. Feel the energy gently travelling up your left arm into your shoulder and spreading across your chest and down your right arm and flowing out of the fingers of your right hand.

11. The energy of the crystal gradually spreads to the whole of your physical body, flowing gently and easily until it slowly flows out of the top of your head and the tips of your toes.

12. At this point you begin to be aware of the space around your body, as the crystal vibration flows all around you, totally enfolding you in a cloud of healing energy. You feel yourself breathing this energy in to your body as well, until there is nothing but the gently oscillating crystal vibration. At this point you just simply relax even more and let go, as you float in your cloud of crystal healing.

13. It is not necessary for your conscious mind to understand - something far deeper has taken over. Your body has a tremendous capacity to heal itself. Strong feelings or emotions may come up; if they do, just acknowledge them and let them go.

14. When you are ready or when the crystal cloud has done its job, you can just relax and allow your body to come back very slowly. Feel the weight of your body on the chair or bed and, when you are ready, become aware of your surroundings and your normal breathing pattern. Allow any feelings of light-headedness to dissipate; this make take a little while. Gently get up. Write down any thoughts or feelings that surfaced during your crystal visualisation.

15. Cleanse your crystal.

Principles of Good Practice

As a crystal therapist you have certain legal and moral obligations to your clients. Health care is delivered through direct interaction between individuals. Those who come into contact with practitioners in the complementary health care sector expect that these practitioners will undertake their duty; this includes being caring and honest, avoiding harm, showing integrity and not exploiting or abusing their power.

Complementary practitioners should show respect for the human condition and its complexity, acknowledging each person's essential humanity. We should welcome our individuality and diversity as the wealth of human experience and hence the need to take the holistic view. This holistic view should include that each human being has a right to expect an environment that is conducive to health and social well-being and that of future generations.

Running a Healing Practice

When practitioners are 'evaluating individual referrals for their appropriateness and clinical priority', one of the criteria they have to meet is that arrangements for the assessment are consistent with the client's clinical priority, their particular requirements and other relevant factors and are confirmed with the client in writing.

This means that the crystal practitioner has to balance a number of competing criteria and demands to achieve the outcome. These arrangements include appointment time, duration of appointment, location, others who need to be present and any necessary physical arrangements within the environment. The clinical priority includes the severity of the client's needs and the likelihood of the client's condition deteriorating. Particular requirements are in relation to the client's personal beliefs and preferences, their physical support and access, including emotional and psychological support, and finally location, transport, time (convenience). It also means evaluating individual referrals for their appropriateness; in other words, never take on a client you feel is beyond your clinical expertise, but always refer them to a more experienced therapist.

Elements of Good Practice:

1. Establish and review clinical crystal and gem therapy - treatments, goals and contracts - with clients.

2. Enable clients and companions to understand the nature, scope and limitations of clinical crystal therapy.

3. Explain very simply the process of crystal and gem therapy, including the physical, mental, emotional and spiritual process of healing.

4. Explore, agree and review with clients the goals they wish to achieve through clinical crystal therapy.

5. Explore with clients factors relating to their health and well-being to support clinical crystal therapy treatments.

6. Explore with clients current contributing factors that are affecting their current state of health and well-being through observation and guided discussion.

7. Investigate with clients their presenting symptoms through external (scanning) examination of the body.

8. Develop holistic client-based profiles from a range of sources.

9. Prepare people, materials and equipment for clinical crystal therapy treatments.

10 Prepare self and work areas for consultation and treatment.

11. Select crystals for treatment.

12. Verify the suitability of crystals with clients.

13. Facilitate clients' own use of crystals for maintenance between visits.

14. Enable clients to emerge from states of altered awareness.

15. Monitor self within the clinical crystal therapy treatment.

16. Differentiate between own internal world and that of clients.

17. Monitor own effects on clients.

18. Ensure continuing self support.

19. Develop ways of enabling understanding of the therapeutic process with clients, their companions, partners, relatives, friends etc. by interaction, e.g. face to face, by telephone, in writing (e.g. letter, information sheets, diagrams).

Performance Criteria

1. The practitioner monitors her/his own physical, mental and emotional health and any conditions which may impede effective therapy.

2. The practitioner's personal presentation aims to promote client confidence and ease.

3. All necessary equipment and crystals are available and in good order ready for use.

4. Heat, light, and ventilation are set and maintained at a level to optimise client and practitioner comfort during therapy.

5. The work area is arranged and prepared in a suitable way to enhance the client's confidence in crystal therapy and to take into account the client's requirements.

6. Work areas comply with relevant current legal and organisational health and safety requirements.

7. Furniture and equipment are arranged in such a way as to facilitate effective therapy.

8. Foreseeable interruptions to the crystal healing session are eliminated.

9. The client is offered the opportunity to use the toilet before the start of the therapy.

10. The client is encouraged and enabled to optimise her/his comfort, without adversely affecting the practitioner's ability to monitor and work with her/him during crystal therapy.

11. Any factors which may cause discomfort or danger to the client during crystal healing are identified and the appropriate action is taken to minimise the risk they pose.

12. Where the practitioner is unable to see the client at the agreed time, the client is given clear information on the likely extent of the delay and any necessary alternative arrangements are agreed.

13. Confidential materials are stored securely when not in use.

14. Clinical records are kept accurately.

Practice Management

Your practice management will also include legal and ethical issues such as client confidentiality. You will also have to be aware of the ways in which holistic treatment differs from conventional treatment. You must also be aware that it is illegal for non-medically qualified personnel to treat sexually transmitted diseases (except Aids) and you cannot claim to be able to cure a disease (e.g. cancer, Brights disease, etc).

Contractual Issues

Contractual issues obviously include practitioner insurance and you must make arrangements with your clients for contact between sessions and the correct procedure and arrangements for cancelling appointments. Your clients must also be made aware of their rights/procedure for making a complaint to your governing body.

Practical Introduction to Commerce

As a complementary medicine practitioner you will also have to understand commercial survival. You could go on a local night school course which would help you to set up a practice. There you will be able to learn about business plans, cash-flows and spread sheets and profit and loss. You will need to keep adequate records of income and expenditure for tax purposes. These records will include a cash book, receipts as proof of expenditure and a separate bank account from your own personal account. Eventually you may need to appoint an accountant to help you. If you have a very successful practice you will have to learn about people management: recruitment, selection and development of staff; supporting and leading, selecting, developing and managing volunteers; how to develop and sustain effective working relationships with people and also understand the law in relation to health and safety at work, contractual obligations and employment legislation.

Part Six

Altars - Creating a Sacred Space

As a crystal or vibrational therapist it is good to have something tangible to focus on. It aids concentration, meditation, inspiration and contemplation and it also facilitates the work we do for ourselves and others, such as personal and spiritual growth, developing intuition, absent or distance healing. An 'altar' is your own personal sacred space; somewhere you can create a celebration or even a ritual, for your chosen work. Our ancestors realised that there was great psychological, spiritual and emotional comfort to be gained from rituals, which is why in institutions from religions and nations to workplaces. In a fast-changing world where ritual and routine seem to be diminishing from our normal way of life, creating a personal or healing altar - no matter how tiny - offers valuable grounding to your work and a chance to explore your creativity and express yourself emotionally, artistically and spiritually.

Through reading the relevant sections on the association with color and crystals and the personal selection of items inspired by meditation, establishing an altar will help you become more mindful of the issues and challenges concerning the particular aspect of your life you are currently working on. Once you have got into the routine of attending to the altar daily - whether to clean, purify or reorganise it, or change some of the sacred objects - it will be much easier to include a set amount of time for meditative thought. Remember, this is your sacred space and you should only include items that have meaning for you. It can be a valuable exercise to meditate on what you might like to include before you start - allowing your 'Divine Essence' or your 'intuitive self' to guide you.

Experiment with the layout; if an item irritates or upset you, or is less than inspiring, remove it. You could place crystals, art, photographs, shells, bells, incense, candles, flowers, oils, religious icons, Angel cards, affirmation cards, shamanic objects, wind chimes, feathers, a small note-book, pencil etc. on your altar. Traditionally there would be a representation of all the elements - air, earth, fire, water, spirit and the human world, plus anything you wanted to bring into your life, such as love, spiritual wisdom, compassion or abundance. Your altar need not be indoors; maybe you could have two, one dedicated to one aspect of your life and one dedicated to another. There is no limit to this exercise and one day you may find that your home has only that which you hold sacred inside, every object chosen with great care for its grace or beauty of purpose.

Feng Shui

The Way of Wind and Water

Feng shui is an 'eco-art' uniting man and his destiny with his environment, whether natural or artificial, cosmic or local. Thousands of years ago, as Chinese civilisation sprang up along the fertile Yellow and Wei river valleys, feng shui's basic premises also developed from the topographical and geographical nature of the area, a mixture of rugged mountains, plateaux, rivers, valleys and large flat plains. Long before there were architects, natural phenomena such as wind and water were viewed as sacred signs mysteriously instructing shamans where the most auspicious place was for a house, an altar, or a grave. Feng shui promotes the modern idea of ecology and conservation. Its message is: harmonize with, do not disrupt, nature. We all know tampering with nature not only disrupts the harmonious flow of the weather but also damages the environment. When we work in harmony with the elemental forces, rather than combating them, we create positive energy in our living and working environments. By focusing on the powerful Universal Life Energy that flows around us, we can begin to bring balance and harmony to every area of our lives.

One of the most popular *nine* feng shui 'cures' is natural crystals. A feng shui cure is simply a ritual, ceremony, technique or item used in a particular way to repel or dispel stagnant or harmful energy. Few people are wealthy enough to use diamonds as a feng shui cure, but a practical, effective and affordable solution is to use the best quality crystal you can. This can be in the form of a hanging crystal, a chandelier, or simply a natural crystal created by the most skilful of artists, 'Mother nature'. As energy encounters a crystal it is transformed. When using crystals in feng shui it is important to place them with a clear intent, also being mindful of the task you want the crystals to accomplish. Obviously a small crystal will not clear a large area such as a living room or office; for these areas, heavy large objects such as carved crystal statues, large clusters, big stones or obelisks are required. Obelisks are especially potent energy enhancers. Used in feng shui placement they magnetize or pull positive energy towards them. Clear quartz gives the optimum power in the obelisk shape, due to its focus and clarity.

In feng shui the color of the stones used is equally as important as the placement: you should only use stones that harmonise with your color scheme and the overall ambience of the room. Clear quartz is most commonly used because it reflects the full spectrum of light and balance. As a general rule, white and blue repel energy and are used for protection. Red is the color of life force and attracts positive energy; this includes the energy of passion. Orange is the color for enhancing creativity, while yellow is used for mental clarity. Green is used for growth and balance, while pink is used for love. Purple or indigo enhances spiritual and psychic energies, including contemplation and meditation. Black is also used for protection, but in a different way from white or blue; black absorbs negative energies, so when using dark crystals please be sure to cleanse them regularly under running water.

The Range of Crystal Cures

Crystals can be used in almost any area to bring in the energy of 'refreshing light'. Hanging crystals strengthen intuition, for they have the ability to not only change the flow of energy but to break up stagnant chi by sending out myriad prisms that dapple the room and fill it with the moving energy of the sun.

Austrian Crystal - Hang a spherical crystal in a window to clear stagnant chi and raise your spirits. If you raise your head to look at the crystal on a regular basis, it will lift your energy. In fact this very movement of looking up will raise your energy. When we are sad or depressed we usually slump our shoulders and take very shallow breaths. If we sit up straight and breathe deeply, it is much more difficult to stay sad or depressed. In this way anything that makes us look physically upwards subtly makes us more open to feeling happy and cheerful in spirit. A sparkling crystal hanging in a window can cast a beautiful rainbow of colors across the walls, bringing beauty, joy and transformation into a space. One of the key regulations in feng shui is to keep energy or chi moving and vibrant, since stagnant chi is unhealthy. Clear, faceted crystals increase and lift chi and have a remarkable capacity to activate energy. One small sphere hanging in a window can have a dramatic effect on a room, especially when it catches the sunlight, and it can add a powerful charge to a particular part of the pa kau (the energy flow of your space). Hang the crystal towards the top of the window in the centre of the pane of glass, suspended from the wooden frame above by a neat pin or nail. Position it about one or two inches away from the glass. Use either a silver thread or invisible twine, or I personally recommend using a red ribbon to enhance this feng shui cure. Whatever you choose to do, make sure it is neat and not a makeshift or botched job. If you have lace curtains in the window, hang the crystal on the inside of the curtain, facing into the room.

Jade - East - Family and Health - Jade has been held in high regard by the Chinese for centuries, being considered more precious than gold or diamonds. It is said to bestow the owner with long life, health, wealth, worldly wisdom, generosity and a peaceful death. It is also said to protect travellers from harm and bring success in matters related to the law. A jade item is best placed in the east of the home (the health area). It may also be worn as jewellery or carried as a potent talisman.

Crystal Ball - North - Career Prospects - A clear glass or good quality crystal ball placed in the career area of your home, the north, will help you with your intuition and making the right career decisions. This 'cure' is also good for improving a boring job or life. The career area is also called the journey, because it relates to everything that you have learnt or experienced so far in life. The north area is also represented by water and gazing into a crystal ball is very reminiscent of gazing into a clear pool of water: you very quickly find yourself totally absorbed in the process of viewing other worlds and realities. Very often when we become 'stuck' or 'stagnant' in our lives, whether in a job or life situation that no longer nurtures us, we need to explore other ways of being and viewing the world.

Citrine - South-East - Wealth and Prosperity - The south-east area of your home is the wealth and prosperity sector. Here it is advisable to place a very large citrine crystal or a large faceted citrine crystal. You should also place a citrine stone on a cash box or till and carry a piece of citrine in your purse or wallet for financial good fortune. The pale variety of citrine can also be worn or carried for spiritual abundance and wisdom. Citrine has long been known as the merchant's stone because of its ability to bring wealth and prosperity to its owner.

Rose Quartz - South-West Marriage and Romantic Happiness - The south-west corner of your home represents marriage and romantic happiness: if you place a large rose quartz crystal in this area everyone in your home will benefit from harmonious relationships. If you place a rose quartz crystal or, even better, a shaped rose quartz heart tied with a red ribbon in the south-west corner of your bedroom you will have a happy relationship with your partner or, if you are single, attract romantic true love. Rose quartz has always been known as the love stone and by wearing a rose quartz pendant you will also attract love and harmonious relationships into your life.

Quartz Pyramid - South - Recognition and Fame - Recognition and fame in the south of your home can be activated by a beautiful clear quartz pyramid. Recognition and fame can also have implications for your promotional prospects, including enlightenment, and how people see you in the community. By placing your quartz pyramid in this area you will be able to progress rapidly up the career ladder, enjoy a good reputation and be well liked.

Carnelian -North-East - Education - Education and knowledge is in the north-east sector of your home: this also relates to studying and learning. Here it is wise to place a bowl of nine tumbled carnelian crystals. Gathering colors like yellow and orange work well in this area. They help us approach situations with an open mind and examine new 'things' before we draw conclusions. When studying it is wise to hold a citrine or carnelian crystal in your hand or place it on the north-east sector of your desk.

Morganite - West - Children - You will find the children area of your home in the west. This area relates to our children's success and failures, their health and energy and whether or not we will have any children. It also influences our pets and our hobbies. For this area morganite crystal is recommended, due to two influences: firstly, the peachy pink color is very nurturing and warming, acting as a stabilising influence on the emotions; secondly, morganite contains the energy of Quan Yin, who is the Goddess of mercy and compassion and also the protector of children. She protects the home and the household from misfortune and ill-health and brings the blessing of children.

Turquoise - North-West - Mentors - Mentors and networking or helpful people, as they are sometimes known, are found in the north- west area of your home. If this area is out of balance you may find yourself too attached to things and find it difficult to forgive and forget easily. You may be quarrelsome and find yourself alone and unsupported. The energy of turquoise crystal will quickly balance the area, bringing healing to any situation, as well as the feelings of universal support. It is very difficult to remain angry with this wonderful crystal to help you. Just looking at a beautiful piece of turquoise will lift your spirits and remind you of beautiful blue skies. In Buddhist visualisations the meditation begins, as do nearly all visualisations, with the appearance of blue sky; the blue sky symbolizes *shunyata*, the true nature of everything, of which all forms are just temporary expressions. Placing your piece of turquoise in a metal bowl will enhance this 'cure' even more, as the north-west area of your home is represented by the metal element.

Left to Right - Energy enters through the left side of your body and exits through the right, so if you want to hold or carry a crystal for its healing properties be sure to place it on the left side for a very simple feng shui 'cure.'

Observing Chi - One way to observe the flow of chi in a room is to light incense or a sage stick to follow the direction of energy the incense takes. If you decide to smudge a room with sage to clear negative energies, don't forget to leave windows open to allow the negative energy a place to leave by.

Part Seven

The A to Z of Crystals

Actinolite - Prase - Nephrite

Chemical Composition: $Ca_2(Mg,Fe)_5Si_8O_{22}(OH)_2$

Crystal System: Monoclinic **Hardness:** 5 - 6

Habit: Usually in long blade or prismatic crystals; sometimes massive, fibrous

Color: Green (White or grey is called tremolite)

Keywords: Sacred Shield

Fibres of actinolite in clear quartz produce the most amazing green rutile quartz. When the fibres are very dense the quartz often appears completely green: this is very often called prase. Prase or 'prasius' has long been used for healing the eyes, bruises and high temperatures. White to grey varieties are called tremolite. Tremis is a characteristic mineral of thermally metamorphosed siliceous dolomite limestones and it occurs in some serpentines. Nephrite, a variety of jade, is usually an actinolite or tremolitic amphibole.

This energy has been successfully used for shielding the entire auric field and is very important in stopping the intrusion of low level energy entering the user's auric shell. When you view a piece of actinolite it is easy to see how this process works; the needles usually go in all directions, scattering throughout the user's aura. This gives an electric-like charge, dispersing and confusing the lower vibration from penetrating the field of energy.

Actinolite is perfect for activating the heart chakra, bringing healing, strength and a sense of 'space' back to the user. It is helpful for understanding what emotions are yours and what emotions are not yours. It also gives you the courage and wisdom to follow your own heart path, bringing stability back to the emotional body. Actinolite works directly on the thymus, but its active therapeutic properties encompass the physical heart as release from the pain of angina. The shoulders and chest, also the lower lungs, have been helped by the piercing electric energy of this crystal.

Actinolite helps dispel negative emotions. A gem aura spray of actinolite used during stormy periods in a relationship will calm and cool the emotions. Actinolite gives direction - so it can be used when you are trying to make up your mind or heart. It brings back focus into your life. It has also been used to heal the kidneys and for eliminating the accumulation of toxins from the physical body, especially those stored in the large intestine.

Actinolite will help you to maintain a balanced heart chakra, the sign that your heart chakra is balanced or you are compassionate, you love unconditionally, your relationships nurture you and others are nurtured by knowing you. If you have a heart chakra that is too open you will find you are possessive, you love others but you have conditions attached to your love and you may punish those you profess to love; on the other hand, if your heart chakra is closed or distorted, you will fear rejection or feel unworthy to receive love.

Affirmation: My sacred shield is an open and balanced heart chakra. I now allow myself to love unconditionally.

Illustrations

Axes of crystal systems with examples of crystal formations of each group

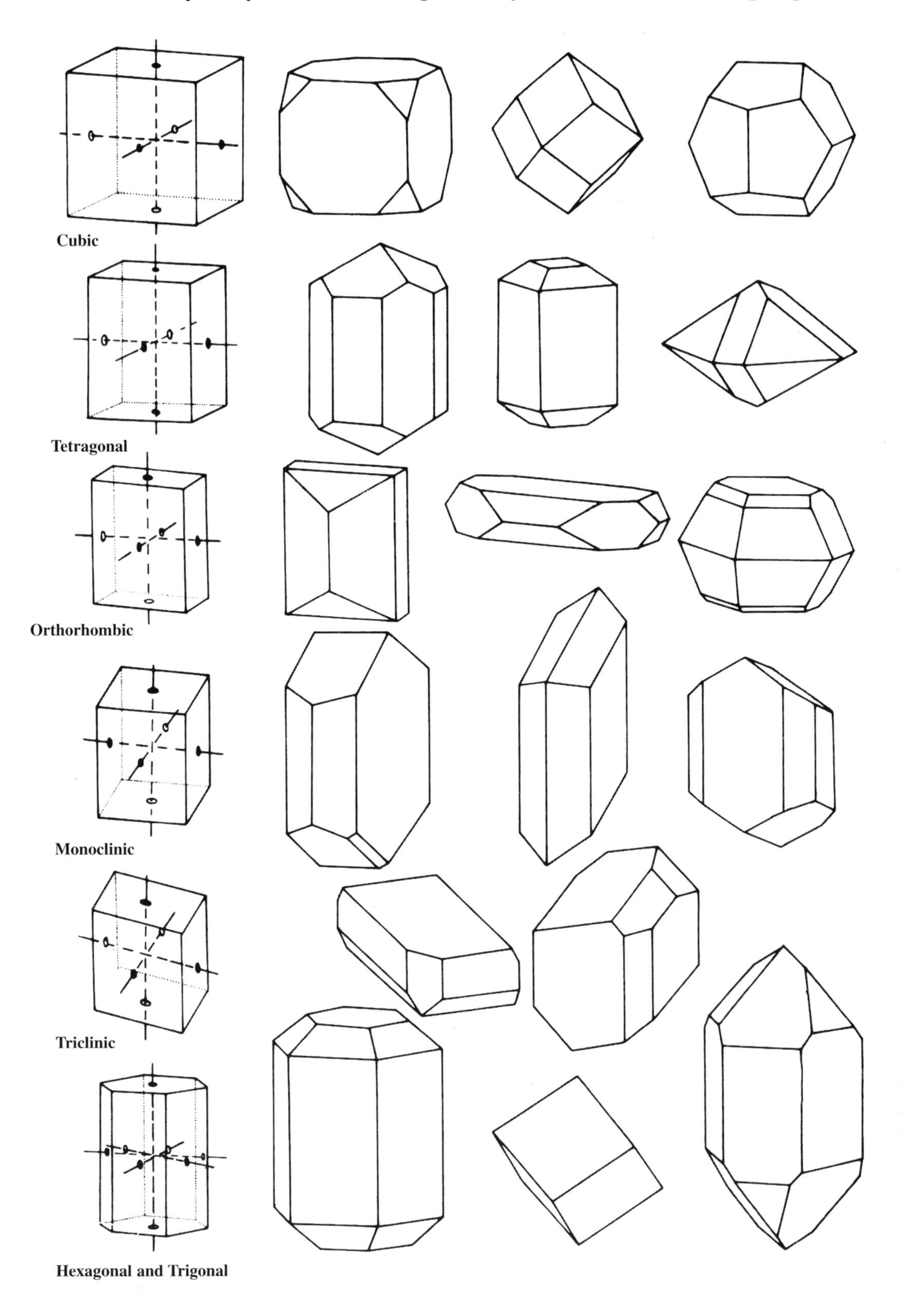

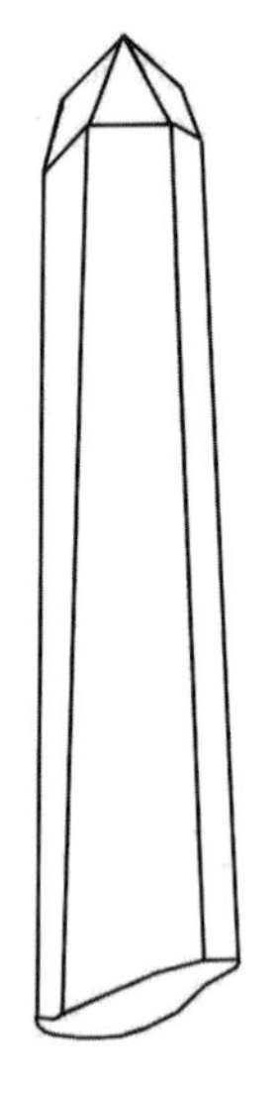

Attunement Crystal

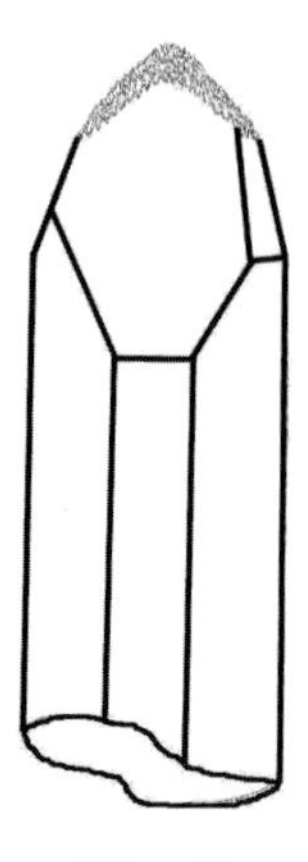

Cathedral Crystal

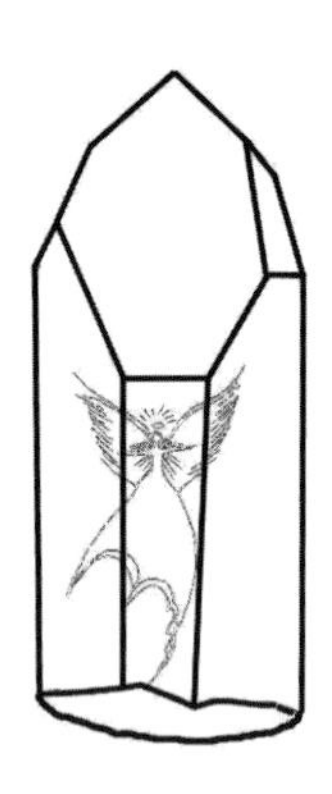

Celestial Writer Crystal

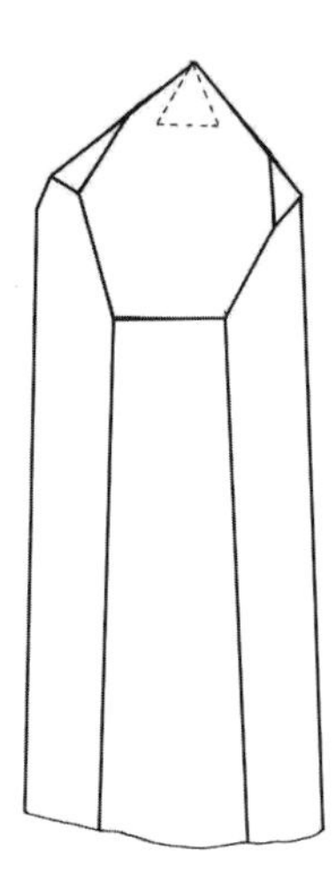

Channelling Crystal

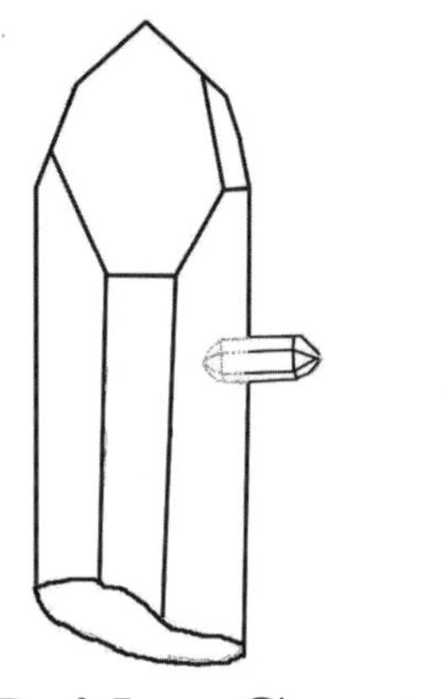

Bridge Crystal

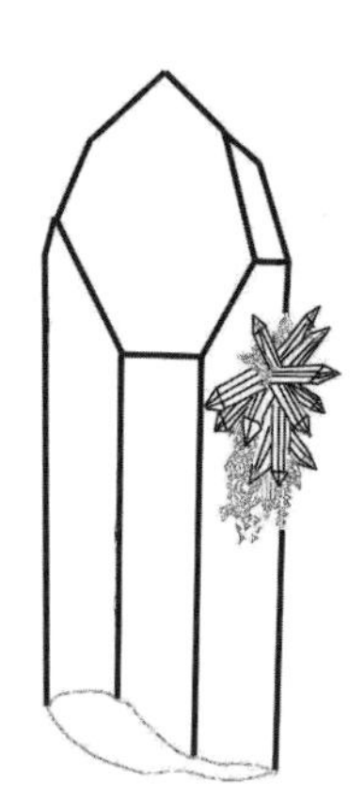

Barnacle Crystal

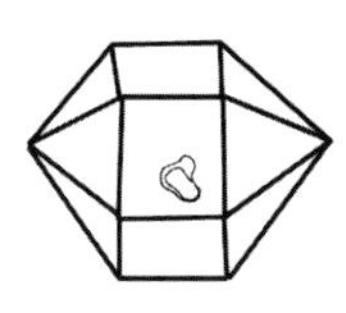

Herkimer Diamond

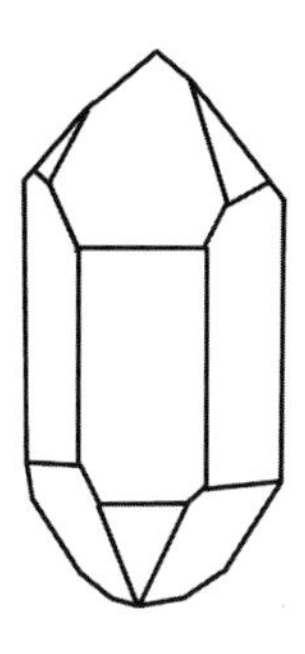

Double Terminated Crystal

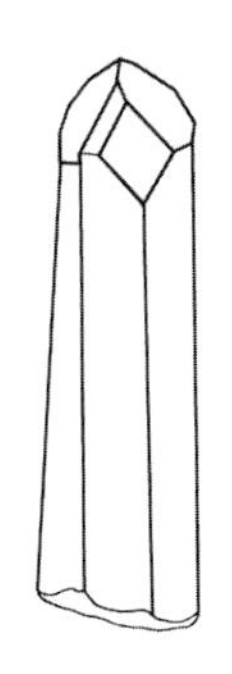

Diamond Crystal

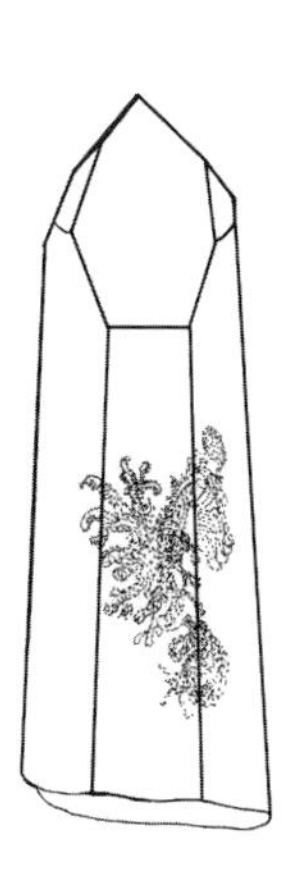

Dendritic Crystal

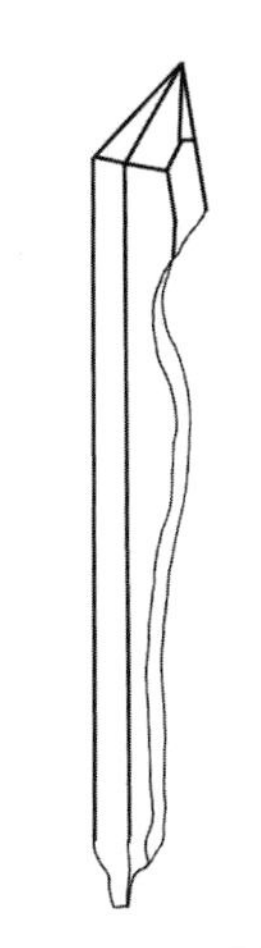

Curves on Crystals

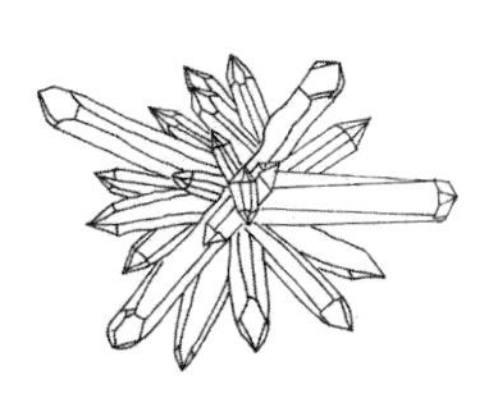

Starburst Crystal

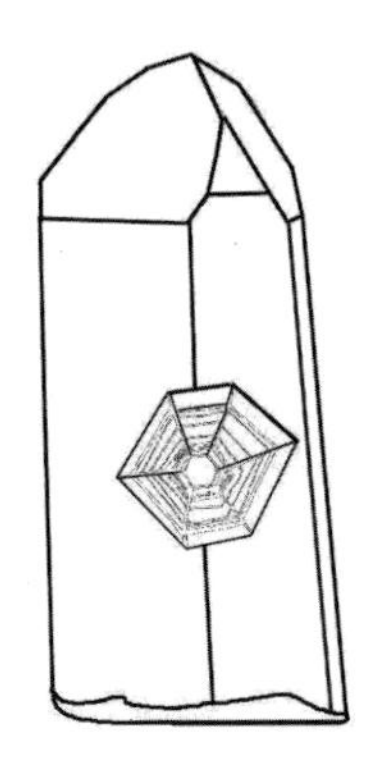

Key Release Crystal

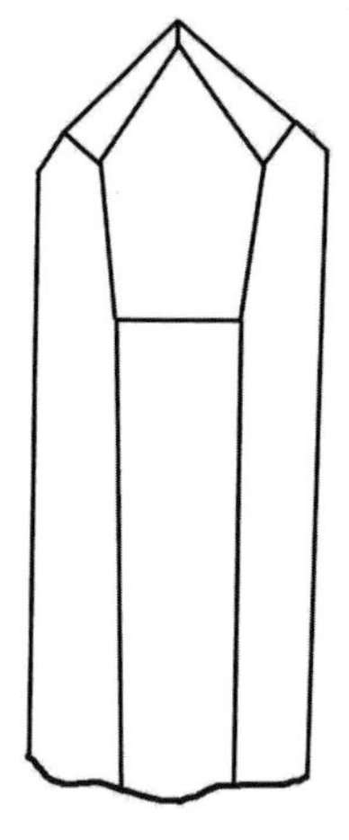

Goddess Crystal

Generator Crystal

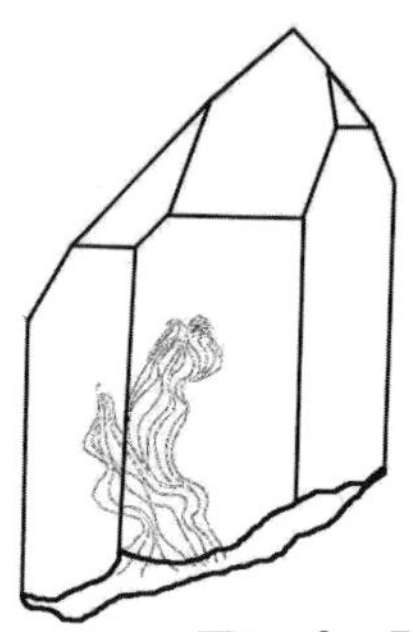

Rainbow Crystal
Fire Crystal

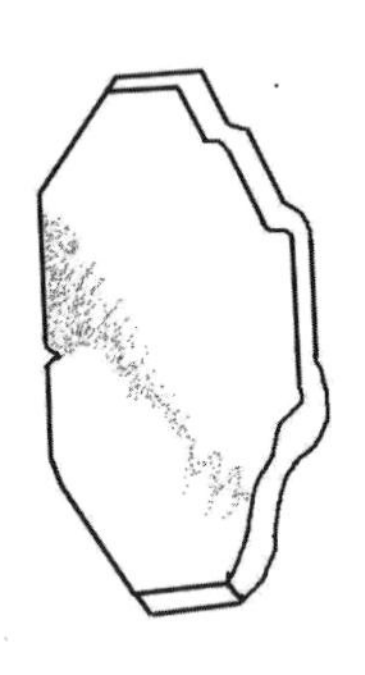

Faden Quartz

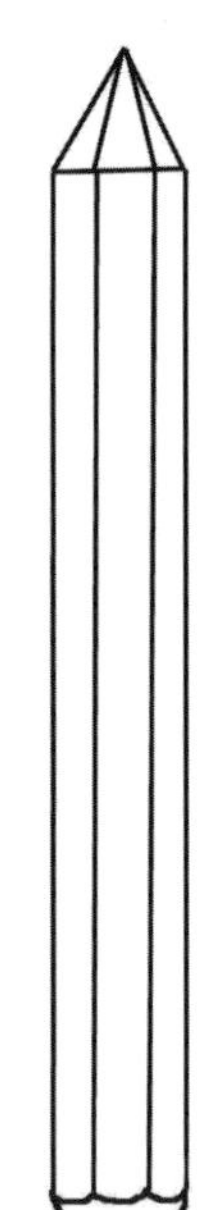

Fashioned Stones
Cut Clear Quartz Wand

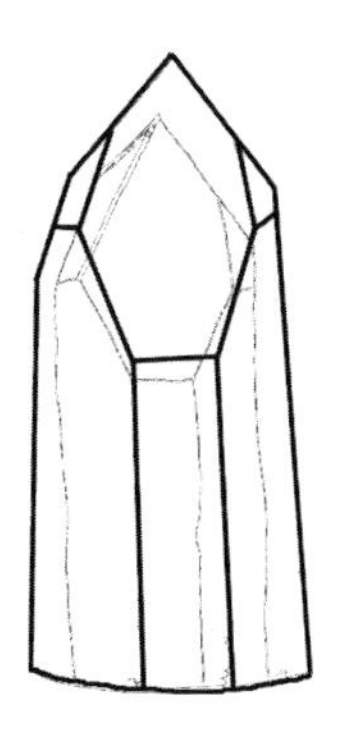

Phantom Crystal

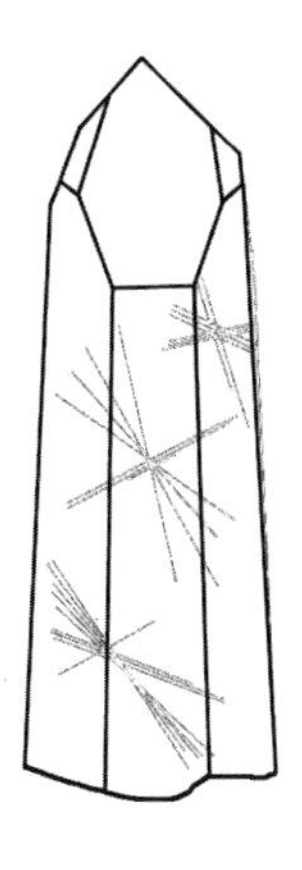

Rutile Crystal

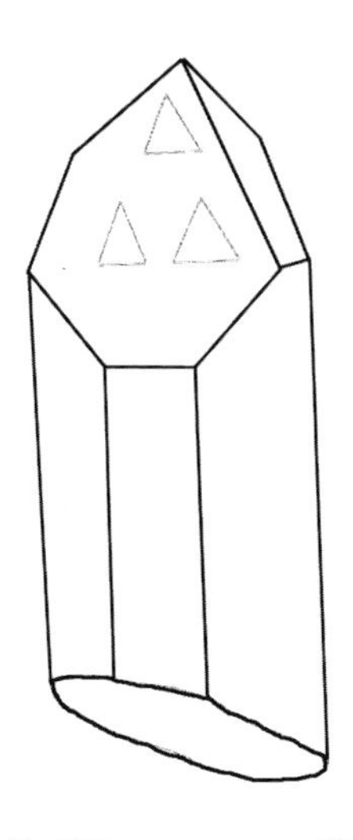

Record Keeper Crystal

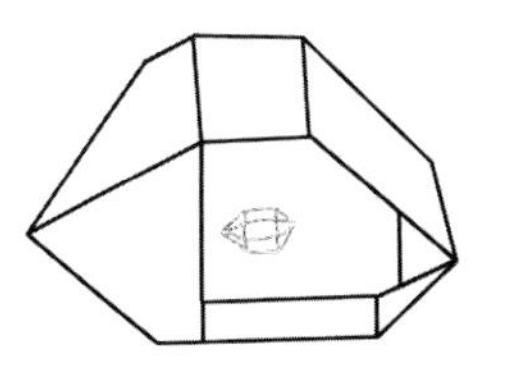

Manifesting Crystal

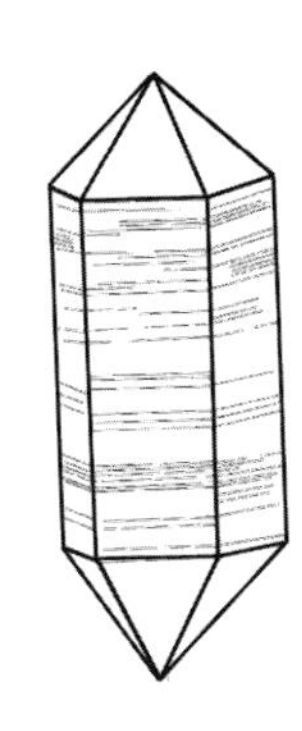

Lines on a Crystal
(striations)

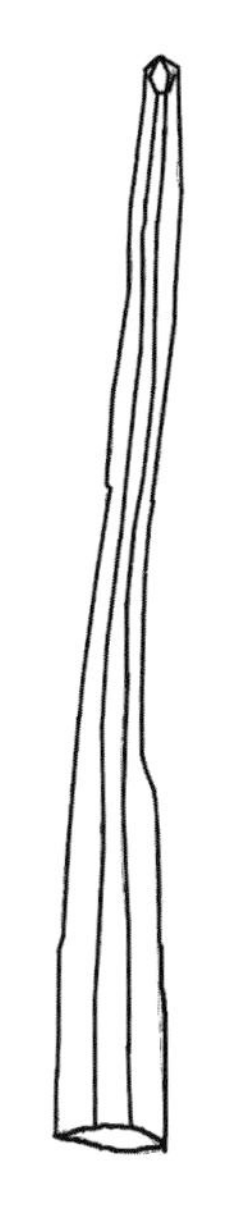

Laser Wand

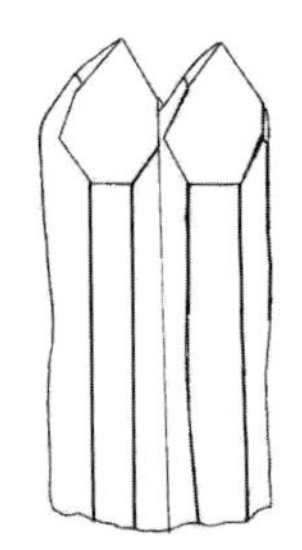

Tantric Twin

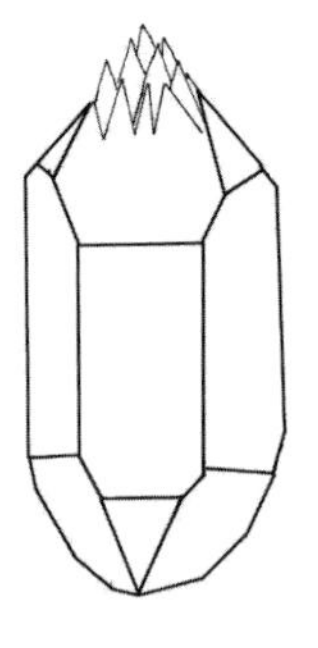

Self-Healed Crystal

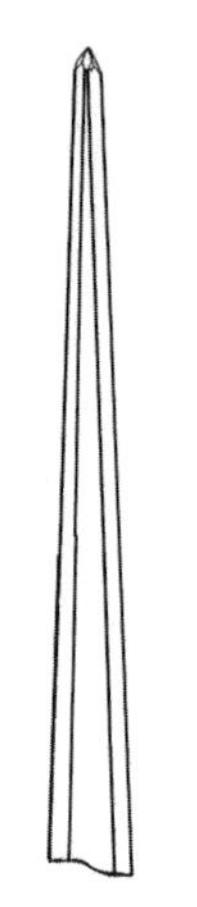

Singing and Toning Crystal

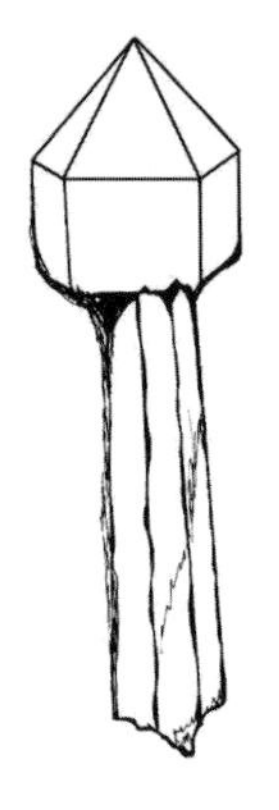

Sceptre Quartz

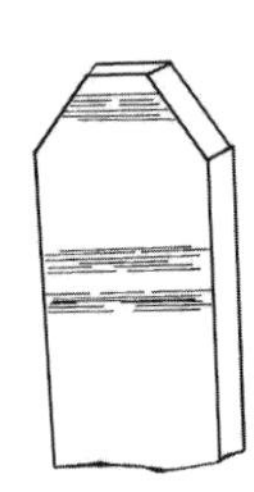

Transcendental Crystal

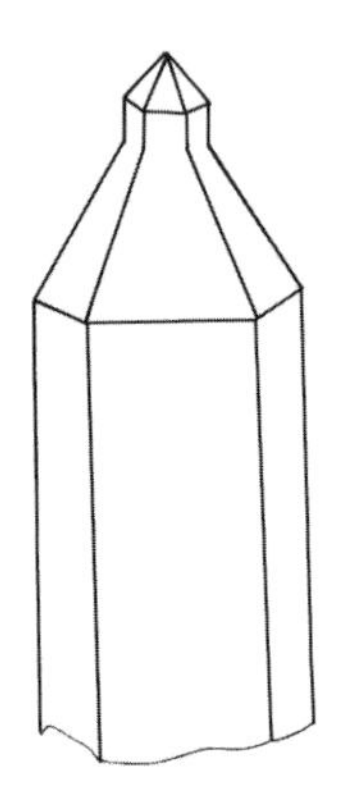

Reversed Sceptre

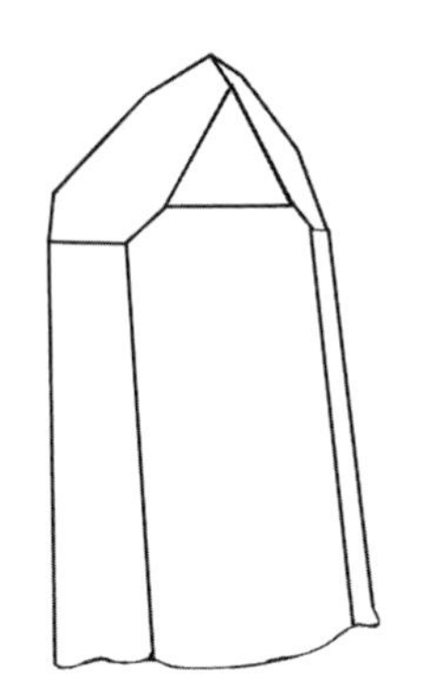

Trans - Channelling Crystal

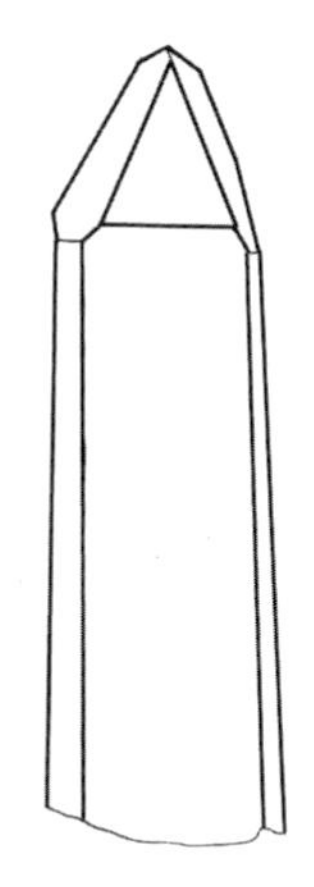

Transmitter Crystal

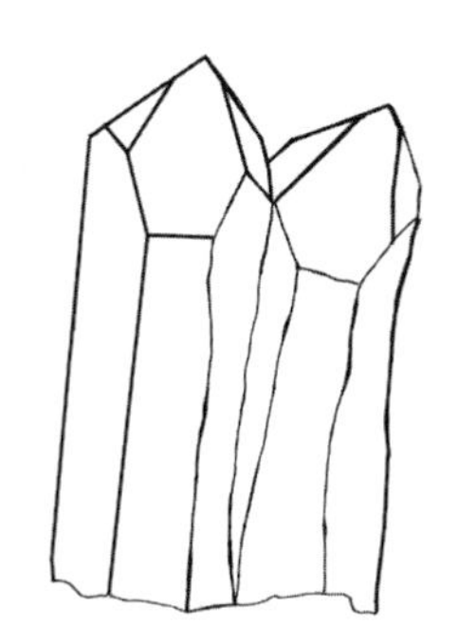

Twin Crystal

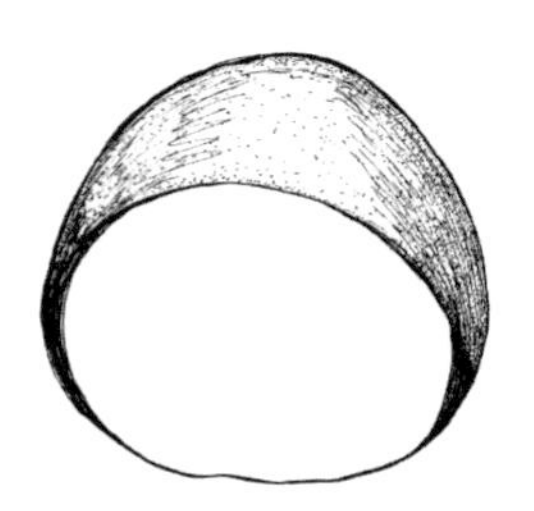

Seer Stone (Dragon's Egg)

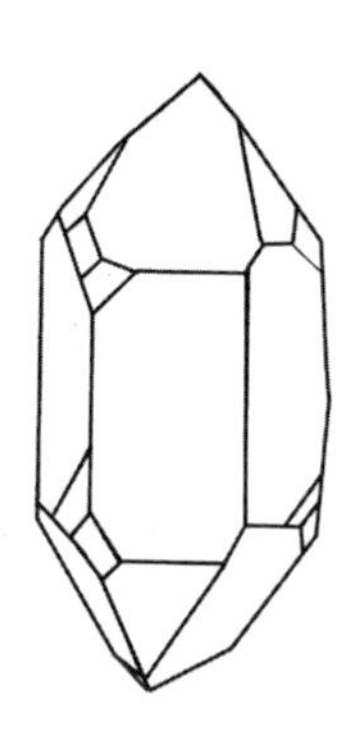

Left Hand Quartz (Time - Link)

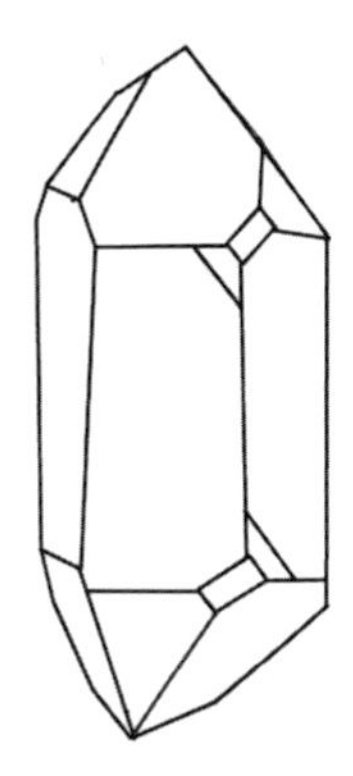

Right Hand Quartz (Time - Link)

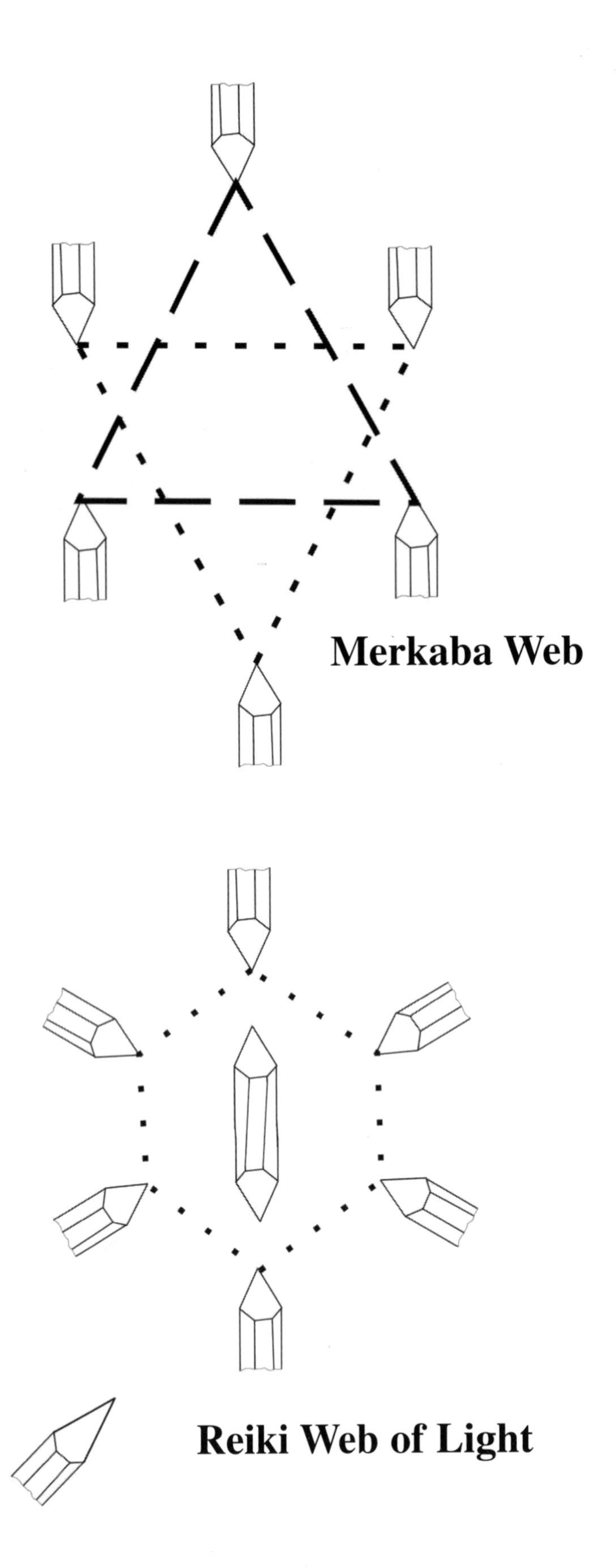
Merkaba Web
Reiki Web of Light

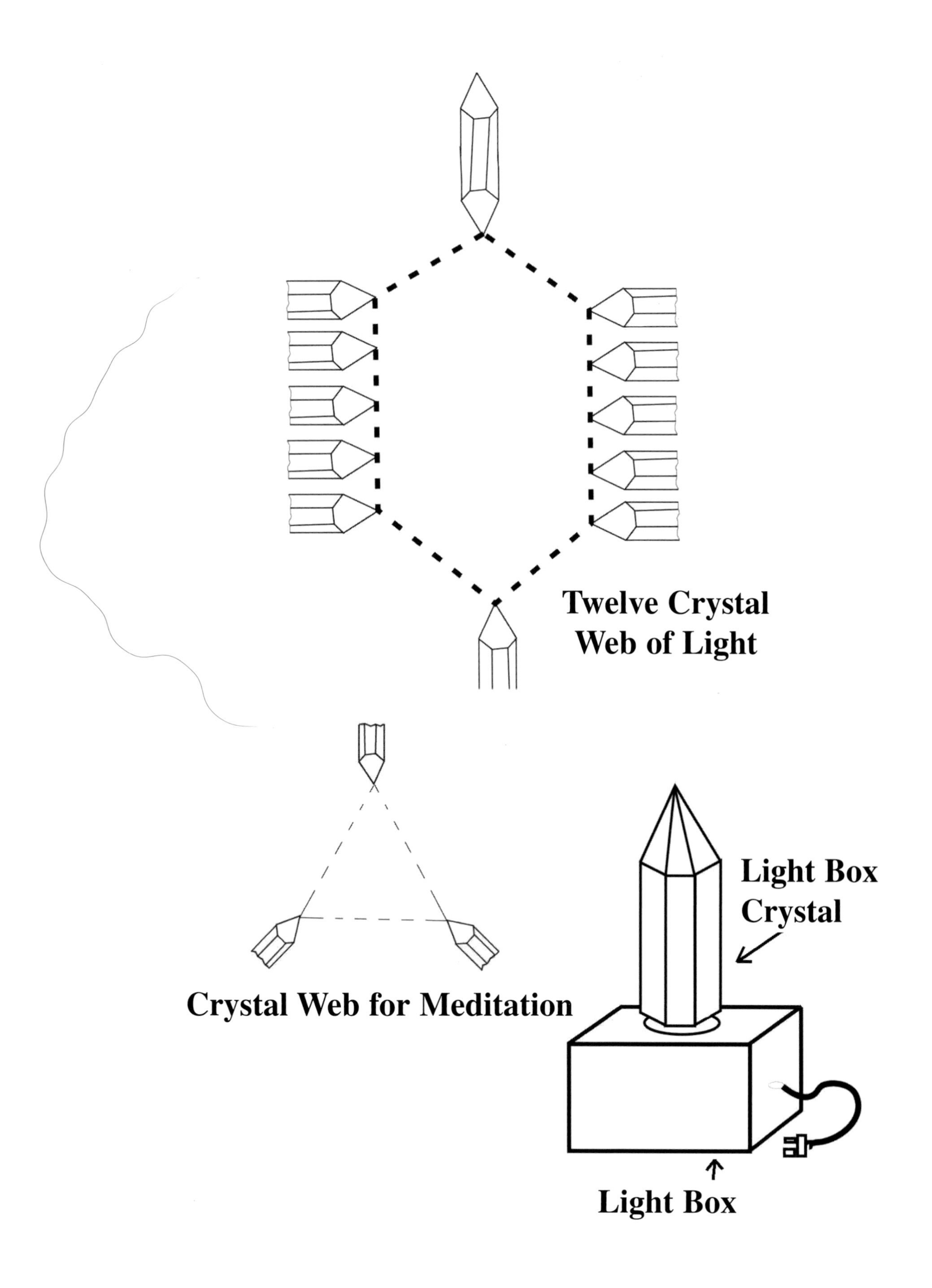
Twelve Crystal
Web of Light
Crystal Web for Meditation
Light Box
Crystal
Light Box

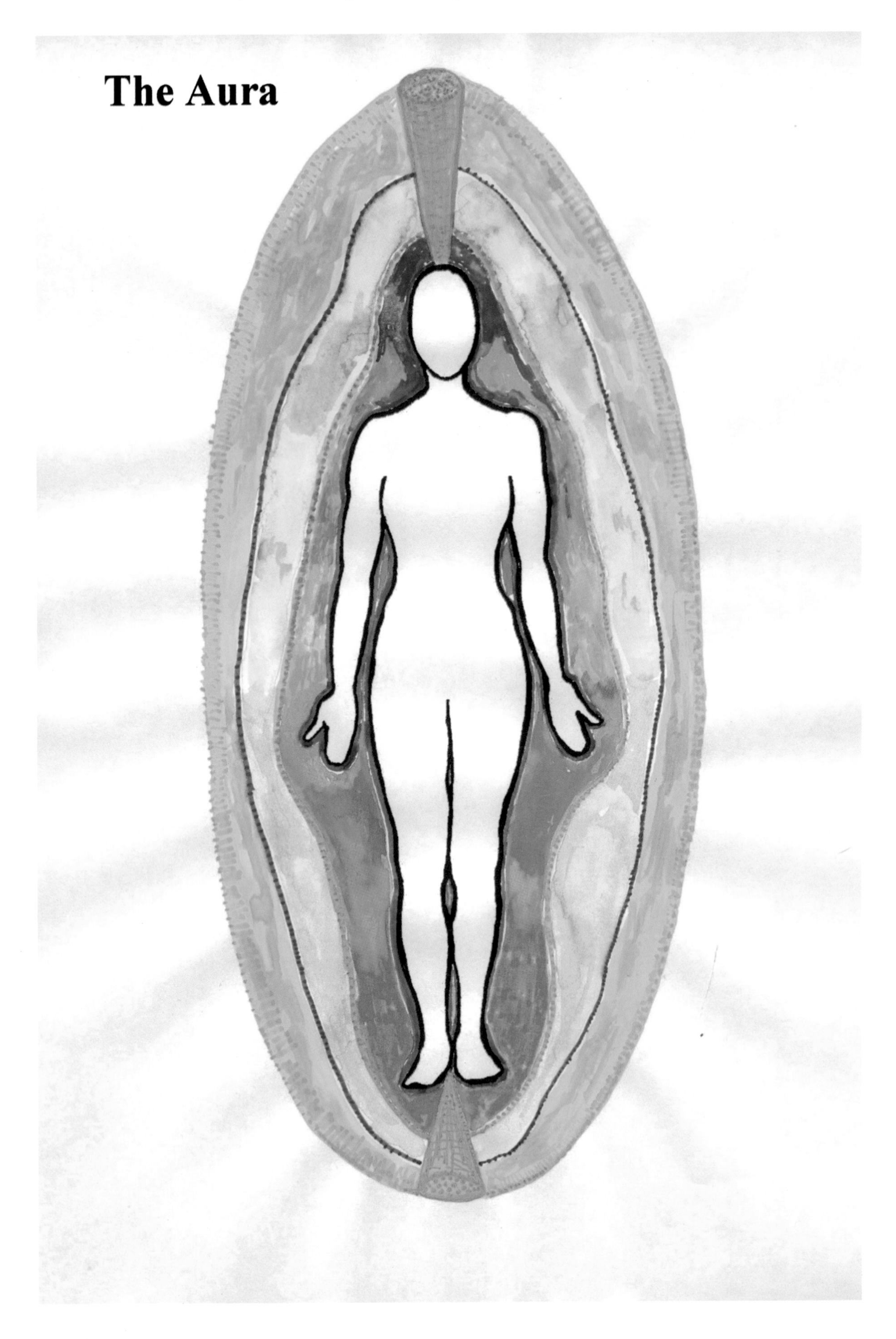
The Aura

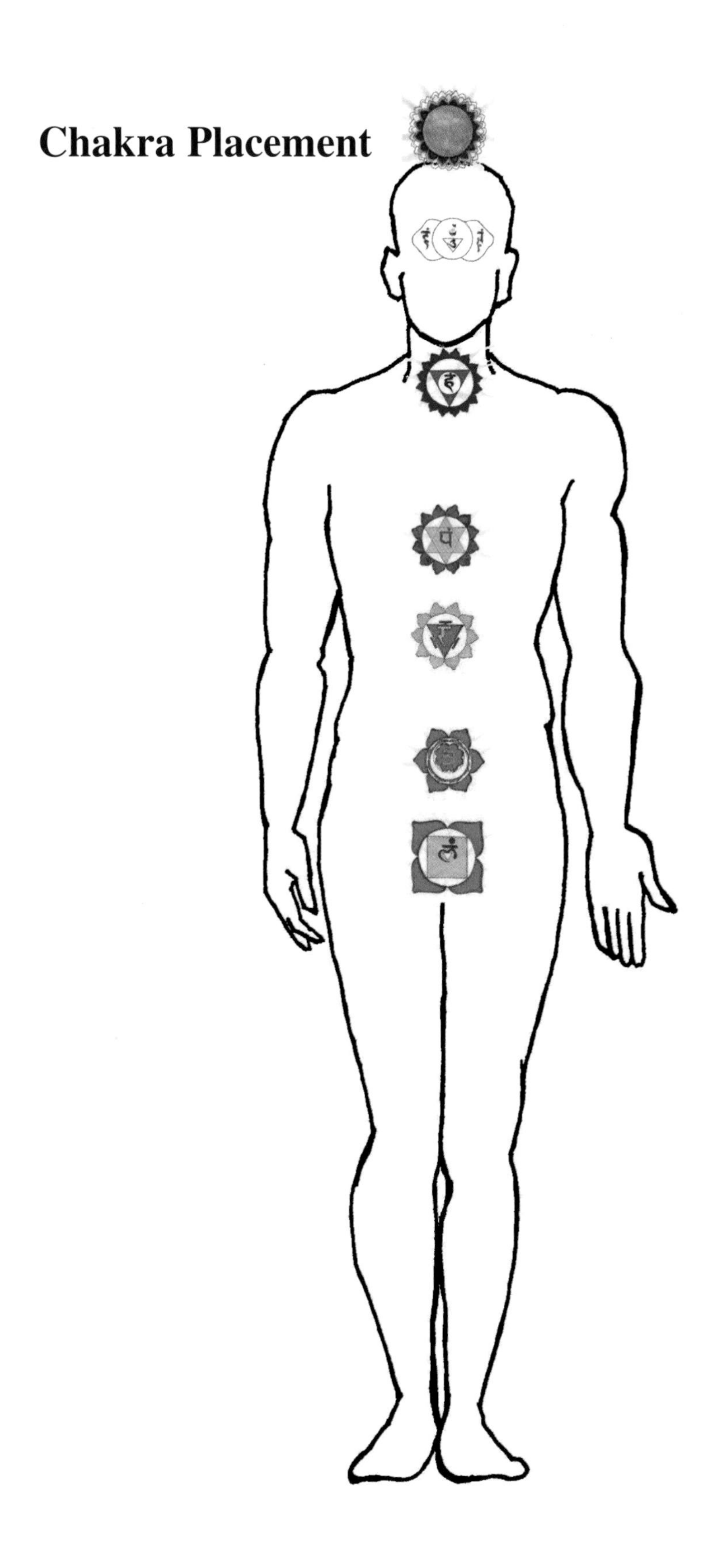
Chakra Placement

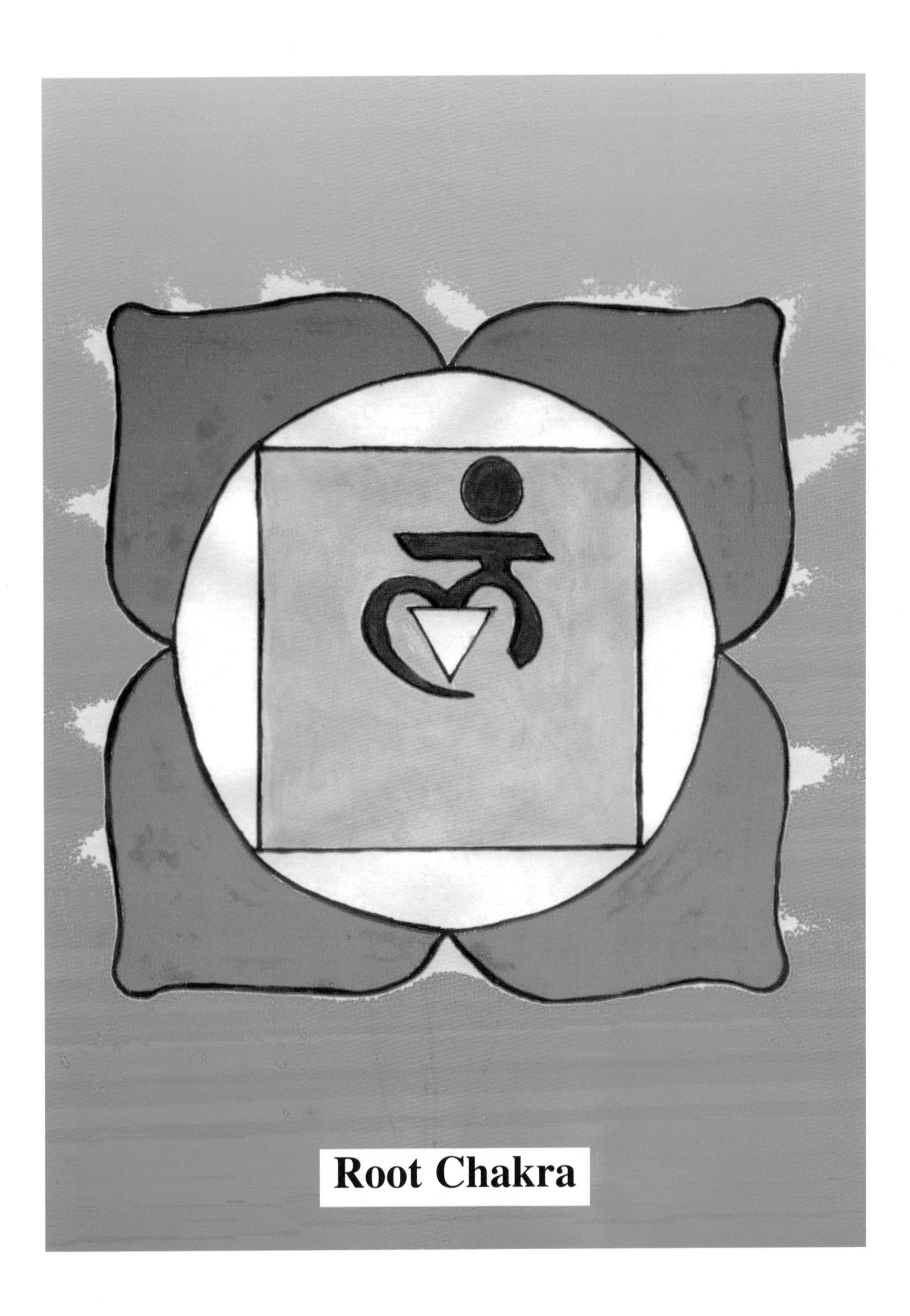
Root Chakra

Sacral Chakra

Solar Plexus Chakra

Heart Chakra

Throat Chakra

Third Eye Chakra

Crown Chakra

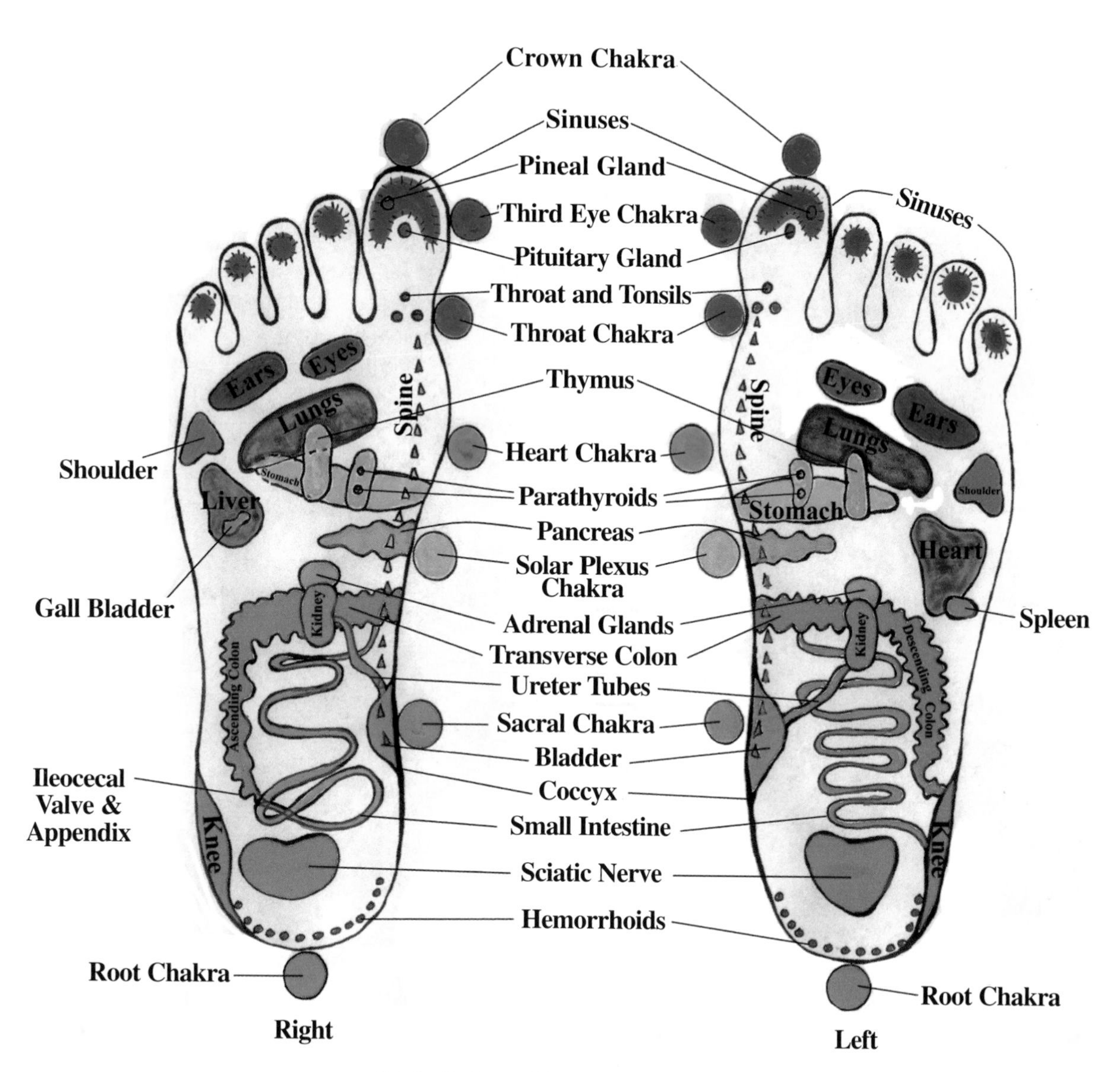

Main Points of Foot Crystal Reflexology

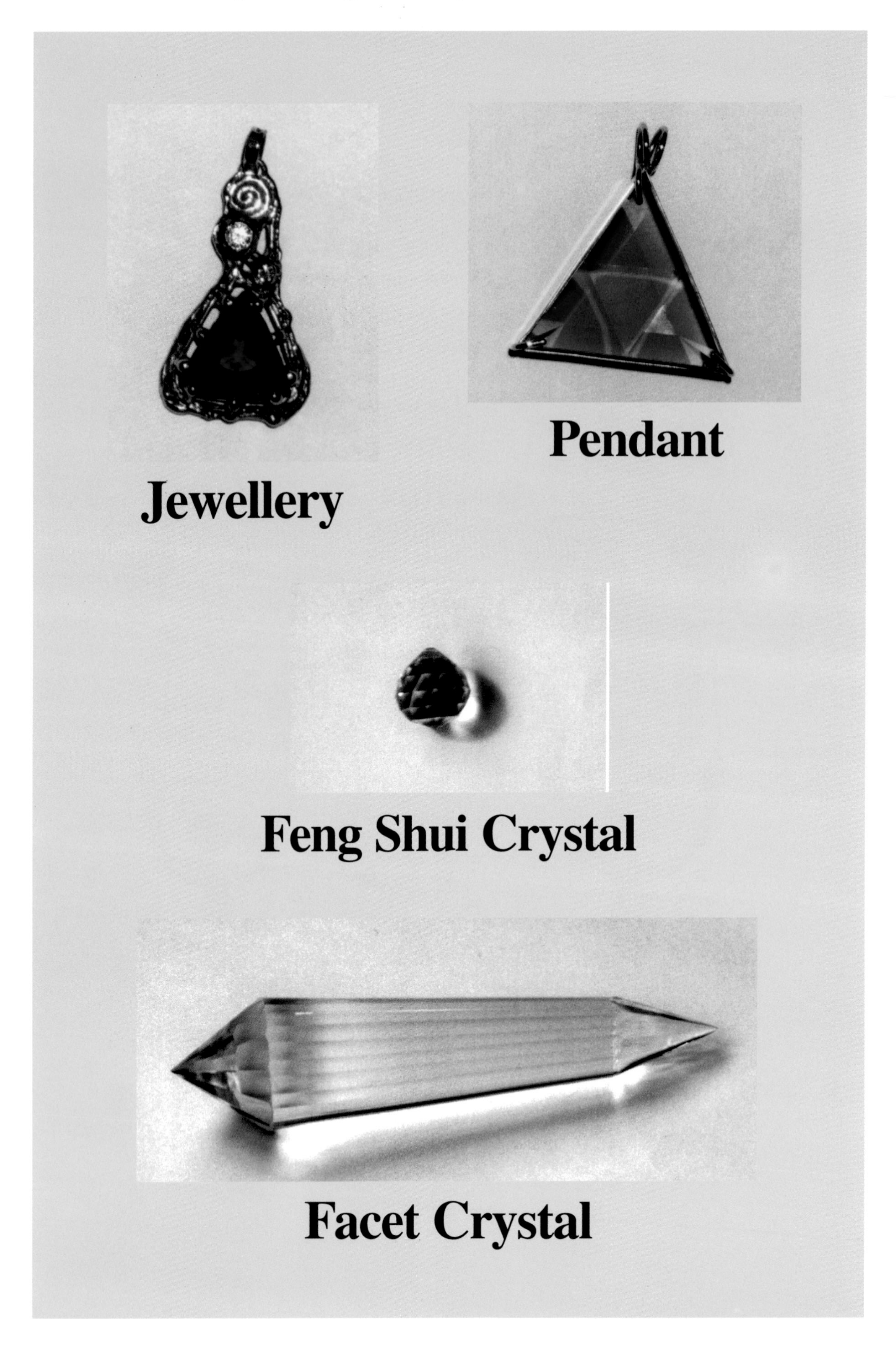
Jewellery
Pendant
Feng Shui Crystal
Facet Crystal

Elestial Quartz

Healing Wand

1. Clockwise from the top:

Actinolite (natural crystal formation)
Boji stones (natural crystal formation)
Agate, Botswana (tumbled)
Hematite (tumbled)
Obsidian, snowflake (tumbled)
Tourmaline, black (natural wand formation)
Quartz, smoky (natural double-terminated crystal)
Tourmaline, black (tumbled)
Agate, black (tumbled)
Moqui marbles/shaman stones (natural crystal formation)
Agate, crazy lace (cabochon)

2. Clockwise from the top:

Calcite, red (rough)
Pietersite (tumbled)
Zircon, red (natural crystal formation)
Tiger eye, red (tumbled)
Chiastolite (tumbled)
Quartz, ruby/green aura (natural single-terminated crystal)
Bloodstone (tumbled)
Garnet, red (tumbled)
Garnet, almandine (natural crystal formation)
Quartz, ruby aura (natural single-terminated crystal)
Ruby (cabochon)

3. Clockwise from the top:

Aragonite (natural crystal formation)
Jasper, red (cut)
Amber (cabochon)
Rhodocrosite (natural crystal formation)
Opal, fire (cabochon)
Sunstone, orange (cabochon)
Garnet, hessonite (tumbled)
Agate, fire (cabochon)
Carnelian (tumbled)
Zincite (natural wand)

4. Clockwise from the top:

Calcite, golden stellar beam (natural crystal formation)
Quartz, sunshine aura (natural single-terminated crystal)
Apatite, yellow (natural crystal formation)
Amblygonite (rough)
Quartz, citrine (natural/untreated cut crystal shape)
Jasper, yellow (tumbled)
Calcite, amber (tumbled)
Tiger eye, yellow (tumbled)
Sunstone, yellow (natural crystal formation)
Labradorite, golden (tumbled)
Topaz, yellow (natural crystal wand)
Pyrite (tumbled)
Quartz, citrine (cut double-terminated wand)
Quartz, citrine (faceted)

5. Clockwise from the top:

Moldavite (natural tektite formation)
Quartz, clear/chlorite phantom (cut crystal shape)
Malachite (tumbled)
Aventurine, green (tumbled)
Prehnite (tumbled)
Peridot (natural crystal formation)
Peridot (faceted)
Hiddenite (natural crystal formation)
Jasper, green (tumbled)
Epidote (tumbled)
Quartz, aqua aura/green aura (natural single-terminated crystal)
Quartz, green (cut double-terminated wand)
Calcite, green (rough)
Emerald (natural)
Dioptase (natural crystal formation)
Tourmaline, green (natural wand)
Agate, green moss (tumbled)
Chrysoprase (cut fancy shape)
Prehnite (natural crystal formation)

6. Clockwise from the top:

Quartz, rose aura (natural)
Tourmaline, pink/violet (natural wand formation)
Rhodocrosite (tumbled)
Morganite (rough)
Kunzite (natural crystal formation)
Smithsonite, pink (natural crystal formation)
Quartz, rose (rough)
Quartz, rose (cut double-terminated wand)
Quartz, rose (natural crystal formation)
Opal, fire/pink (cabochon)
Tourmaline, watermelon (slice)
Tourmaline, pink (natural crystal formation)
Calcite, pink (tumbled)

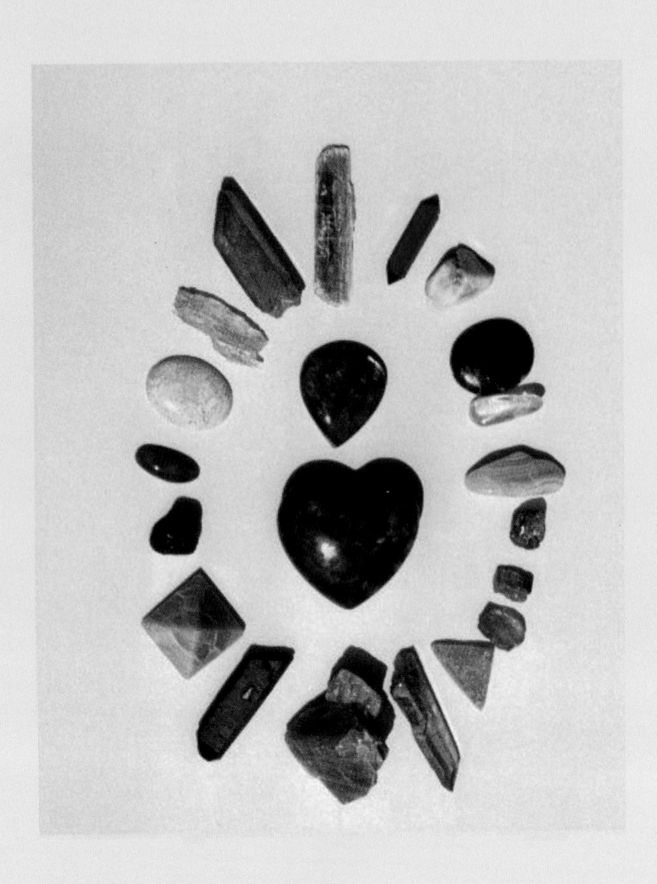

7. Clockwise from the top:

Kyanite (natural blade)
Quartz, Siberian blue (cut double-terminated wand)
Larimar (tumbled)
Lapis lazuli (cabochon)
Topaz, blue (tumbled)
Agate, blue lace (tumbled)
Azurite (natural crystal formation)
Tourmaline, blue (natural)
Apatite, blue (natural)
Chrysocolla, druzy (cut triangle shape)
Quartz, aqua aura (natural single-terminated crystal)
Calcite, blue (rough)
Quartz, rainbow aura (natural single-terminated crystal)
Angelite (cut pyramid shape)
Sapphire, blue (river-washed pebble)
Chrysocolla (cabochon)
Turquoise (cabochon)
Aquamarine (natural crystal formation)
Quartz, aqua aura (natural single-terminated crystal)
Labradorite (cut petal shape)
Chrysocolla (heart shape)

8. Clockwise from the top:

Quartz, amethyst (natural crystal formation)
Quartz, ametrine (tumbled)
Tanzanite (natural crystal formation)
Iolite (natural crystal formation)
Opal, blue/violet (cut fancy shape)
Lepidolite (slice)
Quartz, rainbow aura (natural single-terminated crystal)
Sugilite (cut shape)
Fluorite, purple (natural crystal formation)
Quartz, amethyst (Vera Cruz natural crystal)
Charoite (cut shape)
Quartz, amethyst (faceted)

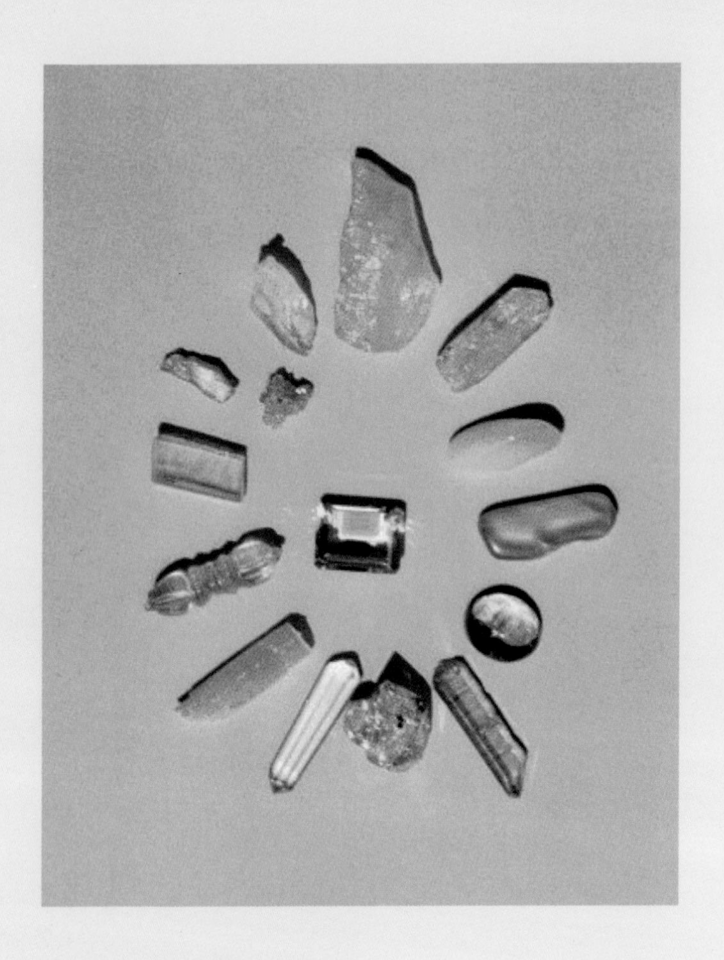

9. Clockwise from the top:

Calcite, white (rough)
Danburite (natural crystal formation)
Quartz, milky/snow (tumbled)
Moonstone (tumbled)
Quartz, rutile (cabochon)
Quartz, opal aura (natural single-terminated crystal)
Quartz, Herkimer diamond (natural double-terminated crystal)
Quartz, clear (cut double-terminated wand)
Selenite (natural wand)
Quartz, clear (carved into a vajra)
Calcite, clear (natural crystal formation)
Azeztulite (rough)
Phenacite (natural crystal formation)
Petalite (rough)
Quartz, clear (faceted)

Agate - Chalcedony

Chemical Composition: SiO_2+

Crystal System: Trigonal **Hardness:** 6.5

Habit: Agate usually forms concentric or irregular layers lining a cavity. Chalcedony is often mamillated, botryoidal or stalactitic. It often lines cavities in rocks

Color: Agate is normally banded, white, milky white or grey, also shades of green, brown, red, blue or black. Commercial agate is often colored artificially. Onyx is a form of agate

Chalcedony is uniform in color: carnelian is red to brownish red; chrysoprase is apple green and heliotrope, also called bloodstone, is green with red spots. Jasper is opaque chalcedony and is generally red, but yellow, brown, green and grey-blue varieties occur. Flint and chert are opaque chalcedony, usually dull grey to black in color. Avalonite is blue druzy chalcedony

Keyword: Strengthening

The names given to the different types of agate are legion and many have local significance only. Agate nodules are of worldwide occurrence. Each type has its own function and therapeutic purpose. Agate was collected in the desert regions around Jebel Abu Diyeiba in Egypt over 3,000 years ago. From ancient times India has supplied agate and the material was also found along the Achates river in Sicily, a river now known as the Drillo. Many types of colorful agates are found in the United States of America. Botswana agate is the most commonly available. Agate occurs typically as a cavity filling in lavas. The layering often follows the form of the cavity and gives place inwards to crystals of quartz. Persian wizards are reputed to have invoked the power of agate to divert storms. A famous collection of thousands of agate bowls, which was accumulated by Mithradates, king of Pontus, shows how highly agate was regarded. Agate bowls were also fashionable in the Byzantine Empire. Collecting agate bowls became a common pastime among European royalty during the Renaissance and many museums in Europe, including the Louvre, have spectacular examples. The mining of agate in the Nahe River valley in Germany, which was already documented in 1497, gave rise to the cutting centre of Idar-Oberstein, Germany. Originally, the river was used to power the grinding wheels. When the Nahe agate deposit was exhausted in the nineteenth century, Idar cutters started to develop the agate deposits of Brazil, which was the catalyst for the exploration and discovery of Brazil's rich deposits of tourmaline, topaz, amethyst, citrine and numerous other fabulous gemstones. It is said to be one of the stones used in the breast-plate of the high priest. Agate amulets were used in Tibet and Nepal.

Agate is used for general strengthening, grounding, stabilizing and centering of physical energies. It can be used for universal healing, bringing vitality, balance and inner harmony. It is slow to work, but agate is especially good for animals, plants and children. In historic times, agate was used in drinking water to heal the body; it also eliminates thirst. If you are using them 'magically' they should have appropriate or special natural 'markings' on them appertaining to and pertinent to their use.

The chalcedony enhydros, or water agates, have a unique significance; they are masses which consist of a shell of cloudy-white chalcedony within which is sealed a quantity of water. This can often be heard splashing about when the pebble is shaken. Sometimes the water is visible. These enhydros are mostly found in Brazil. They are very useful for healing emotional trauma; this is facilitated by holding the enhydro in the receptive hand, or placing it over any painful area of the body until all painful sensation has stopped. Enhydros can be used to heal all fluid functions of the body. They work quickly and have been successfully used in the treatment of liver disorders. The cleansing effect is very beneficial on all organs of the body. Enhydros have a cleansing, supportive, watery, female energy. They equate to the primeval waters, the symbol of the collective unconscious. They have been carried as talismans by pregnant women since the dawn of civilisation.

Remarkable types of agate-filled nodules are the so-called 'Thunder Eggs' - a name given to them by the Native Americans. These nodules are found as spherical masses of silicified claystone and rhyolite with a star-shaped outline of agate. The thunder eggs have been used to facilitate inspiration from other dimensions and connect the user to the 'star nations' for guidance, insight and path-working. They aid meditation, producing deep states of relaxation that would otherwise take years of practice to attain. Thunder eggs contain the energy of the storm, facilitating a synergy of energies to bring about rapid spiritual transformation.

Fire agate consists of platy crystals of an iron mineral over layers of chalcedony. When polished, the rainbow colors of the iridescent layers appear. Fire agates contain the elemental energy of fire, seen by alchemists as the source which operates at the centre of all things, as well as the agent of transmutation, because all things are derived from and return to fire. This energy is seen as the great supernal father energy - the 'seed' force of the universe. It is an expression of spiritual energy and the determination of the spirit. Fire also purifies, burns and destroys the old so that new may emerge. Fire agates are used for spiritual fortitude. They have a fast effective energy, which may be used for vitality, or when you feel your energy is low. They stop 'burn out'. They have also been used for protection: this is facilitated by using the energy as a fire shield. Fire agates are strong, protective and masculine in nature. They relate to the sacral and solar plexus chakras. They are useful to stabilise a 'blown', deformed, wide-open chakra. Successful healing ceremonies have been carried out with fire agates, as their energy quickly burns away the blocks or negative energy in the auric shell.

Green moss agate contains inclusions of other minerals which assume tree-like (dendritic) forms. (Dendritic, is from the Greek word *dendron*, meaning 'tree'). The included 'vegetation' is chlorite. The best known location of green moss agate is the Deccan trap of India. It contains the energy of earth, is slow acting, solid, grounded, physical, stable, passive and feminine. This energy has the power of materialisation and encompasses all activities of productivity, fertility, growth and regeneration. Green moss agate is a wonderful healing stone to use in any situation where the element of earth needs to be fully manifested within the physical realm. It reconnects you back to the earth, bringing stability to all levels and in all situations. It has been used in the treatment of all fungal growths and will help support the immune system by activating the healing and balancing energies within the heart chakra. This action alone will give direct communication with the Divine through the manifestation of a flowing heart energy. Animals and plants thrive in the green moss agate's energy field. It facilitates earth-healing activities and can be used to place a Mandala on the earth for earth-healing ceremonies.

Affirmation: My body is becoming more important to me: I seek to nurture and strengthen it constantly.

Amber - Bernstein - Electron

Chemical Composition: Fossilized resin

Crystal System: Amorphous

Color: Yellow, orange or brown, but may be reddish or whitish, very occasionally blue or green

Keyword: Purification

A time-hardened resin which exuded from certain pine trees, particularly Pinus Succinifera, which flourished in Oligocene times just before the great Ice Age, that is more than 30 million years ago. Amber is in composition a complex mixture of several resins, succinic acid and a volatile oil. It is transparent to translucent and has a greasy lustre. The color range is normally yellow or brown, but may be reddish or whitish; it is often clouded and sometimes fluorescent, very occasionally blue or green.

It is reputed that Stone Age man imbued amber with supernatural properties and used it to wear and to worship with it. Amber took on great value and significance to, among others, the Egyptians, Etruscans, Greeks, Assyrians and Phoenicians.

Many legends surround the origin of amber. Ovid writes that when Phaeton, a son of Phoebus, the sun, convinced his father to allow him to drive the chariot of the sun across the sky for a day, he drove too close to the earth, setting it on fire. To save the earth, Jupiter struck Phaeton out of the sky with his thunderbolts and he died, plunging out of the sky. His mother and sister turned into trees in their grief, but still cried, mourning him. Their tears, dried by the sun, are amber. The Greeks called amber elektron, or sun-made, perhaps because of this story, or perhaps because it becomes electrically charged when rubbed with a cloth and can attract small particles. Homer mentions amber jewellery. The ancient Germans burned amber as incense, so they called it Bernstein, or "burn stone." Clear amber was used for rosary beads in the Middle Ages, due to its silken texture.

Amber works by filling gaps and holes within the auric shell. These may be caused by illness, accident, trauma, medication, stress, depression or psychic or psychological attack. Amber brings balance and stability to the whole energy system, giving immediate strength and stability to the meridian system and etheric body. It facilitates this by gently cleansing away blocks and stagnant or stuck energy. It is a connector, a bridge, polarising and harmonising past, present and future, up-down, yin-yang, etc, clearing stored negative emotions. It will clean and purify the blood. Amber has warm solar energies and provides the goddess energy at its most stable. It is good for birth and rebirthing rooms and can be used to treat the kidneys, bladder and throat. When consciously directed by a crystal therapist, amber has been known to facilitate warmth in the whole auric field; even for those clients who may have suffered for years with 'cold' hands and feet, the 'cold' syndrome has never re-occurred. Historically it was used as a penicillin-type remedy. Amber allows the body to heal itself, by absorbing and transmuting negative into positive. It is calming on the nervous system and lifts the spirits, bringing renewed hope and joy.

Affirmation: I allow my body to purify, heal and renew itself.

Amblygonite

Chemical Composition: $(Li,Na)Al(Po_4)(F,OH)$

Crystal System: Triclinic **Hardness:** 5.5 - 6

Habit: Crystals usually rough and ill-formed, sometimes large, also massive

Color: White to pale green or bluish white; sometimes yellowish or pinkish; transparent to translucent

Keyword: Inspiration

A fluophosphate of lithium and aluminum, amblygonite is a very rare mineral which occurs in granite pegmatites together with other lithium minerals. Energetically these crystals are soothing and inspiring to the mental body, giving a flowing graceful energy of calm and peace. They are very suited to those of an artistic or theatrical nature and give Divine inspiration to those of us who need to, or wish to, express ourselves via writing or poetry. Indeed they are so inspirational that you may find you are almost overwhelmed by the passionate experience, as the ideas and information flow so fast as to cause 'overload'. Using these stones for inspiration is like being tuned into the creative force of the cosmic universal mind of God/Goddess.

Amblygonite does clear the etheric body and can be used to activate any chakra, especially the higher centres above the head. It brings the consciousness of the higher self into the spiritual body and sends your intent out into the universal streams of energy. This stone will also balance your emotional body and is wonderful to work with when you wish to be heart to heart with someone you love. Its message is 'follow your heart, for that is where true joy lies'. For those who wish to acknowledge their creative manifesting gifts for the 'good of all', it will accelerate these altruistic endeavours. Amblygonite combines very well with yellow sapphire and will aid intellectual prowess beyond all former self-imposed limitations. Regardless of anything else this stone will facilitate, its most potent use will be its stress- reducing properties, which are remarkable. It eases stress and anxiety quickly and has been demonstrated to stop feelings of anger, agitation and hostility within minutes. This is a extraordinary feat; it also releases hostility and self hatred whereby those who continually self- sabotage themselves due to low self-esteem have been instantly alleviated of this trait completely. The peaceful flow of this stone is one of being completely de-stressed and inspired. This must be a unique experience for most people and it follows that it is the stone's unique gift or main purpose on the planet at this time. Amblygonite has been used for healing the physical problems of stress, anxiety, stomach disorders, spleen, liver and kidney problems. As well as dispelling fears and phobias caused by wrong mental attitudes, this stone helps you see through the self-limiting illusory world of your own mind. It has been used to view 'masks of the self'. These are often caused by childhood trauma where the 'masked self' was brought up to be seen and not heard, frequently told to 'shut up' and made to feel its opinions were unwanted and useless. The coping mechanism was to hide its 'true self'. This suppressed sad soul remains locked as a child in adult form. It chooses to remain childlike and neglects to take responsibility for its life.

Affirmation: Divine inspiration guides me; I follow my heart, for that is where true lasting joy lies.

Amethyst - *Kataila* or *Jamunia* in Hindi - Rose de France

Chemical Composition: SiO_2 +(Al,Fe,Ca,MgLi,Na)

Crystal System: Trigonal **Hardness:** 7

Habit: Crystals are usually six-sided and are terminated by six faces

Color: From nearly colorless with the faintest of mauve tinges to deep purple

Keyword: Spiritual

The violet and purple varieties of quartz provide the most prized and in many respects the most interesting of the large family of quartz minerals. Amethyst, the name by which this variety of quartz is known, is of ancient derivation. Pliny stated that the gem was so called from the color being near to, but not quite reaching, that of wine. The name is also said to have been derived from the Greek word '*amethustos*', which is translated as 'not drunken', and was assigned to the stone from the belief that the wearer would not suffer from excess consumption of alcohol.

The legend of the origin of amethyst comes from Greek myths. Dionysius, the god of intoxication, was enraged one day by an insult from an insignificant mere mortal and vowed to revenge himself on the next mortal that crossed his path, creating fierce tigers to carry out his wish. Along came unsuspecting Amethyst, a beautiful young maiden on her way to pay tribute to the goddess Diana. Diana turned Amethyst into a statue of pure crystalline quartz to protect her from the brutal claws of the tigers. Dionysius wept tears of wine in remorse for his action at the sight of the beautiful statue. The god's tears stained the quartz purple, creating the gem we know today.

Amethyst was carried into battle to preserve the wearer from harm. As an amulet it was supposed to dispel insomnia and sharpen the intellect and it was also used as an antidote against poison. Leonardo Da Vinci wrote *"Amethyst was able to dissipate evil thoughts and quicken the intelligence"*.

In Tibet, amethyst is considered to be sacred to Buddha and mala beads are often fashioned from it. In ecclesiastical communities the spiritual amethyst has always been held in very high esteem. Many of the finest quality specimens of this variety of quartz are set in the finger rings of bishops. Although amethyst is always violet in hue, the range of color play is very wide, from nearly colorless with the faintest of mauve tinges to a fabulous deep purple. The color is due to an iron impurity via radiation-induced effects. If the earth then heats them, they can turn brown, red or green.

Purple is a dignified color which has long been considered a royal color, so it is not surprising that amethyst has been so much in demand during history. Splendid amethysts are highlighted in the British Crown Jewels; they were also a favourite of Catherine the Great and Egyptian royalty. The pale amethyst colors are sometimes called "Rose de France" and can be seen set in Victorian jewellery. The deep colors are the most valuable, particularly a rich purple with rose flashes. Amethyst is mined in Bolivia, Brazil, Uruguay and Argentina, as well as in Namibia, Zambia and other African countries. Amethyst is the birthstone for February.

'Man is a spiritual being who, in order to be truly spiritual, needs a body' (St Thomas Aquinas).

Amethyst, with its purple polarity, truly embodies these words. It can unquestionably bring out the spiritual properties of those who wear it and work with it. Amethyst is a transformational healer, which will bring spiritual growth and Divine understanding. It purifies all the chakra centres and can be used anywhere on the body and on all levels of the aura, giving relief from addictions and addictive traits within the personality. It works as an amplifier of healing and spiritual energies. When consciously directed it will break down and transform blocked or stuck energies. Its pain-relieving properties have been demonstrated over and over again, so much so that it never seems to fail in drawing out pain.

Amethyst is a very approachable crystal and has been involved in human evolution for eons; as such, it has instigated the activation of many people into the healing properties of gemstones and minerals. The guardian or over-soul of all the amethyst on the planet is probably the most friendly of all the Crystal Angels. Time and time again, if you ask crystal therapists which was the very first crystal they used or wore, you will find the beautiful amethyst at the top of the list. It also helps protect from over-indulgences which have lodged in the emotional body, it calms the mind and thereby aids spiritual and personal growth, giving understanding into the cause of the indulgence.

Amethyst aids comprehension and enhances the faculty of judgement by stimulating the spiritual body, which ultimately brings detachment from worldly concerns. It helps you to retain a good temper, avoid errors and achieve self-discipline and high standards in life. Amethyst encourages you to become your own leader and master. It also gives a stable mind, removes outrage and anxiety and absorbs excessive body heat: as such it is very beneficial to menopausal women who are suffering from hot flushes, due to rapid changes in hormone levels.

Amethyst is full of originality and inspiration and is a great teacher. It is power and humility combined and it will instill these qualities in those who wear it and work with it. Amethyst brings spiritual dedication, which makes it a powerful and positive meditation stone.

Amethyst works on the pineal gland, the top of the head, the crown chakra, the brain and the scalp. Amethyst can be beneficial to help calm people who are emotionally erratic. It treats any kind of internal inflammation. It also treats heart palpitations and hearing disorders, the skeletal system, nervous system, immune system, digestive tract, stomach, heart, skin and teeth, insomnia, mental disorders, eye problems, headaches, migraine and pain. It is used for regression and it links to the unborn child, hence its use in infertility. It protects those who are unable to protect themselves - babies, small children, the sick and vulnerable and the animals. It also affords protection to those who are opening spiritually.

A group or cluster of amethyst will cleanse the environment of large amounts of stuck or blocked energy, easily raising the overall vibratory level to a much higher frequency of light, which is always beneficial to health. In Arabic countries it has been traditionally used to stop nightmares. In In Asia it is a favourite fung shui 'wealth cure' it is common to see amethyst 'caves' being sold, as this is believed to promote harmony and abundance if placed at a "prosperity" area in the room.

Affirmation: I am full of spiritual originality and Divine inspiration.

Ametrine

Chemical Composition: SiO_2 + (Al,Fe,Ca,Mg,Li,Na)

Crystal System: Trigonal **Hardness:** 7

Habit: Crystals are usually six-sided and are terminated by six faces

Color: Purple and yellow combined in the same crystal

Keyword: Synergy

A unique quartz variety which has the colors of both amethyst and citrine contained in the same crystal, it has been found relatively recently only in South America. It has been given the obvious name of ametrine, which emphasises the stone's synergy of energies. This stone, for very good reason, has been eagerly sought by healers and jewellery designers, for not only does it contain the colors of both amethyst and citrine, but also the properties and vibration of both minerals.

Initially the 'new' mineral was said to be from Brazil, but it was later reported to be from Bolivia. The Anahi Mine in Bolivia is the major world producer of ametrine. The mine first became famous in the seventeenth century, when a Spanish conquistador received it as a dowry when he married a princess from the Ayoreos tribe, named Anahi. Ametrine was introduced to Europe through the conquistador's gifts to the Spanish queen.

Ametrine is especially inexpensive when you consider that it comes from only one mine in the world. According to gemmologists, the ferric iron atoms can enter into the quartz crystal structure either by substitution for silicon atoms or interstitially in the gaps between SiO_4 octahedra. One of these replacements provides the color of citrine, while the other causes the amethyst shade, but only after irradiation. The coloration has happened over geological ages, certain conditions occurring in the earth's crust allowing the radiation from surrounding rocks and minerals, though infinitesimal, to create this effect.

What a wonderful crystal ametrine is to work with as a vibrational therapist! Its fast effective action quickly and efficiently dispels negativity from every level of the body and aura.

It speedily fills the spaces with positive Pranic healing energy. In treating long-standing illness and degraded health conditions it is extremely useful, as the amethyst energy works very fast to ease and release pain. It brings understanding as to the cause of the dis-ease harboured within the energy field and purifies on all levels, giving relief from addictions and addictive traits within the personality.

It works as an amplifier of healing and spiritual energies contained within the citrine. The citrine then acts as a positive mental stimulant, clearing the mind and stimulating the mental body into focused concentration. It opens the conscious mind to intuition and guidance from the healer within.

Ametrine promotes mental clarity and mental endurance, balancing, energising and soothing the emotions. It aids digestion and strengthens the digestive system. Ametrine cures burning sensations and problems of the blood, haemorrhoids and jaundice. It also eases gastric upsets, constipation, flatulence, coughs, colds, asthma, apoplexy and tumours and is the best stone of our time for M.E. and relieving energy drain and psychic or psychological attack. Ametrine is expansive and brings abundance on all levels, especially enhancing creative and spiritual abundance. It has been used extensively in the treatment of AIDS patients. It teaches us how to work in a new way, allowing for greater understanding of the brotherhood/sisterhood of the human, animal, plant and mineral kingdoms. Ametrine is also very protective because it contains the protective qualities of amethyst and citrine.

Citrine is brilliant to use with depression. It is particularly useful for fears and phobias and for the process of releasing negative traits, especially the fear of responsibility, which can hinder you - particularly in relationships.

Ametrine will also help you think through your difficulties and encourages you to explore all avenues, leaving no stone unturned until you find the best solution. It stimulates mental wisdom and is very penetrating; it will aid your total concentration. Ametrine loves new ideas and looking at the world with fresh 'eyes', but it hates hesitation, procrastination and ignorance and can be impatient. Ametrine aids communication, so if you sometimes feel 'tongue tied', wear a citrine pendant and you will find you eloquently have no shortage of words. On a higher level, ametrine will aid intuition and telepathy, bringing spiritual wisdom.

Ametrine is a very good crystal to use when counselling others. It tracks deep-rooted reasons why disease occurred. If you give it to your client to hold, it usually brings to the surface what the person needs to look at within their lives. It gets them communicating. Some therapists have found that it helps relieve the symptoms associated with diabetes, rheumatism and anorexia and it clears the mind to help correct forgetfulness.

Affirmation: I am filled with positive Pranic healing energies. My life is transformed.

Angelite - Anhydrite

Chemical Composition: $CaSO_4$

Crystal System: Orthorhombic **Hardness:** 3.5

Habit: Tabular, rectangular box formed by three pinacoids, often elongated in one direction, forming a prismatic crystal; most commonly massive and granular

Color: White, grey or colorless, but also blue to violet

Keyword: Karuna

Anhydrite is a relatively common sedimentary mineral that forms massive rock layers. Anhydrite does not form directly, but is the result of the dewatering of the rock-forming mineral gypsum. This loss of water produces a reduction in volume of the rock layer and can cause the formation of caverns as the rock shrinks. Good mineral specimens of anhydrite were extremely rare, despite its common occurrence. However, fine specimens of anhydrite have been found in Mexico and Peru showing good crystal habit, a nice blue color and even a play of light internally in the crystal. Lilac-blue anhydrite is sometimes called Angelite, for its "Angelic" color.

Anhydrite comes from Mexico; Peru; Germany and New Mexico, but it was adopted by the 'New Agers' as Angelite. This was where it first made its 'appearance' on the New Age crystal scene. This happened when the keepers of 'days' gathered for the Harmonic Convergence of 1986 in Peru. It is used for conscious connection to the Angelic realms via attunement to the heavenly vibration of this pale lilac-blue stone. Angelite brings inner peace, tranquillity, calm and focus to the highest realms of heavenly light. It is one stone that truly holds the energy of the force we know as Karuna: compassion, pity and tenderness. It also implies devoted action to alleviate suffering. It applies itself well to facilitating the practice of *Mantras*, vibrating with high intensity as each chakra is activated with the appropriate sound. With conscious dedicated use it unlocks *Nada* or the inner mystical sounds. When applied to the feet it will also clear the meridians of energy blockages. Angelite's glandular domain is the thyroid and parathyroids. It has also been used for inflammation of the throat and thyroid problems. Its healing vibration is also linked to the upper lungs and arms, the base of the skull and weight. Angelite balances the fluid functions of the body and thereby will release excess body fluid. It has been used as an aura cleanser and activator to bring Angelic attunement.

Blue is the color of the present time, the Aquarian Age. The Aquarian is seen as the truth seeker; however, she or he must go forward in truth, for if they do not go forward, they will go backwards out of fear. Angelite combats this fear. It will help you unlock the secrets of the spoken word, giving voice to your truth. Psychologically, angelite counteracts harshness; if somebody is acting insensitively in a situation, angelite will help them become more compassionate. It also teaches them acceptance of that which cannot be changed. Angelite can be used to relieve pain, both physical and psychological, and combats cruelty and brutality. It has also been used to alleviate the pain of stomach ulcers and sunburn.

Affirmation: The energy of Karuna guides me, I have inner peace and tranquillity.

Apatite

Chemical Composition: $Ca_5(PO_4)_3(F,Cl,OH)$

Crystal System: Hexagonal **Hardness:** 5

Habit: Crystals are common and are usually prismatic or tabular, also massive, granular

Color: Yellow, bluish, green, white, violet, brown or reddish

Keyword: Communication

A superb gemstone with a vast color range of white, yellow, green, blue and violet. It is a calcium phosphate with some fluorine or chlorine in the composition. Apatite is a widely distributed mineral. It occurs as small crystals as an accessory mineral in a wide range of igneous rocks. Large crystals occur in pegmatites and in some high-temperature hydrothermal veins. It also occurs in both regional and contact metamorphic rocks, especially in metamorphosed limestone. In sedimentary rocks, apatite is a principle constituent of fossil bones and other organic matter. The name collophane is sometimes used for such phosphatic material. The name comes from the Greek word *apatao* meaning 'to deceive', because apatite, particularly the gem variety, is easily mistaken for other minerals. Blue apatite helps with communication on all levels, whether it is communication by speech, writing or self-expression through art and music. It has been worn and carried by world-famous musicians who have used its energy for its truly remarkable inspirational qualities. It also aids communication with other realms of existence and has facilitated many past life karmic visions. Many people who have worn or carried the blue apatite have found beneficial high level spirit guides of a humanitarian nature. Blue apatite facilitates true heartfelt communication when used by groups, whereby the altruistic energy has instigated new levels of group love, compassion and wisdom. Blue apatite is connected to the throat and chest. It is the healer of emotions of the heart, it teaches you to 'talk from the heart' and say what you feel instead of what is appropriate. It calms the nerves and is a great crystal to wear if you appear before the public (especially when combined with rose quartz). Large opaque crystals of the blue variety are freely available, but many people are drawn to the rare yellow variety for its beneficial solar energies.

These wonderful yellow stones can be used to energise the solar plexus chakra, which then eases any problems associated with an underactive solar plexus. Blocked or stagnant energy in the solar plexus is exhibited in a myriad of ways, the most common being a lack of energy, depression, M.E., feelings of low self-worth, nightmares, poor digestion and food assimilation, lack of concentration, poor learning abilities, low stamina, restlessness and a short attention span. It helps with problems of the bones and teeth. The yellow variety has successfully been used as an appetite suppressant in the form of a gem essence, as it is good for removing cellulite. Yellow apatite is the great eliminator, it cleans and removes waste from the system. Faulty elimination is the cause of the beginning of most disease. Apatite also works on the pancreas, liver, gall-bladder, spleen and middle stomach. The liver is known as the seat of anger, where our emotional upsets and hurts are stored; yellow apatite can help with the release of this stored anger.

Affirmation: I now communicate my inner truth, I delight in my self-expression and in all my creative pursuits.

Aqua Aura Quartz (See Quartz)

Color: Aqua blue

Keyword: Activator

Aqua aura quartz is a product of advanced twentieth century technology. The beauty of these quartzes is manifested as the 'new' technology enhances the extremely powerful properties of the master healer, clear quartz. It is the product of natural organic quartz and pure gold in a secret process that owes as much to alchemy as it does to science. In high-temperature near-vacuum conditions, atoms of pure gold are pyroelectrically bonded with top grade clear quartz, creating the highly energized stones known as aqua aura. The bonding process of the quartz and pure gold co-mingles the two substances in a permanent way, which results in the dazzling original color. Aqua aura is clear organic quartz combined with gold.

This alliance manifests the most amazing deep vivid sky blue color of vastness, which is free of all limitations. The blue ray works initially on the throat chakra, gently cleansing all stored putrefied negative issues which block the flow of heartfelt communication and the ability to express your emotions in a constructive, positive manner.

It will allow the positive energy of your soul expression to be fully activated within all levels of the chakra, meridian and auric systems. This crystal will activate the original blueprint or Divine matrix, restoring the original energy of vital life to all the cells of the body. This will allow us to anchor our Divine Mandala into the planetary grid, activating our personal and planetary accession into the fifth dimension.

The aqua aura crystal can help with the thymus gland, located between the heart and throat under the sternum, which is now known to play a vital part in maintaining the body's immunity against all diseases. It will cool fevers and bring calm to the aura, allowing for a flowing peaceful energy. Aqua aura is very stimulating when placed on the throat chakra in a gemstone layout, but we find we can safely use this stone on any area of the body. It will release stored stress and induce peace and healing resonance; the process is profound, but gentle. I have personally seen hundreds of people helped by this stone, in fact many would not want to be without it after finding just how transformational its properties are.

This crystal will also safeguard the wearer from psychic or psychological attack. Any unwanted intrusion from outside sources will be quickly dissipated by transmutation into an immaculate pure loving energy which can then be safely used for healing the situation causing the attack. The more outside forces attack your energy field, the more energy will be available to you for healing the cause. This is truly a 'master' vibrational crystal, but as with all energies the conscious use of this energy towards enlightenment is always the prime goal. Aqua aura will help you find your own space again. The aqua aura quartz crystal will bring wisdom to heartfelt communication, encouraging gentleness and discouraging malevolent energies. Aqua aura quartz is even more shielding than an aquamarine crystal, because its gold inclusion within the 'New Crystal Matrix' activates the solar energies, bringing the full force of your soul 'quality' into every level of your being.

Affirmation: I now activate my own 'Divine Essence'. I always speak from the heart.

Aquamarine - Beryl

Chemical Composition: $Be_3Al_2Si_6O_{18}$

Crystal System: Hexagonal **Hardness:** 7.5 - 8

Habit: Crystals are usually prismatic, often with striations parallel to their length; also massive

Color: Beryl (colorless), aquamarine (bluish-green to blue), emerald (light green to dark green), heliodor (yellow), morganite (pink to peachy-pink), goshenite (colorless) and finally very rare red beryl

Keyword: Release

The most popular color for aquamarine is a clear sky-blue, but most are a bluish-green color. This does not affect the healing properties, for both shades are excellent. Under this group may be added the clear green beryls which owe their color to iron and do not have the verdant green of the chromium-colored emerald. Large crystals have been found and sometimes, due to particular growth conditions, striations (lines) are clearly visible on the surface. Aquamarine, the "gem of the sea", derives its name from "sea water". The reference is obvious: aqua sparkles like the sea and its color is pale to medium blue, sometimes with a slight hint of green. Legends say that it is the treasure of mermaids, with the power to keep sailors safe at sea. Aquamarine is said to be a particularly strong charm when immersed in water. The ancients also believed aquamarine gave protection against the wiles of the devil and to dream of aquamarine meant that you would meet new friends.

Aquamarine is always a pastel blue, but the darker the color, the more value it has. Therapists also prefer a pure blue, with no green in it. If you prefer a greenish tinge, you will find that these stones are much less expensive. The word brilliance is probably derived from the ancient Greek word for beryl, *berullos*, which means crystal. Aquamarine is the birthstone for March.

Heliodor, or golden beryl, is named after the Greek words for sun - *helios* - and gift - *doron*. The sunny yellow color of this beryl lives up to its name. Red beryl is the rarest member of the beryl family. It is mined in only one place: the Wah Wah Mountains in Utah. The color is a pure vibrant red. Unfortunately this deposit produces only a small quantity of this gem.

Colorless beryl, which is also known as goshenite, is also relatively rare. It is named after a deposit where it was found in Goshen, Massachusetts. The Greeks used colorless beryl as lenses; the first spectacles were probably beryl.

Very rarely the crystal has the appearance of ancient writing or hieroglyphs on the surface. These special crystals are record keepers. Aquamarine gives freedom from the impressions and influences of others. Calming, soothing to the emotions, cooling and an excellent meditation stone, it helps you go with your own 'flow', finding your perfect karmic path with courage, fortitude and, most of all, compassion for yourself. It will shield the aura from anger, hatred, envy and hostility.

It opens the gateways to understanding the archetypal realms, gives mental and emotional stability, promotes greater understanding of the dramas we may be caught up in and facilitates being able to step out of the drama to see the underlying emotion. Archetypes are universal themes, or models, of the 'human condition'. They are illustrated through myths, fairy stories and even modern plays and films; they serve to provide us with an understanding of our emotional experiences - both what we are and what we would like to become. Once you understand your 'drama' or 'life role' you can then change it for one that is more in tune with the life you really want.

Aquamarine also identifies the underlying patterns we may have embedded into our neural pathways, which are outwardly projected as particular behaviours; we can choose at any moment to discard those that no longer serve us. Aquamarine teaches us to take up our emotional reins and the emotional challenges that face us every day in order that we can choose a different direction and move into a new stage of development.

The throat chakra is also fully activated by aquamarine. Indeed it is very stimulating when placed on the throat chakra in a gemstone layout, but we find we can safely use this stone on any area of the body; it will release stored stress, induce peace and healing resonance. It alleviates all problems of the throat, swollen glands, the teeth, jaw and upper chest. Aquamarine really feeds the central nervous system and calms nervous stress and breakdown. The stillness of aquamarine calms the panic that can follow emotional shock. It stops the person running away from their hurt self and the painful situation. It is a good stone to use when encountering problems in relationships. It encourages you to be able to speak what is in your heart. It is useful in overcoming self-sabotage and in centering oneself.

This stone is said to put you in touch with the dolphins and whales, whose loving energy really makes you look at your resistance to being totally loving and forgiving. Anger or rage initially prepares the body to correct injustice, but it must be released from the body. When it is not released, it solidifies and hardens into hatred. We need to honour and own our emotions, but we also need to elevate our consciousness, which is a conscious act of personal will power. When we know there is someone or something we cannot forgive, we need to ask ourselves what we would have preferred. When we forgive, we rescind our expectations and conditions for loving. We forgive for our own sakes, but our forgiveness will affect the people we have not been able to forgive. If we hold on to resentment, anger, hatred and bitterness, it gives them power over us and eventually these negative emotions make us sick. Sometimes we refuse to forgive in order to punish. A simple way of releasing anger towards someone is to first acknowledge what you are truly feeling about their behaviour or injustice, then consciously choose not to punish yourself for carrying this feeling. You can say "I now intend to let go and release my suffering over the situation". Then visualise the person you need to forgive standing before you. Tell them what you would have preferred to happen and choose to release the expectations. You now want to be free. They are totally accountable for their own actions, good or bad. Unite your consciousness into the light of your cosmic self and imagine and experience the light, compassion and love flowing into you. Experience unconditional love for yourself. As this feeling builds in you, send this love out to the true self of the person and say "I send this love out to you just as you are and have been, I have no expectations regarding your behaviour past, present or future". When you feel honestly and completely at peace with the situation, you are ready to finally release it. Until then, you are bound in karmic chains of hatred and you will be linked to this person or situation for eternity.

Affirmation: I now release and let go of my past suffering and pain, knowing I release others too.

Aragonite

Chemical Composition: $CaCO_3$

Crystal System: Orthorhombic **Hardness:** 3.5 - 4

Habit: Untwinned crystals which are rare are often acicular, though sometimes tabular. Twins stout, prismatic, with marked pseudo-hexagonal symmetry. Also as fibrous, stalactitic and encrusting masses

Color: Colorless, white, grey; also yellowish; green or violet; transparent to translucent

Keyword: Earthing

Aragonite, a dimorphous form of calcium carbonate which crystallises in the orthorhombic system, is very often twinned in its growth. It occurs as a deposit from hot springs and in association with beds of gypsum. The shells of certain molluscs are made of aragonite and many fossil shells now composed of calcite were probably formed originally of aragonite. The name comes from the province in Spain where it was first noted.

This stone has a powerful earth healer energy which is not wildly exciting but is totally stable and safe. It makes you think very deeply, which teaches you to think before acting. Aragonite is used for general strengthening, grounding, stabilizing and centering of physical energies. It connects you to the Goddess and earth healing energies.

It can be used to stabilise the base chakra, attuning you to the positive force of gravity, allowing for your interconnectedness to the earth, your past and childhood. It is good to place on the body to facilitate the grounding process and has been used in this way to access past lives.

It can be used for all the solid elements of the body, including the bones and teeth. It helps mend broken bones and helps with calcium absorption. Aragonite brings immediate warmth to the body when it is chilled from colds or flu, allowing for the full power and passion of the base chakra to be fully activated.

Aragonite gives a cloak of security and earthly support during times of stress. It is soothing; it allows us to snuggle up to the bosom of Mother Nature. An extremely good way of working with aragonite is to go out into nature, where you will feel growth and renewal channelled through the stone and into your energy system. It is very good for spinal problems and will find the root of the problem by gently rooting you back into the earth, where you will feel supported.

One interesting feature of aragonite is its ability to tune you in to the recycling process that is an aspect of conservation. It teaches you moderation in all things, to only 'take' what you need.

Affirmation: I am connected to Mother Earth and know the security of being grounded.

Aventurine (See Quartz)

Color: Green, orange, brown, yellow or grey

Keyword: Comforter

Aventurine is a translucent to opaque massive variety of quartz containing small inclusions of one of several shiny minerals which give the stone a glistening effect. This 'sparkle' effect of aventurine is known as aventurescence. The color of the aventurescence depends on the mineral included in the stone. Mica inclusions give the stone a yellowish or silverish glitter or sheen. Goethite and hematite inclusions give the stone a reddish or greyish glitter or sheen. Fuchsite inclusions give the stone a greenish sheen. Aventurine may be green, orange, brown, yellow or grey. Aventurine received its name from the Italian *a ventura* which means 'randomly', this refers to its randomly spaced mica particles.

All the colors may be used in crystal therapy, but the green type is by far the most popular for its healing properties as a gentle comforter and supporter. Green aventurine has an earth nature like moss. Holding it is reminiscent of being by a stream as the water gently flows slowly over the mossy rocks.

It works with the devic kingdom of nature fairies and as such has been used as a shielding and gridding stone. This is facilitated by placing a triangulation around the garden. This technique has been so powerful that many of my students and former students have very amusing stories to tell of its almost instant effects. (The process also includes asking the devic kingdom for help).

Because of its shielding and reflecting properties it gently stabilizes the emotions by allowing you to find your own heart space again. As such, it is good for all problems of the emotional body, which includes skin conditions, asthma, allergies, the lungs, heart and urogenital tract. It also works on the thymus, heart chakra, shoulders, chest and lower lungs. This crystal restores stability to anything malignant. Malignancy is the result of cells that have accelerated out of control. Green aventurine lowers this over-stimulation. It helps biliousness and is especially useful for ridding the body of infections of the lungs, throat and sinuses. This crystal is also useful for nervous tics and stammering and anyone suffering from severe neurosis.

Aventurine teaches you how to show sympathy and compassion, to yourself and others. It gently encourages you to begin again. Aventurine also helps you to remember what you need to know. This is very important, because most of our physical and psychological illnesses result from events and conditions in our past. This makes it useful for past life regression work. Even in past life work it will always take you to a youthful time of that life, rather than the heavy dramas of the incarnation. It is good for working through non-traumatic lives.

Aventurine has proved beneficial in cases of extreme claustrophobia, where it is soothing and calming.

Affirmation: The love and compassion I feel for myself are unconditional.

Azeztulite (See Quartz)

Keywords: Nameless Light

When this 'New Age' stone first made its appearance on the crystal scene in 1992 very little was known about it apart form the metaphysical properties. Even the name 'azeztulite' was channelled.

Since 1992, hundreds of people have been attracted to this crystal. Originally, the miner who was the source for azeztulite believed it to be a variety of phenacite and many people felt that it channelled a powerful high vibration. Eventually, when the stone received a spectroscopic test, the resulting analysis confirmed it to be a type of quartz, although in a form most people are not familiar with. Regardless of the fact that azeztulite was wrongly identified at first and no more is available, due to the seam being mined out, it just proves the remarkable ability of the quartz vibration to manifest such intense experiences.

The original information is included out of interest in the quartz vibrational spectrum. "Metaphysically it was said to be among the highest vibrations in the Mineral Kingdom". Some people who can attune with it say that it activates the third eye and crown chakras, as well as the chakras above the head in the etheric body. It stimulates the three ascension points at the base of the spine, the middle of the abdomen and the centre of the brain. These points are said to be important for people choosing to consciously enter higher vibrational realms while in the physical body.

Azeztulites, which are colorless, are stones that are said to have been engineered theoretically to carry the energies and communications of a group soul called the 'Azez', who are in non-physical form and station themselves underground in power spots such as Sedona's Cathedral Rock, California's Mount Shasta and England's Glastonbury Tor, bringing to earth a positive energy that they call the nameless light, which assists planets and people in transforming to higher frequencies. The azeztulite is said to be their special conduit for this energy.

Affirmation: I am the ascension in the light.

Azurite

Chemical Composition: $Cu_3(CO_3)_2(OH)_2$

Crystal System: Monoclinic **Hardness**: 3.5 - 4

Habit: Crystals are irregular blades with wedge-shaped terminations. Also, aggregate crusts and radiating, botryoidal, nodular and earthy masses

Color: Azure, deep blue or pale blue if found in small crystals or crusts

Keyword: Vision

Azurite is a very popular mineral because of its unparalleled color, a deep blue called "azure", hence its name. The color is due to the presence of copper (a strong coloring agent) and the way the copper chemically combines with the carbonate groups (CO_3) and hydroxyls (OH). Azurite is transparent if in thin crystals, otherwise it appears translucent to opaque.

Azurite has been used as a dye for paints and fabrics for eons. Unfortunately, at times its color is too deep and larger crystals appear black. Small crystals and crusts show the lighter azure color.

Malachite is closely associated with azurite in many ways. Not only do they frequently occur together, they also have very similar formulae (a difference in structure produces the green color for malachite). Malachite can also replace azurite, making a pseudomorph, or an exact copy of an azurite crystal (only now it would be green). It is also an unimportant ore of copper. Fine crystal clusters, nodular specimens, and interesting and beautiful combinations with malachite are important pieces in anyone's healing collection. Associated minerals are limonite, chalcopyrite, native copper, calcite, cuprite, chrysocolla, malachite and other oxidized copper minerals.

Azurite dissolves and transmutes fear into comprehension. Not only do you release the fear, but understand why you absorbed the fear vibration into your emotional body in the first place. Often when I work with clients I find that their fears or phobias are usually rooted deep within the sub-conscious level, often placed there during the formative years. As children we are extremely impressionable and completely open to the influence of our parents, relatives and teachers. We quickly absorb other people's ideas, thoughts, feelings and emotions; indeed, children are very empathic. By releasing the fear vibration, we quickly find the root cause, allowing true healing to take place.

Azurite has an energy that also brings renewal and can quickly motivate us into action; this is wonderful for all those who feel world weary. Azurite integrates the physical body with the spiritual body for ease of communication and as such has been used for meditation practice.

Azurite has a very powerful healing vibration and combines exceptionally well with other stones for an integrated smooth transmission which facilitates stress-free healing and a gem essence made of azurite is very useful for stopping the side effects of true healing (healing crisis). Azurite is also beneficial for healing stress-related disorders. If you wish to use azurite for meditation assistance, the gem essence, when used externally on the throat and third eye chakras, is a very powerful vision enhancer.

When combined with malachite it is penetrating, bringing up deep, hidden, negative emotional energies, then healing them and cleansing negative thought patterns or miasms that may have become entrenched in the causal body. This stone combination must be used with caution and understanding. Malachite gets to the core of the problem, the very heart of the matter; it fact it will leave no stone unturned in doing so. This makes it a very strong and powerful crystal, an idealist, that can cause heart palpitations if worn, used or carried indiscriminately.

Azurite/malachite does open doors, though, to deep emotional healing - and in its blue/green mantle you will eventually find a sanctuary of peace. Malachite also heals through the realization of the body - mind connection, which has been proved to play a significant role in the origins and exacerbations of many illnesses. The emotions work at a subtle energy level through the influences of the astral body, which feeds into the etheric body. It has become clear that depression and other emotional disorders can cause a suppression of the body's natural defence against illness. This state of immuno-incompetence can later become translated into physical illness through an increased susceptibility to viral and bacterial agents, as well as through internal sources of disease like cancer. Distortions originating at the level of the astral body take time to work their way down through the etheric to the physical levels. This is why it may take weeks, months or even years before changes in the emotional/astral constitution become manifest as physical illness.

Azurite treats skin, bones, teeth, the circulatory system, gall-bladder, liver and kidney problems. It also addresses all problems related to a dysfunctional throat chakra, sore throats, neck-ache, thyroid problems, hearing problems, tinnitus and asthma, also emotional problems such as being over-talkative, dogmatic, self-righteous or arrogant; holding back from self- expression; unreliability and inconsistency of views.

Affirmation: I use my inner vision to reach for the stars and my highest spiritual attainment.

Boji Stone TM

Chemical Composition: FeS_2 +$FeOOH.nH_2O$

Crystal System: Cubic **Hardness:** 7.4

Color: Metallic; metallic rainbow

Keyword: Alignment

Boji StonesTM were named about 50 years ago when Karen Dee Shaw, at age three, was first shown them by her grandfather. Boji StonesTM are only found in the erosional badlands of western Kansas. After the rains they are harvested. Since 1970, Karen, now Karen Dee Gillespie, has marketed Bojis world-wide. Healers from around the world have been drawn to use them for their balanced energy.

Boji StoneTM is the copy-written and registered trademark for concretion stones. Their perfect shape is round, but with some protrusion of platelets. Boji stones come in male, female and androgynous forms and in various sizes. The male stones are characterized primarily by the uneven, sharp, protruding patterns on their surface. The female stones are smooth. The androgynous stones display a point or points of some uneven characteristics, but not as much as displayed on the male stones.

Officially the Bojis are found around the bottom of a natural earth pyramid several storeys high. They are exposed as the earth naturally erodes from them and are found growing on stems. Geologists say this pyramid is on the heart of the United States. When purchasing a Boji stone be sure to receive a 'birth certificate' with it; this is your assurance that it is a genuine Boji.

The Boji will align all the subtle bodies and both balance and align the chakras. It removes energy blockages, increases the wearer's energy field, cleans the aura, charges and fills the voids. It is a wonderful grounding stone and is used for general healing and tissue regeneration. When placed on a painful area it will remove pain. For balance and harmony within the body you must use a pair of Bojis, one crystallized male and one smooth female. Bojis have a balanced polarity, so they may be used on acupuncture or acupressure points. They work through the meridian system of the body.

Affirmation: I now allow balance, harmony and alignment into my life.

Calcite

Chemical Composition: $CaCO_3$

Crystal System: Trigonal **Hardness:** 3

Habit: Crystals are common and extremely varied in habit, more so than any other mineral. The commonest habits are tabular; prismatic; acute; or obtuse rhombohedral; and scalenohedral (dog tooth spar). Also as fibrous, stalactitic or massive

Color: Colorless (Iceland Spar), or white; grey; yellow; green; red; pink; orange; amber; honey; violet; blue; brown; or black. Transparent; translucent to opaque

Keyword: Cleansing

Calcite is a common and widely distributed mineral. It is a rock-forming mineral that is a major constituent in calcareous sedimentary rocks (limestone) and metamorphic rocks (marble). It may be precipitated directly from sea water and it forms the shells of many living organisms which on death accumulate to form limestone. In areas of hot springs it is deposited as travertine or tufa, and stalactites and stalagmites of calcite are common in caves of limestone.

Calcite is the biggest cleanser of negative stored energies within the human system. Its vast array of colors works on all areas of the body and aura, from the gross physical to the finest layers of the etheric.

Clear/rainbow inclusions:

These bring cleansing, clarity and brilliance to all the chakras. Use clear/rainbow calcite when you want to bring about change, major or minor, in your life. Its brilliance allows you to wipe the slate clean, to start again. This shaft of pure cosmic light gives you new beginnings, free of all the old pain and sorrows. Clear calcite gives you the opportunity of bringing the Divine essence of the soul into all the levels of your being to facilitate deep soul healing.

Many crystal therapists make use of clear calcite in healing, as it supports clearer perception of the truth by gently cleansing the eyes - not just the physical eyes, but the third, fourth and fifth eye - so as to fully activate the crown chakra into perfect alignment with the higher self and the Merkaba vehicle for ascension. The first incarnational experiences in this world were ones that were not in bodies such as we now have, and indeed, when we were floating in the ethers and the mists above this world, before it became more solid, that was our true nature, our true geometry, our true bodies, what we would call the light vehicle or the Merkaba.

Clear calcite clears and activates all chakras and heals all conditions: it is a 'cure-all'. Used for detoxification, it is a crystal antiseptic. It also clears a room of negativity; the power of brilliance, iridescent rainbow light, will clear away old blocks and stagnation. It also makes an excellent gem essence, which is used as a 'cure all'.

Red:

This 'gentle' red crystal will work primarily on the genitals and reproductive organs. The glands of the body connected to red calcite are the gonads and ovaries. Deep red calcite understands what prompts the release of adrenaline into the bloodstream when there is danger, aggression or pain - thus its connection to releasing fear. Red calcite will destroy that which is holding up your growth; it is an excellent detoxifier. It releases stagnant energy blocks from every level of your life, not just the physical body, via cleansing and releasing stagnation within the base or root chakra. It is especially useful for healing problems of the hips, legs and feet, bringing stability and strength of will. It also gives you the power to move forward and to take action and it can ease stiff muscles and joints.

Orange:

For stimulation of second chakra sexual energies, clearing negative energies there; regeneration and creativity. Also heals the reproductive system. Orange calcite is useful for any intestinal disorder or irritable bowel syndrome and kidney complaints. It also clears away any mucus or catarrh that may be in the system. Orange calcite can bring relief from emotional fear and emotional paralysis and can be used in cases of mental breakdown, depression, accidents, rape, divorce or suicidal feelings. Orange calcite restores equilibrium by releasing known and unknown fears and phobias.

Amber:

For smoothing the inner disturbances caused by change, especially the menopausal transition, which is very often a time of spiritual awakening. It can be a time of tremendous positive growth, but only for women who believe life is for living and flourishing into your full power. Good for kidneys, bladder and all the female organs. Good as a massage stone. Also eases the stress of children who have problems with bed-wetting.

Yellow:

Joyful, agile and expansive. Activates the solar plexus chakra, which aids mental clarity and concentration. It will balance your will power, by the right use of your Divine will. Brings wisdom, honesty and expansion to the thought processes. Its energy is penetrating and cleansing. Cleansing means healing. Yellow calcite is the great eliminator, thus it can aid digestion and cellular regeneration. As a gem essence it is very uplifting and will energise your whole system.

Green:

Green calcite works on the thymus, heart chakra, physical heart, shoulders, chest and lower lungs. This crystal restores stability to anything malignant. Malignancy is the result of cells that have accelerated out of control. Green calcite lowers this over-stimulation. It helps biliousness and is especially useful for ridding the body of infections of the lungs, throat and sinuses. This crystal is also useful for nervous tics and stammering and anyone suffering from severe neurosis.

Pink:

Sometimes referred to as manganese calcite, is perfect for the heart, releasing old fears and grief, bringing in the essence of unconditional love. The pink ray always works dynamically on the heart chakra, gently cleansing and then transmuting all stored putrefied negative issues of self-worth, self-confidence, self-acceptance and so on. It will allow the integration of positive energy within all levels of the chakra system, the positive energy being love, compassion, understanding of unity within diversity, bringing tolerance, forgiveness and ultimately the complete expression of universal love and self love to every corner of the microcosm and macrocosm. We are all a reflection of the whole, and the more love we can hold within our own being the more will ultimately be reflected outwards to all life and returned to us magnified. It relieves all stress, tension and anxiety, especially about our physical body.

Pink calcite's energy is such that it just melts and dissolves our resistance to loving ourselves enough to honour our body as the temple of our soul. This means taking care of ourselves and choosing food that nurtures us, rather than listening to the negative ego, which only seeks instant gratification regardless of the long-term detrimental effects. Pink calcite is also useful after a person has been assaulted in any way, or if they have had an operation or dentistry. Good for heart conditions, kidney and uterine disorders. It removes fears and eases nightmares.

Blue:

Blue calcite can make you aware of the need for rest and relaxation. It is also a good crystal to help you release stress and anxiety. Soothing, calming, good for frayed nerves. Aids communication and enlightened discussion between individuals who may have opposing views. Treats throat, lungs and thyroid disorders. Blue calcite will lower high blood pressure and give relief from pain. Its soothing blue ray will gently release negative emotions. A gem essence is very helpful for people who may be prone to sore throats or tonsillitis.

Violet:

Of all the shades of calcite perhaps this one is the most exquisite and Divine. The energy of violet calcite has to be experienced to be fully understood. Its energy is silken, smooth and so soothing to the emotional body. Its properties are inspirational beyond words. As a gem essence it calms and soothes the mind, helping with problems of insomnia. Grief and the grieving process are truly understood; whether we are grieving for a 'lost' loved one or the grief of separation from our source, this is the best crystal to bring us Divine understanding of the whole process of death and renewal. It aids the integration of new energies on all levels.

Black:

The void is the home of the 'great mystery' and this crystal will lead you safely through the maze and out of 'castle perilous'. Sometimes we find ourselves in darkness; this can be the dark night of the soul where all that we loved or believed in is swept away in a single moment. Or it can be the deep depression that descends for no known reason, or through the death of a loved one or job loss.

This crystal teaches us that sometimes we need to let go of the old in order for the new to come into our lives. When we lose sight of the light at the end of the tunnel it is very scary; we may lose faith in tomorrow. By using black calcite, followed by the clear calcite, we can begin to release the darkness and step renewed and stronger into the light. Healing begins with a single tiny step. Once the Universal energies know your desire for true healing, they will move heaven and earth to help you; the secret is to recognise and accept all the help you are offered.

Stellar Beam or Dog Tooth Calcite:

This crystal will amplify the user's energy field when used in meditation practice. Its energy is particularly suited for use in the solar plexus area and crown chakras. Many people who have used it have found that it links parallel realities and universes. The energy of the stone is such that it adjusts the user's energy field during meditation, connecting matter to spirit. It will help you to have the courage to hold on to your dreams.

With right use of will, this stone will bring about a sudden and dramatic change in the user's life, catalytic and always for the better. It can be used to realign the earth energies, after they have been damaged by human negativity. It has the potential to clear, activate and align all of the chakras along the spinal column. Stellar beam calcite very often grows with sphalerite, a powerful combination for advanced crystal light workers. This combination of calcite and sphalerite cannot be misused, for if one attempts to abuse the 'power' the crystal simply disappears, or shatters.

Affirmation: I am cleansed of all negative thought patterns; I now allow myself to learn through joy, happiness and success.

Carnelian - Sard (See Agate)

Keyword: Creativity

Carnelian has been historically used in Vedic astrology as a secondary gemstone to correct a badly aspected Mars energy. I have seen many ancient Egyptian scarabs (tomb offerings) carved from carnelian, my Egyptian friend said "they were used to protect the dead on their journey through the underworld". We can deduce from this that they were held in high regard as a protective stone.

Carnelian's signature is strong, stimulating and creative; when used in crystal therapy it has the full potential to balance the sacral chakra completely. The sacral chakra is located in the sexual organs and upwards towards the navel. When the sacral chakra is out of balance, the next chakra above - the solar plexus - and the root chakra below will have a greatly impaired functioning too. A balanced sacral chakra is shown when you trust your own feelings, you are creative and feel good about expressing your creativity. If your sacral chakra is too open you will feel emotionally unbalanced and find yourself living in a fantasy world. The other signs of being too open in the sacral chakra are aggression, sexual manipulation of others or a sex addict. If you are too closed you will be over-sensitive to others' energy, feel guilty for no reason or be frigid or impotent. Carnelian has been used to aid fertility.

Physically, carnelian can help with problems of the lower back, lower intestines, the abdomen, the kidneys, all fluid functions of the body, ovaries, testes, womb and impotency.

Carnelian is also associated with vitality, attraction, desire, emotion, creativity, sexuality and water, fear, shock and guilt. There is a great cleansing potential released when this crystal is used for healing personality disorders related to the emotions.

Carnelian can help to ground and focus thoughts and emotions. It has been utilised to protect the user from hatred, envy and rage. It also lifts the spirits, banishing negativity. For those who suffer from existential fears, past physical abuse, vitality-sapping illness or any long-standing mental anguish, carnelian is a good on-going supplement to their life force and should be carried or worn on a regular basis. Always check with kinesiology for the correct period of wearing duration, as with all crystals you must check on a regular basis the correct time period of use.

Carnelian can also help with the life lessons of uncovering the motivations influencing your choices, which are based on past conditioning. It really helps you fully understand what motivates you. In other words, who or what in your past is pulling your strings now? Carnelian can also accelerate the healing process of broken bones, torn ligaments and strained muscles. You could apply it in a gemstone cream or as a gemstone aura spray, or even wrap a tumbled stone into the bandage.

Affirmation: I trust my own feelings, I am creative and I feel good about expressing my creativity.

Charoite

Chemical Composition: $K(Na,Ca)_{11}(Ba,Sr)Si_{18}O_{46}(OH,F)\text{-}nH_2O$

Crystal System: Monoclinic **Hardness:** 5

Habit: Massive

Color: Purple; violet to lilac; can have black, white or golden patches or swirls

Keywords: Bodhisattvas' Path

Charoite is a mineral and of unique occurrence. It is found in only one location: along the Charo River at Aldan, in Russia, from whence it acquired its name. It formed from alteration of limestone by the close presence of an alkali-rich nephline syenite intrusion. The heat, pressure and, more importantly, the infusion of unique chemicals into the rock is responsible for the transformation into new minerals such as charoite.

Why charoite has not been found in other locations is not understood. It forms a swirling pattern of interlocking crystals. The color of charoite is described as exquisite. The look of charoite is unlike any other mineral and cannot be mistaken. It has the appearance of purple marble, but really defies description. It looks simply etherial.

A stone of vast spiritual transformation and deep personal healing, charoite activates the *Bodhisattva* energy. Whatever methods one uses to bring it about, the *Bodhichitta* can arise and establish itself firmly within one's innermost spiritual heart. Here it grows and becomes the 'path of service'. There are aspirant Bodhisattvas, who are people trying to 'act' as Bodhisattvas, keeping the Bodhisattvas' precepts, which basically are to *'solely pledge to be the unfailing champion and guardian of all life in its battle to overcome suffering'*. Bodhisattvas normally compose their own vows or can use a formula used by previous Bodhisattvas. However, it is one thing to 'feel' the Bodhichitta arise and a great leap of faith and love to 'live' the Bodhisattva vows.

Charoite activates and balances the crown chakra. You can tell when someone has a balanced crown chakra: they have a magnetic personality, they achieve 'miracles' in life, they are at peace within themselves, they transcend the day-to-day worries of ordinary folk. Charoite heals a blocked crown chakra. You can tell when someone's crown chakra is blocked or distorted: they seem to be constantly exhausted, they cannot make decisions and have no sense of belonging. Charoite will also re-balance a crown chakra that is too open or one that spins too fast. You can tell if someone's crown is too open: they are psychotic or manic depressive, they may have a confused sexual expression, or be frustrated and feel a sense of unrealized power.

Charoite has also been known to fully activate and integrate the heart, third eye and throat chakras.

This stone will also facilitate past life recall, not in the spirit of 'look, I was Cleopatra, Queen of the Nile', which only serves to feed the ego, but in the spirit of 'seeing the numerous past lives of all those on the planet'. This view shows us the futility of war, waged over and over again for millennia, with no one ever really winning and the repeated misery and suffering caused by brutality, hatred, prejudice, desire, craving and ignorance. Yes, this is a unique transformational stone!

Since it was discovered in 1976, it has made a huge impact on the vibrational healing scene and has truly 'activated' many 'lightworkers', who can no longer buy into the illusion of the twenty-first century of consumerism, greed, power abuse and corruption, nor the pollution of the planet and the wilful squandering of the earth's beauty and resources.

Charoite also helps infants to sleep peacefully and will give protection from nightmares and insomnia. It releases deep hidden fears. Soothing to the body, it will reduce heat and fevers. Charoite transmutes the symptoms of dis-ease.

It is used for disorders of the eyes, heart and mind. Charoite will improve degraded conditions of the liver (after alcohol abuse) and pancreas (due to excess refined sugars) and regulate the blood. It makes a wonderful gemstone essence and should be kept as a standby remedy for any physical emergency or emotional turmoil, as it will steady the emotional body and ground excess pain and trauma.

Affirmation: I now fully activate and integrate my heart, third eye and throat chakras; this brings spiritual transformation and deep personal healing.

Chiastolite - Andalusite - Cross Stone

Chemical Composition: Al_2SiO_5 +C,Ca,Cr,Fe,K,Mg,MnTi

Crystal System: Orthorhombic **Hardness:** 6.5 - 7.5

Habit: Prismatic, with vertically striated prisms which are nearly square in section and capped with pyramids, but much of the gem material is found as water-worn pebbles

Color: Greenish-brown and brownish-green, to a deep rich green and, very rarely, rose-red

Keyword: Balance

Andalusite is named after the Spanish province of Andalusia, where the mineral was first found. The mineral is an aluminum silicate and is polymorphous (that is, it has the same chemical composition) with the minerals kyanite and fibrolite. The crystals belong to the orthorhombic system and have a prismatic habit, with vertically striated prisms which are nearly square in section and capped with pyramids, but much of the gem material is found as water-worn pebbles. An impure opaque variety of andalusite in which the crystals contain carbonaceous inclusions with cruciform arrangement is known as chiastolite (cross stone). Sections of such crystals are cut and polished for amulets and charms.

The energy of green andalusite is balance; it balances the heart chakra, providing for harmony within the self. It releases deep pent-up hurt, anger and aggression from the heart chakra by bringing the stored blocked energy gently forwards, where it can be safely released. Most people do not even know that they have stored this blocked energy within their shoulder and back muscles. Very often others feel this blocked energy and back off from the person. This blockage stops so many people from having meaningful relationships with others. The chiastolite stone, with its dark cross section, has been used many times over as a heart cleanser. The dark cross section represents the 'dark' hidden emotions, which need to be safely released into the green heart healing andalusite crystal.

The energy field needs to be completely cleansed and this is facilitated by placing the chiastolite crystal on the heart chakra at the front position, by gently breathing deep into the heart space and allowing the stored tension to be eased forwards and safely through the heart chakra. Very often an emotional release is facilitated, with tears or anger acting as the release mechanism. I would strongly suggest this exercise is only carried out with a suitably qualified *crystal* therapist who is trained to use such powerful techniques in a safe, positive manner and an emotionally and spiritually clean environment. *All* therapy and healing is best 'facilitated' by a trained therapist.

Chiasolite has traditionally been worn to deflect the 'evil eye'; as such, its energy is very protective. It is also very helpful in bringing the immune system back into balance and harmony. Many people also use chiastolite in 'medicine' healing ceremonies.

Affirmation: Balance and harmony are now manifesting in every area of my life.

Chrysocolla - Gemmy Chrysocolla - Gem Silica

Chemical Composition: $CuSiO_3$ - nH_2O

Crystal System: Monoclinic **Hardness:** 2 - 4

Habit: Mostly massive forms that can be crusts, stalactites and botryoidal. Also as inclusions in other minerals, such as quartz

Color: Mountain-green, bluish-green, sky-blue and turquoise-blue color

Keyword: Brotherhood

Chrysocolla is an attractive blue-green that provides a unique color to the mineral world. Pure chrysocolla is soft and fragile and therefore not appropriate for use in jewellery. However, chrysocolla often is "agatized" in chalcedony quartz and it is the quartz that provides the stone with its polish and durability. Druzy chrysocolla is a rock composed of agatized chysocolla with a crust of small sparkling quartz crystals in small cavities. Chrysocolla gets its name from the Greek words *chrynos* and *kollo*, which mean 'gold' and 'glue' respectively. The Greeks thought chrysocolla was similar in color to a material used for soldering gold in ancient times.

Chrysocolla cleanses, then energizes, all the chakras. The greatest potential for healing is when we use it at the navel centre: there it removes the deep hidden problems related to negative emotions and deep fears associated with personal power and how we can misuse it. It is useful to ease nervous tension which causes digestive and emotional upsets. If we pause for a moment to understand the process of digestion and assimilation, we perceive that very often when we can't 'stomach' something we respond by being nauseous or violently sick. The other aspect of this digestion and assimilation problem is constipation, where we cannot let go of an issue and constantly 'hold on' to it. Chrysocolla helps us to understand this primary assimilation and rejection process, by which we understand what is good for us and what is not good for us. We release the bad, integrate the good and come to a truer understanding of our assimilation mechanism. It helps to detoxify the liver, kidneys and large intestine, alleviates arthritis and stimulates the lung function, releasing toxins through the breathing process. It is an all-round beneficial cleansing crystal which, when laid on the body, will release miasms - crystallized old patterns of dis-ease and decay.

Many of us feel a deep connection to the earth - this wonderful blue-green stone helps us to consciously connect with the Mother Earth energy, truly understanding the great and exquisite being that she is. This sustains us in every aspect of our life, bringing discretion and wisdom to our Earth walk. Chrysocolla helps with the dispersion of negativity in our homes, places of work, environment and our relationships. It is a good 'witness' stone for group work and will bring the energy of living in harmony as brothers and sisters, sharing our Mother the Earth with every living creature. In this way we will be able to witness the birth of a new world of love, trust and harmony.

Affirmation: I love living in harmony with my brothers and sisters, sharing our Mother the Earth with every living creature.

Chrysoprase - Green Chalcedony (See Agate)

Keywords: Sacred Grove

The most prized of the chalcedonies is the green-colored material called chrysoprase. It varies in color from a lovely vibrant apple-green to a dingy greenish-yellow; the coloration owes its hue to the presence of nickel, either as an oxide or a silicate. It was popular in Greek and Roman times, when it was fashioned into amulets. It has often been confused with jade and I have heard some 'New Age' crystal dealers call it 'new jade'.

The name 'jade' is applied to two distinct minerals: jadeite is one and nephrite is the other. Softer material, such as serpentine, is often sold as jade.

Jade has been held in high regard by the Chinese for centuries, being considered more precious than gold or diamonds. It is said to bestow the owner with long life, health, wealth, worldly wisdom, generosity and a peaceful death. It is also said to protect travellers from harm and bring success in matters related to the law. A jade item is best placed in the east of the home (the health area). It may also be worn as jewellery or carried as a potent talisman.

Chrysoprase brings balance, discrimination, tactfulness, compassion and unconditional forgiveness for oneself and others. Chrysoprase is a bridge: it activates, opens and energizes the heart chakra, bringing in the Divine loving energy through the heart. Carrying or wearing this stone tunes you into the devic realm of nature spirits and fairies. Its energy is as tender and welcome as the new growth in springtime; it has a special appeal to the young and those who are healing their inner child by letting go of childhood deprivation.

It heals relationships, bringing commitment of the heart. It hates jealousy, resentment, selfishness, greed, hypochondria and scarcity, but it will help you to release them and let them go, so you can grow in its green sacred heart space. Chrysoprase is always youthful, bringing the energy of springtime and renewal.

Chrysoprase helps you integrate the two worlds of spirit and matter, as it activates the heart chakra and how we relate compassionately with others, with love. Yet this love is not dependant on others; it is not the tribal love of the root chakra or the sexual love of the sacral chakra, or the materialistic love of the solar plexus chakra, but is a state of being, enduring and constant, regardless of externals - as ethereal as air - the element of the heart chakra.

Chrysoprase heals the thymus, heart, lungs, shoulders and chest. It has the power to renew and restore, brings balance, peace and a peaceful flow of energy to the whole system. Chrysoprase is good for easing the condition known as claustrophobia. It also helps with suppressed emotional issues from childhood.

A gem essence of chrysoprase makes a wonderful calming tonic for the whole system and helps with stomach problems caused by stress and overwork. It is good for detoxification and helping 'diagnose' illness and disease by getting to the root cause of the illness.

Affirmation: The 'Sacred Grove' inside my heart has all the answers.

Citrine - Yellow Quartz (See Quartz)

Keyword: Joy

Natural citrine (yellow quartz) is not common and occurs only sparingly in many large quartz deposits. As such it is greatly prized by crystal therapists and healers.

Most of the yellow and brownish-yellow quartz which in the past was often sold under the misnomer 'topaz' is heat- treated amethyst. Most material comes from Minas Gerais, Brazil, but almost all of the Brazilian material is heat-treated amethyst. Citrine can be found in the Ural Mountains of Russia, in Dauphine, France, and in Madagascar.

Citrine gets its name from the French word for lemon,"citron": many citrines have a pale lemon color. In ancient times, citrine was carried as a protection against snake venom and the evil thoughts of others. Although the darker orange colors of citrine, sometimes called Madeira citrine after the color of the wine, have generally been the most valued, in modern times many people prefer the bright lemony shades.

Occasionally you will hear citrine referred to as 'topaz' quartz, which is inaccurate. This name was used in the past in reference to the color, which is sometimes similar to the color of topaz. Since topaz is a separate mineral, this type of name can be confusing and should not be used. However, 'natural' citrine and golden topaz are considered as alternative secondary 'remedies' to yellow sapphire in Vedic astrology.

Since most citrine on the market started its life as amethyst, which was heated to turn its color to gold, citrine jewellery, as well as amethyst jewellery, should be kept away from prolonged exposure to strong light, sunlight or excessive heat. With this precaution, citrine should keep its color. The yellow quartz, called citrine, varies in color from a pale golden yellow to a reddish-yellow and probably owes its colors to a trace of iron in the ferric state.

Citrine is a lustrous gem of a stone which holds the key to a balanced solar plexus chakra. A balanced solar plexus or power chakra, as it is sometimes known, is shown by the following characteristics: personal power; spontaneity; positive mental attitudes; joy; hope and freedom from emotional hang-ups and inhibitions; a keen thirst for knowledge, wisdom and spiritual understanding. So, if you choose to wear citrine, get ready for a life filled with wonder, delight, enthusiasm, expansion, originality, honesty, justice and self-confidence. People just feel great around citrine energy, of that there is no doubt; it banishes negativity and deep gloom. Yes, citrine certainly holds the answer to depression; it has a general 'feel good' factor.

Citrine will also help you think through your difficulties and encourages you to explore all avenues, leaving no stone unturned until you find the best solution. It stimulates mental wisdom and is very penetrating; it will aid your total concentration. Citrine loves new ideas and looking at the world with fresh 'eyes', but it hates hesitation, procrastination and ignorance and can be impatient. Citrine aids communication, so if you sometimes feel 'tongue tied', wear a citrine pendant and you will find you eloquently have no shortage of words. On a higher level, citrine will aid intuition and telepathy, bringing spiritual wisdom.

If your solar plexus chakra is blocked, underactive or distorted, you will be overly concerned with what others think, be fearful of being alone, insecure and need constant reassurance. If your solar plexus chakra is too open or spinning too fast, you will be angry, controlling, workaholic, judgemental and superior.

Citrine is one of the best stones of our time for M.E. and relieving energy drain. It brings abundance on all levels and has been called the 'merchant's stone', because carrying or wearing a citrine has a positive beneficial effect on cash flows, easing the burdens associated with too little money.

Citrine works first of all on the pancreas, then all the other organs associated with the solar plexus chakra: liver, gall-bladder, spleen and middle stomach. We store anger in the liver and the solar plexus is where our emotional upsets will register first. Citrine knows how to remove this stored pain; it also knows how to rid the body of toxins and cellulite. It is the great eliminator. It relieves constipation. Constipation is holding on to the past.

Citrine tones and cleanses the system, the mind and the emotions. So if you want to let go and lose some mental, emotional or physical weight, join the enlightened crystal weight-watchers and wear a citrine. As a gem essence it is used for menopausal flushes, menstrual difficulties and hormone problems, stomach ulcers, fatigue, allergies and diabetes.

Affirmation: I deserve all the love, respect, joy and prosperity that flows into my life. I am open to receiving all that is good.

Danburite

Chemical Composition: $CaB_2 Si_2O_8$

Crystal System: Orthorhombic **Hardness:** 7

Habit: Includes generally prismatic crystals with a diamond-shaped cross-section. The termination is a steeply slanted dome, producing a wedge look. Crystals can be rather thin to almost acicular or up to a foot long and several inches across

Color: Almost always clear or white, but also can be shades of yellow, pink and brown

Keywords: Karmic Cleanser

Danburite is a calcium borosilicate and the best metaphysical crystals come from Mexico. Danburite is not a well-known mineral, but is growing in popularity. With crystals similar to topaz, its diamond-shaped cross-section and wedge-like termination is a contrast to quartz's hexagonal prisms and pyramidal terminations.

Danburite gets its name from its original locality, which is now buried under the city of Danbury, Connecticut. Danburite is found in Danbury, Connecticut, and Russell, New York, USA; Charcas, San Luis Potosi, Mexico; Kyushu Is, Japan; Mogok, Burma; and Uri, Switzerland.

For metaphysical purposes you need the clear form. The brilliance of danburite carries a very high vibration of the supreme ray; it works to stimulate the third, fourth, fifth eye and crown chakras, plus the 8th to 14th chakras in the etheric body. Danburite can also activate the 'heart' chakra and integrate it with these higher energies.

Danburite can help one to connect to the communication currents of the Angelic Domain. It will also promote lucid dreaming. The brilliance that danburite carries is not a color, it is the original light; not an earthly vibration, but cosmic light representing the Universal Intelligence. It has the purity of the trinity, love, power and wisdom. Danburite clears away any cloudiness in a person's aura to add lustre and beauty. In everyday use, when worn or carried, danburite will give a joyful connection to the Angelic Realms, giving one access to serenity and inner wisdom in one's daily encounters. Danburite can facilitate one's ability to act with a compassionate heart and an activated mind, guided by the true wisdom of one's connection to spirit.

It is said to be useful to those who wish to consciously access inner guidance. In meditation danburites are powerful aids to the attainment of higher states, because of their natural resonance with the higher frequencies of the human vibrational spectrum. We use this stone when we want to bring about change, major or minor, in our lives. Danburite allows us to wipe the slate clean, to start again. The energy of pure danburite will allow us to move on in a new direction. This can be on any level: physical outer changes, emotional changes, or spiritual changes. It is good for those who are making the transition from life to death.

Danburite has the power to modify any condition and some crystal therapists see it as a 'cure all' - it is - it will bring 'healing' in the 'Angels' wake'. Danburite clears allergies and chronic conditions, it removes toxins from the body, heals liver, kidneys and gall-bladder. Danburite even clears karmic burdens, negative karma patterns and miasms. As a gem essence it is excellent and making and using an aura spray will speed up the healing process. I always use it with my clients at the start of the therapy session and during the therapy session.

I have worn a danburite pendant since 1992. Danburite is the main stone in the Angel of Light gem essence I use. As danburite has such a powerful connection to the Angelic Realm, the Angels of Light and Brilliance, and is over-seen by the Ascended Master Serapis Bay, it is useful to keep an Angelic journal when you decide to wear or use it for meditation and dream work. When you choose to use danburite for dream work a natural crystal should be placed in the bedroom. The vibratory signature is so strong that it will transform the entire spiritual climate of the room.

Affirmation: I now choose to release and be cleansed of all negative karma and allow Angelic healing to manifest in my life.

Diamond (*VAJRA* in Sanskrit and *Heera* in Hindi)

Chemical Composition: C

Crystal System: Cubic **Hardness:** 10

Habit: Commonly occurs as octahedral crystals, frequently of flattened habit; more rarely as cubes, often with curved faces

Color: Blue-white, white, brown, green, yellow, canary yellow, pink, red, mauve, black and blue

Keyword: Invincible

The name comes from the Greek word meaning 'invincible' and alludes to the hardness and durability of the diamond. Diamonds first became known from India and it was from old Indian mines that the historically large diamonds such as the Koh-i-nur and the Jehangir were found. The color range is from blue-white, white, brown, green, yellow, canary yellow, pink, red, mauve, black and blue. Except for the pink stones, whose color is attributed to a trace of manganese, the color is thought to be due to lattice defects and not to trace elements, as in most other gemstones. It is crystalline carbon.

Diamond crystals belong to the cubic system of crystal architecture. When showing a perfection of form, they habitually take that of the octahedron, a form which may be described as two equilateral four-sided pyramids base to base.

Reputed to endow the wearer with purity, love and joy, the diamond - the *'adamas'* of the Greeks - is traditionally the emblem of fearlessness. Romantic lore has it as a symbol of the Goddess of love and beauty, Venus. The Italian for diamond, *amante de Dio,* means 'lover of God'. It is the hardest of natural substances. In ancient times it was used to counteract poison. Diamond is the birthstone for April.

Diamond is the ultimate stone, indeed it exemplifies the supreme Ray of Brilliance; it is pure un-corruptible iridescent rainbow light. It contains all the rays and brings them into perfect balance and harmony: as such it is a 'cure all'. It has the power to pierce through any negativity, bringing hope, beauty, light and healing. Diamond's energy is not earthly, it is cosmic. It is the Adamas, invincible. It is the Vajra thunderbolt of the Buddhists. The energy of diamond responds to the Universal Mind from which all energy springs.

Diamond adds lustre and beauty to everything it touches, but it will also show you your flaws; it is the hard bright light that exposes all corruption, shams and evil. Its energy is very intense and it can make you hyperactive and restless if worn indiscriminately.

Diamond works on the aura, first dispelling any darkness that shrouds a person's light. Consciously holding a diamond and attuning to its energies you can instantly see the difference in the aura within seconds. It is fast and swift. Use the energy of diamond when you want to bring about sudden change, minor or major. It will give you a fresh start, hope and new beginnings. Diamond is purity of vision and action.

Crystal therapists make use of the diamond energy to 'heal' any condition; by using this energy you get the process started. It clears allergies, chronic conditions, whatever has darkened your light. It also clears fear and pain. It does it in the name of love, for it is love as exemplified in the lovely energy of Venus that we use to heal ourselves and others. Without love and humility in our hearts we are lost. It also teaches us to let go of the old outworn energies that have held us back.

If you cannot find a good quality diamond you can always clear and recharge your energy system with the diamond brilliance of iridescent rainbow light at any time. Simply visualise a cascade of iridescent rainbow light pouring down through your crown chakra and flooding your whole body and aura. You can also visualise a flow of this light sweeping through a room to clear stagnant or negative energy.

Diamond has been made into gem essence, aura spray and gemstone cream. The therapeutic results have been exceptional. A word of caution, though; please make sure you use the best quality diamond you can afford for healing yourself and others. Also, do not fall into the diamond trap of desire; use the energy wisely with humility.

Affirmation: I now allow the invincible power of love and humility to fully manifest in my heart, so I may be a perfect channel for the light.

Dioptase

Chemical Composition: $CuSiO_2(OH)_2$

Crystal System: Trigonal **Hardness:** 5

Habit: Crystals usually short prismatic, often terminated by rhombohedra; also massive

Color: Emerald-green: transparent to translucent

Keyword: Gateway

This wondrous emerald-green crystal is a copper silicate and has a chemical likeness to chrysocolla. Dioptase is not common, but is found in oxidized parts of copper sulphate deposits. The best deep green dioptase is currently coming out of Russia. The mythology around dioptase is abundant, especially in Germany where it was considered a stone of plenty.

Dioptase works primarily on the thymus, heart, chest, shoulders and lower lungs. It has an intense emerald quality and some healers feel it is a 'young' emerald. As therapists we find that an aversion to the green ray often indicates that we are uncomfortable with our emotions. The key is held in childhood, where our 'conditioning' would have been a 'British' stiff upper lip, no emotions, thank you.

Dioptase is best used as a bridge, a gateway to emotional freedom. Dioptase can reveal the health of your emotional heart and your physical heart. It shows your potential in relating to others. Wearing or carrying dioptase will not only help you gain empathy with others, it will make you more approachable. Often those who are deeply damaged emotionally as children, through severely dysfunctional parents, find it very difficult, if not impossible, to open emotionally as adults. They may even find that when they do open emotionally they get hurt again and again, often very badly and from those they least expect 'abuse' from. This is due to the negative 'victim' energy remaining in the auric shell as negative thought forms. On a subconscious level it is 'read' by everyone they meet and, human nature being what it is, unless they are surrounded by saints, it will be acted upon and they will be punished again. The key to this negative release is held in the shoulders; by applying the beautiful dioptase energy to the shoulders the release mechanism is activated. Dioptase gives direction - so it can be used when you are desperately trying to make up your mind or heart, or both. It is a must for those who don't know what to do next, who feel lost.

Dioptase helps biliousness and soothes headaches. It is a good detoxifier and good for controlling blood pressure and liver complaints. It is excellent for the treatment of fatigue and even shock; it is a soporific and can calm hyperactive children. It is also an excellent nerve tonic. Its beautiful green ray is the ray of the great healers and healing. It will draw positive Pranic healing energy towards those who use it and wear it, restoring their vitality and making them feel glad to be alive. It carries the energy of balance, stability and commitment.

Affirmation: The gateway to unconditional love for myself and others is through my heart chakra.

Emerald - Beryl - *Markat* in Sanskrit and *Panna* in Hindi

Chemical Composition: $Be_3Al_2Si_6O_{18}$

Crystal System: Hexagonal **Hardness:** 7.5 - 8

Habit: Crystals are usually prismatic, often with striations parallel to their length; also massive

Color: Light green to dark green

Keyword: Intelligence

Emerald is a green color variety of the mineral known as beryl. Beryl is a silicate mineral in which the silicate molecule combines with the metals aluminium and beryllium and emerald owes its verdant green color to a trace of chromium, although a trace of vanadium may have some influence on the shade of color. Traces of iron are usually present in emerald and this again may have some bearing on the final shade of color. Chromium is the rare Midas element of gemstones: its presence also gives rubies their fiery redness. Crystals of emerald are rare in large sizes. Other beryls, emerald's cousins, like pale blue aquamarine, pink morganite, golden heliodor and pale green beryl, grow in pegmatites which allow larger crystals to form.

Emerald is steeped in mystic lore. Emerald in Vedic astrology is linked to Mercury, the messenger of the Gods. In other cultures, emerald was dedicated to the Goddess Venus. It is the birthstone for May. It is the symbol of immortality and the symbolisation of faith, and by changing its color is said to reveal the inconsistency of lovers.

The name emerald originated from a Persian word, which later appeared in the Greek as *smaragdos* and then as *smaragdus*. From this derivation the modified forms esmeraude, emeraude and esmeralde were derived, the current form not making its appearance until the sixteenth century. Because the opulent green color of emerald is the color of spring, the ancients endowed it with the properties symbolizing love, renewal and rebirth. Treasured for at least 4,000 years by various cultures all around the world, emerald was said to quicken the intelligence as well as the heart. Legend gives its owner the gift of eloquence.

Cleopatra prized her emeralds more than any other gem. The ancient emerald mines of Cleopatra, long a enigma, were unearthed again a hundred years ago near the Red Sea. Some tools discovered in the mine were dated at 1650 BC, but no valuable emeralds were found: the mines were exhausted thousands of years ago. Egyptian mummies were often buried with an emerald on their necks carved with the symbol for verdure, flourishing greenness, to symbolize eternal youth. The Romans also loved emeralds because, as the ancient scholar Pliny said, "nothing greens greener." Pliny said that emerald was the only gem which delighted the eye without fatiguing it. He said his eyes were restored when gazing at emerald. Emperor Nero wore emerald sunglasses to watch the gladiators.

It is said to be one of the stones used in the breast-plate of the high priest. One legend says that Satan lost the emerald from his crown when he fell. The emerald was shaped into a bowl which the Queen of Sheba sent to Nicodemus. Christ used the bowl at the Last Supper and Joseph of Arimathea used the bowl to catch blood from the cross, founding the order of the Holy Grail.

The majestic Moguls of India, including Shah Jahan, who was the constructer of the Taj Mahal, cherished emeralds and valued them so highly they inscribed them with religious text and wore them as talismans. Some of these sacred stones, called Mogul emeralds, can still be viewed in museums and collections today. Scientists tell us that the human eye is more sensitive to the color green than to any other color ray. Perhaps that is why green is so soothing to the eye. Spring can also be seen in the network of inclusions in the depth of the emerald that the French call the "jardin," or "garden," because it resembles foliage. The inclusions are like a signature, giving each emerald a definite personality. The rarity of transparent emerald is why emeralds can be more valuable than diamonds. Ancient emeralds were from mines in Egypt and perhaps what is now Afghanistan.

But Spaniards arriving on the continent of South America were stunned to see emeralds finer and larger than any ever seen before. They spent years searching for the source of the fantastic green stones favoured by the Incas. They found it finally in what is today Colombia: Chivor, also known as Somondoco or "God of the green gems," then later Muzo and Cosquez, the richest emerald mines in the planet and still the source of the finest stones today. Hernando Cortes, the conqueror of Mexico, was carrying carved emeralds taken from the Aztecs when he was shipwrecked. Many of the finest stones were lost forever. The Incas had an emerald goddess, a fabulous emerald the size of an ostrich egg. In tribute they sacrificed her children: smaller emeralds which were presented to the goddess. Emerald is one of the most difficult gemstones to facet because of the high value of the rough stone and the many inclusions found in crystals.

Emerald embodies wisdom, intellect and clarity of understanding, through the rarest prize of all: an open and balanced heart chakra. That is emerald's gift to those who wear it or work with it in healing others. Emerald loves harmony and abundance; because of this it is valued by healers, as it acts like a magnet, drawing life force to it. Emerald, because of its green ray, is a diagnostic crystal: it gets to the root of the problem.

Emerald helps dispel negative emotions and works on the thymus gland, the heart, shoulders and chest. Also, the lungs will benefit from emerald. Emerald helps biliousness and soothes headaches. It is a good detoxifier and good for controlling blood pressure and liver complaints. It is a soporific and will ease shock and fatigue. The emerald ray restores stability to anything malignant. Malignancy is the result of cells that have accelerated out of control. Green lowers this over-stimulation, but seek professional treatment from a qualified crystal therapist.

Emerald is beneficial for those who suffer from claustrophobia. Emerald is very centering and will bring stability to the emotional body; it releases jealousy, resentment, selfishness, scarcity mentality, greed, frustration and hypochondria. It is a gateway crystal into healing and wholeness. It works with Archangel Raphael and the other Angels of Healing on the green ray. It has a long history of being used for healing eye problems and to quicken the intellect, aiding communication; this includes Divine communication.

Emerald can be worn as jewellery, usually set in gold, or used in chakra layouts, or as an aid to meditation. The gem essence needs to be made from an eye-clear vibrant emerald-green colored gemstone. It has a very swift action and has been used to release malignant energy patterns that may have lodged in the heart chakra or emotional body.

Affirmation: The Divine Intelligence guides me in everything I do.

Epidote - Pistacite - Clinozoisite - Piedmontite - Unakite - Flower Jasper

Chemical Composition: Epidotes have the general common formula $X_2Y_3Si_3O_{12}(OH)$, in which X is commonly Ca, and Y is usually Al and Fe_{3+}, partly replaced by Mg and Fe_2 in some species

Crystal System: Monoclinic **Hardness:** 6 - 7

Habit: Crystals prismatic and often striated parallel to their length; also massive, fibrous or granular

Color: Epidote is yellowish green to black; transparent to nearly opaque. Clinozoisite is usually greenish grey. Piedmontite is reddish or purplish brown to black. Unakite is pink and green

Keyword: Nurturing

The dark brownish-green or pistachio green color of epidote is characteristic of the mineral and gives to the mineral its alternative name of pistacite. Closely related to zoisite, epidote is a calcium aluminum silicate with some iron. The mineral crystallises in the monoclinic system, usually as deep, vertically striated, prismatic crystals which seldom have distinct terminations. The crystals show a brilliant lustre and stones cut from them are a peculiar greenish brown color, which is darker the greater the percentage of iron they contain.

Clinozoisite is an epidote containing less than 10 per cent of the iron molecule and is usually a much lighter green in color. When manganese is a replacing metal in the epidote composition, the mineral piedmontite is produced. This is a red mineral which is the cause of the red color in the red porphyry of Egypt.

An epidote rock, or epidote granite, as it is sometimes called, is usually sold as tumbled or polished pieces under the name 'unakite'. Unakite is a variegated rock in red, pink and green colors, containing quartz, pink feldspar and green epidote, and the rock owes its name to the source in the Unaka range of North Carolina, where it was first found.

The stone okkolite is a similar material. Epidote is a fairly common mineral and is found at many places in the world.

Epidote is good for healing nervous stress, tension and negative emotions which may have lodged in the emotional body; it does this by soothing the emotional body. It then balances the emotional body, bringing it into alignment, ready for the healing process to begin. Epidote then balances the nervous system. It relieves pain and stops trauma. Epidote is a good ally in traumatic situations because it keeps the mind focused; this alleviates mental turmoil. Epidote even stops panic attacks. It amplifies and attracts healing energy. Epidote also amplifies healing abilities by balancing the male/female polarities within the body, especially good for balancing the two hemispheres of the brain.

Epidote focuses the mind, stopping daydreaminess. It is good for pregnant women and has been found helpful in balancing the mother's soul vibration with the incoming soul of the new baby. It is good for all mothers and child minders to wear or carry, due to the harmonising vibrations, especially unakite, as it has the perfect color frequency combination.

Epidote gives a feeling of space to those who feel threatened by overwhelming circumstances. It also helps one to attune to the devic realms of nature. Carrying or wearing a piece will give attunement to tree spirits and guides, especially the trees of apples, cherry and plum. Epidote is good for healing the heart of old emotional wounds and for the newborn. Children feel very comfortable in this stone's energy field, due to its nurturing vibration.

Epidote has the 'medicine' of 'Frog'; it is very cleansing to the whole body, it will ease, refresh and renew. It is good for those who are new to the crystal vibrations; it is an eager and most willing ally for those who truly want to heal themselves. The spirit guide of these stones is gentle but powerful and has a good understanding of working with the human vibration.

Affirmation: I now nurture others: I send love to everyone I know, knowing that they will accept it unconditionally.

Fluorite - Fluorspar - Blue-John

Chemical Composition: CaF_2

Crystal System: Cubic **Hardness:** 4

Habit: Crystals commonly cubic, less common octahedral or rhombdodecahedral. Combinations of cube with octahedral or rhombdodecahedron often have cube faces smooth, others dull or rough, being formed from tiny cube faces in parallel arrangement

Color: Varies greatly: it is often yellow, green, blue, purple; more rarely colorless, pink, red, and black: transparent to translucent. Single crystals may vary in color and, like some fluorite masses, are often banded

Keywords: Auric Cleanser

The name fluorite comes from the Latin word *fluere*, meaning to flow, in reference to its low melting point and use as a flux in metals. Fluorite has given its name to the phenomenon of fluorescence, but it shows this effect only weakly. It is a widely distributed mineral.

Fluorite is too soft to be used as jewellery, but it does produce some beautiful specimens, particularly the color-banded variety known as blue-john. This made it prized as a semi-precious ornamental stone from which vases and ornaments have been fashioned since ancient times.

Purple fluorite is an excellent meditation stone. This is due to its color and crystal nature, very often revealed as the double pyramid formation. The purpose of meditation is to calm and focus the mind. But what is the mind? The mind is neither visible nor tangible. It does not exist in the physical body, as does the brain, but in the astral body. Its magnitude cannot be measured, for it carries all feeling ideas and impressions for this life and from previous lives.

Meditation practice will: unleash your immense potential; it helps you to clear your mind and improve your concentration. This improves your health and can rejuvenate your body.

Blue fluorite will amplify your personal healing power by stimulating harmonious, focused brain activity. Fluorite restores the energy structure of your body and aura. It can awaken healing and personal growth, even improve your creativity. It also brings inner peace, which prevents or can minimize the problems of senility.

Green fluorite can release subconscious hidden knowledge and intuitive forces. We are a magnetic field of energy; we attract what we need. What we dwell on day after day is recorded in our auric field - the data base of the mind. Fluorite teaches you, through one-pointed concentration, to manifest positive energy into your life; it also helps you clear out the negative thoughts, feelings and emotional rubbish that you have dwelt on for years. It is an auric cleanser. As such it will improve all negative, degraded, chronic conditions that have lodged in every level of your being: physical, emotional, mental and spiritual.

When you learn to work with your mind to control and cleanse it, you can change anything you want in your life. Working with the fluorite energy can give a joyous life that works, keying your entire life into a higher vibration. You are more open to experiences of love and joy, to higher emotions, higher thoughts and higher states of consciousness and awareness.

Fluorite has been used in the treatment of respiratory tract infections, colds, flu and sinus problems. It has also proved useful for skin problems and wounds, including the pain of dental surgery. It relieves the pain of stomach ulcers; it is soothing to the digestive tract. It works to calm the nervous system and helps with bones, teeth and joint mobility problems. It has soothed the pain of shingles and other severe nerve pains. As a gem essence or aura spray it is very effective. It can also be used as a room cleanser; this has been facilitated either by the placement of fluorite clusters or as a room spray.

Affirmation: I now ask that my aura be cleansed of past pain, hurt and fragmentation. I fully allow joy, happiness and higher emotions to manifest in my life.

Garnet - Rhodolite - Malaya - Demantoid - Grossular - Hessonite - Spessartite - Almandine - Mandarin - Pyrope - Pomegranate stone - Cinnamon Garnet - Tsavorite - Andradite - Uvarovite - Melanite and combinations between these varieties

Chemical Composition: General formula $X_3Y_2Si_3O_{12}$, where X is commonly Ca, Mn,Mg, or Fe_2+, and Y is Al, Cr or Fe_3

Almandine $Fe_3Al_2Si_3O_{12}$

Andradite $Ca_3Fe_2Si_3O_{12}$

Grossular $Ca_3Al_2Si_3O_{12}$

Hessonite $Ca_3Al_2Si_3O_{12}$

Pyrope $Mg_3Al_2Si_3O_{12}$

Rhodolite $Mg,Fe_3Al_2SiO_4$

Spessartite $Mn_3Al_2Si_3O_{12}$

Uvarovite $Ca_3Cr_2Si_3O_{12}$

Crystal System: Cubic **Hardness:** 6 - 7.5

Habit: Crystal common; usually rhombdodecahedra or icositetrahedra, or combinations of the two; sometimes massive, granular

Color: Varies greatly: dark reds, tangerine orange, yellow green to grass green, vivid lime green, black, pink to purplish red, soft bluish-pink, brown, white; garnets that change color in different light; translucent green garnets that look like jade; garnets with stars

Keywords: Spirit Home

Garnets are a closely related group of gemstones that are available in every color. They have been mined for thousands of years. Garnets have long been carried by travellers to protect against accidents far from home. In legend, garnets light up the night and protect their owners from nightmares. In mythology, Noah used a garnet lantern to navigate the Ark at night. The ancient world is full of praise for the carbuncle, the glowing red coal of a gemstone we now know as garnet.

The name garnet comes from pomegranate. Many ancient pieces of garnet jewellery are studded with tiny red stones that look a lot like a cluster of pomegranate seeds. When you say garnet, most people think automatically of small dark red gemstones, even though this is only one aspect of the family of garnets. Of the varieties available, one of the most popular is rhodolite garnet, which ranges from pink to purplish red in color and is mined in Africa, India and Sri Lanka. Tsavorite garnet is a bright yellow green to grass green and is mined in Tanzania and Kenya. Legendary demantoid garnet combines a bright green with dazzling brilliance that won over the Tsars of Russia, who used it lavishly.

Malaya garnet, another popular mixed variety, ranges from orange to gold and is mined in Tanzania and Kenya. Pyrope garnet is a very saturated red: beautiful small pyrope garnets found in Arizona are called anthill garnet, because they are mined by ants, who carry them up when they are excavating their anthills. One garnet growing in popularity is a newly discovered garnet from Namibia, which is a bright orange spessartite; it is called mandarin garnet because its color is a true orange. Hessonite and spessartite garnets mostly come in golds and oranges and browns that are sometimes called cinnamon garnets. Grossular, the variety of garnets that gives us tsavorite, also is available in pale pinks, greens and yellows.

Almandine red garnet is traditionally the birthstone for January. When you think of the sumptuous, opulent tones of autumn leaves, the glowing, intense red coals of a winter fire, the vivacious, luxurious, sparkling green of summer fields, and the beautiful vibrant pinks of spring flowers, garnet is a gemstone for all seasons. It has always been a warrior's stone - set into shields and sword hilts to give protection in battle. It is known as a stone of health and life force.

Almandine garnets certainly contain the energy of strength, courage, endurance, perseverance, tenacity, durability, forbearance, vigour, fortitude, stamina and self-mastery. These are the signs of a balanced base or root chakra. They keep you grounded, solidly anchored to the earth, bringing a feeling of vigorous good health and boundless vitality. They help you to understand the energy of gravity, allowing you to connect to the vastness of the earth's energy grid. When you are fully 'earthed', nothing can shake you. Without a strong foundation and fortitude you will be blown about like a leaf in the wind. In order to develop metaphysically you must have a sturdy foundation, otherwise you will not be able to grow to great spiritual heights.

The symptoms of an unbalanced base chakra are - when it is too closed, deformed or blocked: emotionally needy, low self-esteem, self-destructive behaviour, fearful. The symptoms of an over-active base chakra are: bullying, over-materialistic, self-centred, engaging in physical foolhardiness. In our present materialistic society we plunder the earth, giving no thought to our children and their future. Garnet teaches you to care for the planet and accept your Divine birthright as a custodian of the earth and guardian of peace.

Garnets also hold a magical key to the Spirit Kingdom of the animals. Meditating or focusing with the powerful earthy energies whilst in this web will activate your passage of power into the 'totem' animal energy or consciousness, where you will find your own animal 'Guardian Angel'; this will be an energy that is wholly trustworthy, completely sincere and reliable. It will work with you in all realms and dimensions as your teacher, mentor and guide.

Pyrope garnet is also helpful for those who have insufficient red energy in their auric shell and as such suffer from fear and survival issues, as well as being good for rheumatism and arthritis.

Hessonite garnet, with its glowing orange-amber color, is used for developing your intuition and creativity. It releases feelings of guilt and shame. It stops you being manipulated by others, especially sexually. It is used for impotence, frigidity, bladder and prostate problems, as well as lower back pain. It has also been used to regulate female hormone production.

Rhodolite garnet, pink to purplish red in color, also has the potential to connect your base chakra with your crown chakra, bringing a flow of positive life force to the whole chakra system. It is good for the 'Kundalini Shakti' yoga activation of the base or root chakra and can be used for all problems of the feet, legs and hips. Rhodolite has proved useful for those who are frigid emotionally, sexually or spiritually.

Affirmation: My body is my spirit's home. I now activate my 'Divine Essence' to guide me on every level.

Gold

Chemical Composition: Au

Crystal System: Isometric **Hardness:** 2.5 - 3

Habit: Includes massive nuggets and disseminated grains; also wires, dendritic and arborescent crystal clusters

Color: Golden 'butter' yellow

Keyword: Purity

Gold is a very stubborn element when it comes to reacting to or combining with other elements. There are very few true gold ores, besides native gold, because it forms a major part of only a few rare minerals, it is found as little more than a trace in a few others or it is alloyed to a small extent with other metals such as silver.

Gold is almost indestructible and has been used and then reused for centuries, to the extent that all gold of known existence is almost equal to all the gold that has ever been mined. Gold is a great medium metal for jewellery, as it never tarnishes. Native gold wires emerging from massive white quartz can make for a visually exquisite specimen. Gold specimens are sometimes artistically stunning.

Gold helps you access knowledge. It has always had an association with wealth, money, energy and power. Gold indicates treasure: the higher treasure of the soul's experience of indestructibility. It never tarnishes and always remains pristine beyond corruption. It reminds you of your true immortal self, that not only lives for ever, but is beyond the mundane day-to-day pettiness and corruption of the physical plane.

Parasites are unable to hang on to the energy of gold, which makes it very useful in healing. It helps you overcome, subdue and release any kind of parasitic entity - emotional as well as physical.

It is strengthening and uplifting, which makes it beneficial for depression, both physical and psychological. It eases suicidal tendencies.

Gold is good for digestive disorders, nervous stomachs and irritable bowel syndrome. It eases rheumatism and all joint pains. Gold is also good for underactive thyroids. Gold helps you purge old pain and hurts; when combined with clear quartz it is a master healer, purifying and refining the energy field of the user till it shines like gold. It raises your feelings of self-worth and aids you in using your personal power wisely.

Gold is nobody's fool. It makes an ideal partner with most gemstones and crystals for jewellery, the only exceptions being pearls and moonstones, which much prefer the feminine energies of silver. As a gem essence it has been used to clear parasites on all levels.

Affirmation: My personal power and purity is becoming stronger each day.

Hematite - Kidney Ore - Tiger Iron - Hematite Rose - Specularite - Oolitic Hematite - Bloodstone

Chemical Composition: Fe_2O_3

Crystal System: Trigonal **Hardness**: 5 - 6

Habit: Crystals are tabular or rhombohedral, sometimes with curved and striated rhombohedral faces; also columnar, laminated or massive, often striking mamillated or botryodial forms

Color: Steel-grey to black, sometimes iridescent. Massive compact varieties vary from dull to bright red

Keyword: Grounding

Hematite is the most important iron source and is widely distributed. In addition to its use as iron ore, hematite is used as a pigment and a polishing powder. The name is derived from the Greek word for blood and is descriptive of the color of the powdered mineral. Ancient superstition held that large deposits of hematite formed from battles that were fought and the subsequent blood that flowed into the ground, hence its ancient name of 'bloodstone'. Hematite has several varieties, each with their own unique names.

Hematite rose is a circular group of bladed crystals giving the appearance of the flower of a rose.

Tiger iron is a sedimentary deposit of approximately 2.2 billion years old that consists of alternating layers of silver-grey hematite and red jasper, chert or even tiger eye quartz.

Kidney ore is the massive botryoidal form and gives the appearance of lumpy kidney-like masses.

Oolitic hematite is a sedimentary formation that has a reddish brown color and an earthy lustre and is composed of small rounded grains.

Specularite is a micaceous or flaky stone that is sparkling silver grey and sometimes used as an ornamental stone.

Hematite reflects back mistakes without distortion, apology or bias. A mistake is only a learning experience and some of our greatest learning experiences come from our mis-takes. Like filming, you just do it again until you get it right. It teaches us to work with what we know, rather than from what we see - for our world is only an illusion, a distorted mirror of the true nature of the universe.

Very often when people open spiritually, they realise what a huge task it is. You very soon realise that the more you 'know' the more you realise just how 'little' you know. We have all spent thousands of lifetimes trying to 'get it right' and learn as much as possible. Your greatest teacher is your own direct personal experience. I realise you will also meet many teachers on your path; each should be working from direct personal experience too.

Hematite is good for calming the nerves and soothing the emotions. It has a strong grounding quality. The spiritual tranquillity associated with hematite brings about a fluid state of consciousness. It calms the hormones. Hematite is good for the functioning of the kidneys, beneficial in use on fluid flows of the body. It will restore equilibrium and stability, so it is good for headaches, dizziness and the feelings of being spaced out.

This stone is also a powerful ally or shield against the negativity of others. When consciously directed it will instantly stop outside intrusive unwanted negative energies affecting your energy field. It is good for stopping nightmares and staunching bleeding.

But be aware it is a very strong stone and if you 'over' use it by always carrying or wearing it on the same area on your body it can begin to give a localised distortion in your energy field, as well as being a skin irritant. The iron energy vibration in hematite will purify and strengthen the blood and aid absorption of iron in the small intestine.

Tiger Iron:

Appears to be very useful for those people who are mentally, emotionally and physically exhausted, whose lives are in need of a major change of direction or a life-style overhaul. It facilitates a space where they can stop and take stock of their lives. The overload is very often due to outside influences; usually money orientated people get 'stuck' in work or family situations that are destroying them.

When someone is very attracted to this crystal, it usually transpires they are suffering from emotional burn-out or mental exhaustion. This stone then helps them to make the necessary life-style adjustments by grounding and energising them into constructive creative action. Physically it will heighten vitality and improve the condition of the blood. It works on the feet, legs, hips and base chakra. It also eliminates toxins from the large intestine.

Affirmation: I now tune in to the great substance of the Earth to give grounding to my spiritual work.

Herkimer Diamond (See Quartz)

Keywords: Dream Stone

Herkimer Diamonds are not diamonds at all, but water-clear quartz from Herkimer County, New York. They grew in soft mud, which did not restrict their growth, and so they often show ideal quartz formation of doubly terminated crystals consisting of a hexagonal prism capped at each end by what may be assumed to be, from their appearance, hexagonal pyramids. These twelve triangular-shaped faces are not, however, pyramidal faces, but equal development of the faces of two rhombohedra of opposite hands or, more correctly, positive and negative rhombohedra.

This makes Herkimers quite extraordinary. They have a very balanced flowing energy that is full of light. They often contain rainbow inclusions, some even contain water and air bubbles. Herkimers are a joy to work with in crystal therapy.

Herkimers are wonderful little dream and vision crystals. With conscious attunement to the light, high, joyful energy you will find they stimulate visions in meditation and dream work. They give access to your unlimited potential and growth, owing to their unique properties, which are due entirely to the formation of Herkimer diamonds, their own birth process being in soft mud which did not restrict their growth and potential.

Herkimers work well in conjunction with the Star-born stone moldavite. Herkimers clear the subtle bodies, which allows you to tap into your soul energy by activating and accessing your own consciousness matrix, which is stored in your DNA. This will fully activate your light body, bringing the conscious connection to the Universal mind. After full activation you will be able to understand your reason for incarnating at this time. You will then slip into the synchronistic energy as you manifest your reality as a day-to-day experience, as a co-creator with God/Goddess the Universal Mind.

If you wish to use Herkimer diamonds for healing others, they work on the supreme ray of brilliance that contains the color of all rays in perfect balance and harmony. The supreme ray will clear and help all dis-ease. As Herkimers contain the trinity energy of love, power and wisdom, they can pierce through the density energy to bring love, light, hope and healing. They are very effective as a gem essence and aura spray.

Affirmation: I now tune in to my dreams and ask my higher self to guide and teach me as I sleep each night.

Iolite - Dichroite - Cordierite

Chemical Composition: $(Mg,Fe)_2Al_4Si_5O_{18}$

Crystal System: Orthorhombic **Hardness:** 7

Habit: Crystals prismatic and pseudo-hexagonal but rather rare; usually as grains, or massive

Color: Indigo or honey yellow, depending on the direction in which it is viewed

Keyword: Prophecy

When Viking explorers ventured far out into the Atlantic Ocean, away from any coastline that could help them determine position, they had a secret gem weapon: iolite. The Viking mariners used thin pieces of iolite as the world's first polarizing filter. Looking through an iolite lens, they could determine the exact position of the sun and navigate safely to the New World. The property that made iolite so valuable to the Vikings is extreme pleochroism. Iolite has different colors in different directions in the crystal. A cube cut from iolite will look a violetish-blue, almost like sapphire, from one side, clear as water from the other, and yellow from the top.

Owing to the sapphire-blue color of gem quality iolite, the material was in earlier days miscalled 'water sapphire'. The name iolite is applied to the stone on account of the blue color of the gem material, the name being derived from the Greek word *ios* for violet. Cordierite is named after PLA Cordier, a French geologist.

Star stone: looking at this stone is like looking at the summer night sky. It has a very high vibrational rate. It is ideal for the awakened 'star children' on the earth plane.

A vision-prophecy stone for the 'Shaman/Shamanka', it contains powerful 'medicine'. It is safe to carry or wear iolite, but when placed on the third eye chakra it gives full psychic activation and integration, though only if the lower five chakras are fully balanced; otherwise there is a danger of over-stimulation. This is why it is 'wise' to consult a suitably qualified crystal therapist who will use this stone in an integrated or full chakra layout. Often we choose to be blind to the potential illuminated by our third eye. In its connection with the higher functions of consciousness, the third eye is a psychic tool reminding us that everything we see, hear, smell, touch or taste started as an inner vision or in-sight.

An unbalanced, blocked, distorted or closed third eye is shown by the person being undisciplined, distrustful; they may fear success and may have a tendency towards schizophrenia or set their sights too low. An unbalanced third eye that is too open or spins too fast is observable by the person being highly logical, dogmatic, authoritarian or having reforming fervour; the religious fanatic or fundamentalist. A balanced third eye chakra means the person is charismatic, highly intuitive, not attached to material possessions and may experience unusual phenomena in meditation.

Iolite is a vision quest guide and guardian to those who go on inner or outer journeys of self-exploration. It awakens innate inner knowledge and wisdom; it assists in reducing confusion by virtue of understanding the life situation that is currently causing the confusion. All confusion arises from the inability to claim one's own 'intuitive power' and act according to the needs of the individual, not the needs of society, or the tribal mentality which one has been born into. (The tribal mentality alludes to your family, friends, work colleagues and any self-limiting group who have a vested interest in your controlled behavioural patterns and the survival of the patterns, which may serve the group, but do not necessarily serve you as an individual).

Iolite teaches us not to get too attached to ritual, but to look for our own path via a balanced third eye chakra; it takes you into the realms of personal inner knowing.

Iolite assists in lessening fatty deposits on the body - the fatty deposits are 'stored negative emotions' - and rids the body of toxins - 'old belief systems'. It alleviates all addiction by virtue of allowing us to understand what an addiction is and why we 'need' this person, food or substance etc. in the first place. It brings the passionate expression of your true potential - 'rather than society's expectations and stereotypes'. Iolite helps with stored anger and pain, bringing relief via the release of the stored anger and pain. It is excellent as a gemstone essence.

Iolite holds the key to the indigo ray of devotion, which is a mixture of dark blue and dark violet. Parts of the body iolite helps are: the pituitary gland; the skeleton; lower brain; eyes and sinuses. Its uses are: aids intuition and spiritual knowledge; strongest painkiller of the rainbow spectrum; releases negativity from the skeletal structure; astral antiseptic and astral toxin release (clears negative thought forms); kills bacteria in food, water or air; clears pollution on all levels; heals chronic sinus complaints (unshed tears); cures insomnia; releases migraine headaches and pain; heals overactive thyroid conditions; breaks up tumours and growths; helps ease kidney complaints.

Indigo-iolite helps to control diarrhoea; eases bronchitis, asthma, lung conditions; lowers high blood pressure; heals back problems, especially sciatica, lumbago, any spinal complaint, or neurological disturbances; transmutes and purifies negativity; is good for spiritual teachers and writers with its great inspirational guidance.

Iolite contains the domain of mystery and psychic understanding. It is the stone of artists and the acting profession; iolite is very theatrical, it teaches you to let go of the 'masked' self to find the inner self.

Affirmation: I now acknowledge my intuitive power and ask it to fully manifest in my life.

Jasper - Turitella Jasper - Basanite - Plasma Stone - Bloodstone - Heliotrope - Mookaite (See Agate)

Color: Usually yellow, red, brown, black or green

Keyword: Stabilising

The variety of quartz known as jasper is a heterogeneous mass of micro-crystallised quartz which is heavily pigmented with colorful minerals. The colors of jasper are mainly due to iron and are usually yellow, red, brown, black or green.

The green jaspers, when of a uniform light shade, are often known as prase, and the darker green as plasma.

Basanite is a velvety-black type of jasper. When plasma contains bright red spots it is commonly called bloodstone or heliotrope.

Much petrified wood (fossil) is jasper, the previously existing wood fibre having been replaced molecule by molecule by silica in the form of jasper.

Mookaite is an Australian jasper with a dark brown coloration. Jasper is of worldwide occurrence. It was said to be one of the stones used in the breast-plate of the high priest. The term jasper is very ancient and comes from the Orient. It was used in Egypt: sacred scarab amulets were carved from red jasper as a symbol of eternal life.

Red jasper is good for clearing blocks in the liver and bile ducts. It energises the solar plexus, sacral and root chakras. It is a good, slow, steady healing stone. The energy is also very protective and may be used in stressful situations when it is important to retain one's own boundaries or when you want to have no outside influence interfering with your energy. This is why it has been revered by 'Shamans' for centuries; they used it for journeying to other realms. It contains a basic 'clay' nature of the red earth from which Adam Cadmon was formed. Red jasper is a useful all-round 'power' tool.

It is excellent as a gemstone essence. Red jasper is a secondary Vedic astrological (Mars) remedial gemstone in place of red coral, though its potency is somewhat reduced. Yellow jasper aids digestion and stomach disorders and will gently ease stomach problems. It should be placed over the area of pain until all painful sensations cease. It is energising, uplifting and sustaining to the whole body. It helps with the release of toxins from the liver and large intestine. It will support you during the releasing process by gently stabilising your energy field, easing the discomfort normally associated with toxin release. It is excellent as a gemstone essence.

Bloodstone or heliotrope is physically cleansing. Even today, finely powdered bloodstone is used as a medicine and aphrodisiac in India. Perhaps that explains why today it is difficult to find fine specimens of bloodstone on the market. Bloodstone is mined in India, Australia and the United States. It completely purifies the blood and detoxifies the organs of the kidneys, liver and intestines. It is perfect for females who choose to connect with the divine Child/ Mother/ Goddess. This stone is excellent for birth or rebirthing. It has been used for centuries to stop bleeding and facilitate healing. It is excellent as a gemstone essence.

Basanite can be used for scrying; its velvety blackness gently draws your attention deep within, its 'softness' allowing you to meld with its energy field, which is conducive to deep states of relaxation and insight. Floating on the cushion of support you will quickly find yourself transported to the hidden realms, as all veils of separation fall away, revealing the core of hidden knowledge which is a pre-requisite for spiritual growth and understanding. Use basanite for prophetic dreams and visions.

Mookaite is grounding and stabilising to the whole body. It strengthens the will to survive. It is also a good, slow, steady healing stone. The energy is also very protective and may be used in stressful situations when it is important to retain one's own boundaries or when you want to have no outside influence interfering with your energy. It also helps with the release of toxins from the liver and large intestine. It will support you during the releasing process by gently stabilising your energy field, easing the discomfort normally associated with toxin release. It is excellent as a gemstone essence.

Affirmation: I am taking responsibility for my life; I can now cope with all situations in a stable responsible way.

Kunzite - Spodumene - Hiddenite

Chemical Composition: $LiAlSi_2O_6$

Crystal System: Monoclinic **Hardness:** 6.5 - 7

Habit: Crystals usually prismatic, often striated along their length, and commonly etched or corroded; also massive, columnar

Color: Kunzite is transparent lilac - pink. Spodumene is usually white or greyish white. Hiddenite is pale green

Keywords: Heart Opener

Kunzite, the pale pink to lilac gem variety of the mineral spodumene, is named as a tribute to George Kunz, the legendary gem scholar, gemmologist, and gem buyer for Tiffany & Co at the turn of the century. The author of 'The Curious Lore of Precious Stones', Kunz searched the globe for old stories and legends about gems as he searched for new varieties and new deposits. Kunzite was first found in Connecticut, USA, but the first commercially significant deposit was discovered in 1902 in the Pala region of California, where morganite beryl was also first discovered. Spodumene occurs typically in lithium-bearing granite pegmatites, together with minerals such as lepidolite, tourmaline and beryl. Very large crystals have been recorded, some reaching 16 metres in length and weighing up to 90 tons.

Kunzite should be protected from heat and continued exposure to strong light which can gradually fade its color. Kunzite carries the energies of the pale pink to lilac ray, which is the ray of spiritual love. It works on all parts of the body, mind and spirit. It is used for the newborn to help them integrate their energies into the earth vibration, for birth and re-birth, for new beginnings and for mid-life crisis as a heart opener. It is also used as a heart consciousness wakener. It comforts and heals the heart and old "heartache". Kunzite has a great balance of compassion, peace and freedom. Kunzite has a hidden magic: it can reveal and heal a lost childhood where, due to circumstances, you had to grow up too soon. Kunzite is good for the immune system and can clear anaesthetics from the system. It is also good for convalescence and aids recovery from long-standing immune system disorders. It makes an excellent gemstone essence.

Spodumene has a green form, hiddenite, that brings in the green ray of tender, gentle heart healing. It is not the powerful emerald green ray, rather the fragile new beginning, a bud just starting to open. It is soft and gentle, like a whisper that holds the promise that all will be well. It will gently dispel negative emotions and feelings by releasing old heartache pain and self- hatred.

Hiddenite releases feelings of failure and it is good for those who put on a brave face when their heart is full of pain; it helps you to honour these feelings and gently release them. Hiddenite works on the thymus, heart, shoulders, chest and lungs. When combined in a gemstone essence with its sister kunzite, it completely stabilizes the emotional body, giving comfort and support.

Affirmation: I now open my heart to receive love.

Kyanite - Disthene

Chemical Composition: Al_2SiO_5

Crystal System: Triclinic **Hardness:** 5.5 - 7

Habit: Crystals usually of flat, bladed habit; also as radiating bladed aggregates

Color: Blue to white, but may be grey or green. Crystals are often unevenly colored, the darkest tints being in the centre. Transparent to translucent, with a pearly covering

Keywords: Sword of Truth

Kyanite occurs typically in pegmatites and quartz veins associated with schists. The name kyanite comes from the Greek word *kyanos*, meaning 'blue'.

A kyanite blade has a very focused swift action: it holds the keys to knowledge, the blue ray of communication. Kyanite works on the following body parts: thyroid and parathyroid; upper lungs; jaw; arms; base of the skull; and body weight. Kyanite integrates the bodies' energies into the head and so can, with conscious attunement, align all the chakras. Kyanite is the seeker of truth and will combat fear of speaking the truth. You can tell if someone has problems expressing themselves: they tend to hold their head down with the chin on the chest. This shows the person is unprotected in the throat chakra. Such people have to clear their throat frequently, because metaphysically they are being choked by the truths they have swallowed. Their voice may be dull or weak, even monotonous in tone. They may try to communicate in group discussions but, because they have problems expressing themselves, very often they go unheard. Anger and frustration can build up for them, causing throat and ear infections.

Kyanite reduces fevers and calms hot conditions where there is too much heat in the body. It also eases stiff necks and stiff-necked attitudes, heals ear and throat infections and is a natural pain reliever. Kyanite can aid weight loss by encouraging communication, thereby releasing stored words and unwanted body weight. It has been used to bring down high blood pressure; also in the sickroom and for those terminally ill.

Kyanite contains the royal color of integrity and is uplifting to the soul as it searches for its maturity. It will bring guidance and faith, giving great encouragement to break loose from the chains of ignorance, desire and hatred. It will aid you in your struggle towards the light of your soul and your soul purpose.

Kyanite works with Archangel Michael and his sword of truth; it is more powerful than *Excalibur*, the legendary sword of King Arthur. Use it to cut away the wrong mental, emotional and spiritual attitudes that have held you captive. It is a double-edged sword, so you can cut away duality and dualistic concepts that have blinded you to the truth. Use it wisely; once you have picked it up, it is very hard to put down until you have ended not only your own suffering (ignorance) but the suffering of all sentient beings.

Affirmation: I use the sword of truth to cut away all illusion that has blocked my spiritual growth.

Labradorite - Feldspar

Chemical Composition: Ca(50-70%) Na(50-30%) (Al, Si)$AlSi_2O_8$,

Crystal System: Triclinic **Hardness:** 6 - 6.5

Habit: Includes blocky crystals that rarely form free of the host rock and therefore do not usually show their full crystal forms. In sliced sections of rock, the labradorite appears as blocky chunks with a predominance of near right-angled corners; also massive, granular

Color: Grey to smoky black, which can produce a colorful play of light across cleavage planes and in sliced sections, called labradorescence. The usually intense colors range from the typical blues and violets through greens, yellows and oranges

Keyword: Enchantment

Labradorite is truly an enchanting, fascinatingly beautiful mineral. It is a mineral whose bewitching charm is not fully noticed and may be overlooked if not viewed from the proper position; generally a drab-looking mineral with no special virtue until the colorful schiller is observed glowing on the surface.

Labradorite can produce a colorful play of light across cleavage planes and in sliced sections, called labradorescence. The usually intense colors range from the typical blues and violets through greens, yellows and oranges. The color display is from lamellar intergrowths inside the crystal. These intergrowths result from compatible chemistries at high temperatures becoming incompatible at lower temperatures and thus a separating and layering of these two phases. The resulting color effect is caused by a ray of light entering a layer and being refracted back and forth by deeper layers. This refracted ray is slowed by the extra travel through the layers and mixes with other rays to produce a light ray coming out that has a different wavelength than when it went in. The wavelength could correspond to the wavelength of a particular color, such as blue.

The labradorescence is truly a one of a kind mineralogical and metaphysical encounter and must be observed in person in order to truly appreciate its beauty. Notable occurrences include Labrador (from where it derives its name), in Canada, and the Scandinavian Peninsula.

Labradorite is metaphysically known as the 'bringer of light', the illumination on the path. It works by dispelling darkness.

Enchanting labradorite is connected to mystery: it points to magic and esoteric knowledge via its labradorescence or luminescence. It contains the mesmerizing dark moon energies of dreaming, of altered states of reality. Labradorite asks you ''where do you go when you sleep?" - then it shows you - where you go - when you are not you. It facilitates initiation into deep hidden sacred knowledge and past life encounters. It is a gateway to other worlds and dimensions.

Labradorite is a shape-shifter, it plays with the light, it moves it and bends it and plays with illusion. It skilfully removes the 'hooks and ensnarements' of other people's mental projections, allowing one to completely clean the auric shell of other people's emotional debris. It removes negativity and depression that have been caused by disappointments in life. It teaches you to look beyond the visible world, to use your sixth sense. Its energy can see beyond the illusion of time and space. It can see right through you - it will expose all your flaws, shams, corruptions and shame, then it teaches you to heal them.

Labradorite heals relationships; it shows you where there is no substance, just delusion and denial. It heals the stress and anxiety related to emotional turmoil. It calms the hormones and is good for the kidneys and all fluid functions of the body. It soothes the digestion.

It has been used as a gem essence and meditation stone with the Goddess groups. It is a powerful, mesmerizing, bewitching female ally and guide. Labradorite is here to offer you in-sight, clairvoyance, truths to the questions of the universe. It teaches you to exercise your third eye, by letting your intuition guide you daily.

Why don't you try using labradorite and keeping an intuitive journal?

Affirmation: I am enchanted as my soul illuminates my path through life.

" 'Come to the edge,' he said.
They said 'We are afraid'.
'Come to the edge,' he said.
They came. He pushed them and they flew."

Guillaume Apollinaire

Lapis Lazuli - Lazurite

Chemical Composition: $(Na, Ca)_8Al_6Si_6O_{24}(S,SO_4)$

Crystal System: Isometric **Hardness**: 5.5

Habit: Dodecahedral crystals have been found, usually massive as a rock (lapis lazuli) forming mineral

Color: Ultramarine blue, brilliant blue with violet or greenish tints

Keywords: Spirit of Truth

Lazurite is a popular but generally expensive mineral. Well-formed, deep blue crystals are rare and valuable. It is more commonly found massive and combined with other minerals into a rock called lapis lazuli.

Lapis lazuli, or lapis for short, is mostly lazurite, but commonly contains pyrite and calcite and traces of some other minerals. The rich blue color is due to the sulphur that is inherent in the structure of lazurite. Small crystals of pyrite are always present in lapis and their brassy yellow color is both attractive and diagnostic in distinguishing lapis from its also blue cousin - sodalite rock, which lacks pyrite and is much cheaper.

The calcite produces white streaks in the lapis and too much calcite will substantially lower the value of the stone. The name lazurite is often confused with the bright blue phosphate mineral lazulite. However, the two minerals cannot be confused with each other identification-wise because of lazulite's typical vitreous lustre and good crystal habit. The beautiful blues in paintings from the Renaissance are thanks to the blue of lapis lazuli, the blue rock cherished by the ancients, from Mesopotamia to Egypt, to Persia, to Greece and Rome.

The ancient city of Ur had a thriving trade in lapis as early as the fourth millennium BC. The name is international, from the Latin, *lapis*, which means stone, and from the Arabic, *azul*, which means blue. When lapis was first introduced to Europe, it was called ultramarinum, which means 'beyond the sea'. Ground lapis was the secret ingredient of the blue in ultramarine, the pigment which painters used to paint the sea and the sky until the nineteenth century. The Romans believed that lapis was a powerful aphrodisiac. In the Middle Ages it was thought to keep the limbs strong and free the soul from error, envy and fear.

Lapis is a high intensity etheric blue stone. It contains the energies of royalty, wisdom, patience, truth, mental attainment, good communication, contentment, artistic inspiration, deep meditation, spiritual and philosophical contemplation, personal integrity and loyalty. It is the 'Spirit of Truth'.

Lapis lazuli will heal an unbalanced throat chakra. How you tell if the throat chakra is un-balanced by being too open or spinning too fast: the person is over-talkative, dogmatic, self-righteous or arrogant. If the throat chakra is too closed, or spinning sluggishly, the person is unreliable, holds inconsistent views and holds back from self-expression. Lapis works on the thyroid, parathyroids, the throat, upper lungs and arms, the base of the skull and body weight.

Lapis teaches you the power of the spoken word. Because the blue ray governs the throat, infections in this area are psychologically related to 'talking inwards', not speaking out. Psychologically speaking, coughing is because a person has swallowed their thoughts and cannot bring themselves to speak out. Lapis teaches you to 'give voice to your truth'. It counteracts harshness. If somebody is acting insensitively in a situation, lapis will help them become more compassionate.

Lapis gives relief from pain, both physical and psychological, and combats cruelty and brutality. Lapis is an interesting stone to meditate with, as its high intensity etheric nature means you really have to reach high to bring your energy into line with its refined vibration. It contains a higher order of intelligence and wisdom, 'intellectual integrity'.

Lapis also heals the martyr syndrome: 'I am going to punish myself in order to make you suffer'. Lapis aids discrimination of wisdom; it is very penetrating and does not suffer fools gladly, or those who are fooling around with other people's spirituality.

Lapis teaches you to reach for the stars and looking at lapis reminds you of a summer night's sky. The small crystals of pyrite which are always present in lapis and the streaks of white calcite produce starry pictures, which will aid your intuition. The white calcite brings in the energies of the crown chakra and the yellow pyrite brings in the energies of the solar plexus chakra to activate, energize, align and integrate the throat chakra.

Lapis teaches you that you have no chance of developing a balanced purified throat chakra until you have successfully worked through and balanced the lower four chakras to obtain the necessary purification to fully activate this centre.

Lapis also teaches the mastery of active listening by integrating the full faculties of hearing. It is a sad fact that active listening is totally neglected in our society. We need to fully develop the outer ear, before the subtle inner ear can be available to us for inner guidance. All too often Divine guidance is not heard, because of not truly listening to the 'wisdom' behind the words.

Lapis makes an excellent gemstone essence which can release a person from emotional bondage and mental suffering.

Affirmation: I allow the spirit of truth to set me free.

Larimar - Blue Pectolite - Dolphin Stone - Atlantis Stone

Chemical Composition: $Ca_2NaHSi_3O_9$

Crystal System: Triclinic **Hardness:** 5

Habit: Found in close aggregations of monoclinic acicular crystals. Pectolite is normally white or greyish only in color

Color: Pale blue-turquoise to greenish-blue coloration

Keyword: Etherial

This variety is actually a rock, being composed of more than one mineral, but is mostly composed of pectolite. It has been given the trade name "Larimar". Only discovered in the Bahamas and Dominican Republic in the last twenty years, it has enjoyed success in the semi-precious stone market. Its translucent sky blue color is attractive and has a loyal following of admirers.

It has a turquoise look to it, although the color is distinctly more blue. Larimar has been used in the same manner as turquoise and is even seen in contemporary Native American jewellery. Pectolite is one of the zeolites and is found in cavities in basalt and other volcanic rocks. It often exhibits chatoyancy.

Larimar is etherial in its nature and has an other-worldly feel. This beautiful heavenly blue stone contains an energy of peace and tranquillity. It gently transmits pure spiritual substance into the higher chakras above the head.

Larimar contains 'Grandmother Earth' energies and will assist you in finding your true path in life. It will also assist you in removing the blocks you have placed on your path to personal power.

For women it will activate your own Goddess energies, bringing understanding of the Divine maiden, mother and crone. It is useful for connecting those who feel disorientated and out of step with the earth.

It has been called the Dolphin stone, due to its watery energy, though this is another aspect of 'mystery' about this stone, as its birth is definitely fire in nature. It is best worn as a pendant for long periods of time; this facilitates its magical properties, allowing them to fully manifest in your life. The best way of understanding larimar's fire is through our own fiery emotions, which very often are released through our watery tears. Our tears are our very own ocean, which has been gifted to us to facilitate our personal cleansing process. The Dolphin energy contained within the stone is also playful in nature and it will activate a deep healing of our emotional inner child or, as has been observed, activate our own Angelic inner child.

Our Angelic inner child has never been damaged and its integrity and purity have remained intact; it is beyond the traumas which may have affected our inner child. Your Angelic inner child will show you the ways of joy, gratitude, playfulness, and nurturing into wholeness. Larimar asks the question "when was the last time you took some time to play? - to explore your inner creative childlike nature?"

Larimar helps in crystal reflexology, as it fully opens the meridians of the feet, so bringing greater awareness of the cause of the initial disease, via the painful area of the foot, which is a reflection of the whole body; just as water is reflective, so is larimar. It may be placed on any area of pain, bringing a cooling, peaceful healing energy into the blocked energy centre.

It is good for all throat ailments and has been effective in healing heart trauma.

Many people have been guided to use larimar as a meditation stone, where it has facilitated deep meditative states, bringing insight and intuition.

It definitely has its own Angelic spiritual guidance and has been used to access the Angelic Realm. It has facilitated contact with the Angels who work with the elements of water and healing. It has been used to contact Dolphins and Whales; this has led to joyful encounters with the guardians of the oceans and the keepers of the sacred records.

Affirmation: I no longer deny my etherial nature and allow it to guide me home.

Lepidolite - Lithia mica

Chemical Composition: $K(Li,Al)_3(Al, Si)_4O_{10}(F, OH)_2$

Crystal System: Monoclinic **Hardness:** 2.5

Habit: Includes tabular to prismatic crystals with a prominent pinacoid termination. Lepidolite's four prism faces and two pinacoid faces form pseudo-hexagonal crystal "books". The sides of the crystal often tend to taper. Also as micaceous, lamellar or granular rock-forming masses

Color: Violet to pale pink or white and, rarely, grey or yellow

Keyword: Relaxation

Lepidolite is a mica and has just in the past decade become available on the mineral market in great quantities. Lepidolite means *scale stone*; it is an ore of lithium and forms in granitic masses that contain a substantial amount of lithium. Lepidolite, like other micas, has a layered structure of lithium aluminum silicate sheets, weakly bonded together by layers of potassium ions. Lepidolite crystals accompany such other lithium-bearing minerals as tourmaline, amblygonite and spodumene and can add greatly to the value of these specimens. Single large plates or 'books' of lepidolite can have appealing violet-lilac color.

Lepidolite can desensitise the nervous system very effectively, thereby numbing pain. It contains an extremely high vibration and works on the brain's pain centres, which helps with drug addiction. It also gives you your own space back, so you can heal, so it is good for convalescence. Lepidolite also clears anaesthetics from the system. It facilitates the energy of no mind, thus relieving stress. It is also used for balancing both sides of the brain. In meditation it feels like a gentle wave of energy flowing through the mind. Lepidolite is especially good for insomnia. The 'Spirit' keeper or Angel of lepidolite facilitates its use as a 'dreamtime' crystal, an astral guide. It changes our way of consciously viewing the world, by accessing other dimensions and realities. Lepidolite is a good space clearer; it can emit an immense force field that will keep anything negative at bay. It has a pushing - pulsing - exploding kind of energy (like popcorn).

It can be used to clear the mind of unwanted debris before meditation, so it aids deep meditation practice. It can fully activate and integrate the crown chakra, bringing alignment to the higher trans-personal chakras above the head. Lepidolite's energy is the positive female aspect of the negative warlike male vibration - Pallas Athena, who sprang fully-armed and protected from the head of her father, Zeus. So lepidolite is beneficial for men who are trying to balance their female polarity and learn to nurture themselves into wholeness. It stops the head ruling the heart, by bringing about a balanced polarity. It teaches us to use an integrated approach.

It stops depression, obsessional thinking and confusion. It alleviates symptoms of sensitivity to pollutants, chronic exhaustion, epilepsy and Alzheimer's. Lepidolite also strengthens the immune system and has great healing powers. It gives a rest for the troubled heart and brings inner peace and emotional healing.

Affirmation: I recognise the need for silence, relaxation and stillness in my life.

Malachite

Chemical Composition: $Cu_2(CO_3)(OH)_2$

Crystal System: Monoclinic **Hardness:** 3.5 - 4

Habit: In its massive forms it is botryoidal, stalactitic or globular. Crystals are acicular or fibrous and form in tufts and encrustations

Color: Banded light and dark green or (if crystalline) just dark green

Keyword: Greenman

The banding of different shades of green easily distinguishes malachite from other green minerals, although it could be confused with the much rarer pseudo-malachite, or opaque green aventurine quartz.

Primarily a hydrated copper carbonate, malachite is formed through the dissolving of copper ores and the subsequent deposition in rock cavities and veins as botryoidal reniform or stalactitic masses. Very occasionally the material shows crystal forms and is most often seen in its botryoidal form, causing the circular banding.

In Egypt, malachite was dedicated to the Goddess Hathor. Malachite is often found with the other copper carbonate, azurite: this beautiful stone is then referred to as azurmalachite. Malachite is also found growing with the copper silicate chrysocolla, and this has been used with positive results in crystal therapy. It is frequently associated with cuprite, which it sometimes replaces.

Malachite can balance and bring harmony to the heart chakra. It brings the ability to experience wholeness and love. It is a gateway, a bridge linking into the ancient Celtic 'Greenman' energies of death, growth and renewal. In the Middle Ages malachite was used to alleviate 'birth' pains.

Malachite is very restorative and tunes you in to the plant kingdom and helps you understand environmental issues, giving you a social conscience.

Malachite gets to the core of the problem, the very heart of the matter; it fact it will leave no stone unturned in doing so. This makes it a very strong and powerful crystal, an idealist, that can cause heart palpitations if worn, used or carried indiscriminately.

Malachite does open doors, though, to deep emotional healing - and in its green mantle you will eventually find a sanctuary of peace. Malachite also heals through the realization of the body - mind connection, which has been proved to play a significant role in the origins and exacerbations of many illnesses. The emotions work at a subtle energy level through the influences of the astral body, which feeds into the etheric body. It has become clear that depression and other emotional disorders can cause a suppression of the body's natural defence against illness. This state of immuno-incompetence can later become translated into physical illness through an increased susceptibility to viral and bacterial agents, as well as through internal sources of disease like cancer. Distortions originating at the level of the astral body take time to work their way down through the etheric to the physical levels. This is why it may take weeks, months or even years before changes in the emotional/astral constitution become manifest as physical illness.

Malachite is a practical idealist and it will help you release the negative aspect of the heart chakra, of coping with unquestioning acceptance, hopelessness, of self denial and self-suppression; a refusal to live life to the full. It will restore stability to anything malignant.

An aversion to malachite or the color green often indicates that we do not feel at ease with our emotions. This is usually due to childhood trauma and a dysfunctional early family background, where emotions had to be denied or hidden, as the trauma of showing emotion was forbidden, a crime, punishable by disapproval and rejection.

On a physical level it will stop biliousness and heal liver complaints, even control blood pressure problems; alleviate rheumatism and help reduce acidification of the tissues. As a gemstone essence it is very potent, so it should only be made and used under the supervision of a qualified crystal or vibrational therapist.

Affirmation: The strong green stem connects the roots below with the bloom above, for perfect balance and emotional integrity.

Moldavite - The Grail Stone - Tektite

Chemical Composition: SiO_2 + Al,Ca,Fe,K,Na

Crystal System: Amorphous **Hardness:** 5 - 6

Habit: Usually small nodules or splinters that vary from simple rounded shapes to very intricate beautiful natural carvings. Many have smooth, scarred or pitted surfaces

Color: Transparent green

Keyword: Transformational

Tektites are still poorly understood. They are irregularly - and at times elaborately - shaped nodules and blobs of a glassy substance. They have no crystal structure and are therefore similar to obsidian, but are not associated with volcanic processes.

Their chemistry is unique and unexplained. The leading theory concerning their origin is the "Meteorite Impact Theory". It is postulated that many odd events occur during a meteor's impact, because of the tremendous heat and pressure produced. Tektites may be fused glass that formed during an impact of a meteor with layers of rock on the earth's surface. Tektites occur in broad bands in specific localities in different parts of the world. These bands produce characteristically similar tektites and are sometimes loosely associated with meteorite craters or suspected craters. Could these fields represent splash material from an impact? Many believe so and this idea is gaining acceptance from many scientists. The odd and diverse chemistry of the tektites could be a result of unique meteorites hitting unique rock types with the combinations producing particular effects.

Tektites, which have been found on every continent, are tar black or blackish brown, while moldavites, which have been found only in the Moldau river valley in Czechoslovakia, are a deep green color. The only known fall of moldavites occurred about 15 million years ago. They were prized by humans at least as long as 25,000 years ago, for archaeologists have discovered moldavite shards and pieces in cave dwellings of that era.

Moldavites are the rarest of gems, perhaps rarer than diamonds, rubies or emeralds. Since their origin is not of the earth, the discovery of new deposits seems unlikely. Moldavites are sometimes cut as gemstones or put into jewellery as natural uncut pieces to show off their often eerie and exquisite intricate shapes.

Although moldavite has been known of as a gem for thousands of years, it remained in obscurity until recently, the only reference being an article in the Lapidary Journal in 1958 about a strange stone with some kind of mystical properties. In 1986 the wonderful book 'Moldavite, Starborn Stone', by Bob Simmons and Kathy Warner, was published. It brought the truly transformational stone moldavite to the attention of millions of 'Light-Workers' around the Planet.

The 5 keys to moldavite's transformational properties are its:

* Amorphous Nature - Inner Structure
* Cosmic Birth - Growth Conditions
* Verdant Green Hue - Color Vibration
* Intense Resonance - Vibration
* 'Spirit' or Angel Guide - Inspiration

Amorphous Nature - Inner Structure

Basically, moldavite has no structure; this means it can take you beyond your self-limiting belief system into uncharted realms of infinite possibilities. Moldavite contains the essence of *shunyata*, the vast emptiness (which contains all potentiality), stretching in all directions, absolutely clear, pristine and radiant. By this clear starry night sky stretching into infinity we can gain an understanding, a feeling for the expansiveness and freedom which could be ours if we did not allow our horizons to become narrow, clouded and limited, if we did not permit our minds to become fixated and hypnotized by cravings and worries centred on what really are empty passing phenomena.

Cosmic Birth - Growth Conditions

Moldavite's chemistry is unique and unexplained. The leading theory concerning their origin is the "Meteorite Impact Theory". They were born from a meteor's impact because of the tremendous heat and pressure produced. This makes the energy of moldavite very fast, hot and cosmic. They were sent here for the awakened 'star children', to help their ascension into the higher realms of cosmic consciousness. This massive vibrational shift is happening right now, that is why so many people feel a magnetic attraction to the cosmic transformational tool of moldavite.

Verdant Green Hue - Color Vibration

Green is a balance color, it is the bridge, a gateway into the heart of the body; the lesson of love that needs to be learned in order to grow spiritually. Green will encourage your spiritual growth. It wants you to take your proper place in life. Green gives you harmony and balance. Green does just not follow rules blindly, it creates better ones where the old ones have failed. Green holds the keys to memory - it can remember that which needs to be re-membered. So it unlocks the deep and hidden that is the cause of our psychological and physical dis-ease. It is the diagnostic color. This makes moldavite one of the best diagnostic crystals we have available. An aversion to moldavite or the color green often indicates that we do not feel at ease with our emotions. It shows a deep fear of opening our heart chakra fully to unlimited unconditional love.

Intense Resonance - Vibration

Metaphysically, we have within us the light body and this contains encodements of information like files. When we hold moldavite this data is released. Very often many people are not consciously aware of the information being unlocked, they just feel what has commonly been called 'the moldavite flush', a huge wave of powerful energy which actually flushes through the body; this can cause sweating or a bright 'red' face. Interestingly, red is the green ray's balance color. Others experience the decoding or download as heat surging up their spine. Still others experience the download as an emotional release of tears or laughter. Others find the vibrational download shift and the resulting rise in their vibrational rate as too intense; they may become fearful. Others experience it as dizziness or headaches. There is no doubt, though, the download does cause massive spiritual growth. It can take years to fully integrate the download of information. In fact the more people resist the integration of their Divine blueprint being decoded from the Akashic records, the longer it takes.

'Spirit' or Angel Guide - Inspiration

When we hold, wear, meditate or carry moldavite our energy field changes. The universal law of resonance says that what we focus on becomes our reality. Like attracts like. When we understand that every thought is sent out and attracts like energy which strengthens it, then comes back to us like a boomerang, we begin to grasp how the higher vibration of moldavite increases our sensitivity and increases our clairaudience and clairvoyance abilities. We literally attract a higher form of guidance. Moldavite does have an Oversoul Spirit Guide, which is a vast cosmic Angel. The moldavite Angel can help in all areas, including connecting you to other high vibrational guides and Ascended Masters. These Cosmic Masters have been around for aeons and are able to work with anyone whose vibration has been raised sufficiently. You don't have to use moldavite, though, to attract Cosmic Masters. Many people who have refined their vibration through meditation have accessed this guidance.

The 'Grail Stone' is another name for moldavite: it is its 'Spirit' name. Legend has it that anyone who touches the 'Grail Stone' will have a spiritual transformation. Those who choose to wear, carry, meditate or heal with moldavite carry the energy of moldavite within their Divine blueprint. This makes them the ambassadors for transformation; indeed their energy is raised to such a high vibration of resonance they become the instruments of the enfoldment of the Divine plan for Planet Earth as she and her children make the vibrational shift into the next dimension.

Affirmation: I release all limiting thought patterns: I am transformed.

Moonstone - Oligoclase - Feldspar

Chemical Composition: Na(90-70%) Ca(10-30%) (Al, Si)$AlSi_2O_8$

Crystal System: Triclinic **Hardness:** 6 - 6.5

Habit: Includes blocky or tabular crystals. Crystals have a nearly rectangular or square cross-section, with slightly slanted dome and pinacoid terminations; also massive, granular

Color: Usually off-white or grey or pale shades of green, yellow, blue, pink or brown

Keyword: Mysterious

Oligoclase is not a well-known gemstone but has been used as a semi-precious stone under the labels of sunstone and moonstone. Sunstone has flashes of reddish color caused by inclusions of hematite. Moonstone shows a glowing shimmer similar to labradorescence, but it is much more subtle. Moonstone is a variety of feldspar and the shimmer, which is called schiller or adularescence, is caused by the intergrowth of two different types of feldspar, with different refractive indexes. Moonstones come in a variety of colors and can range from colorless to grey, brown, yellow, green, blue or pink. The clarity ranges from transparent to translucent. The best moonstone has a blue sheen, perfect clarity and a colorless body color. Sometimes moonstone will have an eye as well as a sheen. Another related feldspar variety is known as rainbow moonstone. In this variety of labradorite feldspar, the sheen is a variety of rainbow hues. Moonstone appears mysterious and magical, with a ghostly shimmering glow floating in a crystalline material. The Romans thought that moonstone was formed out of moonlight. In Europe, moonstone is considered the birthstone for June.

As the talisman of the Goddess, moonstone is the female power stone. Due to its close association with lunar energies it facilitates the wearer's deep understanding and celebration of the cycles of life, of the ebb and flow of birth, death and regeneration - the tides of life. Throughout the ages, people have celebrated the role of the goddess in maintaining balance and harmony. In recent history (the last two thousand years) the goddess has been eclipsed by the solar male energy; she has been subjugated, ignored, humbled and vanquished. People forget that the moon and the goddess energy is in reality our true salvation; by honouring the earth and respecting the feminine we will begin to redress the imbalance. We live in a culture that feeds misogyny - the female holocaust. Moonstone is acceptance and wisdom beyond the energy of duality. It has a soft lustre, an inner strength and hidden power. Moonstone gives personal resilience and calms the mind. It is nurturing to the soul and heals the subtle energy system, by comforting and aiding serene contemplation. Moonstone will lull, soothe, console, comfort, bring personal peace, tranquillity and deep soul connection. Moonstone instigates ceremony and ritual by observation and honouring the feminine: the Divine driving force of the universe. Moonstone makes an excellent gemstone essence and meditation stone. It is good for aiding peaceful sleep and when used in body layouts it is very soothing, except for the peach variety, which is creative and inspiring.

Affirmation: The great mystery guides and nurtures me, it activates my inner strength and hidden power.

Moqui Marbles - Shaman Stones

Color: Brown - to mustard orange-yellow to black

Keyword: Vision Quest

Moqui marbles are also known as Shaman Stones. They have been used for centuries by Shamanic tribes. They get the name Moqui from the Native American tribe of Indians who live in Utah.

Moqui marbles are down to earth, solid and reliable. They can be used for grounding and bringing stability to the energy field. They increase confidence and bring self-assurance. They also help with assimilation and absorption. They bring a cloak of security and earthy support during times of stress.

Moqui marbles hold the seeds of renewal and new growth. When used in healing ceremonies they will align all of the subtle bodies and both balance and align the chakras. They can remove energy blockages and increase the wearer's energy field, clean the aura, charge and fill the voids; they are used for general healing and tissue regeneration, will remove pain when placed on a painful or congested area and are for balance and harmony within the body. It is best to use a pair of Moqui marbles, one walnut-shaped male and one smooth female. Use the female on the left side of the body and the male on the right side.

Moqui marbles have a balanced polarity, so they may be used on acupuncture or acupressure points. They work through the meridian system of the body. They have been used to promote visionary journeys and by Shamans in their shape-shifting ceremonies. For clearing the main energy channel within the spine, place one at the top of the head in the crown chakra, the other between the feet in the earth star chakra, and begin to become aware of your breathing. This allows the natural resonance of the stones to purify the spinal column.

After 15 minutes the purification of the spinal column is complete.

Also Moqui marbles are wonderful dream allies, enhancing dream and inner journey pathworkings. These stones have been used for 'medicine gifts' to one's allies, guides and teachers.

Affirmation: I use my inner vision on my spiritual quest for enlightenment.

Morganite (See Aquamarine - Beryl)

Color: Various shades of peachy-pink

Keywords: Universal Love

Morganite is the pink variety of beryl. Other gemstone color varieties that belong to beryl include emerald, heliodor and aquamarine. Other colors of beryl are simply referred to by their color, such as red beryl. Morganite is colored by trace amounts of manganese that find their way into the crystal structure. It is named after J. P. Morgan, a famous American industrialist.

Morganite is universal love and compassion; the love of humanity, of honouring each being for their own unique expression of their intrinsic Divinity; of unity within diversity. Morganite contains the energy of high affection - affection without ulterior motive. It melts any resistance you may have to being truly in love or truly giving love freely. In crystal therapy morganite clears the way, by preparing the body to receive 'healing'. It soothes the physical body, making it more open and relaxed. This is the beginning and the end of all healing; if your client is not open to 'receiving', all therapy is in vain. Very often someone will give 'lip service' to the notion of healing, but they can't or won't change; being the victim does have its rewards. It makes them special. They may even compete with other victims to see who has suffered the most. Morganite helps these souls to remove the miasm that has lodged within the emotional body and is the source of the pre-disposition towards their victim mentality. These 'casualties' need love, not the co-dependant love of looking outside themselves for the love they crave and looking only to draw strength from others, but the mature love of high affection and deep soul healing; of nurturing into wholeness and self reliance. Easier said than done!

Morganite's signature is very special: it holds the emotional body stable as you let go of pain and painful memories; this is the key to its use. Very often, as people begin to truly heal, they find their emotions are volatile - healing sometimes brings up painful memories; it is easy to get swamped and give up, rather than having the courage to go with the flow. If a crystal therapist uses the vibrational signature of morganite, the emotional backlash is minimised.

Physically, morganite works on the digestive system; affection is nourishment. It also heals any part of the body and emotions we have rejected as being un-lovely or un-lovable. It is a good crystal to use after surgical procedures, especially where a body part has been removed or modified. It is good for those undergoing chemotherapy and long-term conventional drug therapy. It works with the patterns of dis-ease and rejection. Morganite helps clients reassess old ideas and issues, allowing them to melt and dissolve away. It is also good for skin eruptions and rashes.

Spiritually, morganite has a very active and beautiful guide who has worked for aeons to free humanity from the bonds of ignorance and suffering. Avalokiteshvara (Quan Yin), the chief Bodhisattva of Amitabha, whose name means infinite light, the Buddha of the West. Avalokiteshvara is the Bodhisattva of Compassion, who has a heartfelt longing to rescue all living beings from the burning house of *samsara*.

Affirmation: Universal Love, healing and compassion is made manifest in every cell and fibre of my being.

Obsidian - Snowflake - Mahogany - Apache Tears - Marekanite - Silver, Gold, Red, Purple, Green, Blue and Rainbow Obsidian

Chemical Composition: SiO_2; mostly silicon dioxide with large amounts of impurities

Crystal System: Amorphous **Hardness:** 5 - 5.5

Habit: Includes compact nodules or as layers between other volcanic rocks

Color: Dark green to dark brown and black, also can show sheens of gold or green, yellow, blue and/or purple coloration. Sometimes with white inclusions (Snowflake Obsidian)

Keywords: Warrior of Truth

Obsidian is of low significance as a material for gemstones, but the so-called volcanic glasses provide interest for the many uses to which they have been put by aboriginal man and by the enigma of their genesis. Obsidian is formed by the rapid cooling of volcanic lava which, had it been allowed to cool slowly, would have developed a crystalline structure and assumed the character of granitic rocks. There can be no exact chemical composition given for obsidian, for it may vary greatly, but all obsidian has from 66 to 72 per cent of silica and is an extreme modification of rhyolite and dacite rocks.

Obsidian is normally black or grey in color and owes any attraction it may have to an iridescent sheen caused by reflections from minute bubbles or inclusions of water or gas. The silver and gold sheen obsidian is highly prized and much sought after. In the United States of America a variety of obsidian having spherulitic inclusions of a white mineral on the black groundmass is cut and polished and goes under the name of 'flowering obsidian' or 'snowflake obsidian'. A variety banded black and red is known as 'mountain mahogany' or 'mahogany obsidian'.

A transparent leaf-green is also available, but it is extremely rare and most transparent green obsidians are usually found to be moldavites or merely green glass. Red and blue obsidians have also been found, but these are also very rare. Marekanite is the name applied to smoky-brown, grey or black decomposing perlitic obsidian found along the banks of the Mareikanka river at Okhotsk, in Siberia. Glassy pebble-like solid cores of unaltered glass, about an inch or more across, from the decomposed obsidian of the American south-west, are known as 'Apache tears'. The legends around Apache tears are legion.

The fracture of obsidian is extremely conchoidal and it is due to the facility with which the material can be broken into sharp-edged flakes that obsidian was so valued by Stone Age people who lived in areas where it was common, the easily controlled flaking allowing the production of keen-edge spear points, knives and tools. These have been discovered in ancient burial sites. Obsidian has been quarried since the days of the North American Indians, who used it for arrowhead material.

Obsidian was used by the Aztecs and their predecessors for the sharp points of their weapons, for mirrors and masks, and for ear ornaments. They called the material *Iztli* and surnamed it *Teotetl* (Divine stone) because of its diverse uses, one of which was the 'smoking mirror' used by the Mayan priests for scrying to predict the future. Obsidian occurs throughout the world at those places where volcanic activity occurs or has occurred in the past. In Iceland it is known as 'Iceland agate'. It has also been called 'Glass agate', 'Glass lava', 'Montana jet', 'Mountain jet', 'Nevada diamond', 'Nevada topaz', 'Rainbow obsidian', 'Iridescent obsidian' and 'Volcanic glass'. Obsidian derived its name from the Roman Obsius who, according to Pliny, found the stone in present-day Ethiopia. In antiquity, it was regarded as a stone that would drive out and banish demonic entities. In Hawaii it is considered the blood of the 'Mother' as she gives birth, through her volcanic activity.

Obsidian is a master mineral in the art of the hidden, lost or forbidden. It has no restrictions or limitations. This is due entirely to its amorphous structure; it teaches us to let go of our limitations and self-imposed fear restrictions. It teaches us to flow and expand. It has a soul mirror quality that is all its own.

Its 'Spirit' name is the 'Warrior of Truth'. When consciously directed, obsidian reflects our shadow side back to us for deep soul healing. Obsidian then teaches us how to bring more light into our darkness or shadow side. On the path to our own personal wholeness, healing and health, we must confront our deepest fears, phobias, pains, hurts and shame. Very often we desperately try to ignore our shadow side; these are the parts of us that we have judged, rightly or wrongly, to be bad, ugly or shameful. We have been conditioned since our births to conform to other people's ideas of good and bad, right or wrong. This is our personal 'conditioning', our 'robotic programming'. This programming *does* serve a vital function, it makes us easier to control and manipulate. These rules of good or bad constantly change, depending on our personal circumstances and present life situation; they are influenced by our religious beliefs, teachers, parents, relatives, politicians, scientists, the media and our peers. These rules do not represent Eternal Divine Truth, only the current civilisation's accepted truth. As we, as individualised perfect expressions of the sacred life force, claim our Divine birthright and personal power, we will have to confront all our demons of darkness and shine the light of truth into these murky recesses. These demons of darkness will otherwise manifest as illness, pain and feelings of separation from our source of love, inspiration and wisdom.

Obsidian draws the quality of our Divine essence into our physical body; this purges the negativity and activates 'the Divine essence within'. Obsidian will also shield us from all unkind energies which seek to use our energy and manipulate our energy field for their own benefit. It also dissolves all negative energy within our environment. It is an excellent grounding stone for when we feel spaced out or disorientated from reality. It quickly dissolves blocks, trauma, shock, fear and 'reality shock'. It helps us to deal with feelings of betrayal and exploitation.

It has been used for divination and scrying. This is accomplished by the process of soul integration, bringing our spiritual invulnerable self into our consciousness for attunement and integration, until we have a refined clairvoyance that encompasses eternal truth and integrity. Pain is quickly removed when obsidian is placed on the affected area. It has been used in the treatment of arthritis and all joint pain. It easily relieves cramp and the pain from injury or operation scars. It has been used to shrink enlarged prostates and ameliorate the painful side- effects of an enlarged prostate. It removes toxins from the body after exposure to pollution and toxic areas of the earth. It purges negativity from the meridian system and is being used instead of needles in acupuncture. It has helped remove and relieve painful areas in AIDS patients. It is soothing and comforting, but has the ability to deeply penetrate problems and degraded illnesses. Green obsidian is very purifying to the heart and throat chakras.

Because obsidian was used as an implement of death by Stone Age people who lived in areas where obsidian was common - as keen-edged spear points, knives and tools - you may have an initial resistance or fear of its energy. Be assured that the 'Spirit' keeper of obsidian is aware of your fear and will not allow any misuse of its energy.

Obsidian spheres have been used to unwind negative energy from dysfunctional chakras and painful areas of the body. They have also been used in meditation and scrying. An obsidian sphere used for meditation has been likened to an 'iron fist in a black velvet glove', so please have a sphere of clear quartz ready to help you fully integrate the energies a black obsidian sphere can unearth as it shatters your mirror of illusion.

I personally have obsidian as one of my spirit guides. The spirit of obsidian chose me, not the other way round. As we begin to work with crystals, we very often find some of them become 'very' special to us. They choose to act as a personal totem energy or ally. A totem energy is wholly reliable in all situations and acts as a guide on all levels, in all situations, very much like a personal 'Guardian Angel'.

In the late summer of 1990 I was teaching a crystal course in Manchester; it was the first week-end of this particular course, so I had not met all the students. The night before I had a dream in which a beautiful Goddess appeared; she was dressed in flowing iridescent sparkling black clothes and she wore a headdress of black feathers intertwined with shimmering jewels. As she stood before me she held out her hand: on it were three very long strange-looking claws like crystal blades; they were curved, dark, translucent and very exotic-looking. She said "choose one". As I gazed at them in wonder I asked "what are they?" She replied "crows' claws". In the Native American shamanic tradition, Crow Medicine is Truth, Wise Counsel, Wisdom and Resourcefulness. I then chose a 'claw'. The next day, during the lunch-time break in teaching the crystal course, one of the students approached me; she looked very shy, hesitant and a little perplexed. She said "yesterday I was in a crystal shop in London, which is close by where I live, and I was looking at these. I have never seen anything like them before. I was told spiritually to buy three; one is yours". As she stood before me, she held out her hand; on it were three very long exotic-looking claw-like crystal blades; they were curved, dark, translucent and very strange-looking. She said "choose one". Yes, you have guessed it, they were a type of natural obsidian blade I had never seen before. Yes, I was chosen.

Since then I have discovered more about these natural obsidian blades and have purchased them from the lady who 'harvests' them from her obsidian 'mine' in America. Because of the special formation, each blade can take her hours to unearth. They are quite fragile and range in size from a few inches long to huge specimens of 20 inches. I have used them continually in my healing work.

Affirmation: I am a spiritual warrior of truth.

Opal

Chemical Composition: SiO_2-nH_2O

Crystal System: Amorphous **Hardness:** 5.5 - 6.5

Habit: Massive; often as stalactitic, botryoidal and rounded forms; also as veinlets; cavity-fillings such as in fractures and geodes, nodular or as a replacement of other minerals and wood

Color: Variable from colorless through milky white, grey, red, brown, blue, green, pale yellow, pale red, pink, grey or black, when impurities are common. Diffraction can cause flashes of any color of the rainbow (opalescent)

Keywords: Emotional Mirror

The name opal comes from Sanskrit and means 'gem' or 'precious stone'. Opal has been a popular gem for many centuries and has a very interesting structure. Opal is considered a mineraloid because this structure is not truly crystalline. The chemistry of opal is primarily SiO_2 and varying amounts of water. Although there is no crystal structure (meaning a regular arrangement of atoms), opal does possess a structure nonetheless. Random chains of silicon and oxygen are packed into extraordinarily tiny spheres. These spheres in most opals are irregular in size and inconsistent in concentration.

Yet in precious opal, the variety used most often in jewellery, there are many organized pockets of the spheres. These pockets contain spheres of approximately equal size and have a regular concentration, or structure, of the spheres. This has the effect of diffracting light at various wavelengths, creating colors. Each pocket produces a different color, with a different intensity depending on the angle from which a viewer sees it. The multicolored flashes of light which opal emits give it a truly exquisite quality.

Hyalite is colorless, botryoidal opal; wood opal is wood that has been replaced in part by opaline silica; and hydrophane is a variety which becomes transparent when immersed in water. Siliceous sinter and geyserite are opaline deposits formed around geysers or by precipitation from hot waters. They generally form stalactitic and delicate filamentous forms of various colors. Precious opal has a milky white and sometimes black body color. Fire opal is a variety in which red and yellow colors are dominant and produce flame-like reflections when turned.

Opal has been treasured throughout history around the world. Archaeologist Louis Leakey found six thousand-year-old opal artifacts in a cave in Kenya. Roman historian Pliny described the magnificence of opal as the combination of the beauty of all other gems: "There is in them a softer fire than the ruby, there is the brilliant purple of the amethyst, and the sea green of the emerald - all shining together in incredible union. Some by their splendour rival the colors of the painters, others the flame of burning sulphur or of fire quickened by oil."

Opal was much loved and valued highly by the Romans, who called it opalus. In Greek mythology opal is said to have formed out of the tears of joy Zeus cried after his victory over the Titans.

The Aztecs mined opal in South and Central America. Opal was also treasured in the Middle Ages and was called ophthalmios, or eye stone, due to a widespread belief that it was beneficial to eyesight.

Blonde women wore opal necklaces to protect their hair from losing its color. An opal called the orphanus was set in the crown of the Holy Roman Emperor. It was described as follows: "as though pure white snow flashed and sparkled with the color of bright ruddy wine, and was overcome by this radiance." This opal was said to protect the regal honour. Opals are also set in the crown jewels of France. Napoleon gave Josephine a beautiful opal with brilliant red flashes called "The burning of Troy," making her his Helen.

Shakespeare found in the opal a symbol of shifting inconstancy, likening play of color to play of mind in one of the most apt uses of gemstone symbolism in literature. In 'Twelfth Night', he writes: "Now the melancholy God protect thee, and the tailor make thy garments of changeable taffeta, for thy mind is opal."

In India, opal is thought to be the Goddess of rainbows turned to stone when fleeing from the romantic advances of the other Gods. Queen Victoria loved opals and often gave them as wedding presents. Ancient opal came from the mines near Cervenica, Hungary, in what is now Eastern Slovakia, where hundreds of men mined the stone.

Ancient opal devotees never had the opportunity to see the opal of Australia, where the opal of today was born, which far surpasses the beauty of Hungarian opal in fire, color and sheer brilliance. Gold panners in Australia found the first few pieces of precious opal in 1863. Mines at White Cliffs began producing in 1890. The strength of the colors seen in opal also depend on the background body color and the transparency of the stone. Opal is the birthstone for those born in October.

Opal is absorbent, it picks up your emotional energies, positive or negative, and works with the karmic law of return: what you send out is returned amplified like a boomerang. The reason the energy is magnified is very simple: like attracts like! This makes some people very wary of wearing opal, and rightly so - for if you are not sending out positive loving energy and are instead deeply focused on negativity, the last thing you need is even more negativity! But don't blame the beautiful opal, it is just showing you the Universal Law of resonance: what you focus on attracts even more of the same energy; this law makes you very aware of your every thought, word and deed. What you give out will always be yours, you just attract even more of the same! This law can cause havoc when you consider all the 'black' spots on the planet. We have all had enough of killing, of chaos and confusion. I know from my own experience that we can change our field of reality. It is as simple as owning your thoughts, feelings, emotions - your vibratory pattern. Pure mind power - don't be the problem, be the cure. Opals are wonderful emotional healers when you are ready to accept responsibility for owning your own emotional energies and vibratory pattern.

Opal is also used for 'Soul Star' activation in body layouts. The brilliant flashes of light frequency emitted by the opal cause a significant vibrational shift in the chakra immediately above the crown chakra. Although the 'Soul Star' chakra is not actually located on the physical body, its influence and activation will cause a download of 'light vibrational information' that can greatly induce emotional healing and deepen the spiritual results of meditation practice.

Most recently opals have been frequently used to send healing to the Earth's energy matrix; this is activated by sacred sounds or mantras. Each 'Star Seed' on the planet at this time holds a Divine 'key' within their own personal 'Mandala'; as we gather in groups of other 'Light Workers' we should tone our own sacred 'sound key'. This energy is then carried via the opal to the Dolphins and Whales within the Earth's oceans - which will then be anchored into the Earth's energy grid. This will cause a raising of the vibrational energy. By bringing the vibration of the planet into a higher octave, we should find a lessening of aggression and negative frequencies within the 'black spots'. Just as the 'Universal Law of Resonance' works on the human energy field, the same applies to the Earth.

Mysterious opals contain the wonders of the skies - sparking rainbows, fireworks and lightning - shifting and stirring in their depths. They can be extremely inspiring and have been used by artists to gain heavenly Divine inspirational flashes. The opal vibration is very motivating.

Opal can also be used in visualisation practice. As we hold a beautiful opal we begin to visualise ourselves seated on a beautiful white lotus flower set in the midst of an endless perfect blue sky. As we focus on the 'rainbow' opal, its iridescent light begins to enter our heart chakra. There it begins to turn anticlockwise; as it does so, rainbows pour from it, filling our whole body and purifying it, until finally we sit transformed; our gross physical body is now iridescent rainbow light. Having filled our body, the rainbows overspill from the crown of our head and cascade down through our aura. You can stay as long as you like in this visualisation, but please allow all feelings of 'light-headedness' to dissipate before you move about.

Blue Opal (Andean Blue Silica)

Contains no fire. So it is soothing emotionally, it enhances personal courage and confidence. A powerful healer for the etheric blueprint, within the auric field. Realigns you to your highest spiritual purpose this lifetime on the earth plane and gives you the courage to complete. It is a tool for sacred living and sacred gatherings; it is a very sociable crystal. It encourages you to share your heartfelt emotions.

Blue opal is very good for overcoming self-sabotage. It also has a strong affinity with all the sea creatures, including Dolphins, Whales and Mer-fairies.

Pink Opal (Andean Pink Silica)

Contains no fire. Use the pink opal after a person has been assaulted in any way, or after they have had part of their body removed or modified in an operation. Pink opal gets rid of emotional hang-ups. It is spiritually uplifting and creates achievement through love.

It helps you release sorrow with dignity, rather than the distraught expression of emotional turmoil. It enhances your spiritual awakening, bringing Divine joy to all your ventures. It has a beneficial effect on the entire endocrine system. Releases guilt and teaches you to not to be a victim. It is also a good stone to use when the sweetness has gone out of life and has been used to alleviate the symptoms of diabetics.

Fire Opal

Fire opal is used on the area of the lower back and lower intestines, the abdomen and the kidneys. It helps the function of the adrenal glands and is good when used during stressful situations to stop emotional 'burnout'. When someone feels they have been mistreated or are deeply outraged - 'it isn't fair' syndrome - fire opal will bring them up through the shock and emotional turmoil. Fire opal can release deep-seated fears and grief. It helps people to deal with the past and let go. Fire opal frees the spirit and brings optimism and creative power. Fire opal also teaches you self-reliance and to trust your gut instinct regardless of the intellect.

Black Opal

This is used for going into your own personal darkness to discover the Universal Light. It is also used for gazing, providing insight and vision. Also a very high vibration grounding stone, useful when other grounding stones would be too dense a vibration for the energy field of the awakened 'Light Worker'. It is good for souls who have lost faith in tomorrow. Black opal also brings order out of chaos and banishes chaotic thought patterns.

Oregon Opal

This opal is from volcanic deposits in Oregon. It is transparent bluish-white material and rainbow material. It is the gentle form of opal; it is emotionally uplifting and encouraging. It has a lovely lulling quality about it.

Oregon opal tones down the harsh and abrupt. It has a purity and innocence about it; it induces faith and trust in the self. It teaches you to be a free spirit, to break away, to loosen the chains that bind you from reaching your soul's maturity. It is good to use on those souls who are moody with an unforgiving temperament, who needlessly hold on to resentment and hostility.

Affirmation: I now choose to work with the 'Universal Law of Resonance' in a positive loving way.

Opal Aura Quartz (See Quartz)

Color: Pale iridescent rainbow

Keyword: - Brilliance

Opal aura quartz is a product of twentieth century technology, just as aqua aura quartz, ruby aura quartz and sunshine aura quartz are. The beauty of these quartzes is apparent as the 'new' technology enhances the extremely powerful properties of the master healer, clear quartz. Opal aura is clear organic quartz combined with platinum; this combination produces the most amazing pale iridescent rainbow effect. They are a joy to work with and wear.

Rainbows bring joy, light and optimism. Opal aura is an activator of brilliance on all levels of the body and aura. It has been used for aura and chakra clearing, removing 'cords', limited beliefs, wrong mental attitudes, unspoken psychic contracts and astral parasites.

It aligns and purifies all the chakra system, allowing for the 'rainbow light body' activation and integration. The rainbow light body is the full integration of the 'higher self' and leads to enlightenment.

Opal aura allows for deeper meditative states to be reached and knowledge gained to be fully integrated into the 'personality'. During meditation practice, the mind can assume various states of quietude and peace which are often confused and misleading. There is a supersensual bliss that comes with the very lower stages of *samadhi* which, once experienced, leads the meditator to imagine that the final goal has been attained. Opal aura shows you that you should never be satisfied with these lower experiences, but continue onwards towards the experience of full *samadhi* or total union.

Meditation is a lifelong practice, for there will never be a point where there is nothing more to be learned. The last obstacle all who meditate must face, before total union is achieved, is the great void. This too must be crossed by the meditator. It is accompanied by an overpowering feeling of being stripped bare and left totally alone. There is nothing that can be seen or heard. The meditator is beyond seeking solace in others and confronts this illusion themselves. Strength of mind is needed at this juncture and, by drawing courage and strength from within, a triumphant leap of faith is made. Opal aura will give inner rainbow light, strength and courage to those who sincerely seek enlightenment and Cosmic Consciousness.

Affirmation: I cease to limit myself, I now connect my spirit to the source of all knowledge and brilliance.

Peridot - Olivine - Chrysolite

Chemical Composition: $(Mg,Fe)_2SiO_4$

Crystal System: Orthorhombic **Hardness:** 6.5 - 7

Habit: Good crystals are rare; occurs usually as isolated grains in igneous rocks, or as granular aggregates

Color: Various shades of green; olivine is olive green color; sometimes yellowish or brownish to black; reddish when oxidized

Keyword: Springtime

Peridot is the volcanic gem. Small crystals of peridot are often found in the rocks created by volcanoes and also can be found in meteors that fall to earth. A few samples of extraterrestrial peridot have even been faceted into gems. Because the iron which creates the color is an integral part of its structure, it is found only in green, ranging from a summery light yellowish green to bottle green.

Peridot was mined in ancient Egypt on an island called Zeberget. Mining was done at night because legend said that peridot could not be easily seen during the day. The island was infested with serpents who made peridot mining a very dangerous occupation until one Pharaoh finally had them all driven into the sea.

The Romans called peridot 'evening emerald,' since its green color did not darken at night but was still visible by lamplight. Peridot later was also often used to decorate medieval churches. The ancients believed peridot had the power to drive away evil spirits and the power was considered to be even more intense when the stone was set in gold. Peridot was also said to strengthen the power of any medicine drunk from goblets carved from the gemstone.

Although peridot is treasured in Hawaii as the goddess Pele's tears, almost all of the peridot sold in Hawaii today is from Arizona, even though peridot is produced by Hawaii's volcanoes. The island of Oahu even has beaches made out of olivine grains, but unfortunately they are much too small to cut into peridot!

It is mentioned in the Bible under the name of chrysolite. Peridot is considered a secondary 'Vedic' gemstone 'remedy' after emerald for a badly aspected mercury. Although in Vedic Astrology its potency is somewhat reduced, dedication and commitment will bring positive results. In fact the ancient gemological teachings of the East place prime importance on the colour and the quality of the gem crystal.

Peridot is considered in the West the birthstone of those born in August. The springtime energy of peridot is very refreshing to the whole body. It contains vitality and gives the encouragement of renewal - a fresh start. Peridot is helpful for manic depressives. It is also the best crystal for anyone who truly believes that everything wrong in their lives is due to outside circumstances, that someone else is always at fault. It also heals the negative energy of the green ray - jealousy, resentment, selfishness, hypochondria, scarcity, hatred, greed, envy and spite. It is a good crystal for people who are surrounded by disastrous relationships and refuse to acknowledge their part in the problem.

On a physical level it balances the thymus and alleviates problems of the heart, chest, shoulders and lower lungs. Peridot helps dispel negative emotions and can be used when you are trying to make up your mind. It gives direction and wisdom to make the right choice. Peridot can act as a tonic; it eases biliousness, soothes headaches. It is a good detoxifier of the liver. Peridot can purge the system of that which must go for emotional growth and mental stability to manifest.

Rejuvenation, growth and the enthusiasm of youth are the fruits of using peridot. It has also been used for auric protection and to strengthen the energy field of those people who have very little or no green in their aura.

Peridot is a very fiery active crystal to work with, as the crystal therapists who live in Hawaii will vouch for. It does contain the refined energy of the manipura chakra and will help you overcome the fear of fire. It is said she/he who concentrates on this chakra has no fear of fire and is free from disease.

Affirmation: I now release all anger and resentment, so that the fresh new energies of springtime can manifest in my life.

Petalite

Chemical Composition: $LiAlSi_4O_{10}$

Crystal System: Monoclinic **Hardness:** 6 - 6.5

Habit: Crystals are rare; usually massive, showing cleavage

Color: Colorless, white, pink, grey, green or reddish

Keywords: Cosmic Consciousness

Petalite occurs typically in lithium-bearing granite pegmatites along with minerals such as spodumene, tourmaline and lepidolite. Petalite received its name from the Greek word for leaf. Colorless petalite is used to render negative energies impotent. It repels all negative energies, negative entities, evil, black magic, all implants, releases all negative karma and miasms. Petalite releases all binding ties, removes all manipulation. This allows the user to learn discernment in all areas of their life. It teaches you to be aware of every thought, word and deed, to purify and refine your vibration, until your whole system on every level is full of pristine light and glory and you become a conscious channel for the light, a force for good. It encourages wisdom, understanding, truth, dispassion, discrimination, serenity, self-restraint, one-pointedness of mind, purity, forbearance, fortitude, patience, forgiveness, the spirit of service, sacrifice and love for all. Petalite also teaches you to avoid fear, anger, hatred, greed, desire, ego manipulation, pride, boastfulness and laziness. Petalite will activate higher states of cosmic consciousness, where you realise that 'powers' such as clairvoyance and clairaudience are not worth striving for because far greater illumination and peace are possible beyond them. If one regularly practises concentration and meditation, psychic powers are bound to come; but they must not be used for selfish gain, otherwise you become a victim of your own ignorance.

Physically, each gland in the body has a specific color and vibration of its own. Petalite works on all of them by working on the collective functioning of the endocrine system, so it is ideal to use in gemstone layouts over any area that needs clearing of stagnant or stuck energy. Petalite also keeps the skin supple and moist, and directly works on the eyes, especially the whites of the eyes. The state of the whites of the eyes is used in diagnosing physical health. Petalite works well with other crystals and as a basic carrier for other energies. It is also good to use when people have 'frozen emotions', withdrawal, their mind is occupied elsewhere; it begins the process of healing. Petalite has a beneficial cooling quality on the whole system and it eases feelings of frustration and isolation by linking you to your 'Divine Essence'. Pink petalite makes us gentle yet strong; there is no question of pliability or giving in, regardless of any outside pressure that wishes to manipulate our energy field for its own selfish gain. It strengthens the emotional body, by activating the Kundalini energy within the root chakra. This allows us to stay strong, focused and grounded whilst maintaining a balanced open, compassionate heart chakra. Pink petalite is warming to the whole body. It clears the heart meridian, which in turn releases stored emotional baggage. Pink petalite releases us from worry and helps discrimination. It stimulates the blood circulation in the tissues. It fortifies the heart and sexual organs and encourages fertility.

Affirmation: I now activate higher states of Cosmic Consciousness to manifest in my life.

Phenacite - Phenakite

Chemical Composition: Be_2SiO_4

Crystal System: Trigonal **Hardness:** 7.5 - 8

Habit: Crystals are rare; flattened rhombohedral to almost tabular and typically short prismatic crystals, although some prismatic crystals can be rather long

Color: Colorless, white, but can be tinted yellow, brown and pink

Keywords: Light Body Activation

Phenacite is a rare beryllium mineral, but it is found so frequently with precious gemstones that its availability is not in proportion to its rarity. It is found in pegmatitic pockets and is associated with gemstones such as topaz, beryl - especially emerald, chrysoberyl and smoky quartz.

The name phenacite is from a Greek word meaning deceiver, an allusion to its deceptively similar look to quartz. Phenacite is one of the few silicate minerals that has a trigonal symmetry. This symmetry is far more common among carbonates than among silicates. Fine crystals of phenacite can be perfectly clear and, with good hardness, rarity, color and fire, make good choices for gemstones jewellery when you wish to raise your vibratory resonance.

Phenacite is a very rare and beautiful crystal. People who have worked for many years metaphysically with crystals and gemstones classify phenacite as having the highest vibration yet found in any crystal.

It is a powerful activator of the upper chakras, especially the crown and the non-physical 8th to 14th chakras above the head. The Soul Star chakra, which is situated just above the crown chakra, becomes especially energised into full alignment with the higher self.

Phenacite allows entrance only to those who know how to access the energies of this mystical stone. You have to 'aim' very high with phenacite. This stone is only for those who can expand their consciousness far beyond the perceived physical plane and who wish to explore their full potential this lifetime.

Brazilian phenacite is said to have the highest vibration and is associated with the Angelic feminine energies.

The yellow Madagascar phenacite is associated with the extraterrestrial flow and is a powerful tool for manifestation. Colorless Madagascar phenacite is used for grounding the light body into our physical body.

All phenacites help one to activate the light body and to consciously experience one's existence in higher dimensions. Phenacite encourages you to become a spiritual hero in the worldly battlefield, be brave, be undaunted, be a spiritual soldier; to conquer the inner war with the mind and senses, for it is more terrible than the external war; to soar high into the higher regions of bliss.

Clear Madagascar phenacite especially brings this conscious awareness of the Universal Law of resonance, like attracts like. It teaches you to be aware of every thought, word and deed, to purify and refine your vibration, until your whole system on every level is full of pristine light and glory and you become a conscious channel for the light, a force for good. It encourages wisdom, understanding, truth, dispassion, discrimination, serenity, self-restraint, one-pointedness of mind, purity, forbearance, fortitude, patience, forgiveness, the spirit of service, sacrifice and love for all.

Phenacite is a multi-dimensional energy device: it can teach you astral travel. It knows the gateways to other realms and worlds of infinite bliss. Initiation into the ancient mysteries are stored within its vibrational structure. Phenacite gives the full activation and initiation of the ascension process by downloading the information stored within your Divine blueprint on the Akashic records into your energy body.

Phenacite holds the key of the superior human vibration within its structure, for those who choose to use it, to make their ascension in the light. It is a flowing graceful matrix primer of healing, when taken as a gemstone essence. When used to clear the chakra system it is a healer of the soul, heralding the soul force into the vibration of ascension.

Clear faceted stones work the best, the clearer the better, but as with all vibrational energy work your intent and dedication will bring good results, regardless of the clarity or size.

Phenacite, most of all, is the Guardian of the gateway guardians. It has frequently initiated contact with Ascended Masters and Angelic guides for those who choose to work in this way. Cosmic Consciousness is an inherent natural faculty of all women and men. Training and discipline are necessary to awaken the consciousness. It is already present in mankind. It is inactive or non-functioning in the vast majority of human beings on account of the force of *Avidya* or ignorance.

Affirmation: I now activate the Divine blueprint of my light body. I am ascending in the light.

Pietersite - Glaucophane - Riebeckite - Crocidolite - Tempest Stone - Stormstone

Chemical Composition: $SiO_2+Na_2(Mg,Fe,Al)_5(OH/Si_4O_{11})_2$

Crystal System: Trigonal **Hardness:** 5-6

Habit: Good crystals rare; often prismatic or acicular; sometimes fibrous

Color: Pietersite is golden-brown to deep blue-grey

Keywords: Earth Dance

Color and association is distinctive for both glaucophane and riebeckite. Glaucophane occurs typically in sodium-rich schists, derived from geosynclinal sediments which have undergone low temperature/high pressure regional metamorphism. It occurs with minerals such as jadeite, aragonite, epidote, chlorite, muscovite and garnet. Riebeckite occurs mainly in alkaline igneous rocks such as granites. Fibrous riebeckite, known as crocidolite or blue asbestos, occurs as veins in bedded ironstones. Pietersite (tempest stone) is a form of silicified riebeckite with limonite from south-west Africa. It is named after its discoverer, Sid Pieters.

Pietersite has manifested at this time to dispel the elusion created by confusion, the confusion being caused by the following of others' rituals and truths, instead of listening to the still quiet voice within your own heart.

It is a strong stone and this allows you to find your own strength, internal as well as external. It is not always easy to stand in your own truth and take your own earth walk simply by following your own guiding star.

Other people are always opinionated and feel free to not only give advice, but very often thrust their advice upon you. Often they mean well - but pietersite teaches you to look for the truth beneath the words. You and only you know what is best for you. This is because you are so unique, as are your experiences. If we were all the same, there would be no point in so many of us being on the planet at this time; remember we are all expressions of the Divine God/Goddess and are here to have a completely unique earth walk.

This also teaches us not to put our own thoughts and feelings on to others. This is not always easy, when so many on the planet have given their power away and are completely lost. Pietersite will give the 'lost' stability during these stormy periods. This stone possesses a strong male energy, full of vitality, vigour and potent storm power. Holding it gives a feeling of the vast expanse of the African continent. Although 'pietersite' in this form was only recently discovered by Sid Pieters, many who work metaphysically with crystals feel it has been used for centuries by the native medicine people of Africa.

This stone can feel quite challenging to female energies, as holding it one is instantly aware of the powerful spirit that guides and guards the gateway to the ceremonial and ancient energies contained within. We must sometimes face our fears and look deeper when we are confronted by such a powerful spirit guide. When we do, we find it challenging but very enlightening.

In these times of conflict and confusion, it is only by going to the ancient guardians that dwell within the rocks and the very earth herself that our salvation abides. We will make the next shift in consciousness together, whether we are ready or not. This stone's guardian is very protective to those who have the courage and tenacity to fully work with its energies. The over-soul or Angel of pietersite is very powerful. This stone acts as a catalyst to aid vision quests, vision and meditation work. It will quickly dispel confusion, giving a strong guidance, and this is only guidance, not a command; it will not control you, but offer deep insight into current problems that plague your life and stop your spiritual growth towards the perfected state of self-realisation and God/Goddess realisation.

Physically, this stone works on the liver, intestines, feet and legs and helps the blood by purifying the whole body, allowing for greater absorption of nutrients from food. It will regulate hormonal levels, giving potency and fulfilment of all creative pursuits.

It energizes the physical body and aligns the central column, giving an ease and flow to the life force energy. It will open the meridian system, releasing blocks in the energy flow. This will bring all the subtle bodies into perfect alignment.

Pietersite is a strong elemental ally of the Earth Dance; it teaches prayer in motion and can be used by 'Shaman/Shamanka' to quickly bring on altered states of consciousness - from shape-shifting, to shields of perception, to viewing the luminous egg cocoon. You can 'hear' the drumbeat of Mother Earth with this stone.

Affirmation: I am taking responsibility for my life, I now choose to release all confusion and fear and enjoy my earth dance.

Platinum

Chemical Composition: Pt

Crystal System: Isometric **Hardness:** 4 - 4.5

Habit: Nuggets and grains or flakes, rarely showing cubic forms

Color: White-grey to silver-grey, usually lighter than the platinum color of pure processed platinum

Keyword: Environment

Native platinum is an exotic mineral specimen and an expensive metal. Unfortunately, well- formed crystals of platinum are extremely rare. Pure platinum is unknown of in nature as it usually is alloyed with other metals such as iron, copper, gold, nickel, iridium, palladium, rhodium, ruthenium and osmium.

It is typically more expensive by weight than gold, mostly a product of its scarcity. Platinum is very non-reactive and for this reason it is used in chemical reactions as a catalyst. Metallic platinum can facilitate many chemical reactions without becoming altered in the process. It is also used in many anti-pollution devices; most notable is the catalytic converter, and it has been given the nickname the 'Environmental Metal'.

Platinum contains the energies of illumination; it is penetrating and focused, pristine and light. It will reflect negative energies back to their source. It exposes the hidden and untrue, so it is a good 'witness' energy to use in dowsing and kinesiology.

It is good to use in times of stress and stressful situations. It has also been used to bring alignment to the chakra system and facilitate Divine alignment. Its energy is incorruptible, which is why it has terrific potential for cleansing and protecting not only the human energy field but also the environment.

Platinum works on the endocrine system. Platinum supports the life force within all the bodies, physical, emotional, mental, spiritual, etc. and the surrounding auric field, allowing for a greater abundance of vital energy. It gives a feeling of total well-being.

Affirmation: I now begin to harmonise my relationships and environment.

Prehnite

Chemical Composition: $Ca_2Al_2Si_3O_{10}(OH)_2$

Crystal System: Orthorhombic **Hardness:** 6 - 6.5

Habit: Crystals are rare, tabular; usually in globular and reniform masses with a fibrous structure

Color: Colorless to pale green, dark green, yellow, white, brown

Keywords: Spirit of the Home

Prehnite occurs most commonly in veins and cavities in igneous rocks, often in association with zeolites. It is named after Col. von Prehn, who discovered the mineral at the Cape of Good Hope, South Africa.

Prehnite contains the energy to awaken the 'Spirit of the Home'. It makes you look at your personal environment. Your home - is it a place of sanctuary and healing? A place that nurtures your spirit? Does your home calm your mind and soothe your soul? Are you aware of just how great the healing and life-enhancing potential of your physical environment can be? This crystal will inspire you to look at your home and yourself in a whole new light. It will also make you want to take a look at your garden, to create a haven of repose and sanctuary. Do you know how to energize and renew your surroundings?

Prehnite's message is: harmonize with, do not disrupt, nature. We all know tampering with nature not only disrupts the harmonious flow of the weather but also damages the environment. When we work in harmony with the elemental forces, rather than combating them, we create positive energy in our living and working environments. By focusing on the powerful energy that flows around us, we can begin to bring balance and harmony to every area of our lives.

A simple way to begin is to look at your home, room by room. Begin in the rooms you spend the most time in, especially the bedroom. Look at the color section of this book and see if your current color scheme has the correct energies for your needs. If not, change it for a more harmonious color scheme.

I find one of the most important energies you should address on the 'spiritual path' is your clutter. For years I have been teaching that the more 'stuff' you hoard, the harder it is to be spiritual. People spend a lot of time not only cleaning their clutter but protecting it as well. Just think, not only do you have to raise your own energy field, but the energy of your 'stuff' as well. Take a look at the 'Feng Shui' section in part six and begin today by harmonising your personal environment.

Prehnite works on the thymus gland, the heart, shoulders, chest and lungs. Prehnite also restores stability to anything malignant. Malignancy is the result of cells that have accelerated out of control; prehnite lowers this over-stimulation and restores balance and harmony.

Prehnite is a tonic when taken as a gem essence. It is good to take when you feel scattered and frazzled; it brings you back to your centre, your heart, your seat of balance and harmony. For this reason it is also soporific, it has calming qualities, it heals the nerves and gives reassurance. It is good for hyperactive children and those people who suffer from claustrophobia.

Prehnite is also a diagnostic crystal; it takes you to the heart of the problem. Using this crystal raises your perception, it facilitates the energy of taking responsibility for personal as well as global environmental issues, such as over-consumption, over-eating etc.

Prehnite can reveal the state of your heart physically and emotionally: it is a bridge, a gateway to freedom, it teaches you discrimination and personal responsibility. It is good for those who have a scarcity mentality and hoard things; these souls do not believe that the universe will provide for them, that all their needs will be met, so they have to hoard everything, including their love. Hoarding love is the saddest of all; it stops your ability to experience wholeness, balance, harmony and loving relationships on every level.

Affirmation: I now allow myself to heal on every level of my being.

Pyrite

Chemical Composition: Iron pyrites (FeS_2)

Crystal System: Cubic **Hardness:** 6 - 6.5

Habit: Crystals usually cubes, pyritohedral or octahedral, or combinations of these forms. The cubes frequently show striations produced by oscillatory growth of cube and pyritohedron and which are perpendicular to each other; also massive, granular, stalactitic, spheroidal and radiating

Color: Pale brass-yellow: opaque

Keyword: Fire

Pyrite is one of the most widely distributed of sulphide minerals, occurring in a variety of environments. It is present in igneous rocks as an accessory mineral. It is a common mineral in hydrothermal sulphide veins, in replacement deposits and in contact metamorphic deposits. Fossils are often replaced by pyrite. The name comes from the Greek word for fire and alludes to the sparks given off when the mineral is struck sharply. It has been used as a talisman for health and warmth since ancient times.

Pyrite has a very strong powerful male yang energy that will induce intellectual superiority when worn or carried. It is ideal for students and those who wish to improve their academic prowess and memory. It is also ideal for those people who feel subordinate to others or who have an over- abundance of the female yin vibration. It can make those who are very male or yang act almost too aggressively, so they need to be aware of its potency, being conscious at all times to use this mineral in a balanced holistic way.

Pyrite is totally focused and will act like a swift arrow going straight to the physical, mental or emotional disease. There it will facilitate healing but, more than this, it will also make you aware of the cause of the illness or disease and bring about favourable circumstances to find ‘cures’ for the ‘cause’ of the dis-ease. This process is facilitated by a synergy of the higher self and the improved concentrated mind action of the pyrite mineral as it interacts with your energy field.

It will swiftly dispel deep gloom, lift despondency, despair and the drudge mentality. It is also ideal when you feel a severe lack of energy. It is a must for those who display tendencies of low self-worth and subservience. Pyrite teaches you to honour and accept yourself, to work towards self-empowerment, personal freedom and joy.

Pyrite is a very protective stone and will keep your energy field clear of unwanted outside influences. It will stop energy leaks and energy drains from the physical body and auric shell. It will strengthen the meridian system. It is not recommended to be worn as a pendant, as it will irritate the skin, but you could carry it in a ‘medicine’ pouch or use it for meditation.

Affirmation: I accept and honour myself exactly as I am.

Quartz (Clear)

Additional variety specimens include: Amethyst; Citrine; Herkimer Diamonds; Rock Crystal; Rose Quartz and Smoky Quartz

Chemical Composition: SiO_2, Silicon dioxide

Crystal System: Trigonal **Hardness:** 7

Habit: Crystals are usually six-sided and are terminated by six faces

Color: Clear

Keywords: Master Healer

The well-formed quartz crystals which make such beautiful mineral specimens supply such gemstones as rock crystal, amethyst, citrine and cairngorm. Quartz is the most common mineral on the face of the earth. It is found in nearly every geological environment and is at least a component of almost every rock type. It frequently is the primary mineral. It is also the most varied in terms of varieties, colors and forms.

Some macrocrystalline (large crystal) varieties are well-known and popular as ornamental stone and as gemstones. Cryptocrystalline (crystals too small to be seen even by a microscope) varieties are used as semi-precious stones. The water-clear colorless quartz is known as rock crystal and receives its name from the hardy mountain climbers of ancient Greece, who first came upon it gleaming in hidden caves near their sacred mountain, Mount Olympus. They called it *'krustallos'*, meaning ice, for they believed it to be water forever frozen by the Gods.

Colorless clear quartz crystals are profuse and show extraordinary irregularity in size, from crystals so tiny that it would take a hundred thousand to make an ounce to gigantic crystals weighing more than a thousand pounds. Many Native American healers, especially the tribal Shamans of cultures throughout the world, have quartz crystals among their collections of power objects.

Clear quartz is the 'Master Healer' or 'cure all' because it contains the full spectrum of the visible 'white' light (iridescent rainbow cosmic light) and as such it will work on every level of our being, physical, emotional, mental, astral, spiritual, etheric etc. It is acknowledged as the only 'programmable' crystal.

Clear quartz also contains the double helix spiral of Universal Life Energy. Working with, holding or meditating with this 'Master' energy of the supreme ray will unlock not only deep memories but facilitate healing by quickly removing the 'blocks' or stagnant energy which may cause or have caused illness or distress within any level of the body. It is also used for amplifying one's concentrated attention and intent. When healing energy is directed through the clear quartz crystal, it is transmitted into the body of the patient and distributed to the areas most in need of energy balancing. There is an intelligence contained within this focused energy that always directs it to the areas displaying a lower vibration or 'block'.

Quartz crystal allows for easy access to altered states of consciousness and it will assist the movement of energy flowing between the chakras. It can also be used to bring about 'Kundalini' activation. Use clear quartz crystal when you need to bring clarity and light to a situation, or when you need to bring about a change, major or minor. Clear quartz is considered a cure all by many crystal therapists. There are many types and uses. (See part one of this book for a full listing of types, properties, uses and how to programme).

If you wish to begin accessing the crystal knowledge using sacred geometry, the following steps will guide you.

* You will need a crystal that displays one of the three types of sacred geometry:

Diamond Crystal

The diamond crystal is recognised by the presence of a diamond-shaped 'window' located usually in the centre front face of the crystal, although I have seen some diamond crystals with several contained in the same stone. This crystal configuration will help you to see beyond illusion, to read the different layers in a person's aura: the physical, emotional, vitality, mental, spiritual, etheric etc. It will also allow you to define your and others' life purpose or Divine mission. Use this window to see into other realms and dimensions.

Record Keeper Crystal

The record keeper crystal is recognised by one or more perfectly-formed raised triangles on one or more faces. This clearly indicates sacred fire knowledge of creation which, at a vibrational level, is stored within them and within you. These were partially implanted through your ancestry, through your star lineages or, as is sometimes described, your descent into matter.

Left-handed and Right-Handed Quartz Crystal

X-ray study has shown that the atomic structure of quartz, unique among the gem minerals, is helical, and that this spiral arrangement of atoms can be either right-handed or left-handed. This right-hand or left-hand nature of quartz, termed enantiomorphism, is occasionally manifested in crystals by the position of the small trigonal pyramidal faces, if present. These crystals, which are known in New Age terminology as time-link or doorway crystals, may point right (forwards) or left (backwards). They will allow you to travel forwards or backwards in time and space, giving access to different dimensions. Time is merely an illusion of the physical plane, in fact all time is now, but this crystal will allow you, because of its growth conditions, to understand this information clearly and incorporate this concept within your conscious awareness. This will bring a new level of enlightenment to your overall structure of the universe.

* When you are ready to take this step into the world of sacred geometry, first check your motives; why are you drawn to it? If you find your motives are pure and you feel in harmony with the idea of Divine communication, just follow this procedure.
* One of the concepts that you need to access the sacred geometry of crystals is an understanding of how energy vibration, light and sounds work with these particular life forms; in other words, how to 'activate' them. This is an ancient technique of contacting and gaining guidance from the Divine. The use of quartz crystals and sacred geometry to gain access to other dimensions, the astral plane or the Akashic records, goes back to pre-history. Very often when I meet people who have tried activation techniques and failed, it was only because they chose the wrong crystal for them, or they did not prepare enough to facilitate clear, coherent communication with the Divine. The other problem can be fear: fear of failure or fear of the unknown. We will be using eye activation, but you could use sound, or color, just as easily.
* Select a crystal from the list above and one that refracts light well.
* Make sure it feels psychically clean.
* Follow the cleansing procedure as outlined in the relevant section of this book.
* Charge the crystal with positive energy.
* Keep it wrapped in a clean white cloth to protect it from other energies.
* Find a safe space where you can sit comfortably and not be disturbed.
* Turn off the phone, television, radio etc.
* You can use soothing music, a drumming tape, or chanting.

* Light a white candle and turn off the lights (only if you feel comfortable with it).
* Surround or visualise yourself surrounded with a sphere of pure white light and place around that a circle of brilliant blue light for Divine communication.
* Focus on your breathing, then become aware of your heartbeat; do not try and change your breathing, just allow it to become gentle, smooth and easy.
* Allowing the in-breath to follow calmly on the out-breath, continue with 20 connected breaths until you feel your energy field begin to oscillate; allow yourself to fully connect with your higher self.
* Now hold your crystal in your hand of preference and allow your energy field to merge with the crystal's energy field; then place the crystal in front of you with the candle flame behind it, to illuminate its inner chambers. Close your eyes.
* Begin to focus on your question. Be very clear in your intent; do not allow other thoughts to intrude.
* Open your eyes and allow yourself to begin to gaze at your sacred geometry crystal.
* Focus on your triangle, diamond or the trigonal pyramidal face; feel it drawing you closer.
* Allow your mind to move beyond the physical form of the stone; you will feel a change in your energy signature as your resonance begins to move through gateways, portals and other dimensions. You should feel an energetic link with the crystal through your physical eyes. You may also be aware of spiralling or floating - they are all normal - or you may begin to feel asymmetrical or 'light-headed'.
* You will begin to feel a pulse in your eyes and then begin to see the internal light within the crystal activate.
* Keep looking at the light within the crystal. Very often forms will begin to come into view, somewhat like a mini television screen. Keep watching the images and allow other guidance in the form of thoughts or inspiration to inspire you.
* When truly connected you should get impressions and insights. Remember, these have to register on different levels of your being; some people experience them through feelings, others experience them as knowledge, or pictures. There is no right or wrong way. When you go into a meditative state in this way you will experience the information first at the cellular level, then at the feeling level, then eventually on the mental level. So you would probably take a minimum of three sessions to work with a specific crystal, to extract its information into the level of consciousness in which you know it, not just feel it or sense it.
* Do not allow yourself to become exhausted; when you have achieved as much as you can in one sitting, begin the closing down process.
* Wrap your crystal back carefully in its cloth and give thanks to your higher self and the sacred geometry Angels for all the protection, communication and guidance you have just received.
* Blow out your candle.
* Allow yourself plenty of time to come back to everyday reality.
* Centre and earth yourself.
* Keep a written record of the experience.

Affirmation: My consciousness transcends normal thoughts and the ordinary senses. I now move into a deeper state of awareness and personal mastery. I am open to coincidences that add magic to my life.

Rainbow Aura Quartz (See Quartz)

Color: Deep iridescent rainbow

Keywords: Dazzling Rainbows

Rainbow aura quartz is a product of twentieth century technology, just as aqua aura quartz, opal aura quartz, rose aura quartz and ruby aura quartz are. The beauty of these quartzes is apparent as the 'new' technology enhances the extremely powerful properties of the master healer, clear quartz.

Rainbow aura quartz is clear organic quartz combined with gold and titanium; this combination produces the most amazing deep metallic rainbow color. Titanium is a master healer. The energy of titanium is activation; activation of all levels and energy centres. It works by clearing a pathway for the vital life force to flow. Titanium works on the endocrine system. Titanium supports the life force within all the bodies, physical, emotional, mental, spiritual, etc. and the surrounding auric field, allowing for a greater abundance of vital life energy.

Rainbow aura quartz is very energizing and enlivening to all the chakras; it will awaken and activate any energy centre, dispelling sorrow and replacing it with unlimited joy. It can ignite and activate the inner rainbow body of light.

Rainbow aura quartz also helps to heal stressful relationships. All our interactions with others only serve to reflect an aspect of ourselves. This gives us the opportunity to see ourselves more clearly. Taking this into account using rainbow aura quartz can speed up the personal learning process in life. There is also the value of working through conflicts that brings us to opening to wider possibilities. Those who can let go of old belief systems and ways of relating will be rewarded by transformation and regeneration and will find life can flow much more smoothly without pain, resentment and conflict.

Wearing or meditating with this dazzling gemstone will also give new insights to your relationships on all levels; even with your guides and Angels you will find new ways of relating that you may not have thought possible. These could also include hidden talents and Divine gifts.

Affirmation: I am dancing in the dazzling rainbow light of creation.

Rhodochrosite - Rosinca - Inca Rose - Manganese Spar - Raspberry Spar

Chemical Composition: $MnCO_3$

Crystal System: Trigonal **Hardness:** 3.5 - 4

Habit: Includes the rhombohedrons and scalahedrons with rounded faces that can obscure the crystal shape; also botryoidal, globular, stalactitic, layered and granular

Color: Red to pink; raspberry-peachy-pink shades of color, which is variegated and in bands of different shades of peachy-pink

Keywords: Compassion in Action

Rhodochrosite received its name from the Greek for rose colored, but has been known also as 'Rosinca' or 'Inca rose'. In a massive form its pink and white bands are extremely attractive and are often used in semi-precious jewellery. Rhodochrosite is often carved into figurines and tubular stalactitic forms are sliced into circles with concentric bands that are truly unique in the mineral kingdom. Manganese spar is another name associated with rhodochrosite. The material may be likened in its banding, but not color, to malachite. Occasionally very fine quality crystals are found that are transparent; these are usually cut into faceted stones and they have the strongest energy of the peach-rose-pink ray. It is often used with malachite in crystal therapy, where it produces positive results not only in the right use of power, but in this combination it brings in the energy of compassion, so that a greater understanding of the energy of Divine will-power is fully manifested. Rhodochrosite is not the gentle loving energy of the rose quartz pink ray but is the active energy of Divine love in action of the peach-pink ray. It facilitates the energy of compassion, but not pity. It does not encourage the sympathetic use of the pink ray, but rather the dynamic use of the peach-pink ray, whereby a greater understanding of the need to learn through the emotions is fully comprehended. Mankind has a great capacity to learn through the emotions; this has been clearly demonstrated in the twentieth century, where the use of instant communication or global news has moved whole nations as a single soul to end war, famine or disease and brings in the energy whereby the aggressive and destructive behaviour of others can no longer be hidden or tolerated. It is the energy of the enlightened reformer, as has been witnessed so many times this century when we have seen Live Aid, the release of Nelson Mandela, the end of the Vietnam war and the demise of the Iron Curtain. Its message is: let's change the world with enlightened love, as we can no longer tolerate the massive abuse of the solar plexus chakra by the few who manipulate, control and exploit the masses. Rhodochrosite helps ease trauma and clears traumatic events from the heart, solar plexus and sacral chakras. It clears old pains, hurts and memories and will purify the base chakra, sacral chakra, solar plexus chakra and heart chakra. It will restore Divine balance to these areas. Rhodochrosite balances the energies of the heart and reproduction system. It is good for stomach, lungs, heart, reproductive areas, liver, kidneys and the intestines. Rhodochrosite is very enlivening to the mental body; it brings creative self-expression. It really wakes you up and gives boundless energy and enthusiasm. For those of you who are not into compassion, but are turned on by passion or eroticism, rhodochrosite is good for that too; if you feel unloved or unlovely, try the energies of rhodochrosite to give a boost to your love-life.

Affirmation: I am compassion in action.

Rhodonite

Chemical Composition: $(Mn,Fe,Ca)SiO_3$

Crystal System: Triclinic **Hardness:** 5.5 - 6.5

Habit: Includes crystals that have a blocky prismatic habit; typically massive; coarse and fine granular aggregates

Color: Pink to brown, weathers to black

Keywords: Place of the Soul

Rhodonite is an delightful mineral that is often carved and used in jewellery. It is named after the Greek word for rose, *rhodon*. Its rose-pink color is distinctive and can only be confused with rhodochrosite. Rhodochrosite, however, is streaked with white minerals such as calcite. Rhodonite is usually associated with black manganese minerals and pyrite. Crystals of rhodonite, while not in nearly the same abundance as massive rhodonite, are still found and distributed on the mineral markets. Other characteristics: may tarnish to a brown or black color upon exposure. It is also called manganese silicate by some 'New Age' mineral dealers.

Rhodonite is an amazing crystal. Whenever I see someone drawn to it, my first thought is - what have you got bottled up inside you? It always indicates something is lying dormant and buried. If the person works metaphysically, it also means those who don't want to give up anything and lose control. It can show that a person needs to be in control; not just physical and emotional control, but occult control. This crystal also indicates an empty emotional self-destructive life. The black within the pink can also be restriction dominance, depression, with-holding empty power used out of selfishness and weakness. But out of the black can come new beginnings. By seeing that which is hidden, women or men who choose this crystal need to review their emotional health. It is the same with the aura: if you ever view black within a person's aura it indicates disease, illness and darkness of the soul.

When used in healing, this crystal *is* very potent. It will quickly bring these seeds of soul destruction to the surface to be healed with the vibrant rose pink ray of universal love. Rhodonite's rose pink has healing beauty within its vibration. It will support you when you feel betrayed, let down or abandoned, or unloved. It teaches forgiveness and can help you to fulfill your true emotional potential. It will help you develop mature emotional strength and universal love and forgiveness, allowing your heart to become a nurturing place for your soul. This is the life lesson of the heart chakra, forgiveness and compassion for yourself and others.

The emotional dysfunctions of the heart chakra are co-dependency, melancholia, fears concerning loneliness, commitment or betrayal. All dis-ease starts with a lack of love. It should be used with caution by crystal therapists, as it can surface incredible anger, hatred, resentment and bitterness, which must be dealt with in a constructive, empowering manner. Otherwise it can be like 'a loose cannon', you never know when it will go off. Rhodonite's rose pink healing energy is very good for healing skin complaints, cuts and wounds.

Affirmation: My heart is open to healing and love.

Rose Aura Quartz (See Quartz)

Color: Deep iridescent rose pink

Keywords: Divine Love

Rose aura quartz is the dynamic expression of Divine Love. It is a product of twentieth century technology, just as aqua aura, opal aura, ruby aura and rainbow aura quartz are. The beauty of these quartzes is apparent as the 'new' technology enhances the extremely powerful properties of the master healer, clear quartz. Rose aura quartz is clear organic quartz combined with varying quantities of gold and platinum; this combination produces the most amazing dynamic rose pink color. Gold is a master healer, as is platinum. The energy of gold is purity, purity on all levels. This energy, when consciously directed, will clear all negativity from the electromagnetic energy field which flows through and surrounds the human body. The energy of platinum is alignment, aligning all levels and energy centres. It works by clearing a pathway for the life force to flow. Platinum works on the pineal gland. The rose aura ray works dynamically on the heart chakra, gently cleansing and then transmuting all stored putrefied negative issues of self-worth, self-confidence, self-acceptance and so on. It will allow the integration of positive energy within all levels of the chakra system, the positive energy being love, compassion, understanding of unity within diversity, bringing tolerance, forgiveness, and ultimately the complete expression of universal love and self-love to every corner of the microcosm and macrocosm. We are all a reflection of the whole and the more love we can hold within our own being the more will ultimately be reflected outwards to all life and returned to us magnified, using the 'Universal Law of Resonance'.

This crystal will activate the original blueprint or Divine matrix, restoring the original energy of vital life to all the cells of the body. The universe is love: we were created by love, for love. Rose pink is the in-breath of the breath cycle. As this new understanding 'dawns' within each being, the vibration is amplified until we become the 'God/Goddess' of love we truly are. The illusion of separation will vanish as we create the heaven on earth that is our Divine birthright. This will assist us with our own personal and planetary evolution, by allowing us to become a pure channel for higher authority, which is the only true power - the power of love and compassion. The energy of love is the fundamental building block of life. It is the reality behind creation, the force at the beginning of the universe, the reason we became manifest in the first place. Without love in all its aspects we are nothing and fall into the void of illusion and self-deception, which can destroy us on all levels of our being as we look outwards in search of love. We are the only validation we need. If we have true self-love, we are whole and complete. We can then manifest this vibration fully on all levels, ending the vibrations of jealousies, aggression, war, famine and disease. This crystal truly is a blessing at this time, for no other crystal available clearly makes manifest the white and red rays combined into the dynamic rose pink ray, as this one does. It is a world teacher, combining the male and female principles of love. The dynamic rose pink ray is useful in all situations of aggression and aggressive behaviour. When one projects the pink ray at an aggressive person or situation, it will immediately calm the energy (this has been clearly demonstrated by the use of rose pink decor in police cells, calming violent drunks). This crystal can be used for any illness, as all disease starts with a lack of love.

Affirmation: I send Divine unconditional love to everyone I know; all hearts are open to receive my love.

Rose Quartz and Asterised Rose Quartz (See Quartz)

Color: Pale pink to deep pink

Keyword: Love

Rose quartz is one of the most pleasantly seductive varieties of quartz. The pink to rose red color is caused by titanium and iron. Rose quartz is usually too cloudy or pale to be used as a cut gemstone, although a few exceptional pieces are found with enough clarity and color to make fine gems. Most gemmy rose quartz is used as cabochons, where the clarity is not as important as the depth of color. Rose quartz is also a very attractive ornamental stone and is carved into popular spheres, pyramids, healing wands and obelisks.

Rose quartz is found in Brazil, Madagascar, India and several localities in the USA. Brazil is also the only source of true well-formed crystals of rose quartz. All rose quartz was believed to be only massive, found primarily in the cores of pegmatites. This lack of crystals is somewhat of a mystery, because quartz crystallizes into well-formed crystals in all its other macroscopic varieties. So amazing are the crystals of rose quartz that the first ones discovered were dismissed as 'fakes' by mineralogists from around the world.

If needles of rutile are included in the rose quartz, then a star effect or asterism is sometimes present. These stars are most visible when light is viewed through the rose quartz. This is different from asterisms in other gemstones, such as ruby and sapphire, where the stars are seen when light is shown on the gems.

Rose quartz transmits a soft love energy, which is soothing and calming to the emotions. The vibration or resonance signature of rose quartz is good if a person has been assaulted in any way. It is wonderful to use in mid-life crisis when dissolution of old patterns and reassessment is imperative. The paler the rose quartz goes colorwise, the wider, higher and deeper the love vibration extends. The very pale natural rose is highly tuned and sensitive; it carries the promise of spiritual fulfilment.

Rose quartz is very good for children, the new born and those yet to be born. It is also ideal for those who are giving birth to their inner child or any new venture; the red within the pink activates the energy, while the white spiritualises the endeavour.

Rose quartz can fully balance the emotional body. It is used to attune to the love vibration. The rose quartz ray works dynamically on the heart chakra, gently cleansing and then transmuting all stored putrefied negative issues of self-worth, self-confidence and self-acceptance. It contains within its beautiful pink mandala the ray of hope.

The pink warmth melts and dissolves resistance to allowing the full manifestation of love into every corner of the heart. It will allow the integration of positive energy within all levels of the chakra system, the positive energy being love, compassion, understanding of unity within diversity, bringing tolerance, forgiveness, and ultimately the complete expression of universal love and self-love to every corner of the microcosm and macrocosm. Think pink!

The guardian or Angel of rose quartz is very affectionate, deeply understanding and non-judgemental. Many people who tread the Angel path are passionately aware of the potent force of this Divine pink manifestation. It is ideal to carry and wear in stressful situations. It is good to use after operations or dental surgery. Rose quartz is comforting, it mollifies, it is a peace offering. Pour pink on troubled waters.

It is excellent in a crisis and it has been documented many times that the wearer of a rose quartz pendant has had the stone shatter on impact of 'bad news'. This stone really knows how to love you, it will even teach you 'sacrificial love'. It will sacrifice itself for you; rather it breaks, than your heart breaks.

It is affordable and so useful; it is a give-away crystal. Many crystal people carry spare pieces of rose quartz just to give to others in times of stress. Rose quartz is also humble; it teaches humility by truly understanding the unconditional love vibration. It is a good ally in times of anxiety, when life is just one long struggle.

This wonderful stone has also been used to great effect to treat heart problems on all levels, those who are soul weary, Alzheimer's disease, senile dementia, Parkinson's disease. Great benefit has also been gained from easing the pain and speeding the healing of severe burns and scalds. It makes a wonderful gemstone essence and is said to keep the skin young and supple.

The asterised rose quartz is the most powerful gemstone of the pink ray and as such is sought after by crystal therapists and those who work as 'channels for the Angels and Ascended Masters'. The rutile needles contained within the rose quartz structure stop any unwanted outside interference from both the physical and spiritual worlds. Rutile is used for healing and balancing the aura by repelling negative energy. It works on the physical, etheric and astral bodies.

The well-formed crystals of rose quartz from Brazil are so beautiful and seem especially focused for directing the energy of the pink ray. It has been used in gemstone essences, Earth healing ceremonies and pyramid activation. The energy appears to be incorruptible and unlike normal rose quartz never seems to need the same cleansing procedure, only a light cleansing with the intent. It has been placed in several special sites around the planet to affect planetary peace.

Affirmation: My soul dances to the music of universal peace and love.

Ruby - Corundum

Chemical Composition: Al_2O_3

Crystal System: Trigonal **Hardness:** 9

Habit: Crystals usually rough barrel-shaped prismatic forms or tapering spindle-shaped forms; also flat, tabular

Color: Red to pinky-red

Keyword: Passion

Ruby is the fabulous gemstone for those born in the month of July. Ruby is the superb scarlet variety of corundum, the second hardest natural mineral known. The non-red variety of corundum is sapphire. Sapphires are well-known as being blue, but they can be nearly any color. The red color in ruby is caused by trace amounts of the element chromium.

The word red is derived from the Latin for ruby, *rubeus*, which is derived from similar words in Sanskrit, Hebrew and Persian. The intensity of color of a fine ruby is like a glowing coal, probably the most intensely colored substance our ancestors ever saw.

Rubies come from all over the world. Ruby has been the world's most valued gemstone for thousands of years. Ruby was said to be the most precious of the twelve stones God created when he created all things and this "lord of gems" was placed on Aaron's neck by God's command. The Bible says that wisdom is "more precious than rubies".

In the ancient language of Sanskrit, ruby is called *ratnaraj* or "king of precious stones" and *ratnanayaka*, "leader of precious stones." In fact, rubies are today still more valuable and scarce than even the top quality colorless diamonds. It is no wonder they ascribed magical powers to these 'inner fires' that burned eternally. The ancient gemological teachings of the East place ruby under the influence of the Sun. To be completely efficient though they should be free from all impurities, fissures and flaws.

Ruby sometimes displays a three-ray, six-pointed star. These amazing star rubies are cut in a smooth domed cabochon to display the effect. The star is best visible when illuminated with a single light source: it moves across the stone as the light moves. This effect, called asterism, is caused by light reflecting off tiny rutile needles, called "silk," which are oriented along the crystal faces. The ruby mines of Myanmar are older than history: Stone Age and Bronze Age mining tools have been found in the mining area of Mogok.

Ruby instills in the wearer a passion for life, truth, courage, wisdom and perseverance. It introduces dynamic leadership qualities. It emits the energy of cheerfulness and creativity. Ruby is for the pioneers, those who must go first, bravely into uncharted territory. Ruby is raw power, drive and will-power.

Ruby works primarily on the genitals and reproductive organs. The glands of the body connected to ruby are the gonads and ovaries. Ruby also prompts the release of adrenaline into the bloodstream when there is danger, aggression or pain. The blood and the circulation are a focus of the ruby vibration. Muscles, which give the power to act, are also governed by ruby and of course the deep red ray is seen as raw life force, so ruby rules the blood and helps with anaemia; also it will warm the body when it is chilled and they can be used to counteract hypothermia.

Rubies have been worn in the navels of belly dancers and have been used to stimulate sexual power and potency. The signature of ruby is growth at any cost and it can be too powerful for some sensitive souls. You really have to understand the resonance of rubies to be completely comfortable in their vibrational field. If someone is stressed and irritated, avoid ruby completely, as it will inflame the condition.

The bright red scarlet, crimson and flame are clean, pure, pristine forms of ruby; when used spiritually, it is devotion that transfigures Divine love into Divine will. Ruby will stimulate the heart chakra when consciously directed, raising, then transforming the raw power of the base chakra into devotion, piety, adoration, worship, reverence and enlightened religious zeal.

Ruby works very well with those who have a strong 'spiritual devotional' energy to the 'ultimate liberation' of the human race from suffering and ignorance into enlightenment.

Ruby is the gemstone of the Cosmic Christ energy. The ruby ray activates the balanced female energy of love, nurturing, compassion, enlightened attachment, dedication to life, evolved spiritual revolution, personal freedom and joy. The Divine female energy must be ready to help, as the unbalanced male energies on this planet finish fighting each other.

Affirmation: I now allow passion into my life to burn away all obstacles on my spiritual path.

Ruby Aura Quartz (See Quartz)

Color: Magenta to ruby red

Keywords: Divine Passion

Ruby aura quartz is a product of twentieth century technology, just as aqua aura, opal aura, rose aura and rainbow aura quartz are. The beauty of these quartzes is apparent as the 'new' technology enhances the extremely powerful properties of the master healer, clear quartz. Clear quartz is a 'master healer' because it contains the full spectrum of the visible 'white' light and as such it will work on every level of our being, emotional, physical, spiritual, etheric, astral and mental. Ruby aura quartz is clear organic quartz combined with gold and platinum; this combination produces the most amazing deep magenta color.

Gold is a master healer, as is platinum. The energy of gold is purity, purity on all levels. This energy, when consciously directed, will clear all negativity from the electromagnetic energy field which flows through and surrounds the human body. The energy of platinum is alignment, aligning all levels and energy centres. It works by clearing a pathway for the life force to flow. Platinum works on the pineal gland; it supports the life force within all the bodies and the surrounding auric field, allowing for a greater abundance of vital energy.

The crystal known as ruby aura works initially on the base chakra, gently cleansing all stored putrefied negative issues of fear, survival, abuse and not being grounded. It will allow the positive energy of passion, life force, vitality and gravity to be fully activated within all levels of the chakra system. Ruby aura, with its magenta/ruby ray, is the resurrection crystal. This crystal will activate the original blueprint or Divine matrix, restoring the original energy of vital life to all the cells of the body and anchoring our personal Mandala within the Planetary grid.

The transmuting ray for the solar plexus is the ruby/magenta ray; this brings in the energy of the 'Christ', allowing us to fully activate our own 'Christ' consciousness of universal peace and unselfishness. Do not confuse the Christ energy with the 'Martyr's syndrome' though. Martyrdom involves being entrenched in a pit of self-pity with no motivation to shift the negative attitudes contributing to the situation.

The 'Christ' consciousness will assist us with our own personal and planetary evolution, by allowing us to become a pure channel for higher authority, which is the only true power. This will take us beyond the limitations of personal power and the dogma of the twentieth century limited mind set, which has been abused by the patriarchal societies dominating the planet for the last 2,000 years of enslavement, war, famine, disease and pestilence, where brother kills brother through fear and a great need to dominate. Unfortunately this energy is so dense and destructive it pulls in more negative energy. This is resulting in wholesale slaughter of nations, earthquakes, famine, tidal waves, storms and other 'natural disasters' and 'acts' of God. There are those on the planet, though, who realise this imbalance of resonance, the Universal Law of attraction - like attracts like. They are working with pyramid energy to rebalance the negativity.

This ruby/magenta ray also activates the balanced female energy of love, nurturing, passion, peace, harmony, reconciliation, serenity, tranquillity and joy. The Divine female energy must be ready to help, as the unbalanced male energies on this planet finish fighting each other. Hopefully balance returns and 'war' ends. Unfortunately for the unbalanced male energy, it can only find balance through a balanced female energy (this is also very hard to find on the planet at this time), so men* will have to lay their swords to rest and find gentle ways within their own soul. If not, we can only expect more war, death, destruction and possible annihilation.

Physically, the ruby aura crystal, because it wields the invisible energies of infra-red and ultra-violet, can help the entire endocrine system. This ray is nature's antibiotic color, so it can clear fungus, warts and other parasites. It is spiritually uplifting and makes people feel instantly better. Because its powers are unseen, it will safeguard the wearer from psychic attack. Any unwanted intrusion from outside sources will be quickly dissipated by transmutation into a pure loving energy which can then be safely used for healing the situation causing the attack. The more outside forces attack your energy field, the more energy will be available to you for healing the cause.

This is truly a 'Master' vibrational crystal, but as with all energies the conscious use of this energy towards enlightenment is always the prime goal. The ruby aura crystal will bring wisdom to the heart, encouraging gentleness and discouraging violent energies. It is also a very protective stone; it will shield the wearer from the harmful effect of others' violent moods and aggressive tendencies. It will calm nightmares and any fearful situation.

Affirmation: I am at peace with myself, the world and everyone in it.

* There are also many women on the planet at this time who have 'bought' into the unbalanced male energy and are emulating men in their behaviour.

Rutilated Quartz - Sagenite - Venus Hair - Angel Hair - Hair Stone

Chemical Composition: SiO_2+TiO_2

Crystal System: Tetragonal/Trigonal **Hardness:** 6 - 6.5

Habit: Includes eight-sided prisms and blocky crystals terminated by a blunt four-sided or complex pyramid; inclusions of golden rutile needles in clear quartz

Color: Reddish-brown or black in large thick crystals or golden yellow or rusty yellow as inclusions in quartz or in thin crystals

Keyword: Illumination

Rutile is a fascinating mineral; it is very varied. Rutile is a major ore of titanium, a metal used for high technical alloys because of its light weight, high strength and resistance to corrosion. It also forms its own interesting and exquisite mineral specimens. A beautiful stone produced by large inclusions of golden rutile needles in clear quartz is called rutilated quartz. This stone is produced because at high temperatures and pressure $n(SiO_2)$-$n(TiO_2)$ is in a stable state, but as temperatures cool and pressure eases the two separate, with rutile crystals trapped inside the quartz crystals. Rutilated quartz is a semi-precious stone that has been used since ancient times. It was thought to be 'captured sunlight'. The ancient use was for chest infections and as a mood changing crystal.

Rutilated quartz is known as the Illuminator of the Soul. Titanium or rutile needles within the clear quartz structure produce an extremely potent synergy of crystalline vibrations that can be used not only for vibrational healing but unprecedented spiritual growth. Rutilated quartz has a perfect balance of cosmic light.

Use it for illumination and channelling the Universal Intelligence to provide power, wisdom and Divine guidance. It clears the pathway for necessary action by exposing flaws, corruption, negativity and shams. It sustains life and the vital life force. It is used to restore a person's vibrancy and vitality which will lead to the resonance of perfect health. Rutile quartz can provide the energy to break down barriers that have held up your spiritual progress. It helps you to conquer fears and phobias.

Use rutile quartz to bring about a change for healing and new directions. Rutile quartz is a 'cure all'. It clears up and modifies any conditions, including allergies, lung conditions, chronic conditions, negative entities, cell regeneration and personal growth. It activates the aura and fills it with light. Rutile is used for healing and balancing the aura by repelling negative energy. It works on the physical, etheric and astral bodies and dispels unwanted interference from both the physical and spiritual worlds.

Rutile quartz is used for channelling. Seers use rutile quartz, as they know they can trust its vibration; it has vitality, purity and is incorruptible. It expands the power of love, trust and surrender to receive knowledge, wisdom and spiritual treasure.

Rutile quartz is spiritually mature; it throws off parasites on all levels and repels parasites whilst being used in crystal therapy. It has a fast but flowing energy. It also teaches forgiveness by letting go of the past. Holding on to the past is one of the biggest drawbacks on the spiritual path; even talking about negative experiences from the past can tear massive holes in a person's auric shell. Counsellors should always work with rutile quartz to safeguard the energy field of their clients.

Rutile quartz is so full of vitality and healing abundance that it wins against all odds; it is very uplifting. It has also been used to help those who are suicidal, thyroid problems, nervous stomachs, digestive troubles, irritable bowel syndrome, rashes, skin complaints, scars, depression and menopause problems.

Rutile quartz connects you to your 'I Am' presence; it uplifts and fills the aura with light. The light in the aura reflects the inner light of the person. The more luminous and glowing the aura, the more enlightened is the state of consciousness.

Affirmation: I am the light that never fails.

Sapphire - Corundum - Padparadscha

Chemical Composition: Al_2O_3

Crystal System: Trigonal **Hardness:** 9

Habit: Crystals usually rough barrel-shaped prismatic forms or tapering spindle-shaped forms; also flat, tabular

Color: Various shades of blue; pink; yellow; lemon; white; lavender; grey; orange-pink; purple

Keywords: Personal Mastery

Blue sapphire is the birthstone for September. Sapphire is often considered to be synonymous with the color blue: you can easily imagine sapphire seas. However, sapphire is beautiful beyond blue, in every color but red, because red is called ruby.

The other colors of sapphire can be just as beautiful and rare - or even rarer - than the blue. The most valuable other fancy sapphire is an orange-pink or pinkish-orange called "padparadscha" after the sacred lotus blossom. Padparadscha sapphires are extremely rare. Other very popular shades of 'fancy' sapphires are yellows, bright oranges, lavenders and purples, and a bluish-green color. Generally, the more clear and vivid the color, the more valuable the sapphire. Historically, blue sapphire has always been associated with true love and purity; it represents the heavens and Angels. Sapphire gets its name from the Sanskrit word *Sani* (Saturn).

Blue Sapphire:

Blue sapphire encourages you to reach for the stars, for high spiritual attainment. It can release you from emotional bondage. Wearing, carrying or using blue sapphire makes you a seeker of truth. It works primarily on the throat chakra, also the thyroid and parathyroid glands. Its energy vibration also covers the upper lungs and arms and even extends to the base of the skull. It counteracts the psychological problems of speaking in public, of speaking your truth.

Blue sapphire is a great teacher of Universal Truths and the power of the spoken word. Blue sapphire also instills patience and peace. It helps you reason things out slowly and quietly with integrity. The 'Spirit' guide of blue sapphire is a tranquil energy; it teaches higher philosophical thoughts and intellectual integrity. It teaches discretion, moderation, wisdom and discrimination. It is a good meditation stone when you find it difficult to concentrate.

Yellow Sapphire:

Yellow sapphire is mentally and spiritually stimulating. It is very expansive to the mental body and works well to activate and balance the solar plexus chakra. Its vibratory signature balances the pancreas, liver, spleen, gall-bladder and middle stomach.

It also energizes the nervous system and digestive system. It is good for removing cellulite and stored emotional waste and toxins. Elimination is the law of life, faulty elimination is a vital contributing factor to the beginning of most diseases.

Yellow sapphire teaches you to clear your mind of negative thoughts, so it aids concentration and meditation. Emotionally it clears low self-esteem. It also stimulates the lymphatic system. It brings joy and a sunny positive disposition, originality, tolerance and personal honesty and spiritual abundance.

Pink Sapphire:

Pink sapphire is magnetic: it draws and attracts that which you need into your life, so lessons can be learnt quickly. It teaches you mastery of your emotions. It gets rid of emotional hang-ups and aids the digestion by allowing the integration of cosmic affection. It is the stone of universal harmony and cosmic love.

Purple Sapphire:

Purple sapphire works on the pineal gland and the top of the head, the crown, the brain, the scalp and the crown chakra. It is used to calm down those who are emotionally erratic. It is useful for any kind of *internal* inflammation. It is also good for subduing heart palpitations and the pain of neuralgia.

Purple sapphire carries the energies of idealism and the enlightened reformer. It encourages and helps you master the energy of perfection in all things. It contains the spirit of mercy and works with the highest levels of thought - it also aids visionary abilities and psychic perception on an everyday basis.

White Sapphire:

White sapphire is pure and pristine: it is the great spiritual opener. It teaches personal mastery of the energy of spiritual purity, of the universal truths of honour, trust, integrity and openness. It contains a balanced vibration and can be used on any area of the body that needs cleansing of low or painful vibrations. It lifts negativity and is a great protector; like a stream of pure crystal clean water, it washes away all obstacles in your spiritual path.

Green Sapphire:

Green sapphire works on the thymus, the heart, shoulders and chest, including the lower lungs. It teaches compassion and understanding of others' frailty. It contains the energy of trust, decency, honesty and integrity - to honour the trust others may give you to keep their secrets and the integrity not to manipulate others for your own selfish gain; to not be self-centred, greedy, self-indulgent, avaricious and egotistical; to honour others' principles and belief systems, even though they may differ greatly from your own.

Affirmation: Personal mastery can only be bestowed by my own enlightened efforts.

Selenite - Gypsum - Satin Spar - Alabaster

Chemical Composition: $CaSO_4$-2(H_2O)

Crystal System: Monoclinic **Hardness:** 2

Habit: Tabular; bladed or blocky crystals with a slanted parallelogram outline; long thin crystals; massive; fibrous

Color: Usually white, colorless or grey, but can also be shades of red, brown and yellow

Keyword: Remembering

Gypsum is a hydrous calcium sulphate, when well crystallised producing excellent transparent monoclinic crystals, which are often twinned in swallow-tail forms. Such crystals of gypsum are called selenite, for the crystals tend to show moon-like iridescence from the cleavage surfaces.

It is usually formed by the evaporation of an enclosed sea basin, or may be deposited from desert lakes. The massive rock-like variety of alabaster was known from the days of the Phoenicians, Assyrians and Egyptians, who made it into all kinds of beautiful vases and amphorae, and who were also the first to find out and use its splendour as a medium of direct and indirect lighting. The delicately wrought alabaster vases that were found in the tomb of Tutankhamen were used to illuminate the temples in the land of the Pharaohs.

Since it forms easily from saline water, gypsum can have many inclusions of other minerals and even trapped bubbles of air and water. The word selenite comes from the Greek for moon and means moon rock.

Selenite is a stone of communication and communion with the past and present; this includes communication with our guides and Angels. It aids telepathic links with others and contains all sacred knowledge; it often has the appearance of sacred markings on its surfaces to remind us of this fact.

It is used for the remembering of past lives and will help dream and meditation recall. Selenite works by recording information pertaining to all knowledge of all time; this is held within its crystalline structure via its formation by water and evaporation.

The theory goes that nothing can be dis-created, only changed. The water that was on the planet at its formation and the same water that nurtured the early forms of life is the same water the dinosaur drank, which is the same water the ancient peoples drank and it is constantly circulated around the planet by the rainfall and evaporation. So the water that is in you and me has been in everyone and everything. The water sustains and records all the life it touches; nothing on the planet can live without water.

To access the information accumulated by the selenite, you hold your piece of selenite in your hand of preference and ask the Deva, Angel, Spirit or Guardian of the selenite to access the information contained within its structure. You then allow yourself to be open to the subtle thoughts, feelings and emotions that begin to flow through you. When truly connected you should get impressions and insights. Remember, these have to register on different levels of your being. Some people experience them through feelings, others experience them as knowledge, or pictures. There is no right or wrong way. When you go into a meditative state in this way you will experience the information first at the cellular level, then at the feeling level, then eventually on the mental level. So you would probably take a minimum of three sessions to work with a specific crystal, to extract its information into the level of consciousness in which you know it, not just feel it or sense it.

Selenite brings light and healing to every cell in the body. It is a very high vibration stone and crown chakra activator. It will heal all fluid functions of the body. It clears the spinal column of energy blocks via the spinal fluid and gives a flowing healing energy to all it touches. Emotionally it lifts the spirit, bringing Divine joy and playfulness into our lives to enhance the world's light energy.

Affirmation: I am awake to the possibilities of infinite space and time; Divine understanding flows through me and radiates out to all I meet.

Siberian Blue Quartz (See Quartz)

Color: Electric blue

Keywords: Manifests the Impossible

Siberian Blue Quartz is one of the emerging class of stones that is the result of the hybrid energies of man and the mineral world. It has been laboratory grown specifically for linking the third eye to the mental body, which initiates advanced psychic abilities and facilitates a clearer interpretation of the information received. The quartz component of this stone acts as an amplifier and carrier for the energies of the cobalt it has grown with. Siberian blue quartz, or crystal cobalt quartz, allows one to fully access the amazing purity and beauty of the cobalt vibration. This ray is related to the throat and third eye chakras, which embody the qualities of inner vision, clairvoyance and other psychic abilities. Siberian blue quartz manifests the impossible into reality. A miracle!

Anything that takes you beyond your self-limiting belief system, or sentimental tribal conditioning, is seen as a miracle! Everyone has these beliefs. They usually have quite a long list of 'impossible' events that can never happen. Siberian blue quartz has not evolved through the earth vibration, it is new and as such untainted by the human psyche, so it can teach you to be 'new' and untainted by limited beliefs - to be reborn.

When people decide to meditate, to open spiritually, to take responsibility for their own health and well-being, the old belief systems come crashing down, their perception of the world changes radically, their eyes are open to the truth of reality. We call it the reality perception shock! The system that controls and manipulates you will not like you, though; as a free spirit you are very difficult to control and may be considered dangerous, difficult, even a deviant - or worse! The 'system' cannot understand - your care of others, your love of all people, your care of the environment and compassion for all living things including yourself, as you take responsibility for your own health and spiritual and emotional well-being.

You could just use Siberian blue quartz for its wonderful healing properties. It works on the thyroid and parathyroid, the throat, neck, base of the skull, upper lungs and upper arms. The throat and third eye chakras are also activated, the mental body is also stimulated.

Siberian blue quartz also activates the spirit of truth within your vibration, bringing wisdom, patience, mental attainment, spiritual and philosophical contemplation, a quiet peacefulness to the soul vibration. It gives integrity to all your endeavours and loyalty to the truth. It works with the energy of speaking your truth and being heard, self-expression. It does not do this with blind faith, it helps you reason things out slowly and quietly with integrity. It brings peace to your purpose. Siberian blue quartz makes a wonderful gemstone essence and has been used to ease throat infections and reduce fevers. It relieves stress and anxiety, soothes stomach ulcers and internal bleeding. As an aura spray it is good for stiff necks, inflammation, sciatica, sunstroke and sunburn. It can be used to calm down aggressive residue in the environment. It has also been used to ease the passing of the terminally ill.

Affirmation: Manifest the impossible, expect a miracle.

Silver

Chemical Composition: Ag

Crystal System: Isometric **Hardness:** 2.5 - 3

Habit: Massive; disseminated grains; wires and plates as the most common; whole individual crystals are extremely rare, but when present are usually cubes; dodecahedrons and octahedrons; crystal growth as shown on some specimens produces beautiful intricate structures; wires can form coiled clusters

Color: Silver-white with exposed specimens tarnishing black

Keyword: Reflective

Silver has been mined for eons and has always been fashionable in jewellery. Native silver is rare and much silver is produced from silver-bearing minerals such as proustite, pyrargyrite, galena, etc. Specimens of native silver usually consist of wires that are curved and intertwined together, making interesting artistic mineralogical curiosities. Silver illuminates and reflects its energy: it is yin, fluid, soft, feminine, yielding. It is a natural tranquilliser. Silver brings emotional freedom and spiritual harmony. It directs heat and pain away from the area that may be stuck, angry or stagnant. Silver stimulates the activity of body fluids and can ease dizziness and headaches. It reduces feelings of bloatedness and calms the digestive system. It also aids the digestive tract and can clear parasites and parasitic energies. It makes an excellent aura spray. It also mirrors the emotions, so be aware of that energy. It says 'look' and pierces your illusion of reality. The over-soul or Angel of silver works with the 'Mirror of the Kells' - 'Mirror of the Celts' or 'Miracles' - you may find yourself like 'Alice in Wonderland' stepping through the looking glass, even wondering if you are coming or going. It works with the dream time, the seasons and tides of life, waxing and waning. Silver can be slippery and it knows how to bend and distort; it will show you your illusions. The negative aspect of silver is being 'moonstruck', the madness of the March hare. As mad as the hatter! Mirror, mirror, on the wall - into fairy stories and archetypes of good and evil. Silver does encourage the receptive mediumistic side of your nature and brings about tremendous spiritual growth and deep personal insights, especially if you have a sense of humour and can laugh at yourself. Silver reflects back mistakes without distortion. It will show you as you truly are; there is nowhere to hide with silver, it shines its light equally on all. People fall in love with the silver vibration - by the light of the silvery moon - because it reminds them of the silver cord that is said to attach us to the other side. Silver can be used to still the emotions if you feel over-excitable or highly strung and bring tranquillity. It is good for calming the nerves and works on the female hormones to bring stability. All fluid functions of the body can be helped by silver. It is also very beneficial for kidney complaints and rigid fear-based mental attitudes. Silver makes an ideal partner with most gemstones and crystals for jewellery, the only exceptions being red, orange, yellow or green precious gemstones that are being used for their magnetic gathering energies; then the vibrational resonance of gold would be more appropriate to balance and fully integrate the energies. If an all-gold setting is beyond your price range, a good compromise would be a dual setting of gold and silver. If you only like silver jewellery, then your focused 'intent' would still bring beneficial results.

Affirmation: I manifest emotional freedom and spiritual harmony into my life.

Smithsonite

Chemical Composition: $ZnCO_3$

Crystal System: Trigonal **Hardness:** 4 - 4.5

Habit: Botryoidal; rounded rhombohedrons; scalenohedrons

Color: Apple green to blue-green; purple to lavender; yellow; white; tan; blue; orange; peach; colorless; pink; red

Keywords: Child Within

Smithsonite is named for James L. M. Smithson (1754-1829), a British mineralogist and founder of the Smithsonian Institute in Washington. The lustre of smithsonite sets it apart from other minerals: it has a silky to pearly lustre, giving natural specimens a certain play of light across its surface that resembles the lustre of melted wax glowing under a candle flame. The typical crystal habit of smithsonite is an interesting form called botryoidal. This form has the appearance of grape bunches and is the result of radiating fibrous crystals that form from central attachment points and grow outward and into each other. The result is a spherical, bubbly landscape for which smithsonite is considered the perfect classic example. Smithsonite has been and is still being used as an important, although rather minor, ore of zinc.

The pink-lavender varieties of smithsonite have an energy that is soft, gentle, comforting and soothing to the emotional body. It has a heavenly feel of velvety softness. Flowing graceful healing energies are emitted from this stone; it is good for convalescence and works on the brain's pain centres; it helps with alcohol and drug-related disorders.

It has a powerful Angelic guidance. It is used mainly for those who need to let go of trauma or are suicidal. It is full of pink bubbles of joyful healing energy. Smithsonite heals all stress-related conditions; it is a soporific. It heals trauma of the mental and emotional bodies; helps recovery from nervous breakdown; loosens the painful ties of emotional suffering; releases deep-rooted childhood trauma - even the hidden traumas, the ones which are too painful to remember, are released. It brings joy, it brings hope, it gives peace.

Smithsonite is good for birth and re-birthing; it has also been used in regression to acknowledge your child from other lives; in this way it is linked to the unborn child, thus it is used in infertility.

Blue-green smithsonite heals the emotions and helps us to go with the flow, releasing anger and rage in a positive constructive format. It intertwines the etheric and emotional bodies back to a state of Divine grace, bringing in the energy of universal love and peace. The blue variety is like silky watery depths which reveal a healing sanctuary of perfect stillness. It heals all wounds with universal love. This stone gives a joyful feeling of belonging as you are gently nurtured by the universal Angelic energies.

Blue-green smithsonite helps you attain your heart's desire. It promotes friendship and gives the wearer a friendly approachable aura. It will, just like turquoise, balance and centre your energy field; it also 'feeds' the nervous system, allowing you to let go of the fear of opening up, of being yourself. It calms over-emotional tendencies and can ease stress-related panic attacks.

The violet variety gives a feeling of joyful euphoria to your spiritual service. It is perfect for meditation as it holds you gently in a force field of light, guiding you with total certainty and serenity towards higher states of consciousness; it is good for those who are fearful in meditation and fear soul loss, or losing the 'way'. This stone gives total guidance and protection in our meditations and altered states of consciousness. It can show you the future and give you a Divine nudge in the right direction.

The violet variety also releases negative energy and blockages that may have lodged within the energy field; it gently transmutes the negative energy with higher vibrations of love and joy. It is good for all stressful conditions and situations. It helps with the pain of neuralgia and acute inflammation of the nerves. It is linked to the unborn child, thus it is used in infertility and past life regression.

The yellow variety works initially on the solar plexus chakra; it will cleanse, heal, activate, energize, balance and integrate this energy centre. The solar plexus chakra rules the liver, spleen, stomach, gall-bladder and middle stomach; it is related to the mental body; it is where we store our old hurts and emotional wounds; it works with assimilation and digestion of food, as well as mental and emotional nourishment. It also is responsible for a lot of skin and nervous-related problems.

Affirmation: I now nurture my inner child and love myself for who I am.

Smoky Quartz - Cairngorm - Morion - Coon Tail Quartz (See Quartz)

Color: Golden; black; brown

Keywords: Celtic Warrior

Smoky quartz is a popular variety of quartz. It is also popular as an ornamental stone and is carved into spheres, wands, pyramids, obelisks, and eggs. Smoky quartz, a variety itself of quartz, has a few varieties of its own. Cairngorm comes from the Cairngorm Mountains in Scotland. Morion is a very dark black opaque variety of smoky quartz. Coon tail quartz is a smoky quartz with an alternating black and grey banding. The color of smoky quartz is variable from golden-brown to black and sometimes smoky grey-colored specimens are included as smoky quartz. The cause of the color of smoky quartz is in question, but it is almost certainly related to the amount of exposure to radiation that the stone has undergone. Natural smoky quartz often occurs in granitic rocks which have a small but persistent amount of radioactivity. Most smoky quartz that makes its way to crystal shops and to some gem cutters has been artificially irradiated to produce a dark black color. Smoky quartz is the Celtic Warrior; it was carried into battle as late as the first world war. It teaches you the right use of power and keeps you 'grounded' in fearful situations. It stops destructive power that is used out of selfishness, greed, manipulation, evil or weakness. It is very protective. It stops depression and restriction. It connects you to the deep philosophical thoughts, ideals and wisdom of the land - of ancient battles of good versus evil, of the right to hold your own values and stand your ground. But don't think for one moment that it is masculine. Smoky quartz has a balanced polarity of male and female energies. Remember the womenfolk of the Celts went into battle too. Ancient Celtic Queens like Boadicea fought for her land against the might of Rome. It has been used for scrying; it intensifies your visionary ability by releasing your fear, fear of failure or fear of the unknown. Smoky quartz contains hidden riches; it can also throw up energetically a smoke-screen of protection that will temporarily hide you - nothing permanent though, just a breathing space while you gather your scattered emotions and ground yourself or 'go to ground'. Smoky quartz is a great teacher: it can take you deep inside the earth to work with the elementals for healing. It can help you to find your treasure - a strong and healthy body and a calm, peaceful stress-free mind. Smoky quartz can be practical; it likes you to lead a useful life, one in service to others who are less well-off spiritually. Spiritual poverty is rampant today - people with all the money in the world and they are so poor. Smoky quartz teaches the simple pleasure of a happy, joyful heart, of peace and brotherhood/sisterhood. It shows you friendship and trust are worth their weight in spiritual gold. Smoky quartz is stimulating and purifying to the first chakra, so it is good for meditation practice. It can bring you back to earth to everyday normal waking reality. It eases despair, despondency, gloom, melancholy and suicidal tendencies. It can help you bring your dreams into reality. There is nothing weak about smoky quartz. It enhances the survival instinct, it is a life-saver. Smoky quartz allows for clarity of thought and contemplation. It will balance the male/female polarities; it relieves headaches and congestion of the intestines, helps heal the feet and legs and eases lower back pain. It also relieves muscular cramp - not just physical cramp, but soul cramp too. Its pain-relieving properties are wonderful: it just draws out pain. It has been used against the negative effects of radiation, including electrical equipment negativity.

Affirmation: I now free myself from the daily battle to survive; I trust in the Universe to support me in all I do.

Sugilite - Royal Azel - Luvulite - New Age Stone

Chemical Composition: $(K,Na)_2Li_3(Fe,Mn,Al)_2(Si_{12}O_{30})$

Crystal System: Hexagonal **Hardness:** 6 - 6.5

Habit: Rare prismatic crystals; massive

Color: Purple; lilac; lavender, sometimes with black inclusions

Keywords: Third Eye Activator

Sugilite is a very distinctive opaque waxy purple stone. It comes from the Southern states of Africa and Japan. It was discovered in 1944 in Japan by Dr Kenichi Sugi, for whom it was named. It is found in association with manganese and is often streaked with black or bluish lines. Sugilite is the third eye activator; it works on the pineal gland, the top of the head, the crown and heart chakras, as well as the brain and scalp. Sugilite has a potent mature Universal Consciousness. It is very matriarchal and nurturing; it does seem to 'mother' the 'Star Children', giving them feelings of security and protection against the harsh climate of the negative earth vibration of hostility, rage, anger and fear. It is good for those who feel abandoned and dis-connected from their 'home' and source of emotional nourishment. It has also been used by very gentle sensitive souls who find it difficult to screen out the negativity and hostility of others. It is very protective as well as gently grounding. It can integrate the spiritual body to the physical body, which is very helpful for those amongst us who 'space out easily'.

Many people on the spiritual path have utilised sugilite for grounding their spiritual experiences into their everyday life. Above all, sugilite brings peace, dignity, humanitarianism and mental creativity. It really does develop psychic abilities, allowing for mystical experiences. It can develop faith and inner strength. It teaches you personal mastery, that you have a Divine right to your own point of view and inner truth. Sugilite also contains the spirit of mercy and it is very dignified; it allows you to work with the highest levels of thought and gives a thorough understanding of the thought process.

Sugilite is the aristocrat of the purple gemstones; it commands respect as it guides you towards spiritual perfection. It has a richness and quality about it that lead to refined psychic perception. It is good for those who meditate and teach meditation and healing disciplines: its vibration can produce great mystical leaders and enlightened gurus.

Sugilite has been used by cancer sufferers; it has brought relief to many souls. It has helped with all kinds of cancer, from brain tumours to breast cancer; this one use alone deserves complete medical research. It also helps problems associated with the immune system. It has been used to help internal inflammation and skin eruptions. Sugilite can subdue palpitations of the heart and jangled nerves. The lighter shades of sugilite can calm emotional turbulence and help with the pain of neuralgia and acute inflammation of the nerves. Lilac sugilite also has great healing powers; it can strengthen the immune system and is good for convalescence. It also flushes from the system the residue of anaesthetics.

Affirmation: I have a Divine right to my own point of view and inner truth.

Sunshine Aura Quartz (See Quartz)

Color: Bright neon yellow

Keyword: Sunshine

Sunshine aura is the energizer. It is a product of twentieth century technology, just as aqua aura, opal aura, rose aura and rainbow aura quartz are. The beauty of these quartzes is apparent as the 'new' technology enhances the extremely powerful properties of the master healer, clear quartz. They are the product of natural organic quartz; pure gold and pure platinum in a secret process that owes as much to alchemy as it does to science. In a high-temperature near-vacuum environment, atoms of pure gold and pure platinum are pyroelectrically bonded with top grade clear quartz, creating the highly energized stones known as sunshine aura. The bonding process of the quartz and pure gold/platinum co-mingles the two substances in a permanent way, which results in the striking original color of bright sunshine yellow. Clear quartz is a 'master healer' because it contains the full spectrum of the visible 'white' light and as such it will work on every level of our being - emotional, physical, spiritual and mental. Gold is a powerful healer, as is platinum.

The sunshine aura quartz works initially on the solar plexus chakra; it will cleanse, heal, activate, energize, balance and integrate this energy centre. The solar plexus chakra rules the liver, spleen, stomach, gall-bladder and middle stomach; it is related to the mental body; it is where we store our old hurts and emotional wounds; it works with assimilation and digestion of food, as well as mental and emotional nourishment. It also is responsible for a lot of skin and nervous-related problems.

Sunshine aura quartz is a very bright, garish, odd, unnatural-looking crystal, but it is also attractive in a very lively sort of way; it isn't easy to ignore. It seems to 'jump' out at you shouting, I can help! Many people have been attracted to its vibrational healing properties.

It is almost hyperactive as crystal energies go! It appears to be the ultimate cleansing crystal, the great eliminator. As we all know, cleansing means healing - out with the old rubbish, as it cleans and removes toxins and waste from the system. On a physical level it removes toxins and promotes the flow of gastric juices, as well as stimulating the lymphatic system. Sunshine aura really cleanses the system and relieves constipation. Constipation represents holding on to past emotions. On the emotional level it clears low self-esteem and issues of low self-worth and the fear of responsibility. On a mental level sunshine aura clears and stimulates the mind, activating the intellect and intuition. On a spiritual level sunshine aura is very active and expansive. It can really get communication started; it is also good for releasing fears and phobias.

Sunshine aura is also protective, because its energy is so vast, fast and intense; it just shakes off parasitic energy on all levels. It also increases the wearer's capacity for laughter and joy. It appears to be the 'Cosmic Clown' of the healing crystals. It says the best medication as an antidote to illness and disease is a joyful heart.

Affirmation: I deserve all the love, respect, happiness, sunshine and joy that come to me. I am open to receiving all that is good.

Sunstone - Oligoclase - Aventurine Feldspar - Golden Labradorite

Chemical Composition: $NaAlSi_3O_8$-$CaAl_2Si_2O_8$

Crystal System: Triclinic **Hardness:** 6 - 6.5

Habit: Blocky or tabular crystals. Crystals have a nearly rectangular or square cross-section with slightly slanted dome and pinacoid terminations; also massive, granular

Color: Oligoclase is golden yellow; sunstone is orange to reddish

Keyword: Power

Oligoclase is not a well-known mineral but has been used as a semi-precious stone under the names of sunstone and moonstone. Sunstone has flashes of reddish color caused by inclusions of hematite or goethite. Moonstone shows a glowing shimmer similar to labradorescence but lacking in color. The display is produced from lamellar intergrowths inside the crystal. These intergrowths result from compatible chemistries at high temperatures becoming incompatible at lower temperatures and thus a separating and layering of these two phases. The resulting shimmer effect is caused by a ray of light entering a layer and being refracted back and forth by deeper layers before it exits the crystal. This refracted ray has a different character than when it went in and produces the moon-like glow. Oligoclase is a member of the plagioclase feldspar group.

There are two types of 'sunstone' available at the present time. The orange one shows brilliant reflections due to inclusions (usually goethite or hematite); the other, from Oregon in the USA, is a lovely fresh transparent yellow.

The orange sunstone is used in bringing in vibrant solar energies in meditation and body layouts, for connecting with one's own source of light, transmuting dark or negative energies into positive healing energies. It is very yang in nature and emits a strong energy of leadership and positive personal empowerment. It works on the sacral chakra, lower back, lower intestines, abdomen, kidneys, bladder and ovaries. Orange sunstone is very magnetic and attracts the energy of making things happen now. It makes you take action in your life; the time for procrastination and hiding your light away is past; rather than just dreaming of the life you would like, live the life you want to live right now - no more postponement, deferral, delay or stalling.

It is a strong stone, which links you into your intuition. It removes inhibitions, sexual hang-ups, self-imposed constraints, repression and emotional hang-ups, even emotional hook-ups. The emotional hook-ups from others are energies other people have placed within your energy field to control or manipulate you in some way. They can be very debilitating and draining on your energy field. Sunstone gently removes these emotional snares and transmutes them into positive loving energy. Sunstone really makes you look what sacrifice you make to suit others? Dysfunctional relationships are toxic to both people involved. Try saying 'no' next time - you don't even have to explain.

Sunstone also makes you aware of how much you nurture yourself; it asks about taking responsibility for your own health and body, taking regular gentle exercise like walking or Yoga. It also asks 'is your life sweet?' - or has all the sweetness gone out of your life? If it has, sunstone can initiate positive change so you regain your sweetness. If you are not happy in what you do, how can you advance spiritually?

The Oregon sunstone, sometimes known as golden labradorite, is believed to be among the most beneficial stones for the third chakra - the solar plexus - the stomach, spleen, liver, gall-bladder, adrenal glands, nervous and digestive systems. It has a warm sunny nature. It helps you to develop your own originality. It is expansive to the mental body, allowing for integration of knowledge, clarity and wisdom. It is ideal for developing originality and enlightened leadership. It makes you sociable, without being dependant. It gives you the power to be an individual, to be unique, while celebrating your continued connection to humanity.

The spiritual warrior relies on inner strength, tempered by the belief that guidance comes from a Divine force. This strength becomes honed and refined through facing and overcoming external challenges. As you learn to honour and value yourself, the inner chant of "I am not worthy" finds less and less space within your energy field. Only by truly honouring and loving yourself can you hope to act out of love and compassion for others.

Sunstone teaches you that when you suppress your psychic sensitivity it leads to blockages around the solar plexus chakra; these manifest as excess weight around the middle, digestive problems and stomach ulcers. Sunstone is excellent for weight loss and healing digestive problems.

Affirmation: I tune in to the energies of the Sun; my enlightened personal power is becoming stronger every day.

Tangerine Quartz (See Quartz)

Color: Tangerine

Keywords: Soul Retrieval

Tangerine quartz is natural and organic. It has been available for some time, but was extremely rare. Recently a new find has surfaced in Brazil. The tangerine color probably owes its color to a trace of iron in the ferric state (Fe_2O_3). Quartz is crystalline silicon dioxide (silica) which has the formula SiO_2. These natural tangerine quartz have all the usual characteristics of clear quartz and appear to grow in the usual well-formed beautiful mineral specimens. Because of this we must take into account each personal crystal's signature, allowing for the uniqueness of the sacred geometry to be fully manifested within each healing situation. The relevant structures will always apply, i.e. diamond, barnacle, bridge, cathedral, channelling crystal etc. The tangerine quartz can be used for balancing and activating the sacral chakra, easing sexual problems and tensions, impotence or frigidity, also bladder and kidney problems. It eases anger, frustration, aggression, anxiety and blocks in creativity.

It is also the crystal to use after shock or trauma. It will quickly restore the correct flow and the creativity needed to heal the situation. The energy will help with movement and the flow of energy around the sacral chakra - *'Svadhisthana'* in Sanskrit, meaning sweetness. This is one of the most creative energy centres in the body and as such, when our creativity is blocked, we feel congested and ill at ease. All the sweetness has gone out of life and we feel stagnant and impotent, unable to move forward with a sense of purpose.

The energy of (tangerine) quartz is very similar to natural citrine quartz, so it would also be useful in energizing the solar plexus chakra, working with the energy of joy and abundance. My own personal experience with the tangerine quartz was very profound. I was taken to the higher levels and shown how it will help a soul with recovery from trauma and deep shock; also psychic attack or psychic shock. This crystal is to do with *recovery* on a soul level after soul shock or trauma has splintered the soul into fragmentation or soul loss. It has been called 'soul retrieval'. It works very much with the Angels of acceptance and healing through non-judgemental love, showing us that nothing is impossible - if we can conceive it, we can believe it - we can take ourselves beyond our limited belief system and manifest the 'impossible'. When this happens, we call it a miracle. We manifest our belief system every day (whether we are conscious of doing so or not). By changing our limited beliefs we manifest a different reality for ourselves and the world at large - miracles do happen! Nothing is impossible. The tangerine quartz teaches us about magnetism, the law of attraction. We attract into our lives our reality. By changing our signature to a positive vibration we begin to vibrate at a much more refined level and we can then attract energies of love, healing, peace, joy etc. When we become energy aware, we no longer have a victim consciousness and we can take responsibility for our thoughts, words and actions. We become aware of our past karma and can dissolve our past mis-takes; that is just what they are - just like making a movie, you keep doing the same scene over and over again until you get it right. Mis-takes need not be thought of as negative, they do hold a vast learning potential for the soul.

Affirmation: I am magnetic; I attract into my life all I need for my personal happiness and spiritual growth.

Tanzanite - Zoisite

Chemical Composition: $Ca_2Al_3(SiO_4)_3(OH)$

Crystal System: Orthorhombic **Hardness:** 6.5 - 7

Habit: Crystals prismatic

Color: Blue to lavender, deeper along the crystal axis

Keywords: Altered States of Reality

The source of its enchanting color is that tanzanite is trichroic: that is, it shows different colors when viewed in different directions. One direction is blue, another purple, and another bronze, adding subtle tones and depth to the vibrant color. When tanzanite is found in the ground, the bronze color is evident.

The unofficial story has it that the effect of heat was first discovered when some brown zoisite crystals lying on the ground with other rocks were caught in a fire set by lightning that swept through the grass-covered Merelani heartland north-east of Arusha. The Masai herdsmen who drive cattle in the area noticed the beautiful blue color and picked the crystals up, becoming the first tanzanite collectors.

Tanzanite is relatively new on the metaphysical scene. Its blue-lavender color is unique and a wonderful addition to gemstone therapy. Found in Tanzania (hence the name) in 1967, it has since become a well-known, extensively used and highly respected gemstone for crystal therapy. Pleochroism is very pronounced in tanzanite and is seen as three different color shades in the same stone. In viewing a tanzanite stone, the colors dark blue, green-yellow and red-purple can be seen, all a result of pleochroism. Poorer quality stones may have a only brownish color, due to the mixing of blue, purple and green. These stones are usually heat-treated to a deep blue-lavender color. This gemstone is only found in Tanzania.

Metaphysically, Tanzanite is mesmerising. The pleochroism facilitates altered states of reality. These can cause radical shifts in consciousness, by raising the vibratory signature of the user; this expands their personal mandala or 'original blueprint', allowing for 'downloads' of information which is activated from the Akashic records. Tanzanite is then used for inner/outer journeys. Your raised vibratory rate will cause you to see a thinning of the veil between the various planes of consciousness, allowing for clear communication with Ascended Masters, Angels, Spirit guides and other enlightened beings from dimensions not usually available to your normal conscious awareness. Tanzanite facilitates with dedicated use deep meditation, astral journeys and materialisation.

It can activate and integrate the energies of the base, sacral, heart, throat, third eye, fourth eye, fifth eye and crown chakras, as well as the chakras eight to fourteen above the head, facilitating a situation in which the mind and psychic abilities are activated and are guided by the wisdom of an enlightened heart. The energized throat chakra allows for clear communication of this integrated understanding.

Tanzanite works to alleviate problems associated with the upper lungs, throat, ears, thyroid, parathyroid, pineal, head, mouth, upper arms, shoulders, bones and skeletal structure. It holds a lot of healing potential and is carried, worn or used by those who work to alleviate dis-ease in others. As a gemstone essence it has been used for meditation and healing. It combines well with other high vibration gemstones, especially phenacite, danburite, moldavite, azeztulite and quartz.

When combined with aquamarine and moldavite in a gemstone essence it causes old patterns of spiritual dis-ease to simply fall away, which allows for new patterns to be integrated very quickly.

When combined with aquamarine and morganite in a gemstone essence it causes old patterns of emotional dis-ease to simply fall away, which allows for new patterns to be integrated quickly.

When combined with iolite and danburite in a gemstone essence it causes old patterns of karmic dis-ease to simply fall away, which allows for new patterns to be integrated very promptly.

Those crystals that exhibit the full tanzanite spectrum - violet-blue, purple and bronze, or dark blue, green-yellow and red-purple - are very potent in their healing application, as they contain a vast spectrum of possibilities and applications. They make an exceptional gemstone essence which can be used to alleviate problems that have manifested as dis-ease anywhere in the body or aura.

Affirmation: I am open to enlightened altered states of reality; I now choose to transform my life and become free.

Tiger Eye - Crocidolite - Riebeckite - Hawk's Eye - Falcon's Eye - Tiger Iron - Blue Asbestos - Riebeckite - Asbestos

Chemical Composition: $SiO_2 + Na_2(Fe, Mg)_3Fe_2Si_8O_{22}(OH)_2$

Crystal System: Monoclinic **Hardness:** 5 - 6

Habit: Slender prismatic to acicular; aggregated crystals; columnar; granular; fibrous; asbestiform masses

Color: Hawk's eye and falcon's eye dark blue to black; tiger eye dark yellow to black; tiger iron black, brown, yellow and dark red bands

Keyword: Insight

Riebeckite is not a well-known mineral although most people have probably seen stones that at one time were composed of riebeckite crystals. The typically dark blue mineral was named after a famous eighteenth-century German explorer and mineralogist, Emil Riebeck. Riebeckite has a variety called 'crocidolite' that is asbestiform in habit. The largest deposit of crocidolite occurs in South Africa and it is mined there in large quantities. Crocidolite is also known as 'blue asbestos' and 'riebeckite asbestos'. Secondly, crocidolite is often found pseudomorphed by quartz into an attractive stone.

It is popular as a semi-precious stone and is known by many trade names such as tiger eye, hawk's eye and falcon's eye. Blue tiger eye has preserved the original blue color of the riebeckite, while the more common brown color is the result of some oxidation of the iron into limonite inclusions. Although it is wrong to refer to tiger eye as being a form of riebeckite, because there is no riebeckite present in the stone, credit must be given to this mineral for aiding in the production.

Traditionally, tiger eye, hawk's eye and falcon's eye have been carried to give protection from the evil eye. Tiger iron is formed by a metamorphic process from rock containing iron and quartz. Its layers are made up of jasper, hematite and tiger eye.

Tiger Eye:

Tiger eye is dark yellow with brown to dark brown bands. It deals with issues of low self-worth and lack of personal creativity. It aids in clarity of perception, to see one's own faults and understand different perspectives. It can be used to surface any problems of the mind and mental body, where the normal thought patterns and mental processes have gone very wrong. It also deals with fear of responsibility and eating disorders. It has been used to alleviate personality disorders such as aggression, over-sensitivity to criticism, low self-esteem or addictive personality traits. Tiger eye can be used with caution to surface these imbalances for healing. The energies of tiger eye are not recommended to be worn for any length of time as a pendant, due to the intense nature of the stone. It is best used for meditation and as a diagnostic tool.

Hawk's Eye:

The color of this crystal is dark blue to black; it deals with restrictive thought patterns and those of a gloomy, negative or pessimistic disposition. It is definitely the crystal chosen by those who are dissatisfied with their lot in life and choose to blame others. It also indicates locked-up negative emotions. It has been used by some souls for meditation; it will increase clairvoyant ability; it works with elemental energy to aid perception. It has been used to surface 'cold shoulder' and stiff neck problems. The energies of hawk's eye are not recommended to be worn for any length of time as a pendant, due to the intense nature of the stone. It is best used for meditation and as a diagnostic tool.

Tiger Iron:

Appears to be very useful for those people who are mentally, emotionally and physically exhausted, whose lives are in need of a major change of direction or a life-style overhaul. It facilitates a space where they can stop and take stock of their lives. The overload is very often due to outside influences; usually money orientated people get 'stuck' in work or family situations that are destroying them. When someone is very attracted to this crystal, it usually transpires they are suffering from emotional burn-out or mental exhaustion. This stone then helps them to make the necessary life-style adjustments by grounding and energising them into constructive creative action. Physically it will heighten vitality and improve the condition of the blood. It works on the feet, legs, hips and base chakra. It also eliminates toxins from the large intestine.

Affirmation: I now free my mind from logical constraints and trust to my higher self to provide insights to all my questions.

Topaz

Chemical Composition: Al_2,SiO_4 $(OH,F)_2$

Crystal System: Orthorhombic **Hardness:** 8

Habit: Crystals usually prismatic, often two or more vertical prism forms, or with striated prism faces. Also massive, granular

Color: Colorless; golden yellow, pale yellow; pale blue; greenish; and rarely pink

Keyword: Sanctuary

Topaz is a magnificent gemstone that has been used for centuries in jewellery. Topaz is the hardest silicate mineral and one of the hardest minerals in nature. The crystals can reach the incredible size of several hundred pounds. The Ancient Egyptians said that topaz was colored with the golden glow of the all-powerful sun god Ra. This made topaz a very potent amulet that protected the faithful against harm. The Romans associated topaz with Jupiter; so did the Indians in ancient Vedic astrology. Topaz sometimes has the amber gold of fine cognac or the blush of a peach and all the beautiful warm browns and oranges in-between. Some rare and exceptional topaz crystals are pale pink to a sherry red.

Legend has it that topaz dispels all enchantment and helps to improve eyesight. The ancient Greeks believed that it had the power to increase strength and make its wearer invisible in times of emergency. Topaz was also said to change color in the presence of poisoned food or drink. Its mystical curative powers waxed and waned with the phases of the moon: it was said to cure insomnia, asthma and haemorrhages. In Mexico it was used as a truth stone. The most colorful gem, yellow topaz, is the birthstone for those born in November.

Topaz facilitates the deep understanding and acceptance of Universal Laws. These are not man's laws, but cosmic laws. This crystalline energy works through the laws of attraction and manifestation: it's electric! It can 'plug' you into the cosmic web of Divine light. It allows for these cosmic realisations to become manifest in your everyday waking reality. It gives a good perception of the underlying reality behind the truth of personal integrity, ritual, cause and effect and making sure at all times you are energetically pristine. It does not ask for blind devotion though, but it does ask you to open your eyes, to go beyond your self-limiting belief system into the full understanding of personal power, choices and freedom. It does improve your eyesight, inner and outer. A sanctuary of healing awaits you with the topaz vibration.

Yellow Topaz:

Is revitalizing; it has the energy of the ancient Egyptian Sun God Ra. It brings a feeling of energy, power and vitality to the user. It is used for liver, gall-bladder, spleen, pancreas, stomach disorders, anger, emotional upsets, the skin and nervous system; also any problem that is associated with the mental body, toxins and elimination, including negative mental attitudes that have stopped emotional or spiritual growth. It can help with eating disorders, both anorexia and overweight problems; the solar plexus chakra that it governs is responsible for both extremes. It is a powerful stone and, when worn, carried or used in meditation, will bring personal power and self-mastery.

Golden Yellow Topaz:

Can activate contact with your higher self, your Divine aspect, that dwells within each and every one of us. It brings immortality - you are already immortal, but you may have forgotten that you are! You are an eternal being of infinite light, love, compassion, wisdom, truth and joy. This crystal just reminds you of this fact, it then encourages you to behave in the enlightened way.

It manifests healing on all levels. It makes a wonderful gemstone essence, as do all colors of topaz. This gemstone's energy is attraction; it can attract into your life favourable 'happy coincidences' that will advance healing and spiritual growth. It is very beneficial to the meridians and can clear blockages or under-activity very quickly.

Pale Green Topaz:

Is tender, its heart is gentle, it is the fresh start, new beginnings, a learning time; filled with childlike (but not childish) wonder and freshness. It is good for the soul weary, the torch bearers who have carried the energy for so long against overwhelming odds, against ridicule, scorn and negativity. It reminds you that you can refresh and renew yourself moment by moment, as you recreate yourself anew each day.

Pale green topaz gently taps you on the shoulder and reminds you it is not food that keeps you alive, it is the Pranic life force, or have you forgotten to breathe correctly; Pranic breathing is very enlivening. It also works with past life problems and past life regression. It gently cleanses the heart chakra of pain and painful memories, so it is helpful for degraded lung and heart conditions. It also aids assimilation of food and nutrients.

Pale Blue Topaz:

Inspires and uplifts. It also assists your soul in its search for truth. It contains purity and innocence and it is very soothing and calming to the emotional body.

It is a witness stone. Whenever you feel outrage at an injustice, or feel on the receiving end of a 'perceived' wrong, be it on any level, just ask the Angel of the pale blue topaz to act as your witness. The only rule is that you must then in no way, thought or deed behave in a negative manner towards the 'cause' of the injustice. You must be beyond karmic energy and just allow the situation to 'play' itself out, allow the full 'drama' to manifest, as you are merely a silent pristine witness 'viewing' the situation. Using this stone is very useful; it will allow you see what 'movies' you have got caught up in, in the 'theatre' of life.

Natural pale blue topaz is a wonderful 'channelling' gemstone. It can connect you to the Angels of truth and ancient wisdom. It is used physically for the throat chakra and related problems, as well as being calming and soothing to the whole body. The calming and soothing is of a very high vibration, it simply lifts you above the stressful energy by raising your vibratory rate; what was once perceived as stressful, you now rise above.

Pink Topaz:

Works with the energy of hope; it is kind and affectionate, its love is deep, high and wide. Its warmth melts and dissolves resistance, it comforts and mollifies. It is the peace offering. It shows you the face of God/Goddess. When we truly love another person unconditionally we look into the face of God. It is serenity, the peace that passes all understanding, a safe haven. Pink topaz helps old dis-ease patterns simply fall away. Use it on an area of the body that feels congestion or pain. As with all the topaz colors it is a master healer.

London Blue Topaz:

Has the energy of selfless love; it is a universal healer, it reminds you that you can overcome all obstacles. It helps you to remain calm and composed. It teaches you to speak your truth in a dignified manner. It is a very dignified crystal. If you can remain calm and focused in any situation, you will have learned the lesson this crystal is here to teach: detachment. This crystal is good for all problems related to speech, including sore throats, thyroid problems, stiff necks and talking without engaging the mental body.

Clear Topaz:

Teaches you to be aware of every thought, word and deed, to purify and refine your vibration, until your whole system on every level is full of pristine light and glory and you become a conscious channel for the light, a force for good. It encourages wisdom, understanding, truth, dispassion, discrimination, serenity, self-restraint, one-pointedness of mind, purity, forbearance, fortitude, patience, forgiveness, the spirit of service, sacrifice and love for all.

Clear topaz also teaches you to avoid fear, anger, hatred, greed, desire, ego manipulation, pride, boastfulness and laziness. It will activate higher states of cosmic consciousness, where you realise that 'powers' such as clairvoyance and clairaudience are not worth striving for because far greater illumination and peace are possible beyond them. If one regularly practises concentration and meditation, psychic powers are bound to come; but they must not be used for selfish gain, otherwise you become a victim of your own ignorance.

Physically, each gland in the body has a specific color and vibration of its own. Clear topaz works on all of them by working on the collective functioning of the endocrine system, so it is ideal to use in gemstone layouts over any area that needs clearing of stagnant or stuck energy.

Affirmation: I allow myself a sanctuary of peace - a special time every day for personal contemplation and meditation.

Tourmaline - Dravite - Indocolite - Elbaite - Rubellite - Verdelite - Schorl - Paraiba - Watermelon

Chemical Composition: $Na(Mg,Fe,Li,Al,Mn)_3Al_6(BO_3)_3Si_6O_{18}$

Crystal system: Trigonal **Hardness:** 7

Habit: Crystals usually prismatic, often of curved triangular cross-section. The prism faces are often strongly striated parallel to their length and the two ends of the crystal are often differently terminated. Parallel or radiating crystal groups are common; also massive

Color: Dravite is brown; indocolite is blue; rubellite is pink to red; verdelite is green; schorl is black; paraiba is vivid blues and greens; uvite is light to dark brown; elbaite, the gem variety of tourmaline, comes in all colors; watermelon is pink in the centre with a green rind

Keyword: Healing

Tourmaline's name comes from the Sinhalese word 'turmali', which means 'mixed'. Bright rainbow collections of gemstone varieties were called 'turmali' parcels. Tourmaline, occurring in more colors and combinations of colors than any other gemstone variety, lives up to its name. There is a tourmaline that looks like almost any other gemstone! Many stones in the Russian Crown Jewels from the 17th century, once thought to be rubies, are actually tourmalines. Perhaps this is why this gemstone is said to encourage artistic intuition: it has many faces and expresses every mood. The Empress Dowager Tz'u Hsi, the last Empress of China, loved pink tourmaline and bought almost a ton of it. The Dowager went to rest eternally on a carved tourmaline pillow. Tourmaline occurs in every color of the rainbow and combinations of two or three colors. Bicolor and tricolor tourmalines, with bands of colors, are very popular. Sometimes the colors are at different ends of the crystal and sometimes there is one color in the heart of the crystal and another around the outside. In 1989, miners discovered tourmaline unlike any that had ever been seen before. The new type of tourmaline, which soon became known as Paraiba tourmaline, came in incredibly vivid blues and greens.

There are many unique properties of tourmaline. First, they are piezoelectric, which means that when a crystal is heated or compressed (or vibrated) a different electrical charge will form at opposite ends of the crystal (an electrical potential). Conversely, if an electrical potential is applied to the crystal, it will vibrate. It becomes a polarized crystalline magnet and can attract light objects. This property was noticed long ago, before science could explain it: in the Netherlands, tourmalines were called 'aschentrekkers' because they attracted ashes and could be used to clean pipes! Secondly they are pleochroic, which means that the crystal will look darker in color when viewed down the long axis of the crystal than when viewed from the side. This property goes beyond the idea that the crystal is just thicker in that direction. Even equally dimensioned crystals will demonstrate this trait.

Tourmaline is a favourite among crystal therapists. Their rich and varied colors can captivate the eye and enhance the senses. Even the black opaque tourmaline can produce sharp crystal forms. Tourmalines are cut as precious gems, carved into figurines, cut as cabochons or sliced into cross-sections, and natural specimens are enthusiastically added to crystal therapists' healing collections. The tourmaline family as a whole gives off a very focused directional energy; this can be very useful when one wishes to 'work' within a particular chakra that may be too open, blocked, distorted, or split. They can still be used for body layouts to direct the energy flow; they are also good for moving energy between the chakras. For working on the meridian system you need to point the termination in the direction you wish the energy to flow. They also make exceptionally good meditation stones and are used to make wonderful healing gemstone essences.

Red Tourmaline:

Is a powerful healer of the base chakra. It can activate and clear an unbalanced base chakra, bringing inner and outer personal strength, stamina and endurance. Red tourmaline is a good detoxifier; it cleans the blood of impurities, which is vital to the health of the whole organism. It can control muscle spasms and chills, as well as bringing high physical energy and self- mastery. Red tourmaline has a burning desire to probe deeply into any issues you have around the activation of your Kundalini energy and the full mobilisation of your Divine life force that is yours to command. It teaches you the positive form of the ego and its value to the self and others.

Orange Tourmaline:

Is good for the sacral chakra, especially where it has split into more than one wheel, due to operations or personality disorders. A distorted sacral chakra will stop the balance of the whole system, especially the chakras immediately below and above; these three chakras combined are the most magnetic and any dysfunction will result in a greatly depleted life force, where everything is a struggle and life does not seem to move forward. Other indications of distortion are that the person is dreamy, etherial, or lives in a fantasy world of illusion; they can also have nightmares and problems with reality.

Green Tourmaline:

Is deeply nurturing: it quiets the mind and will bring emotional wisdom and balance. It dispels fears, calms nerves, aids sleep; regenerates the heart, thymus and immune system. Green tourmaline is an excellent diagnostic tool - its energy really gets to the root of a problem. It has been helpful when used to combat deep-seated phobias, especially claustrophobia and panic attacks. Green tourmaline makes a good spring tonic, at any time of the year. It is also good for hyperactive children.

Pink Tourmaline:

Is a powerful heart stone that strengthens your wisdom, empathy, compassion and will-power. Your creativity is enhanced as you open yourself to the beauty that surrounds you. You will become aware of the many etheric levels of consciousness and Divine joy. Pink tourmaline will help heart and lung conditions. It is also helpful to those who have a problem with their femininity. It brings spiritual beauty; it is also a good crystal to give your client before a therapy session, as this crystal really makes you feel relaxed, receptive and open to the experience of healing.

Pink/Green or Watermelon Tourmaline:

Is one of the foremost heart chakra healers and helps one release old emotional pains, with love. It treats all stress and nervous conditions. It is especially helpful during stormy periods in a relationship; it will cool, balance and calm the emotions, so it is also good when you are trying to make up your mind; it will bring you back to the centre of yourself. It also melts any resistance or fears you may have to fully healing yourself on every level.

Blue Tourmaline:

Is an emphatic heart healer; it is used on the heart chakra to dispel old fears and hurts. It may even show up fears and hurts that have been suppressed, that were so traumatic you lost them. It has helped those who feel emotionally shattered. Use on any chakra that needs the soothing healing blue ray of this calming stone. The blue ray of this stone is a must for anyone who uses crystals on others, as it protects them from any negativity they may encounter. It is used to stop insomnia and night sweats. Blue tourmaline is helpful for sinus pain and congestion (unshed tears from childhood); its soothing ray is one of nature's pain-killers. It can be used directionally to remove pain and aid healing, as it is also an antibacterial. It is traditionally used on the lungs, throat, thyroid, thymus, larynx, oesophagus and the eyes, although it can be applied to any area of the body that is holding dis-ease patterns, miasms, pain and congestion.

Black Tourmaline:

Gives protection from negativity and heavy energies. It has been used to deflect the negative energy from all electrical equipment and especially computers. It also grounds heavy, stagnant or negative energy; as with all tourmalines it is very directional. It has been used as an energy deflector, as it is an excellent stone for those with potential for exposure to excessive amounts of radiation. It will protect against the negative thought forms and even the evil 'eye' of another. It has been used to help people after operations and chemotherapy. It is used for problems of the spine, feet, legs and for nervous disorders. It is also good for kidney and adrenal problems.

Violet Tourmaline:

Awakens the development of psychic abilities and promotes the desire to act on intuitive information. It is a beneficial stone for stimulating a blocked or under-utilized third eye. It facilitates the opening of an infinite range of mental avenues, increases the ability to concentrate and strips away false illusion. Violet tourmaline also increases the desire for stillness and quiet contemplation. It has been used for past life regression and to clear karmic debris. It also helps with depression, obsessional thinking and confusion. Physically, it eases sensitivity to pollution, eases chronic exhaustion, epilepsy and Alzheimer's disease. It can stimulate the pineal gland and also works on the upper skull, cerebral cortex and skin.

Tourmaline in quartz:

This combination brings the forces of light and darkness into harmony, thereby ending the illusion of duality. It has been used for those who need to heal their shadow side. Also it can be carried or worn by those who have a tendency towards self-sabotage. It can be used to transform negative energy or negative thoughts into positive energy, or deflect negative energies.

Affirmation: I now choose to heal myself on every level and become free of all dis-ease.

Turquoise

Chemical Composition: $CuAl_6(PO_4)_4(OH)_{85}(H_2O)$

Crystal System: Triclinic **Hardness:** 5 - 6

Habit: Includes crystals rarely large enough to see, usually massive, cryptocrystalline forms as nodules and veinlets

Color: Turquoise, but varies from greenish-blue to sky blue shades

Keywords: Great Spirit

Some say that in the thirteenth century turquoise was named in the mistaken belief that it came from Turkey. That may be true or it may be that the name comes from the Persian word for turquoise, *firouze*, since Persia has been a major source of this gemstone for thousands of years. In any case, the blue of this gemstone is so vivid and distinct that it has given its name to the color.

Turquoise is one of the oldest known gem materials. The Egyptians were mining turquoise in 3,200 BC in the Sinai. The blue of turquoise was thought to have powerful metaphysical properties by many ancient cultures.

Montezuma's treasure, now displayed in the British Museum, includes a fantastic carved serpent covered by a mosaic of turquoise. In ancient Mexico, turquoise was reserved for the gods; it could not be worn by mere mortals. The Apache believed that turquoise helped warriors and hunters to aim accurately. The Zuni believed that it protected them from demons.

In Asia it was considered protection against the evil eye. Tibetans carved turquoise into ritual objects, as well as wearing it in traditional jewellery. Ancient manuscripts from Persia, India, Afghanistan and Arabia report that the health of a person wearing turquoise can be assessed by variations in the color of the stone. Turquoise was also thought to promote prosperity.

Turquoise is a mineral usually found in association with copper deposits, so it is sometimes mined as a by-product of copper mining. Turquoise from Iran is often said to be the best because it is sometimes a clear sky blue with no green modifying color and no black veins running through it. Turquoise just as fine is produced in Arizona and New Mexico. In general, the bluer the blue, the more highly valued. A clear even texture without mottling or veins is also preferred. However, some people prefer turquoise with veins, sometimes called spiders'-webs, which set off the color. Sky blue turquoise is considered the birthstone for those born in December.

Turquoise is often imitated by 'fakes', such as the mineral chrysocolla, and poorer turquoise specimens are often dyed or color stabilized with coatings of various resins. The color can change with exposure to skin oils.

Turquoise is a healer for the emotions of the heart. It teaches you to talk from the heart. It loves the sharing of emotional wisdom, heartfelt communication; it loves togetherness, and family. It brings people together and gets them communicating. It is also a good crystal to wear if you have to speak in public. It calms the nerves and 'feeds' the central nervous system. Thus it is helpful in healing situations of nervous stress or breakdown. It helps panic attacks and emotional shock. Turquoise subdues fevers and cools inflammation of the nerves; it is particularly good for the pain of neuralgia.

Turquoise is a good crystal to wear when you have to make decisions, as it encourages self-questioning. It is also a good stone to wear when you wish to overcome self-sabotage; use it to centre yourself.

Turquoise helps you strengthen your voice: a person's voice is a good indication of overall health and vitality. It gently purifies the throat chakra; you can tell if someone's throat is blocked, they have to keep clearing it every few minutes. Turquoise teaches true communication, not idle chatter, but purposeful thought-out communication. It is about personal expression combined with personal responsibility.

Above all, turquoise helps you find your true path in life, your path with heart, so you can walk your talk with truth and dignity.

Turquoise is good for 'channelling' and communication with spirit guides and Angels. Its beautiful blue color is very expansive. It contains the essence of *shunyata*, the vast blue emptiness, stretching in all directions, absolutely clear, pristine and radiant. By this blue sky stretching into infinity we can gain an understanding, a feeling for the expansiveness and freedom which could be ours if we did not allow our horizons to become narrow, clouded and limited, if we did not permit our minds to become fixated and hypnotized by cravings and worries centred on what really are empty passing phenomena.

Turquoise is an excellent meditation stone. It has also been worn and carried as a talisman against demons and evil entities.

Turquoise can be carried, worn, used in body layouts or made into a gemstone essence or aura spray. It aids focused meditation. Physically it has been used for stomach ulcers, fatigue, weight problems, allergies, diabetes, the digestive system, muscles and muscle cramps, heart disease, high blood pressure, cancer, shallow breathing problems, sore throats, neck-ache, thyroid problems, hearing problems, tinnitus, asthma, headaches, nervous complaints, nightmares, dizziness and panic attacks.

Affirmation: Great Spirit, teach me to speak from an enlightened heart.

Zincite

Chemical Composition: ZnO

Crystal System: Hexagonal **Hardness:** 4.5

Habit: Natural crystals very rare; usually massive, foliated, granular

Color: Orange; yellow; red; green; colorless

Keywords: Life Force

Zincite is a zinc oxide compound with a hardness of about 4.5. It has been found in natural formations in New Jersey with willemite and franklinite. Other occurrences include Tuscany, Italy. Natural zincite crystals are very rare, but the more spectacular-looking and larger zincite crystals that are coming from Poland have the following legend attached to them. Informed sources tell us that the Polish zincite is a curious occurrence that was formed as a consequence of zinc smelting, growing spontaneously in the air vents or chimneys of the smelters. If so, these stones might be viewed as a hybrid of natural and synthetic processes. They have a spectacular red/orange and gold color with eye-catching crystal formations.

Metaphysically, the energies are well attuned to the lower three chakras, bringing an enhancement of overall life force, as well as confidence, strength, creativity and courage. Zincite provides for the synergy of personal power, freedom, strength and endurance in all endeavours. Zincite is the 'creative fire' of magnetic manifestation. It encourages activity, it has flamboyance and an air of expectation and excitement around it. It is not for the faint-hearted, if you decide to wear it. Its untiring energy is fearless, as it re-energizes depleted energy systems. If you are feeling pessimistic or dwelling on past events, depressed, or in shock, zincite is a very good crystal to work with. Zincite helps you let go of the past, of painful memories, shock, trauma, psychological paralysis and the fear of moving forward. Zincite is the crystal that pulls you through, breaks down barriers, shatters blocked energies. Its energy is very easy to direct and extremely focused, almost as focused as laser quartz. It has been used extensively in body layouts as a creative fire to not only regenerate depleted energy systems but to energize creativity. Those who have worked with the layouts report that creative abundance has been achieved in all areas of their lives. It is good for menopausal symptoms and the 'empty nest' syndrome; it gives freedom to the spirit and aids intuition - the gut instinct.

Zincite removes energy blocks throughout the system, restoring the natural flow of vitality in the meridian system. It can open the Kundalini channel and is a great re-energizer. With conscious use it will anchor the light body into the physical body. Zincite treats hair, skin and prostate gland problems. It is good for M.E., candida and all immune system disorders, intestinal disorders, assimilation, bowel disturbances, kidney complaints, mucus, catarrh, asthma, bronchitis, epilepsy, mental disorders, rheumatism, torn ligaments, broken bones, infertility and phobias. It has been extensively used to treat AIDS patients and those with severe immune system disorders. Zincite's focused energy has been used to open gateways - portals into other realms of consciousness.

Affirmation: Life can be a succession of wonderful, beneficial experiences - if I choose it to be so.

Zircon - Hyacinth - Jacinth

Chemical Composition: $ZrSiO_4$

Crystal System: Tetragonal **Hardness:** 7.5

Habit: Crystals usually prismatic with bi-pyramidal terminations

Color: Light brown to reddish-brown; yellow, green, blue and colorless

Keywords: Earth Star

Zircon is sometimes confused with the artificial diamond-type simulant cubic zirconia (or CZ).

Zircon can make a very attractive gemstone. The name zircon is very old and may come from Persian words meaning 'golden color'. It is found in reddish-browns and greens, but can be heat- treated to beautiful blue and golden colors. Colorless material is produced in this way as well.

As a mineral specimen, zircon is uncommon in most crystal shops because attractive specimens are rare. However, fine specimens of well-shaped zircons are available and are in demand. The typical simple crystal of zircon is a tetragonal prism terminated with four-sided pyramids at each end. The prism may be lacking and the crystal can look octahedral. More complex crystals have faces of a less steeply inclined prism that taper towards the terminations. Also, a secondary prism may truncate the primary prism by cutting off its edges and producing an octagonal cross-section through the crystal. There is even an eight-sided pyramid (actually a ditetragonal bi-pyramid) that may modify the four-sided pyramids. Hyacinth or jacinth only refers to the reddish-brown varieties of zircon.

The reddish-brown zircon is very grounding, helping you to cope with your physical needs and basic human survival mechanism. It can connect you to ancient knowledge and wisdom. It is used in body layouts and meditation to fully activate not only the base chakra, but the feet chakras and the earth star chakra beneath the feet. Its fiery force burns away blocks and negative energies that may have lodged in the base chakra.

It has also activated Kundalini movement, where this has been appropriate and desirable. Zircon has been used on the knees, ankles and feet to promote flexibility and movement. It loosens rigid patterns of dis-ease that may have lodged in these energy centres. It is very warming to the hands and feet.

Zircon's energy is solid, reliable and caring. It is down to earth; it helps you to understand the positive force of gravity, of being grounded, aware and energetically focused in the moment. It also stops mental lethargy, 'spaciness' and an unfocused mind. It is helpful for those who are incapable of stillness, or who have difficulty achieving their goals. It stops neediness and fearful or self-destructive behaviour patterns. It has also been used to relieve the symptoms of osteoarthritis and other skeletal disorders. It can activate and stimulate the adrenals.

Because zircon's energy is so earthing it can give a beautiful cloak of security and it teaches you the way of healing with the earth's energy field. It also may be used to link into the past - your earliest experiences, including the extent to which your basic needs were met, or not, when you were an infant, are recorded and stored in the root chakra. Psychologists say that babies fed "on demand" learn to trust their needs will be met. These individuals go through life expecting the same and are rarely disappointed. Babies left to cry "till feeding time" learn to distrust and expect and accept disappointments, believing they do not deserve their needs to be met. This can affect them for the rest of their lives. This psychological theory ties in completely with the 'Universal Law of Resonance'. So if you have a lack or disappointment energy field you will attract even more of the same! Zircon can, with conscious attunement, release these hidden blockages from the root chakra.

Affirmation: I now energize my earth star chakra; this activates my Divine matrix within the Earth's planetary grid. This will anchor my Divine presence on Earth.

Glossary

Acupoint: Abbreviation for acupuncture point. An energetic pore in the skin through which subtle energy from the surrounding environment is carried throughout the body via the meridians, supplying nourishing chi energy to the relevant deeper organs, blood and nervous system.

Affirmation: A positive personally inspiring phrase that acts as a powerful therapy tool to counteract previous negative conditioning.

Akashic: Archives of stored information of everything that has ever been or will be within the collective Universal mind of God/Goddess.

Allopathic: Refers to contemporary medical approaches which utilize multiple drugs simultaneously and/or surgery to provide multi-symptom relief and treatment of illness or disease.

Ally: A teacher, guide, totem, spirit, crystal, plant, animal, flower etc. that is wholly reliable and acts as a 'Guardian Angel' on all levels and all dimensions.

Altar: A focal point for contemplation and meditation, usually displaying a personal collection of meaningful possessions. Sometimes a form of ritual may be involved in the process for enhanced experience.

Angel: *see* Devas.

Angelic Realms: *see* Devic Realms.

Archetype: A universal theme, or model of human emotional development or experience. A level of heightened experience on which everything is imbued with rich symbolic meaning.

Astral: Refers to the energy/matter octave or frequency band just beyond the etheric. Because the astral body is strongly affected by emotionality, astral energy is emotionally linked.

Aura: The subtle-energy field surrounding the physical body, invisible to all but gifted/trained individuals and through processes such as aura scans and Kirlian photography.

Bardo: The 'state between' two other states of being.

Bija Mantra: *see* Seed syllable.

Biocrystalline: Refers to the network of cellular elements in the body which have liquid crystal or quartz-like properties. These areas include cell salts, lymphatics, fatty tissue, red and white blood cells, and the pineal gland.

Bioelectromagnetic: The energy generated by living cells, including both conventional magnetic fields and subtle magnetic fields.

Bliss (Great): A state of ecstatic happiness achieved through the realisation of the illusory nature of the ego.

Block/Blockage: A dysfunction in the chakra system inhibiting the smooth, even flow of subtle- energy.

Bodhichitta: The compassionate desire to gain Enlightenment for the benefit of all living beings.

Bodhisattva: A being pledged to become a Buddha so as to be in the best position to aid all other beings to escape from suffering by gaining Enlightenment.

Brilliance: *see* Clear light.

Buddha: A title meaning one who is awake. A Buddha is someone who has gained Enlightenment - the perfection of wisdom and compassion. In particular the title applied to Siddhartha Gautama, also known as Shakyamuni, the founder of Buddhism.

Cerebral Hemispheres: The right and left halves of the cerebral cortex, the highest centres of function within the brain. The left hemisphere controls analytical and linear thought, while the right hemisphere controls symbolic and non-linear thought processes.

Chakra: An integrated system of metaphysical energy centres which affect physical, emotional, mental and spiritual well-being. The chakras process subtle energy and convert it into chemical, hormonal and cellular changes in the body.

Channelling: The phenomenon whereby an individual allows a higher level of consciousness to flow through them, often verbally, as in trance channelling, but also through automatic writing; or channelling the higher self or other 'being' consciously.

Chi: Ancient Chinese term for a nutritive subtle-energy which circulates through the acupuncture meridians.

Clairaudience: The psychic ability of hearing at higher vibrational levels. This usually occurs as a by-product of long-term meditation and involves the energy of a refined throat chakra.

Clairvoyance: The psychic ability of seeing higher subtle-energy patterns (from the French, literally meaning 'clear seeing'). An aspect of the third eye or ajna chakra which usually results after prolonged meditation practice as a by-product of spiritual development or scrying.

Clairvoyant Reality: A state of seeing and feeling that transcends the normal superficial senses. It is an experience of true reality beyond the confines of time and space boundaries, which allows one to experience the interconnectedness of all things.

Clear Light: The experience of the natural state of the mind, of consciousness 'undiluted' by any tendency to move towards sensory experience. Recognition of the nature of this state is synonymous with Enlightenment. Cosmic light. The original light.

Crystal: Solid organic material with ordered internal atomic structure of regular repeating three-dimensional patterns.

Crystal Webs of Light: Crystals arranged in geometric arrays which have an amplified or synergetic effect greater than the sum of the individual crystals, often used for specific healing or meditative practices.

Devas: Long-lived or eternal beings who experience refined and blissful states of mind. They thus inhabit a heavenly realm. These realms can be interpreted as objective or symbolic. Some individuals can contact these heavenly beings.

Devic Realms: These realms can be interpreted as objective or symbolic for states of mind in which human beings can dwell, or which they can 'contact' for guidance and help. Sometimes known as Angelic Realms.

Dharma: A word with numerous meanings, but in the context of this book it stands for all those teachings and methods which are conducive to gaining Enlightenment, and thereby seeing things as they truly are, particularly the teachings of the Buddha.

Dis-Ease: A frequently used term for illness. It implies that sickness is the result of the individual being 'ill at ease' with some aspect of his or her higher self or Divine consciousness. By re-aligning with the higher self, the soul's purpose can be fulfilled and dis-ease disappears.

Distilled Water: Produced by a process of converting the water to steam and condensing the steam back into water, making a very pure product.

Divine Essence Within: The Divine aspect that dwells in each of us, that once acknowledged and integrated is a positive loving guiding force.

DNA: Deoxyribonucleic acid, the helical macromolecule which encodes the genetic information that participates in cellular growth and development at the molecular level. The DNA spiral of life.

Download: Information from the Akashic archives is released into the conscious awareness of the individual.

Dowsing: Another term for radiesthesia. An intuitive skill used for finding hidden or lost objects and mineral resources, and in this book for diagnostic use and healing illness and dis-ease.

Ego: The incarnating personality as expressed through this present physical embodiment.

Emptiness: *see* Shunyata.

Endocrine System: One of the body's major physical control systems that transmits hormones produced from a series of ductless glands throughout the body. The system corresponds roughly to the position of the seven master chakras.

Energy Blockage: A general term referring to the interruption of the natural flow of subtle- energy throughout the human energetic system, often due to abnormal function in one or more chakras.

Enlightenment: A state of perfect wisdom and limitless compassion. The only permanently satisfying solution to the human predicament. The achievement of a Buddha.

Enzyme: A specialized protein molecule which acts to catalyse or accelerate a particular chemical reaction in the body.

Etheric: The frequency band, octave or vibration just beyond the physical realm. Etheric energy vibrates at speeds beyond light velocity and has a magnetic quality.

Grounding: The importance of maintaining connection to the earth in order to be fully centred.

Guru: A spiritual teacher who, through his/her teachings and/or personal example, aids other people to follow the path to Enlightenment.

Higher Dimensions: A term that describes subtle-energy systems which vibrate at speeds faster than light, i.e. non-physical energies.

Higher Self: That part of ourselves from which, once tuned in, we can receive Divine guidance.

Holistic: A synergistic approach which deals with combined physical, mental, emotional and spiritual aspects of human health and illness.

Karma: The reincarnational principle, sometimes stated as 'as ye sow, so shall ye reap'. An energetic system of credits and debits, positive actions or negative actions, which allows the soul to experience the full range of perspectives on life, through learning universal laws of resonances. Literal translation 'action'.

Kosas: *see* Aura.

Kundalini: Mythical serpent goddess said to rise upwards through the chakra system in the journey towards Enlightenment.

Light Body: Another term for subtle body.

Lingam: Hindu phallus, a symbol of the Hindu God, Lord Shiva.

Mala: Buddhist rosary, used for counting, often with 108 beads.

Mandala: An abstract universal symbol used as an aid to meditation practice in inducing higher states of awareness. Also in the context of this book, a personal energy signature or pattern.

Mantra: Mantras, being sacred sound vibrations, are composed of sacred syllables representative of and containing within great spiritual power, or energy. Utilising mantras allows us to concentrate and focus this spiritual energy. The word 'mantra' is composed, in Sanskrit, of two root words: 'man' means 'mind', or 'thinking', and 'tra' to 'release or free or strengthen'. Therefore the meaning is to 'free and strengthen the mind'.

Meridian: A channel through which subtle-energy flows through the body.

Miasm: An energetic state which predisposes an organism to future illness. These can be due to subtle effects of a particular toxic agent or micro-organism. There are four types: acquired, inherited, karmic or planetary in nature.

Mudra: In this book it is used in the sense of a hand gesture imbued with symbolic significance.

Multidimensional: Refers to the total spectrum of human energies or levels: physical, mental, emotional, spiritual, astral and higher spiritual levels.

Nadis: The thread-like subtle pathways of energy flow from the chakras to the various regions of the body and aura.

Paranormal: A term used to describe psychic phenomena, i.e. telepathy, clairvoyance, etc., that are outside the normal materialistic tribal scientific everyday reality.

Parasite: *see* Thought-form.

Piezoelectric: A phenomenon observed in crystals whereby physical pressure is converted into electrical fields.

Prana: An ancient Yogic term for a nutritive subtle-energy thought to be taken in during breathing.

Psychoneuroimmunology: Medical term for the evolving discipline which studies the integrated interaction between the body, mind and the immune system in illness or health.

Purified Water: Distilled water is purified water, but the definition of purified water includes water that has been filtered and/or de-ionised.

Qi: The Japanese term for chi, sometimes spelled Ki. A term for a nutritive subtle-energy which circulates through the acupuncture meridians.

Reiki: Energy 'medicine' where practitioners have been 'attuned' in special 'ceremonies' given by a qualified Reiki Master to become pure channels of Universal Life Force or Reiki energy.

Resonance: The phenomenon of sympathetic vibration between two similarly tuned oscillators.

Samadi: Blissful Divine experience that arises when the ego and the mind are dissolved. It is a state to be attained by one's own enlightened effort. It is limitless, divisionless and infinite, an experience of being and of pure consciousness.

Samsara: The cyclic round of birth and death, marked by suffering and frustration, which can only be brought to an end by the attainment of Enlightenment.

Scrying: *see* Clairvoyance.

Seed Syllable: Subtle sound-symbols through which Enlightened beings can communicate the Dharma to those on advanced stages of the path to Enlightenment. They are often visualized in chakra meditation.

Shakti: Divine cosmic female power. In reality she has no form. It is the coiled-up, sleeping Divine Shakti that lies dormant in all beings.

Shunyata: Literally 'emptiness' or 'voidness'. The ultimate nature of existence, the absolute aspect of all cognizable things. The doctrine of shunyata holds that all phenomena are empty (shunya) of any permanent unchanging self or self essence. By extension it can mean the transcendental experience brought about by the direct intuitive insight into the empty nature of things.

Subconscious: That part of the personality that dwells below the surface of waking consciousness and controls automatic human functions. It subliminally records all information taken in by the senses and is conditioned/programmed by rewards, punishments and messages that subtly build up our internal picture and worth.

Subtle Body: A term referring to any of the subtle-energy bodies which exist in the higher frequency octaves beyond the physical, i.e. the astral, etheric, mental, spiritual.

Subtle-Energy: A general term denoting energy that exists outside the ordinary space/time frame and which moves faster than light.

Superconscious: The part of the higher soul structure which can be 'tuned in' to. It controls the higher wisdom.

Sushumna: Energetic equivalent of the spine; vertical column within which the master chakra system is located.

Sutra: Literal translation - thread.

Tantra: A form of Buddhism making use of yogic practices of visualisation, mantras, mudras and mandalas, as well as symbolic ritual and meditations which work with subtle psychophysical energies. Literal translation - woven.

Thought-Form: A manifestation of a strong thought or emotion as an actual energetic structure within an individual's auric field. It can be caused by personal repeated negative or positive thoughts. It may also be placed there by another individual to control or manipulate the person; in this case it would be parasitic and wholly undesirable.

Universal Life Force: Inexplicable, natural source of all life which plays a vital role in health and healing.

Vajra: A ritual sceptre, which symbolically combines the qualities of both diamond and thunderbolt.

Vibrational: Refers to subtle or electromagnetic energy in varying frequencies and amplitudes.

Vibrational Medicine: That healing philosophy which aims to treat the whole person, i.e. mind, body and spirit complex, by delivering measured quanta of frequency-specific energy to the human multidimensional system.

Visualisation: A method of meditation involving the use of imagination to create vivid symbolic forms.

Witness: A biological specimen or other energetic signature of a patient used as a focal point for attunement by a crystal or vibrational therapist in dowsing or absent healing. It can also be a crystal which acts as a witness in crystal therapy.

Yin and Yang: According to Ancient Chinese philosophy, the two opposing but complementary forces at work in all nature.

Yoga: A Sanskrit word which means 'to link with God' or 'union with God'. It can refer to methods of meditation or physical postures designed to bring about spiritual development.